MIDDLE ENGLISH
ROMANCES
IN TRANSLATION

Sidestone Press

MIDDLE ENGLISH
ROMANCES
IN TRANSLATION

AMIS AND AMILOUN | ATHELSTON | FLORIS AND
BLANCHEFLOR | HAVELOK THE DANE |
KING HORN | SIR DEGARE

KENNETH ECKERT

Published by Sidestone Press, Leiden
 www.sidestone.com

ISBN 978-90-8890-339-7

Layout & cover design: Sidestone Press
Cover images: Detail from King Horn, MS. Harley 2253, British Library;
 Tristan battling fourteen knights, MS. Additional 5474, British Library.

Also available as:
e-book (PDF): ISBN 978-90-8890-340-3

Contents

Acknowledgments

In 1994 I was surprised to hear my now late Grandmother Eckert recite lines from the *Canterbury Tales* which she had probably learned sometime during World War I. As ever, when I write it is partly for her. As well, I owe thanks to teachers and professors who have encouraged me over the years, especially Daniel Thurber (Concordia, Nebraska); Catherine Eddy and Richard Willie (Concordia, Edmonton); William Schipper (Memorial, Newfoundland); my dissertation director, John Bowers (U. of Nevada, Las Vegas) and committee; and my friend Jacquie Elkouz at UNLV. In a book of romances which are often deemed clichéd themselves I will forgo the tired one about standing on giants and simply thank these people for setting me on a path.

In the production of this book I would like to thank Karsten Wentink and Corné van Woerdekom at Sidestone for their kindness and guidance, as well as Hanyang University, Korea for their support of research in Edinburgh and England in 2014. For help I received in inspecting manuscripts I would additionally like to thank the rare book people at the British Library, London.

For their permissions in clearing the use of public domain images and texts I would like to acknowledge the National Library of Scotland, Edinburgh; The British Library, London; the Heidelberg University Library; and the Council of the Early English Text Society, Oxford.

Soli Deo gloria.

Introduction

The Medieval Romances

A wit-besotting trash of books.—Montaigne, on medieval romances.[1]

One frustration of engaging in any branch of European medieval studies as an academic pursuit is that few claim expertise about the ancient or Roman worlds, but seemingly everyone on an internet discussion forum believes him or herself knowledgeable about the medieval period, usually based on patently false beliefs. Outside academia, the popular understanding of the period usually presumes one of two stereotypes. The first is the 'merry olde England' cliché of *Lucky Jim* and the renaissance fair, where undergraduates dress as Vikings with Hagar the Horrible horns and discuss trivial minutiae of medieval weaponry, while flirting with underdressed females who serve mead. Hollywood films similarly depict any English century before the nineteenth as one where knights exclaim "forsooth, varlet" in stilted Victorian accents.

While puerile and anachronistic, the trope is at least benign in comparison to the second common image of the era, which persistently retains the pejorative mislabel *dark ages*. This Monty Pythonesque world reeks of ignorance, plague, war, an

From black-letter edition of Syr Degore, *by Wynkyn de Worde*

---

1   John Florio, trans., *The Essayes of Michael Lord of Montaigne*, 2 vols. (London, 1603), vol. 2, ch. 25, quoted in Nicola McDonald, *Pulp Fictions of Medieval England* (Manchester: University Press, 2004), 3.

oppressive and misogynist church, violence, inquisitions, and witch hunts, hence the slang *get medieval* on someone. The medieval Europeans enjoyed regular baths, but to state that they bathed at all invites incredulity among non-specialists. Yet the medieval church, while far from perfect, fostered our western systems of schools, universities, and hospitals, and the period's supposedly primitive engineering gave us cathedrals and halls which are still standing. One of the bloodiest battles of the European Middle Ages, Agincourt (1415), resulted in about 10,000 deaths–compared to over a million fatalities in the Battle of the Somme in 1916.

Doubly frustrating is the practice among scholars of belittling and misrepresenting the medieval period in order to place other eras in brighter relief. Just as classicists depict Greco-Roman culture as impossibly idyllic and urbane and pass over its rampant slavery, Renaissance humanists imagine a sudden flowering of civilization in post-plague Europe and present, "for purposes of contrast, a grossly simplified image of the preceding age".[2] The prejudice has a long intellectual tradition; the post-medieval appraisal of the period and its literature was consistently disdainful. Just as gunpowder helped make chivalry obsolete, its poetic values were regarded as primitive. Thomas Nashe was typical in writing about *Bevis of Hampton* in 1589 and asking who "can forbeare laughing" at the "worne out absurdities" of its "plodding meeter".[3] Milton disparages poetic rhyme itself as "the invention of a barbarous age, to set off wretched matter and lame meter".[4]

Much of the condemnation was moral. Even in its own time, the romance genre was dismissed as "vayn carpynge" by medieval churchmen, a sentiment going back as far as Alcuin's complaint in 797 to the monks at Lindisfarne, "Quid enim Hinieldus cum Christo?" ("What does Ingeld have to do with Christ?") A homily complains that men who are unmoved by an account of Christ's passion are "stirred to tears when the tale of Guy of Warwick is read".[5] Such reproaches evidently did not go beyond sporadic grumbling, for romances required expensive parchment and clerics to write them, but the condemnations intensified in Elizabethan England even as printing eased their transmission. Churchman Francis Meres cautioned that such wanton stories were "hurtful to youth".[6] The early humanists had equally firm objections against the corrupting example of the sensational plots and heroes of romances. Juan Luis Vives, Spanish humanist and friend to Thomas More, warned that they make their audiences "wylye and craftye, they kindle and styr up covetousnes, inflame angre,

---

2   John A. Burrow, "Alterity and Middle English Literature", *Review of English Studies* 50:200 (1999): 491.
3   Thomas Nashe, *The Anatomy of Absurdity* (1589), in *The Works of Thomas Nashe*, Vol. III, ed. Ronald B. McKerrow (London, 1905), 26.
4   John Milton, Introduction ("The Verse"), *Paradise Lost*, Second Edition (1674), in *The Norton Anthology of English Literature, The Sixteenth Century and Early Seventeenth Century* Vol. B, eighth ed., ed. Stephen Greenblatt (New York: W.W. Norton, 2006).
5   In G.R. Owst, *Literature and Pulpit in Medieval England* (Cambridge, 1933), 14, quoted in Albert C. Baugh, "The Middle English Romance: Some Questions of Creation, Presentation, and Preservation", *Speculum* 42:1 (1967): 2.
6   Francis Meres, *Palladis Tamia, Wits Treasury* (1598), ed. Gregory Smith, *Elizabethan Critical Essays* (Oxford: Clarendon, 1904) 308-309, quoted in Ronald S. Crane, "The Vogue of *Guy of Warwick* from the Close of the Middle Ages to the Romantic Revival", *PMLA* 30:2 (1915): 139.

and all beastly and filthy desyre".[7] Roger Ascham thundered in 1545 that their reading leads to "none other ends, but only manslaughter and baudrye".[8]

Nicola McDonald notes that critics have treated such statements with "humorous detachment",[9] wondering how the genre could ever be seen as threatening enough to exercise its critics so. Like early fulminations against rock music in the 1950s, the remarks seem amusingly quaint. Yet the early moderns were no less hostile to medieval English literature. Partly the criticism originated in post-medieval and anti-Catholic prejudice.[10] Gibbon's *Decline and Fall of the Roman Empire* (1782) is still lauded as a magisterial work in historical analysis. Among other feats, he helped to establish the modern footnote system.[11] Nevertheless, his work extols Rome by juxtaposing it against "the triumph of barbarism and religion"[12] following the empire's decline. For Gibbon's contemporaries who esteemed the Latin of Cicero as the apex of language and rhetoric, modern English was an inferior substitute, and period grammars often forced it into procrustean Latin models.[13] Medieval English romance, mostly treating of non-classical narratives and, even worse, set in a Christian world, would have been beneath contempt.

Thus eighteenth and nineteenth century critics merely shifted the basis of their objections to medieval romance from moral to aesthetic grounds. McDonald again notes that romance's putative friends have been no kinder than its enemies, as scholarship has repeatedly been colored by a "veiled repugnance" to the genre.[14] The first major modern anthology of romance, Thomas Percy's *Reliques of Ancient English Poetry* (1765), was considered a sort of youthful indulgence by its author, who declined to sign his name to later editions upon presumably taking up more serious interests. Similarly, in George Ellis' *Specimens of Early English Metrical Romances* (1805), there is a sort of proper embarrassment at a gentleman slumming among such vulgarisms:

> [Ellis] mocks their long-winded plots, ludicrous emotions and general absurdity, retelling romances like *Guy of Warwick* and *Amis and Amiloun*, with the kind of smug irony that is designed only to assert his, and his reader's superiority over the imagined and denigrated medieval.[15]

---

7   McDonald, 3.
8   Roger Ascham, *Toxophilus*, ed. W.A. Wright, *English Works* (Cambridge, 1904) xiv, quoted in McDonald, 3.
9   McDonald, 3-4.
10 McDonald, 4.
11 Robert J. Connors, "The Rhetoric of Citation Systems, Part I: The Development of Annotation Structures from the Renaissance to 1900", *Rhetoric Review* 17:1 (1998): 35.
12 Edward Gibbon, *History of the Decline and Fall of the Roman Empire* (1782), Vol. 6, Ch. 71, Part 1. Gibbon argues that "the introduction, or at least the abuse of Christianity, had some influence on the decline and fall of the Roman empire. The clergy successfully preached the doctrines of patience and pusillanimity; the active virtues of society were discouraged; and the last remains of military spirit were buried in the cloister" (Vol. 3, Ch. 38, Part 6). While respecting his acumen, some modern historians object that the eastern empire was no less devout and lasted another eleven centuries after Constantine.
13 Celia M. Millward, *A Biography of the English Language* (Orlando, FL: Harcourt Brace Jovanovich, 1988), 210.
14 McDonald, 5.
15 McDonald, 7.

Even among medievalists of the twentieth century, a critical binary prevails with Chaucer, Gower, *Gawain / Pearl*, and devotional texts comprising high culture. English romances, conversely, are the junk food of the period, seen as degenerated pastiches of continental originals cobbled together by "literary hacks".[16] Much late Victorian and pre-World War II criticism analyzed the romances for linguistic or source-hunting purposes, with the story an afterthought. Albert Baugh takes it as a commonplace that "every one knows that the Middle English romances are honeycombed with stock phrases and verbal clichés, often trite and at times seemingly forced".[17] At best their stylized repetition provides juvenile diversion, such as "children feel in The Three Bears".[18] Derek Pearsall once noted his difficulty in comprehending "why poems that are so bad according to almost every criteria of literary value should have held such a central position in the literature culture of their own period".[19]

However, the assumption that educated fourteenth-century audiences also viewed English romances with disdain for their "worn devices of minstrel style" and "stereotyped diction"[20] may betray only modern sensibilities with our different expectations of structure and distaste for formulaic language. These styles, moreover, run deep in 'high' literature as well. Chaucer uses such oral patterns as "the sothe to say" or "tell" twenty-three times in *Troilus*,[21] and the scop of *Beowulf*, no less prone to lengthy digressions, reiterates titles or family lineages with metrical appositives such as "Hroðgar maþelode, helm Scyldinga" ("Hrothgar made a speech, protector of the Scyldings", 370). These stock epithets link to those used by the improvisational guslars documented by Milman Parry in the Balkans, and occur in Homer's *Odyssey* with its repetition of "the blue-eyed goddess Athene".[22] Rhyme and alliterative schemes themselves function as oral and memory devices that are not only pleasurable but add form and meaning to poetry.

Underlying much criticism is the whiff that romance sins by *being* popular, failing to be more rarified or serious in tone for the aesthete or to be more socially subversive for the revisionist. The manuscripts stubbornly survive in numbers larger and more geographically varied than any other medieval English genre, and the recorded libraries of everyone from well-off fishmongers to grocers to aristocrats included them.[23] By the thirteenth century the earliest recorded French bookseller appears with the nickname

---

16 Laura A. Hibbard Loomis, "The Auchinleck Manuscript and a Possible London Bookshop of 1330-1340", *PMLA* 57:3 (1942): 608.

17 Albert C. Baugh, "Improvisation in the Middle English Romance", *Proceedings of the American Philosophical Society* 103:3 (1959): 420.

18 J.S.P. Tatlock, "Epic Formulas, Especially in Layamon", *PMLA* 38:3 (1923): 528-529, quoted in Baugh, "Improvisation", 421.

19 Derek Pearsall, "Understanding Middle English Romance", *Review* 2 (1980): 105, quoted in McDonald, 9.

20 Loomis, "*Sir Thopas*", 491.

21 Nancy M. Bradbury, "Chaucerian Minstrelsy: *Sir Thopas, Troilus and Criseyde* and English Metrical Romance", in *Tradition and Transformation in Medieval Romance*, ed. Rosalind Field (Cambridge: D.S. Brewer, 1999), 120.

22 Baugh, "Improvisation", 419. Athena is actually called *glaukopis* (γλαυκῶπις), "owl-eyed", variously translated as blue and grey.

23 An inventory of two bankrupt London grocers in the 1390s contained four books of romance. Ralph Hanna, *London Literature 1300-1380* (Cambridge: University Press, 2005), 12. See also John Bowers, *The Politics of Pearl: Court Poetry in the Age of Richard II* (Cambridge: D.S. Brewer, 2001), who lists romances in the libraries of Sir Simon Burley and the Duke of Gloucester.

"Herneis le Romanceur".[24] Although perhaps not borne out in fact, a claimed mark of breeding for a knight was reading romances,[25] and Chaucer depicts Creseyde with ladies listening to a reading of the Siege of Thebes (*Troilus* II.82-4). Edward II had fifty-nine books of romance in his library.[26] Well into Elizabethan England the tastes of the literate public remained medieval and romances were among the first popular printed books,[27] providing further materials for ballads and the stage. While by the Restoration the Middle English language had become increasingly antique and difficult, some verse and prose modernizations remained popular into the next century.[28]

McDonald sees a sort of secularized Calvinist guilt in academia, which disparages medieval romances because they are enjoyable, with probably more than a little snobbery due to the sexist stereotype of present-day romances being the province of lovelorn girls and suburban housewives. Yet the themes and content of English medieval romances are not the same as modern exemplars, with their flavor of improbable 'chick-flicks' and Harlequin novels at supermarket checkouts. Medieval romance suffers the additional problem of a lack of scholarly definition, and no consensus has ever been reached on just what comprises a romance. The earliest usage referred more to a story's Old French or Latinate origins, and for many the twelfth-century narratives of Chrétien de Troyes form "the 'paradigm' of romance".[29] Chaucer and his contemporaries also seem to have generalized romances as secular and not specifically historical works in French,[30] though later usage has the broader idea of any "fictitious narratives"[31] involving chivalrous or aristocratic deeds. English romance is thus a blurry designation which bleeds into genres as divergent as Arthurian legend, history, hagiography, and folktale.

Medieval romances often featured some quest or journey, which could be literal but often emotional or spiritual. Such pursuits include marital love, but not categorically– there are almost no women in *Gamelyn*, and the first two romances in this collection, *Amis and Amiloun* and *Athelston*, feature spousal relationships but are more concerned with homosocial bonds of friendship. John Finlayson suggests that romances depict courtly adventures with "little or no connection with medieval actuality... not unlike the basic cowboy film".[32] W.P. Ker states that the old epic warriors always have "good reasons of their own for fighting"[33] which connect to external exigencies, whereas in romance the emphasis falls on the hero's individual achievements, with the causes a background and often perfunctory device. Ralph Hanna asserts the opposite, that

---

24 J.S.P. Tatlock, "The *Canterbury Tales* in 1400", *PMLA* 50:1 (1935): 108.
25 Harriet E. Hudson, "Construction of Class, Family, and Gender in Some Middle English Popular Romances", in *Class and Gender in Early English Literature*, ed. Britton J. Harwood and Gillian R. Overing (Indianapolis: Indiana University Press, 1994), 78. For arguments that the knightly ideal was not reflected in reality see Paul Strohm, *Social Chaucer* (Cambridge: Harvard University Press, 1989), 140.
26 Michael Prestwich, *Plantagenet England 1225-1360* (New York: Oxford University Press, 2005), 54.
27 Roland Crane (132-33) asserts that early English humanists were less concerned with literature than with philosophical or theological matters.
28 See Roland Crane (193) for editions and reworkings of *Guy of Warwick*, which continued to enjoy a readership, albeit increasingly as juvenilia, until the 1700s.
29 Robert M. Jordan, "Chaucerian Romance?" *Yale French Studies* 51 (1974): 225.
30 Susan Crane, *Gender and Romance in Chaucer's Canterbury Tales* (Princeton: University Press, 1994), 9.
31 John Finlayson, "Definitions of Middle English Romance, Part I", *Chaucer Review* 15:1 (1980): 46.
32 Finlayson, Part I, 55.
33 W.P. Ker, *Epic and Romance* (London: MacMillan, 1922), 6.

although romance heroes lack psychological interiority, the narratives symbolically convey such emotions and meanings.[34] I can make no better synthesis than to argue that romances tend to have an escapist ethos which idealizes rather than realistically portrays. Thus while it serves the purpose here to speak of the style as a subgenre, it may be more accurate to call medieval English romance, like satire, a register or mode.[35]

Identifying the class audience of romance has been an equally contentious pursuit. Detractors assert that English romances, with their sentimental themes and oral-based structures, appealed largely to lower-class and non-literate audiences. Ostensibly, French stories were for court audiences and English ones for the hoi polloi,[36] with Latin, French, and English forming a clear downward hierarchy of taste and value regardless of content. English romances frequently feature scenes of civic celebration, and if they were recited at such events–Havelok's coronation features games, music, and "romanz reding on the bok" (2327)[37]–they would have had a broad lay audience. Even if the *Havelok* poet lets the mask slip at the end by mentioning how he stayed up long nights writing the story (2998-9), he presents himself fictively as a minstrel, at ease in a public space with an audience and "a cuppe of ful god ale" (14).

Yet recent scholarship points to a widely heterogeneous audience for English romances which included the lower aristocracy. *Sir Thopas*, albeit in a comic register, is addressed to "knyght and lady free" (*CT* VII.892). English works were not automatically seen as ignoble, as attested by rapidly declining levels of French fluency in the English gentry. Late in the thirteenth century, the *Arthur and Merlin* narrator notes that "mani noble ich have yseiʒe / þat no Freynsche couþe seye" (25-6).[38] Scholars have judged English romances as vulgar corruptions of French originals, often misapplying the standards of Chrétien to a fundamentally different genre. Seaman argues that the English preference for less courtly rigor and more dragons in their romances reflects a distinct and equally valid poetic culture.[39] Where continental romances endorse a more secular value system of chivalry, the English ones are often homiletic.[40] We also forget that many of Chaucer's narratives (and nearly all of Shakespeare's) equally derive from continental originals and were praised for their respect and fidelity to *auctoritee*.

What might Chaucer have thought of these romances? He may possibly have had use of the Auchinleck manuscript (National Library of Scotland Adv. MS 19.2.1), which contains *Amis and Amiloun, Bevis of Hampton, Floris and Blancheflor, Guy of Warwick, Sir Degare,* and *Sir Orfeo.* The prevailing criticism has held that *Sir Thopas* is a "brilliantly bad"[41] parody of the medieval romances. Yet Chaucer's poetic touch

---

34 Hanna, 108-9.
35 Pamela Graden does just this in "The Romance Mode", in *Form and Style in Early English Literature* (London: Methuen, 1971), 212-272.
36 Robert Levine, "Who Composed *Havelok* For Whom?" *Yearbook of English Studies* 22 (1992): 97.
37 For *Havelok* and all other non-Chaucerian romances here I use the editions listed for each chapter as sources unless noted.
38 Quoted in Susan Crane, *Insular Romance: Politics, Faith, and Culture in Anglo-Norman and Middle English Literature* (Berkeley: University of California Press, 1986), 10.
39 Myra Seaman, "Engendering Genre in Middle English Romance: Performing the Feminine in *Beves of Hamtoun*", *Studies in Philology* 98:1 (2001): 51.
40 Dieter Mehl, *The Middle English Romances of the Thirteenth and Fourteenth Centuries* (London: Routledge and Kegan Paul, 1967), 5.
41 Derek Pearsall, *The Life of Geoffrey Chaucer* (Cambridge: Basil Blackwell, 1992), 195.

is too deft for merely a cheap laugh, particularly when he uses romance tropes and phrases in other writings; rather than mocking works such as *Guy* and *Bevis*, the joke may be on Thopas' incompetence at failing to live up to their heroic ideals, and by extension Chaucer pilgrim/poet's failure to relate a better romance. Whether Chaucer and his circle greeted romances with fondness or the equivalent of eye-rolling, they likely knew them as members of the first English-speaking court since Harold Godwineson.[42] Hanna notes that "Chaucerian parody, like all parody, depends upon the accepted status of its target".[43] Whatever their reception, the romances continued to influence "serious" authors. Unlike epic, which Michael Bakhtin categorizes as a completed genre,[44] romance has never ended. It has evolved and grown into modern iterations with heroines ranging from Una to Elizabeth Bennett to Bridget Jones.

However, the texts themselves remain sparsely anthologized and dedicated volumes such as French and Hale (1930) are increasingly out of print. Many of these stories are only accessible online as very dated works in public domain, with the provident exception of the excellent TEAMS editions. Most importantly, until recently few were available in translation beyond the simplified children's versions which seemed to be in vogue in the early twentieth century.[45] Translation is not usually a glamorous pursuit, and few works attain the status of Chapman's *Homer*. Chaucer is available in modernizations, but as with Shakespeare, PDE versions are generally considered nonscholarly, consigned to lay readers or non-native English learners. For romances the situation comprises a vicious circle: they are mostly unpublished because they are obscure, and they are obscure because they are inaccessible in Modern English. A clear academic need stands for close Present Day English (PDE)[46] renderings of these texts in unabridged form for the non-specialist.

I attended sessions at the International Congress on Medieval Studies in Kalamazoo in 2009 and sat in on a discussion of *Beowulf* translations. Opinions varied from grudging acceptance that translations such as Chickering's (1989) were necessary concessions to snide remarks about "Heaneywulf". While Seamus Heaney's version is not textually perfect, it serves as an invaluable access point for the layperson. The alternative is still more execrable movie adaptations and a tiny pool of readers with the training to interpret Old English, and fewer still able to move beyond language issues into appreciating the story as an aesthetic product, which was J.R. Tolkien's call to arms in "*Beowulf*: The Monsters and the Critics" (1936). The same reality is nearing for Shakespeare and long ago arrived for works in Middle English.

---

42 Pearsall, *Life of Chaucer*, 65.

43 Hanna, 108.

44 Mikhail Bakhtin, "Epic and Novel", ed. and trans. Michael Holquist and Caryl Emerson, *The Dialogic Imagination* (Austin: University of Texas Press, 1981), 3.

45 There are a few recent scholarly translations: see Marijane Osborn's *Nine Medieval Romances of Magic: Re-Rhymed in Modern English* (Peterborough, Ont.: Broadview, 2010). Roger Sherman and Laura Hibbard Loomis' *Medieval Romances* (New York: Modern Library, 1957) also has abridged but well-translated texts. For examples of romance juvenilia see F.J.H. Darton, *A Wonder Book of Old Romances* (London: Wells Gardner Darton, 1907); Andrew Lang, ed., *The Red Romance Book* (New York: Longmans and Green, 1921); and Harriot B. Barbour, *Old English Tales Retold* (New York: MacMillan, 1924).

46 Within this book I will use OE, Old English, ME, Middle English, EME, Early Modern English, and OF, Old French. These are understood as loose and flexible divisions. For more discussion of these periods and terms, see Millward.

Amazon.com currently lists a "translation" into Modern English of Bunyan's *Pilgrim's Progress* from 1678!

Happily, the twentieth-century critical disdain for medieval romance as cliché-filled–is becoming a cliché. Perhaps influenced by the general flattening of high-low cultural prejudices wrought by postmodernism, Middle English romances have in the last decade been read with more critical sympathy and respect. The twenty-first century has seen a growth of scholarship and monographs on medieval romances as well as in subfields such as manuscript studies and the emerging law-in-literature interdiscipline. I mentioned Pearsall's reading earlier in past tense, as in 2011 he wittily 'retracted' some of his earlier criticisms of romance, commenting that he now appreciates "its liveliness and brisk pace and sheer appetite for narrative", concluding that "the leap of understanding is in realising that in asking for the wrong things, asking for 'literariness', one misses all that is particular to the pleasure of romance".[47]

McDonald also adds the interesting argument that the relative formulism of medieval romance, with its standard exile/return storylines, evinces not a poverty of imagination but functions as a useful frame within which the author can experiment freely. The predictable happy ending is obligatory but can be very brief and perfunctory, as the story's energy is elsewhere.[48] The more that romance makes itself internally obvious as a self-aware narrative structure by repeatedly telling us "so hit is fonde in frensche tale" (*Bevis* 888), the freer the teller is to invent maidens who are all simultaneously the fairest in the world, to have heroes starve in dungeons for years and not die, for men in heavy armor to battle for days without fatigue, for lone warriors to defeat entire Saracen armies, and for murdered children to spring back to life without shattering the audience's credulity. The heroes inhabit a world where the normal laws of nature are "slightly suspended".[49] This poetic freedom was especially possible in England, where chivalry had never been as pervasive as in France and was increasingly seen through an antique mist.[50]

Moreover, the metafictional sense that exists within many romances suggests a skillful author able to appeal to multiple levels. The numerous references to the storytelling narrator, to other romances the audience is expected to know, and the "citation of bookish sources"[51] requires a certain sophistication to apprehend information above the narrative plane. Chaucer also occasionally drops metafictional touches, telling his "litel book" to *go* (*Troilus* V.1786). The requisite invocation to listen at the beginning of most romances may suggest a traditional oral situation but does not necessarily mean the author is literally a wandering minstrel,[52] any more than the fictional audience of "ye lovers" (*Troilus* I.22) that Chaucer addresses is a real one. Nevertheless, if romances were indeed sung out loud, as the invocation in *King Horn* suggests–"alle beon he blithe / that to my song lythe / a sang ihc schal you singe /

---

47 Derek Pearsall, "The Pleasure of Popular Romance: A Prefatory Essay", in *Medieval Romance, Medieval Contexts*, ed. Rhiannon Purdie and Michael Cichon (Cambridge: D.S. Brewer, 2011), 11.
48 McDonald, 14.
49 Northrop Frye, *Anatomy of Criticism: Four Essays* (Princeton: University Press, 1957), 33, quoted in Diana T. Childress, "Between Romance and Legend: 'Secular Hagiography' in Middle English Literature", *Philological Quarterly* 57 (1978): 313.
50 Mehl, 4.
51 McDonald, 14.
52 Baugh, "Questions", 3.

of Murry the Kinge" (1-4)– their performance may continue the same aristocratic tradition as the *Beowulf* scop who sings heroic lays before Hrothgar and his retainers.[53]

Historians are now unlikely to report, as the *Anglo-Saxon Chronicle* does in 793, that "wæron geseowene fyrene dracan on þam lyfte fleogende" ("fiery dragons were seen flying through the air") in Northumbria.[54] How much a medieval audience might have found actually credible in a romance is difficult to assess. Although many modern readers still share the religious faith of the medieval English, there is now generally less patience for the miraculous in fiction, and a stronger preference for rationalized characters and narratives. A modern reader, not having grown up with the folkloric aptronyms and devices of oral storytelling, might question how Athelston can be so dense as to not suspect someone named "Wicked-mind". The past, being a foreign country, had different sensibilities– gestures of bowing and kneeling in romance may appear to be maudlin affectations but were once common actions predating handshakes.[55]

Nevertheless, the requirement of a considerable suspension of disbelief may have itself been a contemporary feature of medieval romance; Finlayson comments that romance marvels are "a necessary component of the narrative and the character of the 'historical' hero".[56] Just as modern romance readers and movie audiences know that in real life the rich boy does not usually marry the poor girl and not all prostitutes have hearts of gold, a medieval audience was unlikely to be so naïve as to confuse the escapist world of romance with the real one of their own. As the Wife of Bath lectures to her captive husband, it was hardly difficult to find real-life examples of aristocrats behaving shabbily.

Thus the romances contain an amount of nostalgic conservatism mixed with their adventures and peccadilos. The American cowboy 'oaters' of classic film were set in an idealized Old West with the moral clarity of white hats and black hats, and so with romance; Caxton writes in 1483, "O ye knyghtes of Englond, where is the custome and usage of noble chivalry that was used in tho days?"[57] Wilcox equally comments that *Guy of Warwick* is set in a perfected alternative time of the crusades where all the heroes fight honorably.[58] Such sentiments read romance as valorizing a closed past where knights supposedly acted better than the ones its audience would have seen in reality, perhaps in Caxton's case to spur on the latter.

---

53 Baugh, "Questions", 18. Hrothgar's bard is lavishly praised as the "cyninges þegn / guma gilphlæden" ("the king's thane, a man of skilled eloquence"). *Beowulf*, ed. and trans. Howell D. Chickering, Jr. (Toronto: Anchor Books, 1977), lines 867-8.

54 Tony Jebson, ed. *Anglo-Saxon Chronicle, Manuscript E: Bodleian MS Laud 636*, accessed at http://asc. jebbo.co.uk/e/e-L.html

55 Burrow, 488. Burrow believes the gesture of shaking hands in Europe is post-medieval, finding its first OED usage in Coverdale's Bible of 1535 (p. 489).

56 John Finlayson, "The Marvellous in Middle English Romance II", *Chaucer Review* 33:4 (1999) 382.

57 William Caxton, "Exhortation to the Knights of England" (1483), quoted in Larry D. Benson and John Leyerle, ed., *Chivalric Literature* (Kalamazoo: The Board of the Medieval Institute, 1980), xiii.

58 Rebecca Wilcox, "Romancing the East: Greeks and Saracens in *Guy of Warwick*", in McDonald, 221.

Some recent political commentary faults medieval romance for this affirmation of hegemonic values in the feudal period. As Fredric Jameson might say, romances perpetuate the "legitimation of concrete structures of power and domination".[59] Susan Crane notes that romances maintain class divisions through "the conception that social differences order the world hierarchically".[60] Alternatively, Dominique Battles asserts that many romances contain a subtext of native English defiance against the Norman invaders.[61] Yet the romances retain a sense of political subversion not only in their lack of official sanction but also in what they conspicuously omit. Events in an overtly fanciful world where the fair and just always prosper in the end call sharp contrast to the failings of the actual world where they do not. Matthew Holford makes about the same point in noting that *Horn Child and Maiden Rimnild* "uses the past to compensate for the inadequacies of the contemporary world".[62]

Edward Said's famous statement that "we need not look for correspondence between the language used to depict the Orient and the Orient itself, not so much because the language is inaccurate but because it is not even trying to be accurate"[63] can easily be applied to medieval romance. Popular romances indicate a great deal about actual historical circumstances through decoding their audience's idealized desires and values, and not through plots which are often explicitly conceded to be fanciful stories. Yet again, this is not where the energy of the romances lay. Chiefly, a medieval English romance was meant by its author to be a fun diversion of love, adventure, and exotic locales, and like film, was often a shared experience. The audience desired "a tale of myrthe" (*CT* VII.706) as Harry Bailly requests, and its *doctryne* was a commendable but secondary addition to its *solas*.

---

59   In T. A. Shippey, "The *Tale of Gamelyn*: Class Warfare and the Embarrassments of Genre", in *The Spirit of Medieval English Popular Romance*, ed. Ad Putter and Jane Gilbert Jane (Harlow: Longman, 2000). Shippey cites from Fredric Jameson, T*he Political Unconscious: Narrative as a Socially Symbolic Act* (New York: Cornell University Press, 1981).

60   Susan Crane, *Gender and Romance*, 98.

61   Dominique Battles, *Cultural Difference and Material Culture in Middle English Romance: Normans and Saxons* (New York: Routledge, 2013).

62   Matthew L. Holford, "History and Politics in *Horn Child and Maiden Rimnild*", *Review of English Studies* 57:229 (2006): 168.

63   Edward W. Said, *Orientalism: Western Conceptions of the Orient* (London: Routledge & Kegan Paul, 1978), 71.

Textual Notes

In translating these works I have attempted a line-by-line rendering, although at times in order to obtain a natural English syntax, or to accommodate an especially lengthy Middle English line, the line orders may vary slightly. To make the stories as understandable as possible I have modernized character and geographical names where practicable and have attempted to simplify the more arcane details of armament and feudal rank. Some romances, such as *Athelston*, argue a literal reading of placenames, whereas in *King Horn* they are likely poetic and fanciful; the reader may decide. Footnotes are included where the line has a peculiar reading, an evocative allusion, or suggests a figurative expression.

I have attempted to regularize typographical conventions, with the proviso that other editors and the manuscript scribes themselves are far from consistent. Generally, I leave thorn þ (th) as is, and retain yogh ȝ where it approximates a fricative gh/y (but not where it suggests a soft y). Eth ð (th) is rare in ME, especially after 1300, and should not be an issue. I have modernized u where it suggests v (*loue*), v where u/w is likely intended (*vpon, tvay*), i where j is meant (*ioye*), and spelled out ampersands. I have capitalized most proper nouns and religious terms of respect. Lines which are too long for the page column are broken with a caesura. Otherwise I have added only minimal modern punctuation to the original text.

Stylistically, Middle English's main fault as a developing literary language lies not in spelling but in its limited lexicon and grammatical ambiguity. At times pronoun referents are unclear and the repetition of verbs such as *said* can be tedious, and I have made assumptions based on context to communicate subtler shades of meaning. For this reason the translation is often slightly longer than the original. As the romance texts have little syntactic subordination and prefer endless strings of *and,* I have sometimes rephrased. Lastly, despite the metapoetical references of many romances, I have avoided breaking the fourth wall of the translation by exposing it as one, and so I have not used obviously anachronistic expressions or colloquialisms to render medieval idioms. The characters do not tune anyone out or step on the gas. Heroines are attractive but never hot, except for maybe when one is about to be burned at the stake.

In my introductions I reference arguments I have made elsewhere, including "*Amis and Amiloun*: A Spiritual Journey and the Failure of *Treupe*", *Literature & Theology* 27:3 (2013); "Three Types of 'Messengers' in the Middle English *Athelston*", *ANQ* 26:4 (2013); "Growing Up in the Middle English *Floris and Blancheflor*", *The Explicator* 70:4 (2012); "The Redemptive Hero in *Havelok the Dane*," *Philological Quarterly* (In press, 2015); and "Numerological and Structural Symbolism in the Auchinleck Stanzaic *Guy of Warwick*", *English Studies* 95:8 (2014). All Chaucer references are from Larry Benson's *The Riverside Chaucer*, 3rd ed., 1987, and miscellaneous romance citations are from Walter H. French and Charles B. Hale's *Middle English Metrical Romances*, 1964 [1930].

My lineation does not reproduce any "standard" line conventions for the Middle English texts, as I have in some places added lines from other manuscript sources to clarify the narrative. Line numbers are thus here for ease of use in study or for citation. Where I cite scholarship the reference is to the author's line numberings.

Amis and Amiloun

The subject matter and style of romances varied more in the medieval era than in what are called present-day romances, and went far beyond heterosexual courtship. Romances could also explore wondrous tales of the east, the golden age of good kings, or the friendships of men. England in the fourteenth century was considerably different than in the Anglo-Saxon period: the increasing wealth of the emerging classes of tradesmen, entrepreneurs, and urban dwellers was displacing feudal culture and court power; the old bonds of loyalty informed by Christian knighthood were becoming increasingly contractual; popular customary law was being replaced by a creeping bureaucratic legalism. Many would have looked back fondly at a perceived happier pre-Norman time with its traditional social and political mores. One of these past ideals was of *treupe*, the bonds of honor pledged between men in blood-brotherhood. *Amis and Amiloun* (c. 1330) contains numerous folktale elements of evil stewards, wooing women, and trials by combat, but is chiefly a romance dealing with these sacred pledges of honor whereby both heroes are obligated to assist each other and to "be nought ogain thi lord forsworn" (305).

Complications to the protagonists' oaths caused by the steward and the women lead to the story's central conflict where Amiloun must violate *treupe* to save his friend's life. Amis lies about deflowering the duke's daughter, tricks Amiloun's wife,

Herr Goeli, from Codex Manesse 262v,
Heidelberg University Library.

and slays his own children; Amiloun kills the malicious but justified steward and arranges a marriage through a sham act of impersonation. For this *Amis* has been criticized as a problem poem, a sensitive text concerned with complex issues of Christian praxis but seemingly endorsing an indefensible morality.

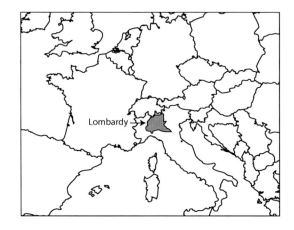

Yet another means of interpreting the poem is to see it as illustrating the problems of *treupe* itself, or at least that debased version which takes the form of proud and cold legalism rather than friendship given freely in Christian love. The medieval church was suspicious of secretive rituals of *treupe* where they engendered exclusive alliances, and using the steward and Amiloun's wife to contrast against and index Amis and Amiloun's progress, the plot tracks the latter two's spiritual maturation as they gradually temper their vows of loyalty into a purer Christian fraternity informed by caritas and humility. In being 'corrected' by heaven for his duplicity, Amiloun patiently endures and overcomes his redemptive punishment and becomes a chivalric *imitatio Christi*. In such a light the poem can be seen as a homiletic romance.

Amis and Amiloun has numerous continental exemplars, surviving in earlier Latin, Norse, and French manuscripts. In English it survives in four manuscripts: Auchinleck, Adv. MS 19.2.1 (c. 1330), Egerton 2862 (c. 1400), Harley 2386 (c. 1500), and Bodleian 21900 (Douce 326) (c. 1500). As my basic textual source I use Eugen Kölbing, ed., *Amis and Amiloun, Altenglische Biblioteck 2* (Heilbronn: Henninger, 1884), checking it against the Auchinleck images. As the Auchinleck text is incomplete, lines 1-52 are from the Egerton manuscript, 53-2401 are Auchinleck, and 2442-2510 are again Egerton.

E: Egerton 2862
A: Auchinleck

1 E	For Goddes love in Trinyte	For the love of the Triune God,
	Al þat ben hend herkeniþ to me	I ask all who are courteous
	I pray ȝow par amoure	To listen to me, for kindness' sake,
	What whilom fel beyond þe see	To hear what once happened across the sea
	Of two barons of grete bounte	To two barons, men of great generosity
	And men of grete honoure.	And high honor.
	Her faders were barons hende	Their fathers were noble barons,
	Lordinges com of grete kende	Lords born of distinguished families
	And pris in toun and toure.	And men esteemed in town and tower.
10	To here of þe children two	To hear about these two children
	How þey were in wele and woo	And how they experienced good and ill
	Ywis it is grete doloure;	Is a great sorrow, indeed;
	In weele and woo how þey gan wynd	How they fared, in good and bad times,
	And how unkouþ þey were of kynd	How humble they were of their lineage—[64]
	Þe children bold of chere	The children, so firm in manner—
	And how þey were good and hend	And how they were good and courteous,
	And how ȝong þei becom frend	And how young when they became friends
	In cort þere þey were	In the court where they stayed,
	And how þey were dobbid knyȝt	And how they were knighted
20	And how þey were trouþ plyȝt	And how they pledged their loyalty,[65]
	Þe children boþ in fere;	Both of the children together;
	And in what lond þei were born	And in what land they were born
	And what þe childres names worn	And what the boys' names were,
	Herkeneþ and ȝe mow here!	Listen and you will learn!
	In Lumbardy y understond	In Lombardy, as I understand,
	Whilom bifel in þat lond	It happened one time in that land
	In geste as we reede	In the romance as we read it,
	Two barouns hend wonyd in lond	That two noble barons lived there,
	And had two ladyes free to fond	And had two ladies of proven nobility,
30	Þat worþy were in wede.	Who were elegant in appearance.
	Uppon her hend ladyes two	From those two courteous ladies
	Twoo knave childre gat þey þoo	They had two boys,
	Þat douȝty were of dede	Who were valiant in deeds,
	And trew weren in al þing.	And were true in all things.
	And þerfore Jesu Hevyn king	And for this Jesus, Heaven's king,
	Ful wel quyted her mede.	Gave them their reward in full.
	Þe children is names as y ȝow hyȝt	I will properly relate in rhyme
	In ryme y wol rekene ryȝt	The children's names, as I promised,
	And tel in my talkyng.	And tell you in my speech.
40	Boþ þey were getyn in oo nyȝt	Both of them were conceived on one night

---

64 *Uncouth they were of kynd*: There is disagreement on what exactly this means. Kölbing (1884) rendered this as "what unknown ancestry they were", but contextually the poet is praising their good nature. Eugen Kölbing, ed., *Amis and Amiloun, Altenglische Bibliotek 2* (Heilbronn: Henninger, 1884).

65 *Trouþ plyȝt*: To swear one's troth in friendship, duty, or marriage is to make a serious and unbreakable vow of fidelity. The word 'truth' only later added the modern meaning of 'accordance to fact'. See R.F. Green, *A Crisis of Truth: Literature and Law in Ricardian England* (Philadelphia: University of Pennsylvania Press, 1999); see also *Athelston*, line 24 for another friendship pledge.

And on oo day born a plyȝt	And born the same day, in fact,
For soþ wiþ out lesyng;	Truthfully, without a lie;
Þat oon barons son ywys	One of the baron's sons, in fact,
Was ycleped syre Amys	Was named Amis
At chyrche at his Cristenyng;	At his christening in church;
Þat oþur was clepyd syre Amylyoun	The other was called Amiloun,
Þat was a childe of grete renoun	Who was a child of great renown
And com of hyȝe ofspryng.	And descended from a high lineage.
Þe children gon þen þryve	The children began to thrive.
50 Fairer were never noon on lyve	There were none fairer alive,
Curtaise hende and good.	More courteous, handsome, and good.
When þey were of ȝeres fyve	When they were five years old,
. . . .	. . . .
A Alle her kyn were of hem bliþe	All their family was pleased with them,
So mylde þey were of mode.	They were so gentle in their manners.
When þey were seven ȝere old ywis	When they were seven years old,
Every man hadde of hem blis	Every man took pleasure in
To beholde þat frely fode.	Beholding those admirable children.
When þey were twelve winter old	When they were twelve years old,
In al þe londe was þer non hold	There were none in the land
60 So faire of boon no blode.	Regarded so highly in flesh and blood.
In þat tyme ich understond	In that time, as I understand,
A duk was lord of þat lond	A duke resided in the land,
Prys in toun and tour.	Esteemed in town and castle.
Frely he let sende his sond	He graciously sent his invitation
After erles barouns fre and bond	To earls and barons, free and bound,
And ladies bryȝt in bour.	And ladies shining in their bowers.[66]
A ryche fest he wald make	He was to host a rich feast
Al for Jesu Cristes sake	All for Jesus Christ's sake,
Þat is oure saveour.	Who is our savior.
70 Muche folk soþe to say	He sent his invitation that day
He lete sende þeder opon a day	To many people, to tell the truth,
Wiþ myrth and gret honour.	With celebration and great ceremony.
Þe two barouns þat were so bold	These two barons that were so valiant,
And her sones þat y of told	And their sons that I spoke of,
To court þey com ful ȝare.	Came promptly to the court.
When þey were samned ȝong and old	When they were gathered, young and old,
Mony men hem gan bihold	Of the lordings who were there,
Of lordynges þat þer ware	Many men looked upon them:
How gentyl of body þai were apliȝt	How elegantly shaped they were in body,
80 And how þai were yliche of siȝt	And how fair they were in sight,
And how wise þai were of lare.	And how wise they were in learning.

---

66   *Ladies bryȝt in boure*: A recurring poetic phrase. A bower is a lady's bedroom, whereas a chamber usually refers to any room in a castle. Like *toun and tour* (9) and *worthy in wede* (30), this sort of alliterative doublet is omnipresent in ME romances, perhaps a holdover from Anglo-Saxon poetic modes. Chaucer only uses the expression once in his writings, fittingly in *Sir Thopas* (*CT* VII.742).

Alle þey seide wiþ outen les	And they all said, without a lie,
So faire children al so þai wes	That they had never before seen
In worlde never þai nare.	Finer young men than they were.
In al þe court was þer no wiȝt	In all the court there was no one,
Erl baron swain no kniȝt	Earl, baron, squire, or knight,
Neiþer lef ne loþe	Neither fair nor foul,
So lyche were þai boþe of siȝt.	Like them in their appearance.
And of on waxing ypliȝt	And in stature, I swear to you
90 I tel ȝow for soþe	That I tell you the truth,
In al þing þey were so liche	In every way they were so alike
Þer was neiþer pouer no riche	That there was no one, rich or poor,
Who so beheld hem boþe	Father or mother,
Fader ne moder þat couþe sain	Who beheld them both who could tell
Þat knew þe hendi childrew twain	The two handsome youths apart
But by þe coloure of her cloþe.	Except by the color of their clothes.
Þat riche douke his fest gan hold	That rich duke held his festivities,[67]
Wiþ erls and wiþ barouns bold	With earls and with brave barons,
100 As ȝe may listen and liþe	As you may listen and learn,
Fourtenniȝt as me was told	For fourteen nights, as I have been told,
Wiþ meete and drynke meryst on mold	With food and drink, the finest on earth,
To glad þe bernes bliþe.	To gladden the merry men.
Þer was mirþe and melodye	There was entertainment and melody
And al maner of menstracie	And all types of musicians
Her craftes for to kiþe.	There to show off their skills.
Opon þe fiftenday ful ȝare	On the fifteenth day, with earnestness,
Þai token her leve for to fare	They made their goodbyes to leave
And þonked him mani a siþe.	And thanked him many times.
110 Þan þe lordinges schuld forþ wende	When the gentlemen had set forth,
Þat riche douke comly of kende	That splendid duke, noble in lineage,
Cleped to him þat tide	Called to him on that occasion
Þo tway barouns þat were so hende	The two barons, who were so courteous,
And prayd hem also his frende	And urged them as his friend
In court þai schuld abide	That they should permit
And lete her tway sones fre	Their two fine sons to stay in the court
In his servise wiþ him to be	And be with him in his service,
Semly to fare bi his side.	To live fittingly by his side.
And he wald dubbe hem kniȝtes to	And he would dub them both knights
120 And susten hem for ever mo	And support them forevermore,
As lordinges proude in pride.	As lords proud in honor.[68]

---

67   *That riche douke*: In early Middle English the Old English articles / demonstratives se, seo, and þæt were gradually replaced by the definite article *the* (þe), and at times *the* and *that* seem poorly distinguished. Recurring formulas such as *that rich duke* might have been grandfathered for poetic reasons. A similar process was happening in Old French where Latin *ille*, *illa* (that) had become *li, la* (the). Rich in ME has a variety of nuances, from "powerful" or "high-ranking" to the modern sense of "wealthy".

68   The duke is proposing that the boys enter into an apprenticeship where they will serve him and be trained as pages, squires, and then knights. For noble boys to enter service in a great house was a common medieval arrangement, and could also be a route to other prestige appointments in court, as it was for Chaucer. Horn in *King Horn* receives a similar preferment.

Þe riche barouns answerd ogain
And her leuedis gan to sain
To þat douke ful ȝare
Þat þai were boþe glad and fain
Þat her levely children twain
In servise wiþ him ware.
Þai ȝave her childer her blisceing
And bisouȝt Jhesu Heven-king
130 He schuld scheld hem fro care
And oft þai þonked þe douke þat day
And token her leve and went oway
To her owen cuntres þai gun fare.
Þus war þo hende childer ywis
Child Amiloun and child Amis
In court frely to fede
To ride an hunting under riis.
Over al þe lond þan were þai priis
And worþliest in wede.
140 So wele þo children loved hem þo
Nas never children loved hem so
Noiþer in word no in dede.
Bitwix hem twai of blod and bon
Trewer love nas never non
In gest as so we rede.
On a day þe childer war and wiȝt
Treweþes togider þai gun pliȝt
While þai miȝt live and stond
Þat boþe bi day and bi niȝt
150 In wele and wo in wrong and riȝt
Þat þai schuld frely fond
To hold togider at everi nede
In word in werk in wille in dede
Where þat þai were in lond.
Fro þat day forward never mo
Failen oþer for wele no wo.
Þerto þai held up her hond.
Þus in gest as ȝe may here
Þo hende childer in cuntre were
160 Wiþ þat douke for to abide.
Þe douke was bliþe and glad of chere
Þai were him boþe leve and dere
Semly to fare bi his side.

The elegant barons gave their answer,
And their ladies began to speak
To the duke with enthusiasm,
That they were both glad and eager
That their two beloved children
Should be in service with him.
They gave their children their blessing
And entreated Jesus, Heaven's king,
That He would shield them from harm,
And they thanked the duke many times that
Day, and they took their leave and went.
They set off to journey to their own lands.
Thus those lovely boys, in truth,
Child Amiloun and Amis,
Were free to dine in the court,
And to ride and hunt under the boughs.
In all the land, they were respected
And held as worthiest in appearance.
So well did each love the other that
Never were children so close to each other,
Neither in word nor in deed.
Between the two, in blood and bone,
There was never truer friendship,[69]
In the stories that we read. On one day
The young men, keen and brave,
Pledged their loyalty together,
That while they might live and stand,
By both day and night,
In good and ill, in right and wrong,
They would freely endeavor
To hold together in every need,
In word, in action, in will, in deed,
Wherever they were in the land.
From that day forward they would never
Fail the other, neither for better or worse.
To this they held up their hands.
So in the story as you may hear,
These gentle young men of that country
Were living with the duke.
The duke was pleased and glad at heart,
And they were beloved and dear to him,
And fared honorably by his side.

---

69 ME is fairly poor in words for friendship, usually resorting to *love*. Throughout the text I am reading in various synonyms, as the repeated allusions to marital fidelity in homosocial relationships would not have suggested anything to a romance audience beyond deep *amicus*. Not everyone agrees: see Sheila Delaney, "A, A, and B: Coding Same-Sex Union in *Amis and Amiloun*", in *Pulp Fictions of Medieval England*, ed. Nicola McDonald (Manchester: University Press, 2004), 63-81.

Þo þai were fiften winter old
He dubbed boþe þo bernes bold
To kniȝtes in þat tide
And fond hem al þat hem was nede
Hors and wepen and worþly wede
As princes prout in pride.
170 Þat riche douke he loved hem so.
Al þat þai wald he fond hem þo
Boþe stedes white and broun
Þat in what stede þai gun go
Alle þe lond spac of hem þo
Boþe in tour and toun
In to what stede þat þai went
To justes oþer to turnament
Sir Amis and Sir Amiloun
For douhtiest þai were in everi dede.
180 Wiþ scheld and spere to ride on stede
Þai gat hem gret renoun.
Þat riche douke hadde of hem pris
For þat þai were so war and wiis
And holden of gret bounte.
Sir Amiloun and Sir Amis
He sett hem boþe in gret office
In his court for to be.
Sir Amis as ȝe may here
He made his chef botelere
190 For he was hend and fre
And Sir Amiloun of hem alle
He made chef steward in halle
To diȝt al his meine.
In to her servise when þai were brouȝt
To geten hem los þam spared nouȝt
Wel hendeliche þai bigan.
Wiþ riche and pouer so wele þai wrouȝt
Al þat hem seiȝe wiþ word and þouȝt
Hem loved mani a man.
200 For þai were so bliþe of chere
Over al þe lond fer and nere
Þe los of love þai wan
And þe riche douke wiþouten les
Of alle þe men þat olive wes
Mest he loved hem þan.
Þan hadde þe douke ich understond
A chef steward of alle his lond
A douhti kniȝt at crie
Þat ever he proved wiþ niþe and ond

When they were fifteen years old,
He dubbed both of the youths
As knights on that occasion,
And gave them all that they needed,
Horses and weapons and fine clothes,
As princes who were proud in bearing.
That rich duke loved them so.
All that they wished for he provided,
Steeds for both, white and brown,
So that in whatever place they went,
All the land would speak of them later,
Both in tower and in town,
At whatever place that they went,
To jousts or to tournaments,
Sir Amis and Sir Amiloun, for they were
The bravest in every deed. With shield
And spear, as they rode on steeds,
They won great fame for themselves.
That regal duke had great regard for them,
For they were so keen and wise
And esteemed for their great generosity.
He set Sir Amiloun and Sir Amis,
Both of them, in key offices,
In order to be in his court.
Sir Amis, as you may hear,
Was made his chief butler,
For he was courteous and gracious.
And Sir Amiloun was made
Chief steward of the hall over everyone
To keep his household in order.
When they were placed in their positions,
They spared nothing to earn themselves
Praise, and they performed very graciously.
They served rich and poor so admirably
That all who saw them, many a man,
Cherished them in word and thought.
For they were of such good cheer
That over all the land, near and far,
They won praise for their devotion,
And the mighty duke, without a lie,
Of all the men that were alive,
Loved them most of all then.
At the time the duke, as I understand,
Had a chief steward of all his land,
A formidable knight at his call, who
Constantly schemed, with spite and hate,

210 For to have brou3t hem boþe to schond	To have them both brought to shame
Wiþ gile and trecherie.	With guile and treachery.
For þai were so gode and hende	For they were so good and so gracious,
And for þe douke was so wele her frende	And because the duke was so close a friend
He hadde þerof gret envie.	He had great jealousy because of it.
To þe douke wiþ wordes grame	With biting words to the duke,
Ever he proved to don hem schame	He continually tried to bring them shame
Wiþ wel gret felonie.	With some outrageous crime.
So wiþin þo 3eres to	So then, within two years
A messanger þer com þo	A messenger arrived there,
220 To Sir Amiloun hende on hond	Skillful in hand, to Sir Amiloun
And seyd hou deþ hadde fet him fro	And said how death had taken from him
His fader and his moder also	His father and his mother as well
Þurth þe grace of Godes sond.	Through the grace of God's command.
Þan was þat kni3t a careful man	Then that knight was a sorrowful man.
To þat douke he went him þan	He took himself to the duke
And dede him to understond	And had him understand
His fader and his moder hende	That his father and his gracious mother
War ded and he most hom wende	Were dead, and he had to travel home
For to resaive his lond.	In order to receive his land.
230 Þat riche douke comly of kende	That stately duke, of a noble family,
Answerd o3ain wiþ wordes hende	Answered in reply with kindly words
And seyd, "So God me spede	And said, "So help me God,
Sir Amiloun now þou schalt wende	Sir Amiloun, now that you must go
Me nas never so wo for frende	I was never so sad to see a friend
Þat of mi court out yede.	Go out of my court.
Ac 3if ever it bifalle so	But if it ever happens so
Þat þou art in wer and wo	That you are at war or in woe
And of min help hast nede	And have need of my help,
Saveliche com or send þi sond	Just come or send your word,
240 And wiþ al mi powere of mi lond	And with all the powers in my land
Y schal wreke þe of þat dede".	I will avenge you of that injury".
Þan was Sir Amiloun ferli wo	Then Sir Amiloun was bitterly sad
For to wende Sir Amis fro	To part from Sir Amis.
On him was al his þou3t.	On him were all his thoughts.
To a goldsmitþe he gan go	He made his way to a goldsmith
And lete make gold coupes to.	And had two gold cups made.
For þre hundred pounde he hem bou3t	He paid three hundred pounds for them,[70]
Þat boþe were of o wi3t	So that both were the same weight,
And boþe of o michel y pli3t.	And both were the same size, truly.
250 Ful richeliche þai were wrou3t	They were very richly fashioned,
And boþe þai weren as liche ywis	And both were as alike, I know,
As was Sir Amiloun and Sir Amis;	As Sir Amiloun and Sir Amis were;

---

70 According to the UK National Archives website, £300 in 1340 is roughly £160,000 or US$250,000 in modern money, a preposterous amount only credible in a medieval romance. Even the extravagantly lavish ring Havelok gives Ubbe is mentioned as worth £100. Accessed at http://www.nationalarchives.gov.uk/currency/.

Þer no failed riȝt nouȝt.
When þat Sir Amiloun was al ȝare
He tok his leve for to fare
To wende in his jorne.
Sir Amis was so ful of care
For sorwe and wo and sikeing sare
Almost swoned þat fre.

260 To þe douke he went wiþ dreri mode
And praid him fair þer he stode
And seyd, "Sir par charite
Ȝif me leve to wende þe fro
Bot ȝif y may wiþ mi broþer go
Mine hert it brekeþ of þre!"
Þat riche douke comly of kende
Answerd oȝain wiþ wordes hende
And seyd wiþouten delay
"Sir Amis mi gode frende

270 Wold ȝe boþe now fro me wende?
"Certes", he seyd, "nay!"
"Were ȝe boþe went me fro
Þan schuld me waken al mi wo
Mi joie were went oway.
Þi broþer schal into his cuntre.
Wende wiþ him in his jurne
And com oȝain þis day".
When þai were redi forto ride
Þo bold bernes for to abide

280 Busked hem redy boun.
Hende herkneþ is nouȝt to hide
So douhti kniȝtes in þat tide
Þat ferd out of þat toun
Al þat day as þai rade
Gret morning boþe þai made
Sir Amis and Amiloun.
And when þai schuld wende otwain
Wel fair togider opon a plain
Of hors þai liȝt adoun.

290 When þai were boþe afot liȝt
Sir Amiloun þat hendi kniȝt
Was riȝtwise man of rede
And seyd to Sir Amis ful riȝt
"Broþer as we er trewþe pliȝt
Boþe wiþ word and dede
Fro þis day forward never mo
To faily oþer for wele no wo
To help him at his nede.

There was no defect in them at all.
When Sir Amiloun was all ready,
He made his goodbyes to set forth,
To travel on his journey.
Sir Amis was so full of sadness,
That for sorrow and woe and bitter sighs,
That sensitive man almost fell faint.
He went to the duke in dreary spirits
And addressed him reverently where he
Stood, and said, "Sir, for charity's sake,
Give me permission to travel from you.
Unless I may go with my brother,
My heart, it will break in three!"
The regal duke, of a noble family,
Answered in reply with gracious words
And said without delay,
"Sir Amis, my good friend,
Would you both now leave me?"
"Surely not!" he said.
"If you were both gone from me,
Then all my sorrows would be awakened
And my joys would be gone away!
Your brother will go to his country.
Accompany him on his journey
And come back again this day".
When they were ready to ride,
Those brave men readied
Themselves for the journey. Gentle
People, listen! There's nothing to hide.
So these sturdy knights, at that moment,
Traveled out of the town.
All that day, as they rode on,
They both made great mourning,
Sir Amis and Amiloun.
And when they had to part in two,
They dismounted from their horses
Gallantly together upon a plain.
When they were both on foot,
Sir Amiloun, that faithful knight,
Was a just man of counsel,
And said straightaway to Sir Amis,
"Brother, as we pledged loyalty before,
Both in words and deeds,
From this day on we will promise
To never fail the other, for better or worse,
To help him in his need.

Broþer be now trewe to me	Friend, be true to me now,
300 And y schal ben as trewe to þe	And I will be as true to you,
Also God me spede!	As God may help me to!
Ac broþer ich warn þe biforn	But brother, I warn you beforehand,
For his love þat bar þe croun of þorn	For His love, who wore a crown of thorns
To save al mankende	To save all mankind,
Be nouȝt oȝain þi lord forsworn	Do not swear falsely against your lord
And ȝif þou dost þou art forlorn	In any way. And if you do, you are lost
Ever more wiþouten ende.	Forevermore without end.
Bot ever do trewþe and no tresoun	But always be true and never treasonous;
And þenk on me Sir Amiloun	And think of me, Sir Amiloun,
310 Now we asondri schal wende.	Now that we must travel apart.
And broþer ȝete y þe forbede	And friend, again I warn you against
Þe fals steward felawerede.	Fellowship with the false steward.
Certes he wil þe schende!"	He will surely bring you to harm!"
As þai stode so þo breþeren bold	As they stood so, the brave brothers,
Sir Amiloun drouȝ forþ tway coupes of gold	Sir Amiloun drew out the two gold cups,
Ware liche in al þing	Which were alike in every way,
And bad Sir Amis þat he schold	And asked that Sir Amis would
Chese wheþer he have wold	Choose which one he wished for,
Wiþouten more dwelling	Without any more delay.
320 And seyd to him "Mi leve broþer	And he said to him, "My dear friend,
Kepe þou þat on and y þat oþer.	Keep that one and I will the other.
For Godes love Heven-king	For the love of God, Heaven's king,
Lete never þis coupe fro þe	Let this cup never go from you,
Bot loke heron and þenk on me.	But look on it and think of me.
It tokneþ our parting".	It is a token of our parting".
Gret sorwe þai made at her parting	They made great sorrow at their leaving
And kisten hem wiþ eiȝen wepeing	And kissed each other with weeping eyes,
Þo kniȝtes hende and fre.	Those knights, noble and free. Each
Aiþer bitauȝt oþer Heven-king	Commended the other to Heaven's king,
330 And on her stedes þai gun spring	And they jumped on their steeds
And went in her jurne.	And went on their journeys.
Sir Amiloun went hom to his lond	Sir Amiloun went home to his land
And sesed it al into his hond	Which his ancestors had held,
Þat his elders hadde be	And claimed it all into his hand,
And spoused a leuedy briȝt in bour	And wedded a lady, beautiful in her bower,
And brouȝt hir hom wiþ gret honour	And brought her home with great ceremony
And miche solempnete.	And much stately formality.
Lete we Sir Amiloun stille be	We will leave Sir Amiloun alone
Wiþ his wiif in his cuntre.	With his wife in his country.
340 God leve hem wele to fare!	God grant that he fare well!
And of Sir Amis telle we.	And we will talk of Sir Amis.
When he com hom to court oȝe	When he came back home to the court,
Ful bliþe of him þai ware.	They were very pleased to see him.
For þat he was so hende and gode	For he was so gracious and good that

Men blisced him boþe bon and blod
Þat ever him gat and bare
Save þe steward of þat lond.
Ever he proved wiþ niþe and ond
To bring him into care.
350 Þan on a day bifel it so
Wiþ þe steward he met þo
Ful fair he gret þat fre.
"Sir Amis", he seyd, "þe is ful wo
For þat þi broþer is went þe fro
And certes so is me.
Ac of his wendeing have þou no care
3if þou wilt leve opon mi lare
And lete þi morning be.
And þou wil be to me kende
360 Y schal þe be a better frende
Þan ever yete was he.
"Sir Amis", he seyd, "do bi mi red
And swere ous boþe broþerhed
And pli3t we our trewþes to.
Be trewe to me in word and dede
And y schal so God me spede
Be trewe to þe also".
Sir Amis answerd, "Mi treuþe y pli3t
To Sir Amiloun þe gentil kni3t
370 Þei he be went me fro.
Whiles þat y may gon and speke
Y no schal never mi treuþe breke
Noiþer for wele no wo.
For bi þe treuþe þat God me sende
Ichave him founde so gode and kende
Seþþen þat y first him knewe;
For ones y pli3t him treuþe þat hende
Whereso he in warld wende
Y schal be to him trewe.
380 And 3if y were now forsworn
And breke mi treuþe y were forlorn
Wel sore it schuld me rewe.
Gete me frendes whare y may
Y no schal never bi ni3t no day
Chaunge him for no newe".
Þe steward þan was egre of mode
Almest for wretþe he wex ner wode
And seyd wiþouten delay
And swore bi Him þat dyed on rode
390 "Þou traitour unkinde blod!

Men blessed them, both flesh and blood,
Who had conceived and given birth to him,
Except for the steward of that land.
Continually he tried with spite and hostility
To bring him into trouble.
Then one day it so happened
That he met with the steward,
And greeted the noble man courteously.
"Sir Amis", he said, "it is very sad for you
That your friend has gone from you,
And certainly it is the same for me.
But do not be troubled by his going,
If you will live by my advice,
And let your mourning pass.
You will be kin to me,
And I will be a better friend to you
Than he ever was.
Sir Amis", he said, "do as I advise,
And swear our brotherhood together
And pledge our fidelity as well.
Be true to me in word and deed,
And I will to you, so help me God,
Be true as well".
Sir Amis answered, "I gave my word
To Sir Amiloun, the noble knight,
Though he has departed from me.
While I can walk and talk,
I will never break my vow,
Neither for better or worse.
For by the truth that God sends me,
I have found him so good and kind
From the time I first knew him;
Since I have pledged him loyalty,
That gentle man, wherever he goes
In the world, I will be true to him.
And if I now swore against him
And broke my oath, I would be lost.
I would regret it bitterly.
Though I get friends where I may,
I will never by night or day
Exchange him for someone new".
Then the steward was in a furious mood;
He almost grew mad with rage
And said, without any pause,
And swore by Him who died on the cross,
"You common-blooded traitor!

Þou schalt abigge þis nay!
Y warn þe wele", he seyd þan
"Þat y schal be þi strong foman
Ever after þis day!"
Sir Amis answerd þo
"Sir þerof ȝive y nouȝt a slo!
Do al þat þou may!"
Al þus þe wrake gan biginne
And wiþ wretþe þai went atwinne
400 Þo bold bernes to.
Þe steward nold never blinne
To schende þat douhti kniȝt of kinne
Ever he proved þo.
Þus in court togider þai were
Wiþ wretþe and wiþ loureand chere
Wele half a ȝere and mo.
And afterward opon a while
Þe steward wiþ tresoun and gile
Wrouȝt him ful michel wo.
410 So in a time as we tel in gest
Þe riche douke lete make a fest
Semly in somers tide.
Þer was mani a gentil gest
Wiþ mete and drink ful onest
To servi by ich a side.
Miche semly folk was samned þare
Erls barouns lasse and mare
And leuedis proude in pride.
More joie no miȝt be non
420 Þan þer was in þat worþly won
Wiþ blisse in borwe to bide.
Þat riche douke þat y of told
He hadde a douhter fair and bold
Curteise hende and fre.
When sche was fiften winter old
In al þat lond nas þer non yhold
So semly on to se
For sche was gentil and avenaunt.
Hir name was cleped Belisaunt.
430 As ȝe may liþe at me.
Wiþ leuedis and maidens briȝt in bour
Kept sche was wiþ honour
And gret solempnite.
Þat fest lasted fourten niȝt

You will pay for this snub!
I warn you well", he said then,
"That I will be your sworn enemy
Forevermore after this day!"
Sir Amis answered then,
"Sir, I don't give a berry about it![71]
Do as you like!"
And so their emnity began to rise,
And in wrath they went their ways,
Those two bold young men.
The steward would never cease,
Always attempting to shame
That valiant knight of honor.
Thus in court they coexisted
With hostility and surly glares
Well more than half a year.
And afterward, on one occasion,
The steward caused great woe for him
With treason and guile.
So one time, as the story says,
The rich duke held a feast,
Fittingly in summertime.
There were many noble guests
With the finest food and drink
Served all around.
Many worthy people were gathered there,
Earls, barons, high and low,
And ladies magnificent in appearance.
There could be no greater joy
Than there was in that stately place,
With the pleasures to enjoy in the castle.
This grand duke, which I spoke of,
Had a daughter who was fair and bold,
Courteous, attractive, and generous.
When she was fifteen years old,
There was no one in all the land believed
So lovely to look on,
For she was graceful and beautiful.
If you may listen to me,
Her name was called Belisaunt.
She stayed with the ladies and maidens,
Shining in their bowers, in honor
And great dignity.
The feast lasted fourteen nights,

---

71 *Sloe*: a tart plum-like fruit resembling a blueberry. As the berries were of little value, the idiom is close in meaning to PDE "I don't give a crap".

Of barouns and of birddes briȝt
And lordinges mani and fale.
Þer was mani a gentil kniȝt
And mani a seriaunt wise and wiȝt
To serve þo hende in halle.
440 Þan was þe boteler Sir Amis
Over al yholden flour and priis
Trewely to telle in tale
And douhtiest in everi dede
And worþliest in ich a wede
And semliest in sale.
Þan þe lordinges schulden al gon
And wende out of þat worþli won
In boke as so we rede
Þat mirie maide gan aske anon
450 Of hir maidens everichon
And seyd, "So God ȝou spede
Who was hold þe douȝtiest kniȝt
And semlyest in ich a siȝt
And worþliest in wede
And who was þe fairest man
Þat was yholden in lond þan
And douȝtiest of dede?"
Her maidens gan answere ogain
And seyd, "Madame we schul þe sain
460 Þat soþe bi seyn Savour
Of erls barouns kniȝt and swain
Þe fairest man and mest of main
And man of mest honour
It is Sir Amis þe kinges boteler.
In al þis warld nis his per
Noiþer in toun no tour.
He is douhtiest in dede
And worþliest in everi wede
And chosen for priis and flour".
470 Belisaunt þat birdde briȝt
When þai hadde þus seyd ypliȝt
As ȝe may listen and liþe
On Sir Amis þat gentil kniȝt
Ywis hir love was al aliȝt
Þat no man miȝt it kiþe.
Wher þat sche seiȝe him ride or go
Hir þouȝt hir hert brac atwo
Þat hye no spac nouȝt wiþ þat bliþe
For hye no miȝt niȝt no day
480 Speke wiþ him þat fair may

With barons and beautiful lasses
And lords, numerous and abundant.
There was many a gentle knight
And many a servant, strong and wise,
To serve those noble people in the hall.
But the butler, Sir Amis,
Held the flower and prize over all,
To speak truly in the tale,
And most valiant in every deed,
And worthiest in all appearance,
And the most dignified in the hall.
When it was time for the lordings to leave
And depart from that stately dwelling,
In the book as we read it,
The merry maid asked right away
Each one of her maidens,
And said, "So help you God,
Who was considered the bravest knight
And finest in every aspect,
And worthiest in appearance,
And who was seen as the fairest man
In the land at the time,
The most valiant of deeds?"
Her maidens answered in return
And said, "My lady, we will tell you
The truth, by our Holy Savior.
Out of earls, barons, knights, and youths,
The fairest man and greatest of might,
And the man of highest honor,
Is Sir Amis, the king's butler.
In all this world he has no peer,
Neither in town nor castle.
He is bravest in deed
And worthiest in all appearance
And takes the prize and flower".
Belisaunt, that beautiful lass,
When they had spoken so,
As you may listen and learn–
Her heart was all set on fire, truly,
For Sir Amis, the noble knight,
With a love no man could fathom.
Wherever she saw him ride or walk,
She thought her heart would break in two,
For she never spoke with that elegant man
Because she had no chance by night or day
To speak with him, that fair maid,

Sche wepe wel mani a siþe.   And so she wept many a time.
Þus þat miri maiden ying   Thus the merry young maiden
Lay in care and love-morning   Lay in sadness and lovesickness
Boþe bi niȝt and day.   Both by day and night.
As y ȝou tel in mi talking   As I tell you in my speaking,
For sorwe sche spac wiþ him no þing   In sorrow she said nothing to him,
Sike in bed sche lay.   But lay ill in bed.
Hir moder come to hir þo   Her mother then came to her
And gan to frain hir of hir wo   And asked her about her malaise,
490 Help hir ȝif hye may.   To help her if she could.
     And sche answerd wiþouten wrong   And she answered without deceit
     Hir pines were so hard and strong   That her pains were so hard and strong
     Sche wald be loken in clay.   She wanted to be buried in the earth.
     Þat riche douk in o morning   One morning, that majestic duke,
     And wiþ him mani a gret lording   Along with many a great lording,
     As prince prout in pride   As princes proud in their bearing,
     Þai diȝt hem wiþouten dweling   Prepared themselves without delay
     For to wende on dere hunting   To go out deer hunting,
     And busked hem for to ride.   And so they dressed themselves to ride.
500 When þe lordinges everichon   When every one of the lordings
     Were went out of þat worþli won   Was gone out of that regal residence–
     In hert is nouȝt to hide   There's nothing in one's heart to hide–[72]
     Sir Amis wiþouten les   Sir Amis, without a lie,
     For a malady þat on him wes   Because of a minor illness he had,
     At hom he gan to abide.   Stayed behind at home.
     When þo lordinges were out ywent   When the lordings were all gone out
     Wiþ her men hende and bowes bent   With their men, skillful and bows bent,
     To hunte on holtes hare   To hunt in the deep woods,
     Þan Sir Amis verrament   Then Sir Amis, in truth,
510 He bileft at hom in present   Was left at home for the day
     To kepe al þat þer ware.   To attend to all who were there. Then
     Þat hendi kniȝt biþouȝt him þo   The gracious knight thought to himself
     Into þe gardin he wold go   That he would go into the garden
     For to solas him þare.   To relax himself there.
     Under a bouȝ as he gan bide   Under a bough as he rested,
     To here þe foules song þat tide   To hear the birds sing in that moment
     Him þouȝt a blisseful fare.   Seemed a peaceful state to him.
     Now hende herkneþ and ȝe may here   Now, gentle people, listen and you will hear
     Hou þat þe doukes douhter dere   How the duke's dear daughter
520 Sike in hir bed lay.   Lay in distress in her bed.
     Hir moder com wiþ diolful chere   Her mother came in doleful spirits
     And al þe leuedis þat þer were   With all the ladies that were there
     For to solas þat may.   To give comfort to that maiden.

---

72 The narrator may also be referring to the lordings, i.e. they rode out in good faith without any ulterior motives at heart.
    The parallel trope of the hero being 'hunted' at home by lusty ladies while the lords are also out hunting is a popular one
    in romance, also seen in *King Horn* and in *Sir Gawain and the Green Knight*.

"Arise up", sche seyd, "douhter min
And go play þe in to þe gardin
Þis semly somers day.
Þer may þou here þe foules song
Wiþ joie and miche blis among
Þi care schal wende oway!"
530 Up hir ros þat swete wiȝt
Into þe gardine sche went ful riȝt
Wiþ maidens hende and fre.
Þe somers day was fair and briȝt
Þe sonne him schon þurth lem of liȝt
Þat semly was on to se.
Sche herd þe foules gret and smale
Þe swete note of þe niȝtingale
Ful mirily sing on tre.
Ac hir hert was so hard ibrouȝt
540 On love-longing was al hir þouȝt
No miȝt hir gamen no gle.
And so þat mirie may wiþ pride
Went into þe orchard þat tide
To slake hir of hir care.
Þan seyȝe sche Sir Amis biside
Under a bouȝ he gan abide
To here þo mirþes mare
Þan was sche boþe glad and bliþe.
Hir joie couþe sche noman kiþe
550 When þat sche seiȝe him þare
And þouȝt sche wold for noman wond
Þat sche no wold to him fond
And tel him of hir fare.
Þan was þat may so bliþe o mode
When sche seiȝe were he stode.
To him sche went þat swete
And þouȝt for alle þis warldes gode
Bot ȝif hye spac þat frely fode
Þat time no wold sche lete.
560 And as tite as þat gentil kniȝt
Seiȝe þat bird in bour so briȝt
Com wiþ him for to mete
Oȝaines hir he gan wende.
Wiþ worde boþe fre and hende
Ful fair he gan hir grete.
Þat mirie maiden sone anon
Bad hir maidens fram hir gon
And wiþdrawe hem oway.
And when þai were togider alon

"Rise up, daughter of mine", she said,
"And go play in the garden
This lovely summer's day.
There you can hear the birds sing
With joy and great bliss among them,
And your troubles will pass away!"
That sweet creature rose up.
She went straightaway into the garden
With her maidens, graceful and noble.
The summer's day was fair and bright.
The sun shone down in a gleaming light,
Which was pleasant to see.
She heard the birds, great and small.
The sweet notes of the nightingale
Sang merrily in the tree.
But her heart was so heavily burdened
That all her thoughts were on love-longing,
And she could not play or enjoy herself.
And so that lovely maid went
Elegantly into the orchard that moment
To relieve herself of her troubles.
When she saw Sir Amis nearby
Under a bough where he had settled
To better hear the singing,
Then she was both glad and overjoyed.
She could not express her joy to any man
When she saw him there, and she knew
She would not stop for anyone
In order to make her way toward him
And tell him about her feelings.
Then the maiden's spirits were so light
When she saw where he stood.
She went to him, that sweet one,
And thought that, for all this world's goods,
She would not let that time pass without
Speaking to the gallant young man.
And just as soon as the gentle knight
Saw that lass, so beautiful in her bower,
Coming across to meet with him,
He made his way toward her.
With words both noble and gracious
He greeted her courteously.
The merry maiden quickly
Told her ladies to go from her
And take themselves away.
And when they were alone together,

570 To Sir Amis sche made hir mon	She made her plea to Sir Amis
And seyd opon hir play	And said coquettishly,
"Sir kniȝt on þe mine hert is brouȝt	"Sir Knight, my heart is set on you.
Þe to love is al mi þouȝt	To love you is all my desire,
Boþe bi niȝt and day.	Both by night and day.
Þat bot þou wolt mi leman be	Unless you will be my sweetheart,
Ywis min hert brekeþ a þre	My heart will break into three for sure![73]
No lenger libben y no may".	I will not live any longer".
"Þou art", sche seyd, "a gentil kniȝt	"You are a gallant knight", she said,
And icham a bird in bour briȝt	And I am a woman, shining in my bower,
580 Of wel heiȝe kin ycorn.	Born into a noble family.
And boþe bi day and bi niȝt	And both by day and by night,
Mine hert so hard is on þe liȝt	My heart has fallen for you so hard
Mi joie is al forlorn.	That my joys are all lost.
Pliȝt me þi trewþe þou schalt be trewe	Pledge me your vow that you will be true
And chaunge me for no newe	And will not exchange me for anyone new
Þat in þis world is born	Who is born into this world,
And y pliȝt þe mi treuþe also.	And I'll pledge you my vow as well.
Til God and deþ dele ous ato	Until God and death part us in two,
Y schal never be forsworn".	I will never break my promise".
590 Þat hende kniȝt stille he stode	That gentle knight stood still
And al for þouȝt chaunged his mode	And, deep in thought, changed his mood
And seyd wiþ hert fre	And said with a generous heart,
"Madame for Him þat dyed on rode	"My lady, for Him who died on the cross,
Astow art comen of gentil blode	If you have come from noble blood
And air of þis lond schal be	And will be heir of this land,
Biþenke þe of þi michel honour!	Think of your high position!
Kinges sones and emperour	The sons of kings and emperors
Nar non to gode to þe.	Are none too good for you.
Certes þan were it michel unriȝt	Surely, it would be a great wrong
600 Þi love to lain opon a kniȝt	For your love to be given to a knight
Þat naþ noiþer lond no fe.	Who has neither land nor income.
And ȝif we schuld þat game biginne	And if we should begin to court,
And ani wiȝt of al þi kinne	And anyone from all your family
Miȝt it undergo	Would discover it, we would lose
Al our joie and worldes winne	All our joys and pleasures of this world,
We schuld lese and for þat sinne	And for that sin
Wretþi God þerto.	Anger God by doing so.
And y dede mi lord þis deshonour	If I did my lord this dishonor,
Þan were ich an ivel traitour.	Then I would be an evil traitor.
610 Ywis it may nouȝt be so!	Surely it cannot be so!

---

73 Medieval hearts seem to break into two, three, or five with no particular significance, although there may be a reference either to the Trinity or to other significant numbers in scripture. I discuss this in "Numerological and Structural Symbolism in the Auchinleck Stanzaic *Guy of Warwick*", *English Studies* 95:8 (2014), 849-859; see also Russell A. Peck, "Number as Cosmic Language", 24, in *Essays in the Numerical Criticism of Medieval Literature*, ed. Carolyn D. Eckhardt (Lewisburg, PA: Bucknell University Press, 1980).

Leve madame do bi mi red	Dear lady, do as I advise
And þenk what wil com of þis dede:	And think what will come of this deed:
Certes noþing bot wo".	For certain, nothing but sorrow".[74]
Þat mirie maiden of gret renoun	The lovely lady of great renown answered,
Answerd, "Sir kniȝt þou nast no croun!	"Sir Knight, you have no tonsure![75]
For God þat bouȝt þe dere	By God who redeemed you dearly,
Wheþer artow prest oþer persoun	Are you some priest or parson,
Oþer þou art monk oþer canoun	Or are you a monk or clergyman
Þat prechest me þus here?	That preaches to me so here?
620 Þou no schust have ben no kniȝt,	You shouldn't have been a knight,
To gon among maidens briȝt;	Mingling among us fair maidens;
Þou schust have ben a frere!	You should have been a friar!
He þat lerd þe þus to preche	Whoever taught you to sermonize so,
Þe devel of Helle ichim biteche	The devil can take him to Hell,
Mi broþer þei he were!"	Even if he were my brother! But",
"Ac", sche seyd, "bi him þat ous wrouȝt	She continued, "by Him who created us,
Al þi precheing helpeþ nouȝt	All your preaching accomplishes nothing,
No stond þou never so long!	No matter how long you resist!
Bot ȝif þou wilt graunt me mi þouȝt	Unless you grant me my desires,
630 Mi love schal be ful dere abouȝt	My love will be paid for dearly
Wiþ pines hard and strong.	With pains, hard and strong.
Mi kerchef and mi cloþes anon	My headscarf and my clothes,
Y schal torende doun ichon	I will tear all of them off at once
And say wiþ michel wrong	And say with great deception
Wiþ strengþe þou hast me todrawe!	That you violated me by force!
Ytake þou schalt be þurth londes lawe	You will be taken by the law of the land
And dempt heiȝe to hong!"	And condemned to hang high!"
Þan stode þat hendy kniȝt ful stille	Then the noble knight stood still
And in his hert him liked ille;	And he was troubled at heart;
640 No word no spac he þo.	He spoke no words then.
He þouȝt, "Bot y graunt hir wille	He thought, "Unless I grant her will,
Wiþ hir speche sche wil me spille	She will destroy me with her words
Er þan y passe hir fro.	Before I move away from her.
And ȝif y do mi lord þis wrong	And if I do my lord this wrong,
Wiþ wilde hors and wiþ strong	I will be drawn behind wild horses
Y schal be drawe also".	With violence as well".[76]
Loþ him was þat dede to don	He was loath to do that deed,

---

74 Amis believes that his rank and status are too low to become romantically involved with the king's daughter, and that doing so would be a punishable act of disloyalty. He is also continuing to keep his vow to Amiloun, "Be nought ogain thi lord forsworn" (304).

75 *Tonsure:* the partly-shaved hairstyle common to medieval clergy. Belisaunt makes fun of Sir Amis by suggesting that he is acting like a celibate monk. As stereotypical friars in medieval humor were suave womanizers, her subsequent joke that Amis should have been a friar instead of a knight is especially cheeky. Medieval women were often depicted as having more sexual desire than men; see also line 1167.

76 Sir Amis is referring to the capital punishment for high treason of being hanged and drawn–dragged along the ground by horses–for Belisaunt's false charge of rape. Sir Amis's squire mentions being ripped apart in 2046, perhaps the final punishment of quartering, having the body cut into four pieces.

And wele loþer his liif forgon.
Was him never so wo.

650 And þan he þouȝt wiþouten lesing
Better were to graunt hir asking
Þan his liif for to spille.
Þan seyd he to þat maiden ying
"For Godes love Heven-king
Understond to mi skille!
Astow art maiden gode and trewe
Biþenk hou oft rape wil rewe
And turn to grame wel grille
And abide we al þis sevenniȝt!

660 As icham trewe gentil kniȝt
Y schal graunt þe þi wille".
Þan answerd þat bird briȝt
And swore, "Bi Jhesu ful of miȝt
Þou scapest nouȝt so oway!
Þi treuþe anon þou schalt me pliȝt
Astow art trewe gentil kniȝt
Þou schalt hold þat day".
He graunted hir hir wil þo
And pliȝt hem trewþes boþe to

670 And seþþen kist þo twai.
Into hir chaumber sche went ogain
Þan was sche so glad and fain
Hir joie sche couþe no man sai.
Sir Amis þan wiþouten dwelling
For to kepe his lordes coming
Into halle he went anon.
When þai were comen fram dere hunting
And wiþ him mani an heiȝe lording
Into þat worþly won

680 After his douhter he asked swiþe.
Men seyd þat sche was glad and bliþe;
Hir care was al agon.
To eten in halle þai brouȝt þat may.
Ful bliþe and glad þai were þat day
And þonked God ichon.
When þe lordinges wiþouten les
Hendelich were brouȝt on des
Wiþ leuedis briȝt and swete
As princes þat were proude in pres

And more unwilling to lose his life.
He was never so woeful.
And then he thought, without lying,
It would be better to grant her plea
Than to lose his life.
Then he said to that young maiden,
"For the love of God, Heaven's king,
Listen to my reasons!
If you are a good and true maiden,
Think how often haste is regretted
And turns into fearful disaster,
And let us wait these seven nights!
So long as I am a true noble knight,
I will grant you your will".
Then that beautiful lass answered,
And swore, "By Jesus, full of might,
You do not get away so easily!
You will pledge your vow to me at once.
If you are a true and noble knight,
You will hold to that day".
He granted her will to her then,
And pledged loyalty between them both,
And then the two kissed.
She returned to her chamber.
Then she was glad and content;
No man could comprehend her joy.[77]
Sir Amis, without more delay,
In order to prepare for his lord's arrival,
Went into the hall at once.
When the duke returned from deer hunting
Into that stately dwelling,
And with him many a high lord,
He straightaway asked about his daughter.
Men said that she was cheerful and at ease;
Her troubles were all gone. They brought
The maiden to dine in the hall.
They were very relieved and glad that day,
And everyone thanked God.
When the lordings, without a lie,
Were escorted courteously to the table
As princes that were proud in battle,
With ladies beautiful and sweet,

---

77 *Hir joie sche couthe no man sai*: This, along with 475, 549, and 1239, is a problematic line. The meaning may be that Belisaunt is too coy or timid to reveal her joy, but it seems unlike her if she passionately threatens Sir Amis with a false accusal of rape and then flirts with him at the supper table. The poetic idea may be that her joy is so overwhelming that it is beyond anyone's understanding.

690 Ful richeliche served he wes	They were served splendidly
Wiþ menske and mirþe to mete.	With grace and enjoyment at dinner.
When þat maiden þat y of told	When the maiden that I spoke of
Among þe birdes þat were bold	Sat there in her seat,
Þer sche sat in her sete	Among the lasses who were merry,
On Sir Amis þat gentil kniȝt	She cast her sight a hundred times
An hundred time sche cast hir siȝt.	On Sir Amis, that noble knight.
For noþing wald sche lete.	She would not cease for anything.
On Sir Amis þat kniȝt hendy	On Sir Amis, that handsome knight,
Ever more sche cast hir eyȝe;	She continually cast her eye;
700 For noþing wold sche spare.	She would not stop for anything.
Þe steward ful of felonie	The steward, full of wickedness,
Wel fast he gan hem aspie	Began to watch them attentively
Til he wist of her fare	Until he observed her situation,
And bi her siȝt he parceived þo	And by her look he then perceived
Þat gret love was bitwix hem to.	That there was great love between the two.
And was agreved ful sare	He was sorely aggrieved
And þouȝt he schuld in a while,	And thought he might in a while,
Boþe wiþ tresoun and wiþ gile	With both treason and guile,
Bring hem into care.	Bring them into trouble.
710 Þus ywis þat miri may	Thus, indeed, that sweet maiden
Ete in halle wiþ gamen and play	Ate in the hall with sporting and fun
Wele four days oþer five	Well over four or five days,
Þat ever when sche Sir Amis say	So that always, when she saw Sir Amis,
Al hir care was went oway;	All her cares were gone away;
Wele was hir o live.	It was good to her to be alive.
Wher þat he sat or stode	Whether he sat or stood,
Sche biheld opon þat frely fode	She openly watched that noble youth,
No stint sche for no strive.	Nor did she hold back for any danger.
And þe steward for wretþe sake	And the steward, for wrath's sake,
720 Brouȝt hem boþe in ten and wrake	Brought them both to pain and harm.
Wel ivel mot he þrive!	May he have foul fortune![78]
Þat riche douke opon a day	The rich duke, on one afternoon,
On dere hunting went him to play	Took himself out deer hunting again,
And wiþ him wel mani a man.	And many men went with him.
And Belisaunt þat miri may	And Belisaunt, the merry maiden,
To chaumber þer Sir Amis lay	Went to the chamber where Sir Amis lay,
Sche went as sche wele kan.	As she knew the way well.
And þe steward wiþouten les	And the steward, without a lie,
In a chaumber bisiden he wes	Was in a chamber nearby
730 And seiȝe þe maiden þan	And saw the maiden then
Into chaumber hou sche gan glide.	And how she breezed into the room.
For to aspie hem boþe þat tide	In order to spy on them both that moment,
After swiþe he ran.	He ran quickly after them.

---

78 *Wel ivel mot he thrive*: "May he thrive evilly". A moderately strong curse often found in ME, along with "Datheit hwo recke" ("Curse anyone who cares".)

When þat may com into þat won	When the maiden came into the room,
Sche fond Sir Amis þer alon.	She found Sir Amis there alone.
"Hail", sche seyd þat leuedi briȝt.	"Hello", she said, that beautiful lady.
"Sir Amis", sche sayd anon	"Sir Amis", she continued at once,
"Þis day a sevenniȝt it is gon	"Today seven nights have passed
Þat trewþe we ous pliȝt.	Since the vow that we pledged.

740
Þerfore icham comen to þe	Therefore I have come to you to know—
To wite astow art hende and fre	If you are courteous and true,
And holden a gentil kniȝt	And trusted as a noble knight—
Wheþer wiltow me forsake	Whether you will reject me
Or þou wilt trewely to me take	Or you will take me faithfully
And hold as þou bihiȝt".	And keep me as you promised".
"Madame", seyd þe kniȝt ogain	"My lady", said the knight again,
"Y wold þe spouse now ful fain	"I would marry you now gladly
And hold þe to mi wive.	And keep you as my wife.
Ac ȝif þi fader herd it sain	But if your father heard it said

750
Þat ich hadde his douhter forlain	That I had slept with his daughter,
Of lond he wald me drive.	He would drive me out of the land.
Ac ȝif ich were king of þis lond	But if I were king of this realm
And hadde more gode in min hond	And had more possessions in my hand
Þan oþer kinges five	Than five other kings,
Wel fain y wald spouse þe þan.	I would happily marry you then.
Ac certes icham a pouer man	But I am, in honesty, a poor man!
Wel wo is me o live!"	It is woe for me to be alive!"
"Sir kniȝt", seyd þat maiden kinde	"Sir Knight", said that elegant maiden,
"For love of seyn Tomas of Ynde	"For the love of Saint Thomas of India,[79]

760
Whi seystow ever nay?	Why do you keep saying no?
No be þou never so pouer of kinde	No matter how poor your family was,
Riches anouȝ y may þe finde	I can find riches enough for you,
Boþe bi niȝt and day!"	By both night and day!"
Þat hende kniȝt biþouȝt him þan	The noble knight thought to himself
And in his armes he hir nam	And then took her in his arms
And kist þat miri may.	And kissed the sweet maiden.
And so þai plaid in word and dede	And so they played in word and deed,
Þat he wan hir maidenhede	So that he won her virginity
Er þat he went oway.	Before he went away.

770
And ever þat steward gan abide	And all the time the steward waited
Alon under þat chaumber side	Alone alongside the chamber
Hem for to here.	In order to overhear them.
In at an hole was nouȝt to wide	Through a hole, which was not very wide,
He seiȝe hem boþe in þat tide	He saw them both in that moment

---

79   *Seyn Tomas of Ynde*: Christ's disciple, the 'doubting Thomas' who was also obstinate in questioning Jesus. There were medieval traditions that Thomas later evangelized in India. Edward E. Foster, ed. *Amis and Amiloun, Robert of Cisyle, and Sir Amadace* (Kalamazoo, MI: Medieval Institute Publications, 1997), http://www.lib.rochester.edu/camelot/teams/amisfr. htm.

	Hou þai seten yfere.	And how they sat together.[80]
	And when he seyȝe hem boþe wiþ siȝt	And when he saw them both with his eyes—
	Sir Amis and þat bird briȝt	Sir Amis and that lovely lass,
	Þe doukes douhter dere	The duke's dear daughter—
	Ful wroþ he was and egre of mode	He was vengeful and fierce at heart,
780	And went oway as he were wode	And stole away, as if he were mad,
	Her conseil to unskere.	In order to expose their secrets.
	When þe douke com into þat won	When the duke came into the residence,
	Þe steward oȝain him gan gon	The steward hurried up to him
	Her conseyl forto unwrain.	To betray their secret.
	"Mi lord þe douke", he seyd anon	"My lord, Sir Duke", he said at once,
	"Of þine harm bi seyn Jon	"By Saint John, I am very eager[81]
	Ichil þe warn ful fain!	To warn you about any harm to you!
	In þi court þou hast a þef	In your court you have a thief,
	Þat haþ don min hert gref	Who has done my heart grief,
790	Schame it is to sain.	It is a shame to say.
	For certes he is a traitour strong	For, certainly he is a foul traitor
	When he wiþ tresoun and wiþ wrong	When he has, with treason and injustice,
	Þi douhter haþ forlain!"	Bedded your daughter!"
	Þe riche donke gan sore agrame.	The great duke became greatly incensed.
	"Who haþ", he seyd, don me þat schame?	"Who has", he said, "done me this shame?
	Tel me y þe pray!"	Tell me, I order you!"
	"Sir", seyd þe steward, "bi seyn Jame	"Sir", said the steward, "By Saint James,
	Ful wele y can þe tel his name.	I can full well tell you his name.
	Þou do him hong þis day!	Have him hanged this day!
800	It is þi boteler Sir Amis.	It is your butler, Sir Amis.
	Ever he haþ ben traitour ywis;	He has always been a traitor, truly;
	He haþ forlain þat may.	He has deflowered that maiden.
	Y seiȝe it me self for soþe	I saw it myself, to tell the truth,
	And wil aprove biforn hem boþe	And will swear it before both of them,
	Þat þai can nouȝt say nay!"	So that they cannot deny it!"
	Þan was þe douke egre of mode.	Then the duke was in a livid rage.
	He ran to halle as he were wode;	He ran to the hall as if he were mad;
	For no þing he nold abide.	He would not stop for anything.
	Wiþ a fauchoun scharp and gode	With a curved sword, sharp and good,
810	He smot to Sir Amis þer he stode	He slashed at Sir Amis where he stood,
	And failed of him biside.	But failed to strike him.
	Into a chaumber Sir Amis ran þo	Sir Amis ran into a chamber

---

80 Delaney sees sexual jealousy toward Amis in the steward, who behaves "like the proverbial scorned woman" (68) after Amis's rejection of his invitation to exclusively replace Amiloun in his affections. Equally, the steward has no real need to spy on Amis and Belisaunt the entire duration they are together (line 770), and perhaps his voyeurism has a secondary purpose: "he likes to watch" (69). Delaney points to historical same-sex unions such as that of the young Edward II and Piers Gaveston as possible influences, and finds the A-A (same) / B (Belisaunt, different) figuration suggestive. Delaney, 66.

81 *Seyn Jon*: Swearing by saints was common in romances, just as modern French expletives favor religious epithets over sex or bathroom functions. Often the choice of saint is meaningful, but not always. Ford argues that particular saints are sometimes invoked simply to fit the poetic line. John C. Ford, "A New Conception of Poetic Formulae Based on Prototype Theory and the Mental Template", *Neuphilologishche Mitteilungen* 103 (2002): 218–24.

And schet þe dore bitwen hem to	And shut the door between the two of them
For drede his heued to hide.	To hide his head for fear.
Þe douke strok after swiche a dent	The duke struck such a blow at him
Þat þurth þe dore þat fauchon went	That the blade pierced through the door,
So egre he was þat tide.	So furious was he that moment.
Al þat ever about him stode	All who stood around him
Bisouȝt þe douke to slake his mode	Begged the duke to control his emotions,
820 Boþe erl baroun and swain.	Both earl, baron, and servant. But he
And he swore bi Him þat dyed on rode	Swore by Him who died on the Cross
He nold for al þis worldes gode	That he would not stop for all the world
Bot þat traitour were slain.	Unless that traitor was slain.
"Ich have him don gret honour	"I have given him great honors
And he haþ as a vile traitour	And he has behaved like a vile criminal
Mi douhter forlain!	And slept with my daughter!
Y nold for al þis worldes won	I wouldn't turn away for all the world
Bot y miȝt þe traitour slon	Until I might slay this traitor
Wiþ min hondes twain!"	With my own two hands!"
830 "Sir", seyd Sir Amis anon	"Sir", Sir Amis pleaded at once,
"Lete þi wretþe first overgon	"Let your rage die down first,
Y pray þe par charite!	I beg of you, for charity's sake!
And ȝif þou may prove bi Sein Jon	And if you can prove, by Saint John,
Þat ichave swiche a dede don	That I have done such a thing,
Do me to hong on tre!	Have me hanged on a tree!
Ac ȝif ani wiþ gret wrong	But if anyone has defamed the two of us
Haþ lowe on ous þat lesing strong	With a foul lie, with great injustice–
What bern þat he be	Whatever man that he be
He leiȝþ on ous wiþouten fail	Who lies about us–without fail,
840 Ichil aprove it in bataile	I will prove it in combat,
To make ous quite and fre".	To clear ourselves as innocent".[82]
"ȝa", seyd þe douke, "wiltow so?"	"So!" said the duke, "Will you do so!"
"Darstow into bataile go	"You dare to go into battle
Al quite and skere you make?"	To acquit and clear yourself?"
"ȝa certes sir", he seyd þo	"Yes, certainly, sir!" he replied then,
"And here mi glove y ȝive þerto:	"And here I give my glove to you:
He leiȝe on ous wiþ wrake".	This man lies about us in hatred".
Þe steward stirt to him þan	The steward bolted to him then
And seyd, "Traitour fals man!	And yelled, "Traitor! False man!
850 Ataint þou schalt be take!	You will be seized and condemned!
Y seiȝe it me self þis ich day	I saw it myself this very day
Where þat sche in þi chaumber lay.	Where she lay in your chamber.
ȝour noiþer it may forsake!"	Neither of you can deny it!"
Þus þe steward ever gan say	The steward continually charged so,
And ever Sir Amis seyd, "Nay	And Sir Amis always said, "No,

---

82 Sir Amis is proposing that he prove his innocence through combat against the steward, who argues instead for summary justice while the duke has lost his temper. The fact that Amis is telling a lie forms the moral conundrum of the poem when Amiloun defends him.

Ywis it nas nouȝt so".

Þan dede þe douke com forþ þat may

And þe steward wiþstode alway

And vouwed þe dede þo.

860 Þe maiden wepe hir hondes wrong

And ever swore hir moder among

"Certain it was nouȝt so!"

Þan seyd þe douke, "Wiþouten fail

It schal be proved in batail

And sen bitwen hem to".

Þan was atwix hem take þe fiȝt

And sett þe day a fourtenniȝt

Þat mani man schuld it sen.

Þe steward was michel of miȝt;

870 In al þe court was þer no wiȝt

Sir Amis borwe durst ben.

Bot for þe steward was so strong

Borwes anowe he fond among

Twenti al bidene.

Þan seyd þai alle wiþ resoun

Sir Amis schuld ben in prisoun

For he no schuld nowhar flen.

Þan answerd þat maiden briȝt

And swore bi Jhesu ful of miȝt

880 Þat were michel wrong.

"Takeþ mi bodi for þat kniȝt

Til þat his day com of fiȝt

And put me in prisoun strong.

Ȝif þat þe kniȝt wil flen oway

And dar nouȝt holden up his day

Bataile of him to fong

Do me þan londes lawe

For his love to be todrawe

And heiȝe on galwes hong!"

890 Hir moder seyd wiþ wordes bold

Þat wiþ gode wil als sche wold

Ben his borwe also

His day of bataile up to hold

Þat he as gode kniȝt schold

In truth, it was not so".

Then the duke had the maiden come forth

And the steward persisted all the time

And vowed on the deed.

The maiden wept, she wrung her hands,

And her mother continually defended her,

Saying "For sure, it was not so!"

At last the duke said, "Without a doubt,

It shall be proved in battle

And seen between the two of them".[83]

Then the fight was arranged between them,

And set for the day after fourteen nights,

So that many men should see it.

The steward was great in might;

In all the court there was no one

Who dared to be Sir Amis' guarantor.[84]

But because the steward was so strong,

He found warrants enough among them,

Twenty altogether.

Then they all said that for good reason,

Sir Amis should be in prison,

For he should not flee anywhere.

Then the beautiful maiden protested

And swore by Jesus, full of might,

That it would be a great injustice.

"Take my body for that knight,

Until his day comes to fight,

And put me in a strong prison.

If the knight flees away

And does not dare to keep his day,

To face the steward in combat,

Then do to me the law of the land,

And have me drawn apart for his love

And hanged high on the gallows!"

Her mother said, with bold words,

That, in good faith, she would

Be his surety as well,

To guarantee his day of battle,

So that he would, as a good knight should,

---

83 Trial by combat was an established practice in Germanic law, with the victor assumed to be in the right. The practice had faded away in England by the late Middle Ages in favor of trial by jury and would have been slightly antique even in Auchinleck's time, but dueling continued up to the twentieth century, even in America.

84 *Borwe*: The steward intends to find supporters who will assume legal responsibility if he absconds, but Sir Amis does not find a guarantor as the court believes he will flee from the steward's formidable strength. Skeat etymologizes *bail* as coming from OF *baillier*, to keep in custody. As with the Anglo-Saxons, the system seems to have been originally based on hostages and not money. The fact that no one helps Sir Amis after the affection shown him earlier (342-5) may thematically underscore the fact that he is in the wrong, but also highlights Sir Amiloun's unquestioning loyalty in comparison.

Fiȝt oȝain his fo.
Þus þo leuedis fair and briȝt
Boden for þat gentil kniȝt
To lain her bodis to.
Þan seyd þe lordinges everichon
900 Þat oþer borwes wold þai non
Bot graunt it schuld be so.
When þai had don as y you say
And borwes founde wiþouten delay
And graunted al þat þer ware
Sir Amis sorwed niȝt and day.
Al his joie was went oway
And comen was al his care
For þat þe steward was so strong
And hadde þe riȝt and he þe wrong
910 Of þat he opon him bare.
Of his liif ȝaf he nouȝt
Bot of þe maiden so michel he þouȝt
Miȝt noman morn mare;
For he þouȝt þat he most nede
Ar þat he to bataile ȝede
Swere an oþ biforn
Þat also God schuld him spede
As he was giltles of þat dede
Þat þer was on him born.
920 And þan þouȝt he wiþouten wrong
He hadde lever to ben anhong
Þan to be forsworn.
Ac oft he bisouȝt Jhesu þo
He schuld save hem boþe to
Þat þai ner nouȝt forlorn.
So it bifel opon a day
He mett þe leuedi and þat may
Under an orchard side.
"Sir Amis", þe leuedy gan say
930 "Whi mornestow so wiþouten play?
Tel me þat soþe þis tide.
No drede þe nouȝt", sche seyd þan
"For to fiȝt wiþ þi foman!
Wheþer þou wilt go or ride
So richeliche y schal þe schrede
Þarf þe never have of him drede
Þi bataile to abide".
"Madame", seyd þat gentil kniȝt
"For Jhesus love ful of miȝt
940 Be nouȝt wrorþ for þis dede.

Fight against his foe.
Thus those ladies, fair and bright,
Pledged to offer both of their bodies
For that gentle knight.
Every one of the lordings said
That they needed no other guarantors,
And granted that it should be so.
When this was done, as I say to you,
And warrants were arranged without delay,
And all who were there were had agreed,
Sir Amis grieved night and day.
All his joy had gone away,
And all his troubles had multiplied,
For the steward was so formidable
And was in the right, and he was guilty
Of the offence that was laid upon him.
He did not care about his life,
But he thought so much about the maiden
That no man might mourn more;
For he knew that he would be obligated,
Prior to going to battle,
To swear an oath beforehand,
That so help him God,
He was guiltless of the deed
Which he had been accused of.
And then he resolved, without wrong,
That he would rather be hanged
Than to swear falsely.
But he continually called on Jesus
That He would save both of them
So that they would not be lost.
So it happened that one day
He met the lady and the maiden
Under the shade of an orchard.
"Sir Amis", her mother began to say,
"Why do you grieve so without any joy?
Tell me the truth this time.
Do not be afraid", she continued,
"To fight with your enemy!
Whether you walk or ride,
I will equip you so lavishly
That you need never have fear of him
In awaiting your battle".
"Madam", said that gracious knight,
"For Jesus' love, full of might,
Do not be angry for what I have done.

	Middle English	Modern English
	Ich have þat wrong and he þe riȝt	I am in the wrong and he is in the right,
	Þerfore icham aferd to fiȝt	And for this I am afraid to fight,
	Also God me spede!	So help me God![85]
	For y mot swere wiþouten faile	For I must swear, without fail,
	Also God me spede in bataile	That so may God help me in battle,
	His speche is falshede!	His words are falsehoods!
	And ȝif y swere icham forsworn	And if I swear, I swear falsely,
	Þan liif and soule icham forlorn.	And then in life and soul I am lost.
	Certes y can no rede".	For sure, I know no answer!"
950	Þan seyd þat leuedi in a while	Then after a while the lady said,
	"No mai þer go non oþer gile	"Is there no other trick that will work
	To bring þat traitour doun?"	To bring that traitor down?"
	"Ȝis dame", he seyd, "bi seyn Gile!	"Yes, my lady", he said, "by Saint Giles![86]
	Her woneþ hennes mani a mile	Many a mile from here, there lives
	Mi broþer Sir Amiloun.	My brother in arms, Sir Amiloun.
	And ȝif y dorst to him gon	And if I dare to go to him,
	Y dorst wele swere bi seyn Jon	I would swear by Saint John,
	So trewe is þat baroun	That baron is so loyal that
	His owhen liif to lese to mede	He would help me in my need,
960	He wold help me at þis nede	Even if he lost his own life in reward,
	To fiȝt wiþ þat feloun".	To fight with that murderer".
	"Sir Amis", þe leuedi gan to say	"Sir Amis", the mother said,
	"Take leve tomorwe at day	"Leave tomorrow at daybreak
	And wende in þi jurne.	And go on your journey.
	Y schal say þou schalt in þi way	I will say that you are on your way
	Hom into þine owhen cuntray	Home to your own country
	Þi fader þi moder to se.	To see your father and your mother.
	And when þou comes to þi broþer riȝt	And when you come to your friend,
	Pray him as he is hendi kniȝt	Insist to him that if he is a noble knight
970	And of gret bounte	And of great generosity,
	Þat he þe batail for ous fong	That he accept the battle for us
	Oȝain þe steward þat wiþ wrong	Against the steward, who will unjustly
	Wil stroie ous alle þre!"	Destroy all three of us!"
	Amorwe Sir Amis made him yare	In the morning Sir Amis readied himself
	And toke his leve for to fare	And took his leave to travel
	And went in his jurnay.	And went on his journey.
	For noþing nold he spare.	He would not stop for anything.
	He priked þe stede þat him bare	He spurred the horse that carried him
	Boþe niȝt and day.	Both day and night.
980	So long he priked wiþouten abod	So long did he spur the steed
	Þe stede þat he on rode	That he rode on, without rest,

---

85 *So God me spede*: ME is full of emphatic oaths and this phrase is a recurring one in romance.

86 *Dame*: From Latin *domina*, *dame* is difficult to translate here as the sense is highly contextual in ME. It can be a formal title, serving as the female counterpart to Sir (Lady), or it can simply mean a matron or mistress of a household (madam, ma'am). Saint Giles (c. 650-c. 720) was a patron of cripples and was famed for kindness to animals, and is probably only referenced here to supply a rhyme.

In a fer cuntray
Was overcomen and fel doun ded.
Þo couþe he no better red.
His song was "Waileway!"
And when it was bifallen so
Nedes afot he most go.
Ful careful was þat kniȝt.
He stiked up his lappes þo
990 In his way he gan to go
To hold þat he bihiȝt.
And al þat day so long he ran
Into a wilde forest he cam
Bitwen þe day and þe niȝt.
So strong slepe ȝede him on
To win al þis warldes won
No ferþer he no miȝt.
Þe kniȝt þat was so hende and fre
Wel fair he layd him under a tre
1000 And fel in slepe þat tide.
Al þat niȝt stille lay he
Til amorwe men miȝt yse
Þe day bi ich a side.
Þan was his broþer Sir Amiloun
Holden a lord of gret renoun
Over al þat cuntre wide
And woned fro þennes þat he lay
Bot half a jorne of a day
Noiþer to go no ride.
1010 As Sir Amiloun þat hendi kniȝt
In his slepe he lay þat niȝt
In sweven he mett anon
Þat he seiȝe Sir Amis bi siȝt
His broþer þat was treweþe pliȝt
Bilapped among his fon.
Þurth a bere wilde and wode
And oþer bestes þat bi him stode
Bisett he was to slon.
And he alon among hem stode
1020 As a man þat couþe no gode.
Wel wo was him bigon.
When Sir Amiloun was awake
Gret sorwe he gan for him make
And told his wiif ful ȝare
Hou him þouȝt he seiȝe bestes blake

That in a faraway place
It was overcome and collapsed dead.
Then he knew no other course.
His refrain was "Alas the day!"
And when it had happened so,
He had to go on foot.
That knight was sorely aggrieved.
He tucked up the hems of his coat[87]
And began to go on his way
To keep what he had promised.
And so all the day long he ran
Until he came into a wild forest
Between day and the night.
Such a strong weariness came upon him
That for all this world's possessions
He could not go any farther.
The knight, who was so gracious and noble,
Laid himself carefully under a tree
And fell asleep at that moment.
All the night he lay still
Until the morning when men might see
The day on all sides.
At the time his brother, Sir Amiloun,
Was honored as a lord of great renown
Over all that wide country
And lived only half a day's journey,
Whether on foot or riding,
Away from where he lay.
As Sir Amiloun, that gallant knight,
Lay asleep that night,
In his nightmare he dreamed at once
That he saw Sir Amis with his own eyes,
His brother, who was bound by loyalty,
Surrounded by his enemies.
Because of a bear, wild and crazed,
And other beasts that stood nearby him,
He was about to be killed.
And he stood among them alone
As a man who hoped for no help.
He was in great despair.
When Sir Amiloun woke up,
He felt great sorrow in himself
And told his wife immediately
How he dreamed he saw dark beasts

---

87   *Lappes:* Leach explains that "knights wore long coats that had to be tucked up for walking or riding" (quoted in Foster).
MacEdward Leach, ed., *Amis and Amiloun*, EETS OS 203 (London: Oxford University Press, 1937).

About his broþer wiþ wrake
To sle wiþ sorwe and care.
"Certes", he seyd "wiþ sum wrong
He is in peril gret and strong
1030 Of blis he is ful bare".
And þan seyd he, "For soþe ywis
Y no schal never have joie no blis
Til y wite hou he fare".
As swiþe he stirt up in þat tide.
Þer nold he no leng abide
Bot diȝt him forþ anon.
And al his meine bi ich a side
Busked hem redi to ride
Wiþ her lord for to gon.
1040 And he bad al þat þer wes
For Godes love held hem stille in pes.
He bad hem so ich-chon
And swore bi Him þat schop mankende
Þer schuld no man wiþ him wende
Bot himself alon.
Ful richeliche he gan him schrede
And lepe astite opon his stede;
For noþing he nold abide.
Al his folk he gan forbade
1050 Þat non so hardi were of dede
After him noiþer go no ride.
So al þat niȝt he rode til day
Til he com þer Sir Amis lay
Up in þat forest wide.
Þan seiȝe he a weri kniȝt forgon
Under a tre slepeand alon.
To him he went þat tide.
He cleped to him anonriȝt
"Arise up felawe it is liȝt
1060 And time for to go".
Sir Amis biheld up wiþ his siȝt
And knewe anon þat gentil kniȝt
And he knewe him also.
Þat hendi kniȝt Sir Amiloun
Of his stede liȝt adoun
And kist hem boþe to.
"Broþer", he seyd, "whi listow here
Wiþ þus mornand chere?
Who haþ wrouȝt þe þis wo?"
1070 "Broþer", seyd Sir Amis þo
"Ywis me nas never so wo

Raging around his friend,
Ready to kill with sorrow and grief.
"Surely", he said, "by some wrong
He is in peril, great and strong.
He is barren of any joy!"
And then he said, "For sure, in truth,
I will never have happiness or rest
Until I know how he is doing".
Just as quickly he started up that moment.
He would not wait there longer,
But prepared himself at once.
And all his company, on each side,
Readied themselves to ride in order
To set forth with their lord.
But he ordered all who were there
For the love of God, to be still and quiet.
He called to every one of them
And swore by Him who made mankind
That no man should go with him
But himself alone.
He dressed himself splendidly
And leaped as quickly upon his steed;
He would not wait for anything.
He had forbidden all of his people
So that none were so daring
As to walk or ride after him.
So all that night he rode until daylight,
Until he came where Sir Amis lay
Up in the wild forest.
He saw a weary knight, lost,
Sleeping under a tree alone.
He went to him that instant.
He called to him at once,
"Rise up, fellow, it is light
And time to go!"
Sir Amis looked up with his eyes
And knew at once the noble knight
And he recognized him as well.
The noble knight, Sir Amiloun,
Got down off his horse
And the two of them kissed.
"Brother", he said, "why are you lying here
With such a mournful face?
Who has brought you this unhappiness?"
"Friend", Sir Amis then said,
"For sure, I was never so troubled

Seþþen þat y was born.	Since the day I was born.
For seþþen þat þou was went me fro	For since the time that you went from me,
Wiþ joie and michel blis also	I have served before my lord
Y served mi lord biforn.	With joy and great happiness as well.
Ac þe steward ful of envie	But the steward, full of jealousy,
Wiþ gile and wiþ trecherie	And with guile and treachery,
He haþ me wrouȝt swiche sorn!	Has brought me such sorrow!
Bot þou help me at þis nede	Unless you can help me in my need,
1080 Certes y can no noþer rede.	For sure, I know no other course.
Mi liif it is forlorn!"	My life, it is lost!"
"Broþer", seyd Sir Amiloun,	"Brother", said Sir Amiloun,
"Whi haþ þe steward þat feloun	"Why has the steward, that villain,
Ydon þe al þis schame?"	Done you all this shame?"
"Certes", he seyd, "wiþ gret tresoun	"For sure", he replied, "with great infamy
He wald me driven al adoun	He wants to drive me down
And haþ me brouȝt in blame".	And has brought me into blame".
Þan told Sir Amis al þat cas	Then Sir Amis explained all his situation,
Hou he and þat maiden was	How he and the maiden were
1090 Boþe togider ysame	In each other's company,
And hou þe steward gan hem wrain	And how the steward had accused them,
And hou þe douke wald him have slain	And how the duke would have slain him
Wiþ wretþe and michel grame.	With fury and hot rage.
And also he seyd ypliȝt	And he also said, truly,
Hou he had boden on him fiȝt	How he had offered to fight him,
Batail of him to fong	To face him in combat,
And hou in court was þer no wiȝt	And how in the court there was no one
To save þo tway leuedis briȝt	Except those two beautiful ladies
Durst ben his borwe among	Who dared to be among his guarantors,
1100 And hou he most wiþouten faile	And how he must, without fail,
Swere ar he went to bataile	Swear before he went to battle
It war a lesing ful strong.	That it all was a foul lie.
"And forsworn man schal never spede.	"And a false man will never succeed.
Certes þerfore y can no rede	Therefore, for certain, I know no answer.
Allas may be mi song!"	My song will be 'Alas'!"
When þat Sir Amis had al told	When Sir Amis had told all,
Hou þat þe fals steward wold	How that false steward intended to
Bring him doun wiþ mode	Bring him down with angry passion,
Sir Amiloun wiþ wordes bold	Sir Amiloun swore with bold words:
1110 Swore: "Bi Him þat Judas sold	"By Him that Judas betrayed
And died opon þe rode	And who died upon the cross,
Of his hope he schal now faile	He will soon fail in his hopes,
And y schal for þe take bataile!	And I will take the battle for you!
Þei þat he wer wode	Even if he is a madman,
Ȝif y may mete him ariȝt	If I can meet him to his face,
Wiþ mi brond þat is so briȝt	With my blade, which is so bright,
Y schal sen his hert blode!"	I will see his heart's blood!"

"Ac broþer", he seyd, "have al mi wede
And in þi robe y schal me schrede
1120 Riȝt as þe self it ware.
And y schal swere so God me spede
As icham giltles of þat dede
Þat he opon þe bare!"
Anon þo hendi kniȝtes to
Alle her wede chaunged þo
And when þai were al ȝare
Þan seyd Sir Amiloun, "Bi seyn Gile
Þus man schal þe schrewe bigile
Þat wald þe forfare!"
1130 "Broþer", he seyd, "wende hom now riȝt
To mi leuedi þat is so briȝt
And do as y schal þe sain.
And as þou art a gentil kniȝt
Þou ly bi hir in bed ich niȝt
Til þat y com ogain
And sai þou hast sent þi stede ywis
To þi broþer Sir Amis
Þan wil þai be ful fain.
Þai wil wene þat ich it be;
1140 Þer is non þat schal knowe þe
So liche we be boþe twain!"
And when he hadde þus sayd ypliȝt
Sir Amiloun þat gentil kniȝt
Went in his jurnay.
And Sir Amis went hom anonriȝt
To his broþer leuedi so briȝt
Wiþouten more delay
And seyd hou he hadde sent his stede
To his broþer to riche mede
1150 Bi a kniȝt of þat cuntray.
And al þai wende of Sir Amis
It had ben her lord ywis
So liche were þo tway.
When þat Sir Amis hadde ful yare
Told hem al of his care
Ful wele he wend þo
Litel and michel lasse and mare
Al þat ever in court ware

"But friend", he said, "Take all my clothes,
And I will dress myself in your robe,
Right as if it were yourself.
And I shall swear, so help me God,
That I am guiltless of that deed
Which he charged upon you!"[88]
At once those two wily knights
Exchanged all their clothes.
And when they were all ready,
Sir Amiloun said, "By Saint Giles,[89]
Thus so a man will trick the criminal
Who would destroy you!"
"Brother", he said, "now go right home
To my lady, who is so beautiful,
And do as I tell you to do.
And if you are a virtuous knight,
Lie beside her in bed each night
Until I come back again.
And say you have sent your steed, in truth,
To your brother, Sir Amis.
Then I will be very glad.
They will assume that you are me;
The two of us are so alike
That there is no one who will know you!"
And when he had spoken so, indeed,
Sir Amiloun, that noble knight,
Went on his journey.
And Sir Amis went home at once
To his brother's lady, who was so beautiful,
Without any more delay,
And he explained how he had sent his steed
To his brother as a rich gift
Via a knight of that country.
And all of them thought that Sir Amis
Was their lord, in fact,
So alike were the two of them.
When Sir Amis had fully
Told them all about his labors,
He surmised full well that
Small and great, high and low,
All who were ever in the court,

---

88 Sir Amis' moral conundrum is that they have sworn to be truthful to their lords, and he will be a liar if he swears to the court that he never slept with Belisaunt. The steward is justified in accusing Amis, however spiteful his motives. Sir Amiloun's trick is to impersonate Sir Amis, as Amiloun will technically be telling the truth if he vows that *he* has not seduced the king's daughter.

89 *Seyn Gile*: Saint Giles (c. 650-710), a hermit saint from Athens associated with cripples and beggars.

Þai þou3t it hadde ben so.

1160 And when it was comen to þe ni3t
Sir Amis and þat leuedi bri3t
To bed þai gun go.
And when þai were togider ylayd
Sir Amis his swerd out braid
And layd bitwix hem two.
Þe leuedi loked opon him þo
Wroþlich wiþ her ei3en two.
Sche wend hir lord were wode.
"Sir", sche seyd, "whi farstow so?
1170 Þus were þou nou3t won to do.
Who haþ changed þi mode?"
"Dame", he seyd, "sikerly
Ich have swiche a malady
Þat mengeþ al mi blod.
And al min bones be so sare
Y nold nou3t touche þi bodi bare
For al þis warldes gode".
Þus ywis þat hendy kni3t
Was holden in þat fourtenni3t
1180 As lord and prince in pride.
Ac he for3at him never a ni3t
Bitwix him and þat leuedi bri3t
His swerd he layd biside.
Þe leuedi þou3t in hir resoun
It hadde ben hir lord Sir Amiloun
Þat hadde ben sike þat tide.
Þerfore sche held hir stille þo
And wold speke wordes no mo
Bot þou3t his wille to abide.
1190 Now hende herkneþ and y schal say
Hou þat Sir Amiloun went his way.
For noþing wold he spare
He priked his stede ni3t and day
As a gentil kni3t stout and gay.
To court he com ful 3are
Þat selve day wiþouten fail
Þat was ysett of batail
And Sir Amis was nou3t þare.
Þan were þo leuedis taken bi hond
1200 Her juggement to understond

Believed that it had been so.

And when it came to the night,
Sir Amis and that shining lady
Made their way to bed.
And when they were laying together,
Sir Amis drew out his sword
And laid it between the two of them.
The lady looked at him crossly
With her two eyes.[90]
She thought that her lord was mad.
"Sir", she said, "why are you behaving so?
You have never acted like this.
What has changed your mood?"
"My lady", he answered, "for certain,
I have such an illness
That it troubles all my blood.
And all my bones are so sore
That I would not touch your bare body
For all this world's goods".
In this way, indeed, that righteous knight
Stayed for those fourteen days
Honorably as lord and prince.
But he never forgot for one night
To lay his sword in the middle
Between him and that beautiful lady.
The lady thought in her mind
That it was her lord, Sir Amiloun,
Who was sick at that time.
Therefore she kept herself content
And did not speak any more about it,
Only wishing to abide by his will.
Now, good people, listen and I will say
How Sir Amiloun went his way.
He would not stop for anything.
He spurred his steed by night and day,
As a noble knight, sturdy and cheerful.
He came to the court in haste
The same day, without fail,
That was set for the battle,
And Sir Amis was not there.
Then the two ladies were seized by hand
To undergo their judgment,

---

90   Again, unlike Victorian literature, medieval women are often depicted (and criticized in homilies) as sexually libidinous. Here the wife of Sir Amiloun is depicted with particular annoyance over her apparent husband's refusal, predicting her later petulance and selfishness, in contrast to Belisaunt who becomes more patient and generous. See also Faramerz Dabhoiwala, *The Origins of Sex: A History of the First Sexual Revolution* (New York: Oxford University Press, 2012).

Wiþ sorwe and sikeing sare.
Þe steward hoved opon a stede
Wiþ scheld and spere bataile to bede.
Gret bost he gan to blawe.
Bifor þe douke anon he ȝede
And seyd, "Sir so God þe spede
Herken to mi sawe!
Þis traitour is out of lond ywent.
Ȝif he were herein present
1210 He schuld ben hong and drawe!
Þerefore ich aske jugement
Þat his borwes be tobrent
As it is londes lawe".
Þat riche douke wiþ wretþe and wrake
He bad men schuld þo leuedis take
And lede hem forþ biside.
A strong fer þer was don make
And a tonne for her sake
To bren hem in þat tide.
1220 Þan þai loked into þe feld
And seiȝe a kniȝt wiþ spere and scheld
Com prikeand þer wiþ pride.
Þan seyd þai everichon ywis
"Ȝonder comeþ prikeand Sir Amis!"
And bad þai schuld abide.
Sir Amiloun gan stint at no ston.
He priked among hem everichon
To þat douke he gan wende.
"Mi lord þe douke", he seyd anon
1230 "For schame lete þo leuedis gon
Þat er boþe gode and hende!
For ich am comen hider today
For to saven hem ȝive y may
And bring hem out of bende.
For certes it were michel unriȝt
To make roste of leuedis briȝt.
Ywis ȝe eren unkende".
Þan ware þo leuedis glad and bliþe.
Her joie couþe þai noman kiþe;
1240 Her care was al oway.
And seþþen as ȝe may list and liþe
Into þe chaunber þai went aswiþe
Wiþouten more delay
And richeliche þai schred þat kniȝt

With sorrow and bitter sighing.
The steward leaped upon a horse
With shield and spear to offer battle.
He began to chatter great boasts.
He quickly appeared before the duke
And said, "Sir, so God protect you,
Listen to my words!
This traitor has run out of the land.
If he were here in person,
He would be hanged and drawn!
Therefore I ask for judgment,
That his guarantors be burned,
As it is the law of the land".
The rich duke, with wrath and anger,
Ordered men to take hold of the ladies
And bring them forth beside everyone.
A raging fire was readied there,
And a barrel for them to wear,
To burn them on that day.
Then they looked toward the field
And saw a knight, with spear and shield,
Come spurring there gallantly.
Then everyone said, indeed,
"Here comes Sir Amis riding!",
And asked that they would wait.
Sir Amiloun did not rest at any milestone.
He rode past each one of them,
Making his way toward the duke.
"My lord, the duke", he said at once,
"For shame, let those women go,
Who are both good and noble!
For I have come back here today
In order to save them, if I can,
And bring them out of bondage.
For, certainly, it would be a great wrong
To make a roast of beautiful ladies.
You go against nature, indeed".[91]
Then the ladies were glad and relieved.
No man could fathom their joy;
Their troubles had all departed.
And then, as you may listen and learn,
They went into the chamber as quickly
Without any more delay,
And they dressed that knight splendidly

---

91 *Unkende* can mean either cruel or unnatural (i.e. to one's own kind), though here both senses overlap and fit the context.

Wiþ helme and plate and brini briȝt.	With helmet and armor and shining mail.
His tire it was ful gay.	His clothing was magnificent.
And when he was opon his stede	And when he was upon his steed,
Þat God him schuld save and spede	Many men prayed that day
Mani man bad þat day.	That God would save and aid him.
1250 As he com prikand out of toun	But as he came galloping out of town,
Com a voice fram Heven adoun	A voice came down from Heaven,
Þat noman herd bot he	Which no one heard but him,
Say, "þou kniȝt Sir Amiloun	And said, "You knight, Sir Amiloun!
God þat suffred passioun	Christ, who suffered pains,
Sent þe bode bi me!	Sends you a warning through me![92]
ȝif þou þis bataile underfong	If you go through with this battle,
Þou schalt have an eventour strong	You will have a great reckoning
Wiþin þis ȝeres þre.	Within the next three years.
And or þis þre ȝere ben al gon	And before these three years are all gone,
1260 Fouler mesel nas never non	There will never have been a fouler leper
In þe world þan þou schal be!	In all the world than you will be! But
Ac for þou art so hende and fre	Because you are so gallant and generous,
Jhesu sent þe bode bi me	Jesus sent this proclamation through me
To warn þe anon:	To warn you at once:
So foule a wreche þou schalt be	You will be so foul a wretch,
Wiþ sorwe and care and poverte.	With sorrow and trouble and poverty.
Nas never non wers bigon	There was never a worse one before,
Over al þis world fer and hende.	Over all this world, near and far.
Þo þat be þine best frende	Those who were your best friends
1270 Schal be þi most fon	Will be your greatest foes,
And þi wiif and alle þi kinne	And your wife and all your kin
Schul fle þe stede þatow art inne	Will flee the room that you are in,
And forsake þe ichon".	And desert you, every one".
Þat kniȝt gan hove stille so ston	The knight remained as still as a stone
And herd þo wordes everichon	And heard every one of the words,
Þat were so gret and grille.	Which were so grave and stern.
He nist what him was best to don	He did not know what was best to do,
To flen oþer to fiȝting gon.	To flee or to go on fighting.
In hert him liked ille.	He was aggrieved at heart.
1280 He þouȝt, "ȝif y beknowe mi name	He thought, "If I reveal my name,
Þan schal mi broþer go to schame.	Then my brother will go to shame.
Wiþ sorwe þai schul him spille".	They will kill him, in sorrow. For sure",
"Certes", he seyd, "for drede of care	He said, "for fear of worse trouble,
To hold mi treuþe schal y nouȝt spare.	I will spare nothing to keep my pledge.
Lete God don alle His wille".	Let God do all that He wills".
Al þe folk þer was ywis	All the people who were there, indeed,

---

92   The angel's speech has caused critical difficulties. If heaven is displeased, Amiloun should not *win*, "since the trial by combat is predicated upon the belief that the right will be shown by God's fighting on its side". Ojars Kratins, "The Middle English *Amis and Amiloun*: Chivalric Romance or Secular Hagiography?" *PMLA* 81 (1966): 347-54 [350]. But the angel may also be indicating a sort of bargain, that Amiloun's victory will come at the cost of a redemptive divine punishment.

Þai wend it had ben Sir Amis
Þat bataile schuld bede.
He and þe steward of pris
1290 Were brouȝt bifor þe justise
To swere for þat dede.
Þe steward swore þe pople among
As wis as he seyd no wrong
God help him at his nede.
And Sir Amiloun swore and gan to say
As wis as he never kist þat may
Our Leuedi schuld him spede.
When þai hadde sworn as y ȝou told
To biker þo bernes were ful bold
1300 And busked hem for to ride.
Al þat þer was ȝong and old
Bisouȝt God ȝif þat He wold
Help Sir Amis þat tide.
On stedes þat were stiþe and strong
Þai riden togider wiþ schaftes long
Til þai toschiverd bi ich a side.
And þan drouȝ þai swerdes gode
And hewe togider as þai were wode
For noþing þai nold abide.
1310 Þo gomes þat were egre of siȝt
Wiþ fauchouns felle þai gun to fiȝt
And ferd as þai were wode.
So hard þai hewe on helmes briȝt
Wiþ strong strokes of michel miȝt
Þat fer biforn out stode.
So hard þai hewe on helme and side
Þurth dent of grimly woundes wide
Þat þai sprad al of blod.
Fram morwe to none wiþouten faile
1320 Bitwixen hem last þe bataile
So egre þai were of mode.
Sir Amiloun as fer of flint
Wiþ wretþe anon to him he wint
And smot a stroke wiþ main.
Ac he failed of his dint
Þe stede in þe heued he hint
And smot out al his brain
Þe stede fel ded doun to grounde.
Þo was þe steward þat stounde
1330 Ful ferd he schuld be slain.
Sir Amiloun liȝt adoun of his stede
To þe steward afot he ȝede

Thought that it was Sir Amis
Who was to offer battle.
He and the renowned steward
Were brought before the justice
To swear on that deed.
The steward swore in front of the people
That may God help him in his need,
For certain he spoke no wrong.
And Sir Amiloun affirmed and said
That may our Lady aid him,
For certain he never kissed that maid.
When they had pledged as I told you,
The men were very eager to fight
And readied themselves to ride.
All who were there, young and old,
Beseeched God that He would
Help Sir Amis in that moment.
On steeds that were firm and strong, they
Rode against each other with long spears,
Until on both sides they were shattered.
And then they drew out good swords
And clashed together as if they were mad.
They would not stop for anything.
These warriors, who were a fierce sight,
Began to fight with deadly curved swords
And fared as if they were crazed.
So hard did they strike on shining helmets
With powerful blows of great might
That fiery sparks flew out from them.
So hard did they hack at helmets and body
That through the blows of many grisly
Wounds they were all covered with blood.
From morning to noon, without fail,
The battle lasted between them,
So fierce were they in spirit.
Sir Amiloun, like sparks from flint,
Went straight at the steward with anger
And landed a blow with force.
But he failed in his aim.
He hit the steed in the head
And struck out all its brains,
And the horse fell dead to the ground.
Then the steward was, at that moment,
Greatly afraid he would be slain.
Sir Amiloun came down from his steed.
And went to the steward on foot

And halp him up ogain.
"Arise up steward", he seyd anon
"To fiȝt þou schalt afot gon
For þou hast lorn þi stede.
For it were gret vilani bi seyn Jon
A liggeand man for to slon
Þat were yfallen in nede".
1340 Þat kniȝt was ful fre to fond
And tok þe steward bi þe hond
And seyd, "So God me spede
Now þou schalt afot go
Y schal fiȝt afot also.
And elles were gret falshed".
Þe steward and þat douhti man
Anon togider þai fiȝt gan
Wiþ brondes briȝt and bare.
So hard togider þai fiȝt þan
1350 Til al her armour o blod ran;
For noþing nold þai spare.
Þe steward smot to him þat stounde
On his schulder a gret wounde
Wiþ his grimly gare
Þat þurth þat wounde as ȝe may here
He was knowen wiþ reweli chere
When he was fallen in care.
Þan was Sir Amiloun wroþ and wode
Whan al his armour ran o blode
1360 Þat ere was white so swan.
Wiþ a fauchoun scharp and gode
He smot to him wiþ egre mode
Also a douhti man
Þat even fro þe schulder-blade
Into þe brest þe brond gan wade
Þurthout his hert it ran.
Þe steward fel adoun ded.
Sir Amiloun strok of his hed
And God he þonked it þan.
1370 Alle þe lordinges þat þer ware
Litel and michel lasse and mare
Ful glad þai were þat tide.
Þe heued opon a spere þai bare.
To toun þai diȝt hem ful ȝare

And helped him up again.
"Rise up, steward", he said at once,
"You will walk on foot to fight,
For you have lost your mount.
For it would be great villainy,
By Saint John, to slay a prostrate man
Who had fallen into helplessness".[93]
The knight was gallant in need
And took the steward by the hand
And said, "So help me God,
Now you will go on foot
And I will fight on foot as well.
Otherwise it would be great unfairness".
The steward and that sturdy man
At once began to fight together
With blades that were shining and bare.
So hard did they battle each other
Until all their armor ran with blood;
They would not stop for anything.
At that moment the steward struck on him
A great wound on his shoulder
With his fearsome weapon, so that
Through that wound, as you may hear,
He knew, with a remorseful face,
When he had fallen into trouble. Then
Sir Amiloun became wild and enraged,
As all his armor ran with blood
Which was before as white as a swan.
With a curved sword, sharp and fine,
He struck at the steward,
As a hardy man with a fierce heart,
So that even from the shoulder blade
Into the breast the blade traveled
And ran through his heart.
The steward fell down dead.
Sir Amiloun cut off his head,
And then thanked God for it.
All of the lordings who were there,
Small and great, low and high,
Were greatly pleased that moment.
They bore the head upon a spear.
They made their way to town excitedly

---

93 Medieval armor could be so heavy that a warrior thrown from his horse might only get up off the ground with difficulty. Sir Amiloun shows a chivalric sense of fair play in lifting the steward and being willing to fight on foot, not wanting to cheapen his victory by killing a nearly helpless man. A horse being killed is an everpresent romance cliché, perhaps enabling the hero to show off his physical prowess on foot. See also *Sir Degare*, 940.

For noþing þai nold abide.	And would not wait for anything.
Þai com oȝaines him out of toun	They came toward him outside the town
Wiþ a fair processioun	In a grand procession,
Semliche bi ich a side.	Splendid on every side.
Anon þai ladde him to þe tour	Soon they escorted him to the tower
1380 Wiþ joie and ful michel honour	With joy and great honor,
As prince proude in pride.	As a prince proud in nobility.
Into þe palais when þai were gon	When they had gone into the palace,
Al þat was in þat worþli won	All who were there in that stately dwelling
Wende Sir Amis it ware.	Thought it was Sir Amis.
"Sir Amis", seyd þe douke anon	"Sir Amis", the duke at once spoke,
"Bifor þis lordinges everichon	"Before every one of these lords,
Y graunt þe ful ȝare	I readily grant you Belisaunt,
For Belisent þat miri may	That merry maiden,
Þou hast bouȝt hir ful dere to day	For you have bought her dearly today
1390 Wiþ grimli woundes sare.	With sore and horrible wounds.
Þerfore y graunt þe now here	Therefore I grant you here now
Mi lond and mi douhter dere	My land and my dear daughter,
To hald for ever mare!"	To hold forevermore!"
Ful bliþe was þat hendi kniȝt	The noble knight was overjoyed
And þonked him wiþ al his miȝt.	And thanked him with all his might.
Glad he was and fain.	He was glad and pleased.
In alle þe court was þer no wiȝt	In all the court there was no one
Þat wist wat his name it hiȝt	Who knew what his real name was,
To save þo leuedis twain.	Except for the two ladies.[94]
1400 Leches swiþe þai han yfounde	They quickly found doctors
Þat gun to tasty his wounde	Who treated his wounds
And made him hole ogain.	And made him whole again.
Þan were þai al glad and bliþe	Then everyone was glad and relieved
And þonked God a þousand siþe	And thanked God a thousand times
Þat þe steward was slain.	That the steward was slain.
On a day Sir Amiloun diȝt him yare	The next day Sir Amiloun hastily readied
And seyd þat he wold fare	Himself and said that he would travel
Hom into his cuntray	Home to his country
To telle his frendes lasse and mare	To tell his friends, low and high,
1410 And oþer lordinges þat þere ware	And other lords that were there,
Hou he had sped þat day.	How he had fared that day. The duke
Þe douke graunted him þat tide	Gave him permission in that moment
And bede him kniȝtes and miche pride	And offered him knights and great
And he answerd, "Nay".	Ceremony, but he answered, "No".
Þer schuld noman wiþ him gon	No man should go with him,
Bot as swiþe him diȝt anon	But with equal speed he prepared himself
And went forþ in his way.	And went forth on his way.
In his way he went alone	He went alone on his journey.

---

94 Whether Belisaunt and her mother know about Amis's impersonation at this point is not clear. An alternate reading is "who had saved the two ladies", though some manuscripts omit *to*. See also line 1625.

Most þer noman wiþ him gon	No other man could go with him,
1420 Noiþer kniȝt no swain.	Neither knight nor servant.
Þat douhti kniȝt of blod and bon	The knight, sturdy of flesh and blood,
No stint he never at no ston	Did not rest at any milestone
Til he com hom ogain.	Until he came home again.
And Sir Amis as y ȝou say	And Sir Amis, as I tell you,
Waited his coming everi day	Waited for his coming every day
Up in þe forest plain.	Up in the forest plain.
And so þai mett togider same	And so they met together in reunion,
And he teld him wiþ joie and game	And he told him with joy and laughter
Hou he hadde þe steward slain	How he had slain the steward,
1430 And hou he schuld spousy to mede	And how in reward he would marry
Þat ich maide worþli in wede	That same maiden, noble in appearance,
Þat was so comly corn.	Who was of such excellent birth.
Sir Amiloun liȝt of his stede	Sir Amiloun descended from his steed,
And gan to chaungy her wede	And they exchanged their clothes
As þai hadde don biforn.	As they had done before.
"Broþer", he seyd, "wende hom ogain".	"Brother", he said, "go back home".
And tauȝt him hou he schuld sain	And he told him what he should say
When he com þer þai worn.	When he returned there.
Þan was Sir Amis glad and bliþe	Then Sir Amis was happy and glad
1440 And þanked him a þousand siþe	And gave thanks a thousand times
Þe time þat he was born.	For the day that his friend was born.
And when þai schuld wende ato	And when they had to part ways,
Sir Amis oft þonked him þo	Sir Amis continually thanked him
His cost and his gode dede.	For his trouble and his good deed.
"Broþer", he seyd, "ȝif it bitide so	"Friend", he said, "if it happens so
Þat þe bitide care oþer wo	That you encounter trouble or woe,
And of min help hast nede	And need my help,
Savelich com oþer sende þi sond	Just come or send your message,
And y schal never lenger wiþstond	And I will delay no longer,
1450 Also God me spede!	So help me God!
Be it in periil never so strong	No matter how much the danger,
Y schal þe help in riȝt and wrong	I will help you, in right or wrong,
Mi liif to lese to mede".	Even if I lose my life in reward".
Asonder þan þai gun wende.	They then parted from each other.
Sir Amiloun þat kniȝt so hende	Sir Amiloun, that knight so gentle,
Went hom in þat tide	Went home at that time
To his leuedi þat was unkende	To his lady who was unwitting,
And was ful welcome to his frende	And who was so welcoming to his friend,
As prince proude in pride.	As a prince proud in bearing.
1460 And when it was comen to þe niȝt	And when it came to the night,
Sir Amiloun and þat leuedi briȝt	Sir Amiloun and that beautiful lady
In bedde were layd biside.	Were lying beside each other in bed.
In his armes he gan hir kis	In his arms he began to kiss her
And made hir joie and michel blis	And gave her joy and great happiness.

For noþing he nold abide.
Þe leuedi astite asked him þo
Whi þat he hadde farn so
Al þat fourtenniȝt
Laid his swerd bitwen hem to
1470 Þat sche no durst nouȝt for wele no wo
Touche his bodi ariȝt.
Sir Amiloun biþouȝt him þan
His broþer was a trewe man
Þat hadde so done apliȝt.
"Dame", he seyd, "ichil þe sain
And telle þe þat soþe ful fain
Ac wray me to no wiȝt".
Þe leuedi astite him frain gan
For His love þat þis warld wan
1480 Telle hir whi it ware.
Þan astite þat hendy man
Al þe soþe he teld hir þan
To court hou he gan fare
And hou he slouȝ þe steward strong
Þat wiþ tresoun and wiþ wrong
Wold have his broþer forfare;
And hou his broþer þat hendy kniȝt
Lay wiþ hir in bed ich niȝt
While þat he was þare.
1490 Þe leuedi was ful wroþ ypliȝt
And oft missayd hir lord þat niȝt
Wiþ speche bitwix hem to
And seyd, "Wiþ wrong and michel unriȝt
Þou slouȝ þer a gentil kniȝt!
Ywis it was ivel ydo!"
"Dame", he seyd, "bi Heven-king
Y no dede it for non oþer þing
Bot to save mi broþer fro wo
And ich hope ȝif ich hadde nede
1500 His owhen liif to lesse to mede
He wald help me also".
Al þus in gest as we sain
Sir Amis was ful glad and fain
To court he gan to wende.
And when he com to court oȝain
Wiþ erl baroun kniȝt and swain
Honourd he was þat hende.
Þat riche douke tok him bi hond
And sesed him in alle his lond
1510 To held wiþouten ende.

He would not leave for anything.
The lady then straightaway asked him
Why he had behaved so
All those fourteen nights,
Laying his sword between the two of them
So that she dared not, for good or ill,
Touch his body at all.
Sir Amiloun was then assured
His friend was a faithful man
Who had done this, truly.
"My lady", he said, "I will tell you
And explain the truth to you gladly.
But betray me to no one".
The lady at once began to pester him,
For the love of Him who redeemed the
World, to tell her what happened.
Then as promptly that gentle man
Told her all the truth,
How he had traveled to the court,
And how he had killed the fierce steward,
Who would have destroyed his brother
With treason and with injustice;
And how his friend, that gallant knight,
Had laid with her in bed each night
While he was there.
The lady was very irate, truly,
And continually berated her lord that night
In speech between the two of them,
And protested, "You killed a noble knight
With foul and great injustice!
For certain, it was done in evil!"
"Lady", he said, "by Heaven's king,
I did it for no other reason
But to save my brother from grief.
And I hope, if I had need, that even if
He shortened his own life as a reward,
He would help me also".
Meanwhile, in the story as we read it,
Sir Amis was glad and at ease
And he traveled to the court.
And when he came back to the court
He was honored, that good man,
By earl, baron, knight, and servant.
The rich duke took him by the hand
And endowed him with all his land
To hold without end.

And seþþen wiþ joie opon a day	And afterward with joy, upon one day,
He spoused Belisent þat may	He married Belisaunt, that maiden
Þat was so trewe and kende.	Who was so loyal and kind.
Miche was þat semly folk in sale	There were many fine guests in the hall
Þat was samned at þat bridale	Who were gathered at that wedding
When he hadde spoused þat flour:	When he wedded that flower:
Of erls barouns mani and fale	Earls, barons, numerous and plenty,
And oþer lordinges gret and smale	And other gentlemen, great and small,
And leuedis briȝt in bour.	And ladies, beautiful in their bowers.
1520 A real fest þai gan to hold	They held a royal feast
Of erls and of barouns bold	With earls and brave barons,
Wiþ joie and michel honour.	With joy and stately honor.
Over al þat lond est and west	Over all the land, east and west,
Þan was Sir Amis helden þe best	Sir Amis was esteemed as the best
And chosen for priis in tour.	And lauded with praise in the highest place.
So wiþin þo yeres to	So within those two years,
A wel fair grace fel hem þo	They were blessed with grace,
As God Almiȝti wold;	As God Almighty willed;
Þe riche douke dyed hem fro	The rich duke was taken from them
1530 And his leuedi dede also	And his lady passed away as well,
And graven in grete so cold.	And buried in the ground so cold.
Þan was Sir Amis hende and fre	Then Sir Amis, noble and generous,
Douke and lord of gret pouste	Became a duke and lord of great authority
Over al þat lond yhold.	Throughout all the land he held.
Twai childer he biȝat bi his wive	He fathered two children with his wife,
Þe fairest þat miȝt bere live	The fairest that might bear life,
In gest as it is told.	In the story as it is told.
Þan was þat kniȝt of gret renoun	Then that knight was of great renown
And lord of mani a tour and toun	And lord of many a tower and town
1540 And douke of gret pouste.	And a duke of great power.
And his broþer Sir Amiloun	But his brother, Sir Amiloun,
Wiþ sorwe and care was driven adoun	Who was so noble and valiant before,
Þat ere was hende and fre.	Was weighed down with sorrow and cares.
Also þat angel hadde him told	Just as the angel had told him,
Fouler messel þar nas non hold	There was no leper in the world
In world þan was he.	Regarded so foully as he was.
In gest to rede it is gret rewþe	To read the story is great sadness,
What sorwe he hadde for his treuþe	What misery he had for his faithfulness
Wiþin þo ȝeres þre.	Within those three years. And before
1550 And er þo þre ȝere com to þende	Those three years came to an end,
He no wist whider he miȝt wende	He was so burdened by affliction
So wo was him bigon;	He did not know where he might go;
For al þat were his best frende	For all who were his best friends,
And nameliche al his riche kende	And, namely, all his rich family,
Bicom his most fon.	Became his worst foes.
And his wiif for soþe to say	And his wife, to say the truth,

Wrouȝt him wers boþe niȝt and day
Þan þai dede everichon.
When him was fallen þat hard cas
1560 A frendeleser man þan he was
Men nist nowhar non.
So wicked and schrewed was his wiif
Sche brac his hert wiþouten kniif
Wiþ wordes hard and kene.
And seyd to him, "þou wreche chaitif
Wiþ wrong þe steward les his liif;
And þat is on þe sene!
Þerfore bi seyn Denis of Fraunce
Þe is bitid þis hard chaunce!
1570 Daþet who þe bimene!"
Wel oft times his honden he wrong
As man þat þenkeþ his liif to long
Þat liveþ in treye and tene.
Allas allas þat gentil kniȝt
Þat whilom was so wise and wiȝt
Þat þan was wrouȝt so wo
Þat fram his leuedi fair and briȝt
Out of his owhen chaumber aniȝt
He was yhote to go.
1580 And in his owhen halle oday
Fram þe heiȝe bord oway
He was ycharged also
To eten at þe tables ende.
Wald þer no man sit him hende;
Wel careful was he þo.
Bi þan þat half ȝere was ago
Þat he hadde eten in halle so
Wiþ gode mete and wiþ drink
His leuedi wax ful wroþ and wo
1590 And þouȝt he lived to long þo
Wiþouten ani lesing.
"In þis lond springeþ þis word
Y fede a mesel at mi bord!
He is so foule a þing
It is gret spite to al mi kende.
He schal no more sitt me so hende
Bi Jhesus Heven-king!"
On a day sche gan him calle
And seyd, "Sir it is so bifalle
1600 For soþe y telle it te
Þat þou etest so long in halle
It is gret spite to ous alle.

Treated him worse, by day and night
Than everyone else did.
When he had fallen into that hard state,
Men did not know a more friendless man
Anywhere than he was.
His wife was so wicked and cunning
That she pierced his heart without a knife,
With words that were hard and sharp.
She said to him, "You miserable wretch,
The steward lost his life wrongly;
It's clear to see what you've done!
And so, by Saint Denis of France,
This hard luck is meant for you!
Damn whoever pities you!"
Continually he wrung his hands
As a man who thinks his life too long,
Who lives in trial and pain.
Alas, alas! That gentle knight,
Who once was so wise and manly,
Who was ordained such sorrow
That away from his lady, so fair and bright,
Out of his own chamber at night,
He was forced to go.
And in his own hall, one day
He was ordered away as well
From the high table
To eat at the bench's end.
No man there would seat him honorably;
He was all the more miserable then.
By the time half a year was gone
That he had eaten this way in the hall
With good food and drink,
His lady grew angry and resentful,
And thought he had lived too long,
Without any lie.
"Talk is spreading throughout this land
That I feed a leper at my table!
He is so foul a thing,
It is a great disgrace to all my kin.
He will no longer sit near at hand to me
By Jesus, Heaven's king!"
One day she called for him
And said, "Sir, it has come to happen—
I tell it to you, in truth—
You have eaten for so long in this hall
That it is a great disgrace to us all.

Mi kende is wroþ wiþ me".
Þe kniȝt gan wepe and seyd ful stille
"Do me where it is þi wille
Þer noman may me se.
Of no more ichil þe praye
Bot of a meles mete ich day
For seynt charite".
1610 Þat leuedi for hir lordes sake
Anon sche dede men timber take.
For noþing wold sche wond.
And half a mile fram þe gate
A litel loge sche lete make
Biside þe way to stond.
And when þe loge was al wrouȝt
Of his gode no wold he noȝt
Bot his gold coupe an hond.
When he was in his loge alon
1620 To God of Heven he made his mon
And þonked Him of al his sond.
Into þat loge when he was diȝt
In al þe court was þer no wiȝt
Þat wold serve him þare
To save a gentil child y pliȝt.
Child Owaines his name it hiȝt.
For him he wepe ful sare.
Þat child was trewe and of his kende;
His soster sone he was ful hende.
1630 He sayd to hem ful ȝare
Ywis he no schuld never wond
To serven him fro fot to hond
While he olives ware.
Þat child þat was so fair and bold
Owaines was his name ytold;
Wel fair he was of blode.
When he was of twelve ȝere old
Amoraunt þan was he cald
Wel curteys hende and gode.
1640 Bi his lord ich niȝt he lay
And feched her livere ever day
To her lives fode.
When ich man made gle and song
Ever for his lord among

My family is angry with me".
The knight began to weep and said softly,
"Have me put where it is your will,
Where no man may see me.
I will ask no more of you
Than a meal's ration each day,
For holy charity".
The lady at once had men
Take wooden timbers for her lord's sake.
She would not hesitate for anything.
And half a mile from the gate,
She had a little cabin made,
To stand alongside the way.
And when the lodge was all built,
He would have nothing of his possessions
But his gold cup in his hand.
When he was in his lodge alone,
He made his lament to God of Heaven
And thanked Him for all his blessings.
In all the court there was no one
Who would serve him there
In that cabin where he was placed,
Except for one noble child, in truth.[95]
His name was called Child Owen.
For him the boy wept bitterly.
The youth was faithful and from his kin;
His sister's son, he was very gracious.
He said to them freely,
For certain, he would never hesitate
To serve him hand and foot
While he was alive.
That child, who was so fair and bold,
Was said to be named Owen;
He was from very good blood.
When he was twelve years old,
He was then called Amoraunt,
A courteous, noble, and good youth.
He lay by his uncle each night
And fetched his provisions every day
For their lives' food. When each man
Made celebration and song,
He always kept a sober manner

---

95   *Child*: Child is problematic in ME as it may refer commonly to children or be used as a title for a young knight in training.
     In Owen's case, he is later promoted to the rank of squire. In Germanic culture there is often a special closeness between
     uncles and matrilineal nephews. See Stephen O. Glosecki, "*Beowulf* and the Wills: Traces of Totemism?", *Philological*
     Quarterly (78:1/2) 1999, 15-47.

He made dreri mode.
Þus Amoraunt as y ʒou say
Com to court ich day
No stint he for no strive.
Al þat þer was gan him pray
1650 To com fro þat lazer oway
Þan schuld he the and þrive.
And he answerd wiþ milde mode
And swore bi Him þat dyed on rode
And þoled woundes five
For al þis worldes gode to take
His lord nold he never forsake
Whiles he ware olive.
Bi þan þe twelmoneþ was al gon
Amorant went into þat won
1660 For his lordes liveray.
Þe leuedi was ful wroþ anon
And comaunde hir men everichon
To drive þat child oway
And swore bi Him þat Judas sold
Þei his lord for hunger and cold
Dyed þer he lay
He schuld have noiþer mete no drink
No socour of non oþer þing
For hir after þat day.
1670 Þat child wrong his honden twain
And weping went hom ogain
Wiþ sorwe and sikeing sare.
Þat gode man gan him frain
And bad him þat he schuld him sain
And telle him whi it ware.
And he answerd and seyd þo
"Ywis no wonder þei me be wo
Mine hert it brekeþ for care!
Þi wiif haþ sworn wiþ gret mode
1680 Þat sche no schal never don ous gode.
Allas hou schal we fare?"
"A God help!" seyd þat gentil kniʒt.
"Whilom y was man of miʒt
To dele mete and cloþ
And now icham so foule a wiʒt
Þat al þat seþ on me bi siʒt
Mi liif is hem ful loþ.
"Sone", he seyd, "lete þi wepeing
For þis is now a strong tiding;
1690 Þat may we se for soþ!

Among them for his lord.
Thus Amoraunt, as I tell you,
Came to court each day.
He did not cease for any difficulty.
All who were there advised him
To abandon that leper,
For then he would thrive and prosper.
And he answered in a gentle manner
And swore by Him who died on the cross,
And suffered five wounds,
That he would never forsake his lord
For all this world's goods in his hand
While he was still alive.
When twelve months had passed,
Amoraunt went into the residence one day
For his lord's supplies.
The lady at last become furious
And commanded each of her men
To drive that boy away,
And swore by Him that Judas sold,
Even if his lord died where he lay
For hunger and cold,
He would have neither food nor drink,
Nor the aid of any other thing,
From her after that day.
The young man wrung his two hands
And went home again weeping,
With sorrow and bitter sighing.
That good man questioned him
And asked him to speak to him
And tell him what had happened.
Then he answered and said,
"Truly, it's no wonder that I am woeful,
For my heart, it breaks from worrying!
Your wife has sworn in a fierce temper
That she will never do us any more good.
Alas, how will we live?"
"Ah, God help us!" said that noble knight.
"Once I was a man of might,
One to deal out food and clothing,
And now I am so foul a creature
That for anyone who sees me by sight,
My life is loathsome to them.
Son", he said, "stop your weeping,
For this is serious news;
We can see that for sure!

For certes y can non oþer red	For sure, I know no other course;
Ous bihoveþ to bid our brede.	We are obliged to beg our bread.
Now y wot hou it goþ".	Now I know how it must go".
Amorwe astite as it was liȝt	In the morning, as soon as it was light,
Þe child and þat gentil kniȝt	The youth and that noble knight
Diȝt hem for to gon	Prepared themselves to go,
And in her way þai went ful riȝt	And they went straight on their way
To begge her brede as þai hadde tiȝt	To beg their bread, as they had determined,
For mete no hadde þai none.	For they had no food at all.
1700 So long þai went up and doun	For a while they went up and down
Til þai com to a chepeing toun	Until they came to a market town,
Five mile out of þat won	Five miles away from that area,
And sore wepeand fro dore to dore	And they wept bitterly from door to door
And bad her mete for Godes love.	And begged their food for God's love.
Ful ivel couþe þai þeron!	They had little experience of that!
So in þat time ich understond	So in that time, as I understand,
Gret plente was in þat lond	There was great plenty in that land,
Boþe of mete and drink.	Both of food and drink.
Þat folk was ful fre to fond	The people were generous in giving
1710 And brouȝt hem anouȝ to hond	And brought them enough to their hand
Of al kines þing	Of all kinds of things,
For þe gode man was so messais þo	For the good man was so wretched then,
And for þe child was so fair also	And the young man was so fair as well,
Hem loved old and ying	That young and old pitied them
And brouȝt hem anouȝ of al gode.	And brought them enough of all necessities.
Þan was þe child bliþe of mode	Then the child was cheerful in spirit
And lete be his wepeing.	And let his weeping pass.
Þan wex þe gode man fete so sare	Then the good man's feet grew so sore
Þat he no miȝt no forþer fare	That he could travel no further
1720 For al þis worldes gode.	For all this world's goods.
To þe tounes ende þat child him bare	The youth carried him to the town's edge
And a loge he bilt him þare	And built him a cabin there,
As folk to chepeing ȝode.	Where people passed by to the market.
And as þat folk of þat cuntray	And as the locals of that country
Com to chepeing everi day	Came to buy and sell every day,
Þai gat hem lives fode.	They received their sustenance.
And Amoraunt oft to toun gan go	And Amoraunt often walked to town
And begged hem mete and drink also	And begged them for food and drink as well
When hem most nede atstode.	When they stood in greatest need.
1730 Þus in gest rede we	And so we read in the story
Þai dwelled þere ȝeres þre	That they stayed there for three years,
Þat child and he also	The youth and him also,
And lived in care and pouerte	And lived in hardship and poverty
Bi þe folk of þat cuntre	Through the people of that land
As þai com to and fro	As they came to and fro,
So þat in þe ferþ ȝere	Until the fourth year,

Corn bigan to wex dere.
Þat hunger bigan to go
Þat þer was noiþer eld no ȝing
1740 Þat wald ȝif hem mete no drink.
Wel careful were þai þo.
Amorant oft to toun gan gon
Ac mete no drink no gat he non
Noiþer at man no wive.
When þai were togider alon
Reweliche þai gan maken her mon
Wo was hem o live.
And his leuedi for soþe to say
Woned þer in þat cuntray
1750 Nouȝt þennes miles five
And lived in joie boþe niȝt and day
Whiles he in sorwe and care lay.
Wel ivel mot sche þrive!
On a day as þai sete alon
Þat hendi kniȝt gan meken his mon
And seyd to þe child þat tide
"Sone", he seyd, "þou most gon
To mi leuedi swiþe anon
Þat woneþ here biside
1760 Bid hir for Him þat died on rode
Sende me so michel of al mi gode
An asse on to ride
And out of lond we wil fare
To begge our mete wiþ sorwe and care
No lenger we nil abide".
Amoraunt to court is went
Bifor þat leuedi fair and gent.
Wel hendeliche seyd hir anon.
"Madame", he seyd, "verrament
1770 As mensanger mi lord me sent
For himself may nouȝt gon
And praieste wiþ milde mode
Sende him so michel of al his gode
As an asse to riden opon
And out of lond we schulen yfere
No schal we never com eft here
Þei hunger ous schuld slon".
Þe leuedi seyd sche wald ful fain
Sende him gode asses twain
1780 Wiþ þi he wald oway go
So fer þat he never eft com ogain.
"Nay certes dame", þe child gan sain

When grain began to grow scarce.
Hunger started to spread,
So that there was no one young or old
Who would give them food or drink.
They were very wretched then.
Amoraunt often walked to town,
But he got no food or drink,
Neither from man nor woman.
When they were together alone,
They would ruefully lament
That it was woe to be alive.
And the knight's lady, to tell the truth,
Lived there in that country
Not five miles away,
And lived in ease both day and night
While he lay in sorrow and suffering.
May she have foul fortune!
One day, as they sat alone,
That kindly knight began his plea
And said to the child at that moment,
"Son", he said, "you must go
At once to my lady,
Who lives nearby here.
Ask her, for Him who died on the cross,
To send me so much of my goods
As a donkey to ride on,
And we will travel out of the land
To beg our food in sorrow and hardship.
We will not stay any longer".
Amoraunt went to the court
Before that beautiful and well-born lady.
Straightaway he addressed her courteously.
"My lady", he said, "truly,
My lord has sent me as his messenger,
For he himself cannot travel,
And he pleads in a gentle manner
For you to send him so much of his goods
As a donkey to ride on,
And we will journey out of the land.
Nor will we ever come back here,
Even if hunger should finish us".
That lady said she would very gladly
Send him off with two good donkeys
Provided that they would go away
So far that they never came back again.
"No, for certain, my lady", the boy said,

"Þou sest ous never eft mo".	"You will never see us again".
Þan was þe leuedi glad and bliþe	Then the lady was pleased and glad
And comaund him an asse as swiþe	And as promptly ordered him a donkey[96]
And seyd wiþ wretþe þo	And then ordered angrily,
"Now ȝe schul out of lond fare.	"Now you shall travel out of the land.
God leve you never to com here mare	God allow that you never come back here,
And graunt þat it be so!"	And grant that it be so!"
1790 Þat child no lenger nold abide.	The young man did not linger any longer.
His asse astite he gan bistride	He immediately got on his donkey
And went him hom ogain	And took himself home again
And told his lord in þat tide	And told his lord at that moment
Hou his leuedi proude in pride	How his lady, haughty in her pride,
Schameliche gan to sain.	Had spoken so shamefully.
Opon þe asse he sett þat kniȝt so hende	He set that gentle knight on the donkey
And out of þe cite þai gun wende.	And they began to ride out of the city
Þerof þai were ful fain.	And were very content to do so.
Þurth mani a cuntre up an doun	Through many a land, up and down,
1800 Þai begged her mete fram toun to toun	They begged for their food from town
Boþe in winde and rain.	To town, both in the wind and the rain.
Over al þat lond þurth Godes wille	Over all the land, through God's command,
Þat hunger wex so gret and grille	Their hunger grew sharp and intense
As wide as þai gun go.	As they travelled farther.
Almest for hunger þai gan to spille;	They were almost dying from hunger;
Of brede þai no hadde nouȝt half her fille.	They did not have half their fill of food.
Ful careful were þai þo.	They were very miserable then.
Þan seyd þe kniȝt opon a day	Then one day the knight said,
"Ous bihoveþ selle our asse oway	"We need to sell our donkey away,
1810 For we no have gode no mo	For we have no goods anymore,
Save mi riche coupe of gold.	Except my rich cup of gold.
Ac certes þat schal never be sold	But for sure that will never be sold
Þei hunger schuld me slo".	Even if hunger should kill me".
Þan Amoraunt and Sir Amiloun	Then early the next morning,
Wiþ sorwe and care and reweful roun	With sorrow and worry and doleful words,
Erliche in a morning	Amoraunt and Sir Amiloun
Þai went hem til a cheeping toun.	Took themselves to a market town.
And when þe kniȝt was liȝt adoun	And when the knight had dismounted,
Wiþouten ani dwelling	Without any delaying,
1820 Amoraunt went to toun þo.	Amourant went into the town.
His asse he ladde wiþ him also	He led the donkey with him as well

---

96 Sir Amiloun's wife has just agreed to *asses tuain* (1779), but either there is an error or the poet wishes to emphasize her grudging parsimony in promising two but only delivering one donkey out of his riches.

And sold it for five schilling.
And while þat derþ was so strong
Þerwiþ þai bouȝt hem mete among
When þai miȝt gete no þing.
And when her asse was ysold
For five schilling as y ȝou told
Þai dwelled þer dayes þre.
Amoraunt wex strong and bold.
1830 Of fiftene winter was he old
Curtays hende and fre.
For his lord he hadde grete care
And at his rigge he diȝt him ȝare
And bare him out of þat cite.
And half a ȝere and sum del mare
About his mete he him bare.
Yblisced mot he be!
Þus Amoraunt wiþouten wrong
Bar his lord about so long
1840 As y ȝou tel may.
Þat winter com so hard and strong
Oft "Allas!" it was his song
So depe was þat cuntray.
Þe way was so depe and slider
Oft times boþe togider
Þai fel doun in þe clay.
Ful trewe he was and kinde of blod
And served his lord wiþ mild mode
Wald he nouȝt wende oway.
1850 Þus Amoraunt as y ȝou say
Served his lord boþe niȝt and day
And at his rigge him bare.
Oft his song was "Waileway!"
So depe was þat cuntray
His bones wex ful sare.
Al her catel þan was spent
Save twelf pans verrament.
Þerwiþ þai went ful ȝare
And bouȝt hem a gode croude-wain.
1860 His lord he gan þerin to lain
He no miȝt him bere namare.

And sold it for five shillings.[97] And while
The bad harvest was so biting, they
Bought food among themselves with it
When they could not beg anything.
And when their donkey was sold
For five shillings, as I told you,
They stayed for three days there.
Amoraunt had grown strong and hardy.
He was fifteen years old,
Courteous, handsome, and gallant.
For his uncle he had great concern,
And he placed him cheerfully on his back
And carried him out of the city.
For half a year and somewhat more
He bore him about for his food.
May he be blessed for it!
Thus Amoraunt, without fail,
Carried his lord around for so long,
As I may tell you.
The winter arrived so hard and fiercely
That "Alas!" was constantly his song,
So deep was the country in snow.
The way was so slushy and slippery
That they often both together
Fell down into the dirt.
But he was faithful and kind-natured
And served his lord with a gentle spirit
And would not turn away.
Thus Amoraunt, as I tell you,
Served his lord both night and day
And carried him on his back.
His refrain was continually "Woe is us!"
So deep was the snow in that land
That his bones grew sore.
All their money was spent then,
Except for twelve pennies, in truth.
With that they readily went
And bought themselves a sturdy pushcart.
He laid his lord inside it,
For he could carry him no longer.

---

97   *Five schilling*: About £130 (US$200) in modern money (UK National Archives). This is two days' wages for a knight, but
enough for simple provisions for a long time. Hodges gives the typical price of a chicken in 1338 at two for one penny (1/12
of a shilling, £2.25 in modern money). Kenneth Hodges, "Medieval Sourcebook: Medieval Prices", *Fordham University
Center for Medieval Studies,* mirrored at http://faculty.goucher.edu/eng240/medieval_prices.html. The Lombards would
of course have used florins or other coins rather than shillings and pounds, but romance audiences would have cheerfully
ignored such inaccuracies just as Shakespeare's did with his Italian settings.

Þan Amoraunt crud Sir Amiloun
Þurth mani a cuntre up and doun
As ȝe may understond.
So he com to a cite-toun
Þer Sir Amis þe bold baroun
Was douke and lord in lond.
Þan seyd þe kniȝt in þat tide
"To þe doukes court here biside
1870 To bring me þider þou fond.
He is a man of milde mode.
We schul gete ous þer sum gode
Þurth grace of Godes sond.
"Ac leve sone", he seyd þan
"For His love þat þis world wan
Astow art hende and fre
Þou be aknowe to no man
Whider y schal no whenes y cam
No what mi name it be".
1880 He answerd and seyd, "Nay".
To court he went in his way
As ȝe may listen at me
And bifor al oþer pouer men
He crud his wain into þe fen.
Gret diol it was to se.
So it bifel þat selve day
Wiþ tong as y ȝou tel may
It was Midwinter tide.
Þat riche douke wiþ gamen and play
1890 Fram chirche com þe riȝt way
As lord and prince wiþ pride.
When he com to þe castel gate
Þe pouer men þat stode þerate
Wiþdrouȝ hem þer beside.
Wiþ kniȝtes and wiþ seriaunce fale
He went into þat semly sale
Wiþ joie and blis to abide.
In kinges court as it is lawe
Trumpes in halle to mete gan blawe.
1900 To benche went þo bold.

Then Amoraunt carted Sir Amiloun
Through many a land, up and down,
As you might understand.
And so they came to a walled city,[98]
Where Sir Amis, the brave baron,
Was duke and lord of the land.
Then the knight said at that moment,
"Try to bring me forth
To the duke's court near here.
He is a man of a gentle nature.
There we will get us some help
Through the grace of God's blessing.
But, dear son", he added then,
"For His love, who redeemed this world,
If you are courteous and well-bred,
Do not let it slip to any man
Where I am going, or where I am from,
Or what my name is".
He answered and said, "No, I will not".
They went on their way to the court
As you may hear from me,
And before all the other poor men
He pushed his cart through the mud.
It was a great sorrow to see.
So it happened that same day,
As I may tell you with my tongue,
That it was the Midwinter festival.[99]
The rich duke, with good cheer
And laughter, came that way from church
As lord and prince with honor.
When he came to the castle gate,
The poor men who stood there
Withdrew themselves out of the way.
With knights and many attendants
He went into that fine hall
To dwell in joy and ease.
In the king's court, as was the custom,
Trumpets in the hall announced dinner.
The bold men went to their benches.

---

98 *Cite-toun*: ME terms for municipalities are not yet clearly distinguished. They generally anticipate modern usages based on size, growing from *hamlet / village* to *toun / cite*, often indicating whether a church or see is present, but some words such as *borwe* may describe a semi-rural district, an incorporated town, or a fortified settlement. A *cite-toun* is possibly a capital, or at least an important center, to rate a city wall. See James Tait, *The Medieval English Borough* (Manchester: University Press, 1936; 1968).

99 *Midwinter*: The winter solstice immediately before Christmas, and a festive time of celebration. Just as Odysseus appears as a beggar to his decadent household, the poet here also contrasts Sir Amiloun's extreme hardship against the drunken revelry of Midwinter in the court.

When þai were semly set on rowe
Served þai were opon a þrowe
As men miriest on mold.
Þat riche douke wiþouten les
As a prince served he wes
Wiþ riche coupes of gold.
And he þat brouȝt him to þat state
Stode bischet wiþouten þe gate
Wel sore ofhungred and cold.
1910 Out at þe gate com a kniȝt
And a seriaunt wise and wiȝt
To plain hem boþe yfere.
And þurth þe grace of God Almiȝt
On Sir Amiloun he cast a siȝt
Hou laiþ he was of chere.
And seþþen biheld on Amoraunt
Hou gentil he was and of fair semblaunt
In gest as ȝe may here.
Þan seyd þai boþe bi seyn Jon
1920 In al þe court was þer non
Of fairehed half his pere!
Þe gode man gan to him go
And hendeliche he asked him þo
As ȝe may understond
Fram wat lond þat he com fro
And whi þat he stode þer þo
And whom he served in lond.
"Sir", he seyd, "so God me save
Icham here mi lordes knave
1930 Þat liþ in Godes bond.
And þou art gentil kniȝt of blode
Bere our erand of sum gode
Þurth grace of Godes sond".
Þe gode man asked him anon
Ȝif he wald fro þat lazer gon
And trewelich to him take;
And he seyd he schuld bi seyn Jon
Serve þat riche douke in þat won
And richeman he wald him make.
1940 And he answerd wiþ mild mode
And swore bi Him þat dyed on rode
Whiles he miȝt walk and wake
For to winne al þis warldes gode
His hende lord þat bi him stode
Schuld he never forsake.
Þe gode man wende he hadde ben rage

When they were fittingly seated in rows,
They were served in a moment,
As the merriest men on earth.
That elegant duke, without a lie,
Was served as a prince
With rich cups of gold.
And he who brought him to that state
Stood shut outside the gate,
Sore with hunger and cold.
Out of the gate came a knight
And a servant, strong and able,
To amuse themselves together.
And through the grace of God Almighty
They cast their eyes on Sir Amiloun,
Seeing how hideous he was to look on.
And then they beheld Amoraunt and saw
How noble he was, and how fair in
Appearance, in the story as you may hear.
Then they both said, by Saint John,
In all the court there was no one
Half his equal in handsomeness!
The good man went up to him
And then courteously asked him,
As you might understand,
What land he had come from,
And why he stood there then,
And who he served in the land.
"Sir", he said, "so God help me,
I am the servant of my lord here,
Who endures in God's bonds.
If you are a gracious knight in blood,
Bring some good out of our efforts,
Through the grace of God's plenty".
The good man asked him at once
If he would leave that leper
And stay with him faithfully;
And he said, by Saint John, that he should
Serve the rich duke in that residence
And he would make him a prosperous man.
The youth answered with a gentle manner
And swore by Him who died on the cross
That while he could live and breathe,
For all this world's goods
He would never forsake
His beloved lord, who stood nearby him.
The good man believed he was mad,

Or he hadde ben a fole sage
Þat hadde his witt forlorn
Oþer he þou3t þat his lord wiþ þe foule visage
1950 Hadde ben a man of hei3e parage
And of hei3e kinde ycorn.
Þerfore he nold no more sain
Bot went him into þe halle ogain
Þe riche douke biforn.
"Mi lord", he seyd, "listen to me
Þe best bourd bi mi leute
Þou herdest seþþen þou were born!"
Þe riche douke badde him anon
To telle biforn hem everichon
1960 Wiþouten more dwelling.
"Now sir", he seyd, "bi seyn Jon
Ich was out atte gate ygon
Ri3t now on mi playing.
Pouer men y sei3e mani þare
Litel and michel lasse and mare
Boþe old and 3ing
And a lazer þer y fond.
Herdestow never in no lond
Telle of so foule a þing!
1970 Þe lazer liþ up in a wain
And is so pouer of mi3t and main
O fot no may he gon.
And over him stode a naked swain
A gentiler child for soþe to sain
In world no wot y non.
He is þe fairest gome
Þat ever Crist 3af Cristendome
Or layd liif opon
And on of þe most fole he is
1980 Þat ever þou herdest speke ywis
In þis worldes won".
Þan seyd þe riche douke ogain
"What foly", he seyd, "can he sain?
Is he madde of mode?"
"Sir", he seyd, "y bad him fain
Forsake þe lazer in þe wain
Þat he so over stode
And in þi servise he schuld be.
Y bihete him boþe lond and fe
1990 Anou3 of warldes gode.
And he answerd and seyd þo
He nold never gon him fro.

Or that he had been a court fool
Who had lost his wits.
Or else, he thought that foul-looking lord
Might have been a man of noble lineage
And born from aristocratic kin.
Therefore he said no more,
And only went into the hall again
Before the stately duke.
"My lord", he said, "listen to me
About the funniest thing, by my word,
You ever heard since you were born!"
The rich duke asked him at once
To describe it before every one of them
Without more delaying.
"Now sir", he said, "By Saint John,
I was just outside the gate
Right before now to have some fun.
I saw many poor men there,
Small and great, low and high,
Both young and old,
And I found a leper there.
You will never have heard of
Such a foul thing in any land!
The leper sits up in a cart
And is so poor in strength and vigor
That he cannot go on foot.
And over him stood a half-dressed worker,
A nobler youth, to tell the truth,
Than any I know in the world.
He is the fairest creature
That Christ ever gave Christendom
Or endowed with life,
And one of the biggest fools
That you ever heard speak, in truth,
In all this world's lands".
Then the rich duke said again,
"What nonsense does he say?" he asked,
Is he mad in his manners?"
"Sir", he answered, "I gladly invited him
To abandon the leper in the cart
That he stood over so,
And said he should be in your service.
I offered him both land and a living,
And enough of worldly goods.
And he answered and said then
That he would never go from him.

Þerfore ich hold him wode".
Þan seyd þe douke, "þei his lord be lorn
Par aventour þe gode man haþ biforn
Holpen him at his nede
Oþer þe child is of his blod yborn;
Oþer he haþ him oþes sworn
His liif wiþ him to lede.
2000 Wheþer he be fremd or of his blod
Þe child", he seyd, "is trewe and gode
Also God me spede!
3if ichim speke er he wende
For þat he is so trewe and kende
Y schal quite him his mede".
Þat douke astite as y 3ou told
Cleped to him a squier bold
And hendelich gan him sain
"Take", he sayd, "mi coupe of gold
2010 As ful of wine astow mi3t hold
In þine hondes twain
And bere it to þe castel 3ate.
A lazer þou schalt finde þerate
Liggeand in a wain.
Bid him for þe love of seyn Martin
He and his page drink þis win
And bring me þe coupe ogain".
Þe squier þo þe coupe hent
And to þe castel gat he went
2020 And ful of win he it bare.
To þe lazer he seyd verrament
"Þis coupe ful of win mi lord þe sent.
Drink it 3ive þou dare".
Þe lazer tok forþ his coupe of gold;
Boþe were 3oten in o mold
Ri3t as þat selve it ware.
Þerin he pourd þat win so riche.
Þan were þai boþe ful yliche
And noiþer lesse no mare.
2030 Þe squier biheld þe coupes þo
First his and his lordes also
Whiles he stode hem biforn
Ac he no coupe never mo
Chese þe better of hem to
So liche boþe þai worn.
Into halle he ran ogain.

For this I believe he is mad".
Then the duke said, "Though his lord
Is wretched, by chance the good man
Helped him in his need before,
Or the youth is born from his blood;
Or he has sworn him oaths
To lead his life with him.
Whether he is a stranger or his kin",
He said, "The youth is loyal and good,
So help me God!
If I can speak to him before he goes on,
I will give him his reward
For being so faithful and good-natured".
Just as quick, as I tell you,
The duke called a bold squire to him
And said to him graciously,
"Take my gold cup", he said,
"With as much wine as it can hold,
In your two hands,
And deliver it to the castle gate.
You will find a leper there,
Lying in a cart.
Invite him, for the love of Saint Martin,[100]
To drink this wine with his page
And bring me the cup back again".
The squire then took the cup
And went to the castle gate,
Bearing the cup, full of wine.
He said to the leper, in truth,
"My lord sends you this cup of wine.
Drink it, if you dare".
The leper took out his gold cup;
Both were made from one mold,
Right as if they were the same.
He poured in the rich wine.
Then they were both exactly alike,
And neither more nor less.
The squire looked at the cups,
First the leper's and his lord's as well,
While he stood before them,
But he could no longer
Choose the better one of them,
They were both so alike.
He ran back into the hall.

---

100 *Seyn Martin*: Martin of Tours (316-397), a Christian saint who tore his soldier's cloak to split it with a beggar, leading to his conversion. Here the choice of saint is likely thoughtful.

"Certes sir", he gan to sain
"Mani gode dede þou hast lorn
And so þou hast lorn þis dede now!
2040 He is a richer man þan þou
Bi þe time þat God was born".
Þe riche douke answerd "Nay".
"Þat worþ never bi niȝt no day.
It were oȝaines þe lawe!"
"ȝis sir", he gan to say
"He is a traitour bi mi fay
And were wele worþ to drawe!
For when y brouȝt him þe win
He drouȝ forþ a gold coupe fin
2050 Riȝt as it ware þi nawe.
In þis world bi seyn Jon
So wise a man is þer non
Asundri schuld hem knawe".
"Now certes", seyd Sir Amis þo
"In al þis world were coupes nomo
So liche in al þing
Save min and mi broþers also
Þat was sett bitwix ous to
Token of our parting.
2060 And ȝif it be so wiþ tresoun
Mine hende broþer Sir Amiloun
Is slain wiþouten lesing!
And ȝif he have stollen his coupe oway
Y schal him sle me self þis day
Bi Jhesu Heven-king!"
Fram þe bord he resed þan
And hent his swerd as a wode man
And drouȝ it out wiþ wrake
And to þe castel gat he ran.
2070 In al þe court was þer no man
Þat him miȝt atake.
To þe lazer he stirt in þe wain
And hent him in his honden twain
And sleynt him in þe lake
And layd on as he were wode
And al þat ever about him stode
Gret diol gan make.
"Traitour", seyd þe douke so bold
"Where haddestow þis coupe of gold
2080 And hou com þou þerto?
For bi Him þat Judas sold
Amiloun mi broþer it hadde in wold

"For certain, sir", he cried,
"You have wasted many good deeds,
And so you have wasted this one now!
He is a richer man than you are,
By the time that God was born!"
The rich duke answered, "No!"
"That could never happen, by night or day;
It would be against the law!"
"It's true, sir", he answered,
"He is a thief, by my faith,
And fully deserves to be pulled apart!
For when I brought him the wine,
He drew out a fine golden cup,
Right as if it were your own.
In all this world, by Saint John,
There is no man so wise
That he could tell them apart".
"Now, for sure", Sir Amis said then,
"In all this world there are no cups
So alike in every way,
Except for mine and my brother's as well,
Which were given between us two
As a token of our parting.
And if it is so, my gracious friend
Sir Amiloun was killed, with treason,
Without a lie!
And if this man has stolen his cup away,
I shall slay him myself this day,
By Jesus, Heaven's king!"
He reared up from the table
And seized his sword as a madman
And drew it out in fury,
And he ran to the castle gate.
In all the court there was no man
Who might overtake him.
He went to the leper in the cart
And grasped him by his two hands
And slung him into the lake
And attacked him as if he were crazed,
And all who stood around there
Began to make a great commotion.
"Thief!" cried the duke in boldness.
"Where did you get this golden cup?
And how did you get it?
For by Him that Judas betrayed,
My brother Amiloun used to have it

When þat he went me fro!"
"ʒa certes sir", he gan to say
"It was his in his cuntray
And now it is fallen so.
Bot certes now þat icham here
Þe coupe is mine y bouʒt it dere
Wiþ riʒt y com þer to".
2090 Þan was þe douke ful egre of mod.
Was noman þat about him stode
Þat durst legge on him hond.
He spurned him wiþ his fot
And laid on as he wer wode
Wiþ his naked brond.
And bi þe fet þe lazer he drouʒ
And drad on him in þe slouʒ.
For no þing wald he wond
And seyd, "þef þou schalt be slawe
2100 Bot þou wilt be þe soþe aknawe
Where þou þe coupe fond!"
Child Amoraunt stode þe pople among
And seye his lord wiþ wouʒ and wrong
Hou reweliche he was diʒt.
He was boþe hardi and strong
Þe douke in his armes he fong
And held him stille upriʒt.
"Sir", he seyd "þou art unhende
And of þi werkes unkende
2110 To sle þat gentil kniʒt.
Wel sore may him rewe þat stounde
Þat ever for þe toke he wounde
To save þi liif in fiʒt.
And ys thi brother Sir Amylioun
Þat whilom was a noble baroun
Bothe to ryde and go
And now with sorwe ys dreve adoun!
Nowe God þat suffred passioun
Breng him oute of his wo!
2120 For the of blysse he ys bare
And thou yeldyst him all with care
And brekest his bones a two.
Þat he halp the at thi nede
Well evell aquitest thou his mede.
Alas whi farest thou so?"
When Sir Amis herd him so sain
He stirt to þe kniʒt ogain
Wiþouten more delay

When he went away from me!"
"Yes, for certain, sir", the leper answered.
"It was his in his country,
And now it has passed on so.
But as sure as I am here,
The cup is mine, and I paid for it dearly,
And I came to it rightfully".
Then the duke was in a furious temper.
There was no one would stood near him
Who dared to lay a hand on him.
He kicked him with his foot
And attacked him, as if he were mad,
With his naked sword.
And by the feet he dragged the leper
And raged over him in the mud.
He would not stop for anything,
And said, "Thief, you will be slain
Unless you make known the truth
About where you found that cup!"
Young Amoraunt stood among the people
And saw how badly his lord was treated,
With wretchedness and injustice.
He was both hardy and strong;
He seized the duke in his arms
And held him still upright.
"Sir", he said, "you are ungrateful
And ignorant of what you are doing
To slay that gentle knight.
He might well sorely regret the time
That he ever suffered wounds for you
To save your life in battle.
For this is your brother, Sir Amiloun,
Who once was a noble baron
Both as he rode and as he walked,
And is now driven down by sorrow!
Now may God, who suffered anguish,
Bring him out of his woe!
Because of you he is deprived of joy,
And you only burden him with trouble
And break his bones in two.
After he helped you in your need,
You reward him so foully.
Alas, why do you act this way?"
When Sir Amis heard him say this,
He leaped toward the knight again
Without any more protest

And biclept him in his armes twain	And clasped him in both his arms
2130 And oft "allas!" he gan sain.	And began to cry "Alas!"
His song was "waileway!"	His constant refrain was "Woe is me!"
He loked opon his scholder bare	He looked upon Amiloun's bare shoulder
And seiȝe his grimly wounde þare	And saw his savage wound there,
As Amoraunt gan him say.	As Amorant began to explain.
He fel aswon to þe grounde	He fell faint to the ground
And oft he seyd "Allas þat stounde!"	And repeatedly cried, "Alas the moment!"
Þat ever he bode þat day.	This he proclaimed all that day.
"Allas", he seyd, "mi joie is lorn!	"Alas!" he said, "My joys are lost!
Unkender blod nas never born!	More shameful blood was never born!
2140 Y not wat y may do!	I do not know what I will do!
For he saved mi liif biforn	For he saved my life before,
Ichave him ȝolden wiþ wo and sorn	And I have repaid him with pain and
And wrouȝt him michel wo.	Sorrow and caused him great woe.
"O broþer", he seyd, "par charite	"My brother", he cried, "for charity's sake,
Þis rewely dede foryif þou me	Forgive me this terrible deed,
Þat ichave smiten þe so!"	That I have struck you so!"
And he forȝave it him also swiþe	And he forgave him just as quickly
And kist him wel mani a siþe	And kissed him many times over,
Wepeand wiþ eiȝen two.	Weeping from both eyes.
2150 Þan was Sir Amis glad and fain.	Then Sir Amis was glad and joyful.
For joie he wepe wiþ his ain	He wept from his eyes with happiness
And hent his broþer þan	And embraced his friend then,
And tok him in his armes twain	And held him in his two arms
Riȝt til he com into þe halle oȝain.	Right until they came back into the hall.
No bar him non oþer man.	No other man carried him.
Þe leuedi þo in þe halle stode	The lady stood in the hall
And wend hir lord hadde ben wode.	And thought that her lord had gone mad.
Oȝaines him hye ran.	She ran toward him.
"Sir", sche seyd, "wat is þi þouȝt?	"Sir", she cried, "what are you thinking?
2160 Whi hastow him into halle ybrouȝt	By Him who saved the world,
For Him þat þis world wan?"	Why have you brought him into the hall?"
"O dame", he seyd, "bi seyn Jon	"Oh, my lady!" he said, "by Saint John,
Me nas never so wo bigon	I was never so full of remorse,
Ȝif þou it wost understond!	If you would only understand!
For better kniȝt in world is non	For there is no better knight in the world,
Bot almost now ichave him slon	But I have almost killed him
And schamely driven to schond.	And have shamefully brought him to harm.
For it is mi broþer Sir Amiloun	For it is my brother, Sir Amiloun,
Wiþ sorwe and care is dreven adoun	Who has been ruined by sorrow and
2170 Þat er was fre to fond".	Hardship, who was once so valiant in trial".
Þe leuedi fel aswon to grounde	The lady fell faint to the ground
And wepe and seyd, "Allas þat stounde!"	And wept and said, "Alas the moment!",
Wel sore wrengand hir hond.	Sorely wringing her hands.
As foule a lazer as he was	As foul a leper as he was,

Þe leuedi kist him in þat plas;
For noþing wold sche spare
And oft time sche seyd "Allas!"
Þat him was fallen so hard a cas
To live in sorwe and care.
2180 Into hir chaumber sche gan him lede
And kest of al his pouer wede
And baþed his bodi al bare
And to a bedde swiþe him brouȝt
Wiþ cloþes riche and wele ywrouȝt.
Ful bliþe of him þai ware.
And þus in gest as we say
Twelmoneþ in her chaumber he lay.
Ful trewe þai ware and kinde.
No wold þai nick him wiþ no nay.
2190 What so ever he asked niȝt or day
It nas never bihinde.
Of everich mete and everi drink
Þai had hemselve wiþouten lesing
Þai were him boþe ful minde.
And bi þan þe twelmonþ was ago
A ful fair grace fel hem þo
In gest as we finde.
So it bifel opon a niȝt
As Sir Amis þat gentil kniȝt
2200 In slepe þouȝt as he lay
An angel com fram Heven briȝt
And stode biforn his bed ful riȝt
And to him þus gan say
Ȝif he wald rise on Cristes morn
Swiche time as Jhesu Crist was born
And slen his children tway
And alien his broþer wiþ þe blode
Þurth Godes grace þat is so gode
His wo schuld wende oway.
2210 Þus him þouȝt al þo þre niȝt
An angel out of Heven briȝt
Warned him ever more
Ȝif he wald do as he him hiȝt
His broþer schuld ben as fair a kniȝt
As ever he was biforn.
Ful bliþe was Sir Amis þo
Ac for his childer him was ful wo
For fairer ner non born.
Wel loþ him was his childer to slo
2220 And wele loþer his broþer forgo

The lady kissed him in that place;
She would not cease for anything,
And continually she cried "Alas!"
That he had fallen into such a hard state
To live in misery and worry.
Into her chamber she brought him
And threw off all of his ragged clothing
And bathed his naked body,
And brought him quickly to a bed with
Clothes that were rich and finely made.
They were overjoyed to have him.
And thus in the story as we know it,
He stayed twelve months in her chamber.
They were very devoted and kind.
They would never say no to him.
Whatsoever he asked for, day or night,
It was never slow in coming.
With every dish and every drink
They had themselves, without a lie,
Both had him fully in mind.
And by the time twelve months had passed,
A wondrous blessing came to them,
In the story as we find it.
So it happened one night
As Sir Amis, that gracious knight,
Lay asleep, that he dreamed
An angel came from bright Heaven
And stood right before his bed,
And began to say to him that if
He would rise on Christmas morning
At the same time as Jesus Christ was born,
And slay his two children
And anoint his brother with the blood,
Through God's grace, that is so good,
His disease would fade away.
Thus he dreamed all through the night
That an angel out of Heaven's radiance
Advised him for evermore
That if he would do as he was ordered,
His brother would be as fair a knight
As he ever was before.
Then Sir Amis was very gladdened,
But was very sad for his children,
For none were ever born who were so fair.
He was greatly loath to kill his children,
But more unwilling to deny his friend,

Þat is so kinde ycorn.
Sir Amiloun met þat niȝt also
Þat an angel warned him þo
And seyd to him ful yare
Ȝif his broþer wald his childer slo
Þe hert blod of hem to
Miȝt bring him out of care.
Amorwe Sir Amis was ful hende
And to his broþer he gan wende
2230 And asked him of his fare.
And he him answerd oȝain ful stille
"Broþer ich abide her Godes wille
For y may do na mare".
Also þai sete togider þare
And speke of aventours as it ware
Þo kniȝtes hende and fre
Þan seyd Sir Amiloun ful ȝare
"Broþer y nil nouȝt spare
To tel þe in privite.
2240 Me þouȝt toniȝt in mi sweven
Þat an angel com fram Heven.
For soþe he told me
Þat þurth þe blod of þin children to
Y miȝt aschape out of mi wo
Al hayl and hole to be".
Þan þouȝt þe douk wiþouten lesing
For to slen his childer so ȝing
It were a dedli sinne.
And þan þouȝt he bi Heven-king
2250 His broþer out of sorwe bring;
For þat nold he nouȝt blinne.
So it bifel on Cristes niȝt
Swiche time as Jhesu ful of miȝt
Was born to save mankunne
To chirche to wende al þat þer wes
Þai diȝten hem wiþouten les
Wiþ joie and worldes winne.
Þan þai were redi for to fare
Þe douke bad al þat þer ware
2260 To chirche þai schuld wende
Litel and michel lasse and mare
Þat non bileft in chaumber þare
As þai wald ben his frende.
And seyd he wald himselve þat niȝt
Kepe his broþer þat gentil kniȝt
Þat was so god and hende.

Who had so noble a birth.
Sir Amiloun also dreamed that night
That an angel addressed him then
And said to him directly
That if his brother slayed his children,
The heart's blood of the two
Might bring him out of his troubles.
In the morning Sir Amis was gracious
And made his way to his friend
And asked him how he was.
And the other answered back softly,
"Brother, I wait here for God's will,
For I can do no more".
As they sat together there,
And spoke of the adventures that had been,
Those noble and gracious knights,
Sir Amiloun then said in earnestness,
"Brother, I will not hesitate
To talk to you in private.
I dreamed last night in my sleep
That an angel came from Heaven.
In truth, he told me
That with the blood of your two children
I might escape from my affliction,
To be all healthy and whole".
The duke thought, without a lie,
That to kill his children, so young,
Would be a deadly sin.
But then he resolved, by Heaven's king,
To bring his brother out of hardship;
From that he would not flinch.
So it happened on Christmas Eve,
At such time as Jesus, full of might,
Was born to save mankind,
That all who were there readied themselves,
Without a lie, to go to church
With joy and all earthly pleasure.
When they were ready to set forth,
The duke commanded all who were there
That they should go on to church,
Small and great, less and more,
So that if they were his friends,
None would be left in the chamber there.
He said he would himself that night
Keep his brother, that noble knight
Who was so good and kind.

Þan was þer non þat durst say nay.
To chirche þai went in her way
At hom bileft þo hende.
2270 Þe douke wel fast gan aspie
Þe kays of þe noricerie
Er þan þai schuld gon
And priveliche he cast his eiʒe
And aparceived ful witterlye
Where þat þai hadde hem don.
And when þai were to chirche went
Þan Sir Amis verrament
Was bileft alon.
He tok a candel fair and briʒt
2280 And to þe kays he went ful riʒt
And tok hem oway ichon.
Alon him self wiþouten mo
Into þe chaumber he gan to go
Þer þat his childer were
And biheld hem boþe to
Hou fair þai lay togider þo
And slepe boþe yfere.
Þan seyd himselve, "Bi seyn Jon
It were gret reweþe ʒou to slon
2290 Þat God haþ bouʒt so dere!"
His kniif he had drawen þat tide;
For sorwe he sleyntt oway biside
And wepe wiþ reweful chere.
Þan he hadde wopen þer he stode
Anon he turned oʒain his mode
And sayd wiþouten delay
"Mi broþer was so kinde and gode
Wiþ grimly wounde he schad his blod
For mi love opon a day.
2300 Whi schuld y þan mi childer spare
To bring mi broþer out of care?"
"O certes", he seyd, "nay".
"To help mi broþer now at þis nede
God graunt me þerto wele to spede
And Mari þat best may!"
No lenger stint he no stode
Bot hent his kniif wiþ dreri mode
And tok his children þo.
For he nold nouʒt spille her blode
2310 Over a bacine fair and gode

There were none there who dared to say no.
They went on their way to church
And left those noble men at home.
The duke had swiftly located
The keys to the nursery
Before they were to go,
And he secretly cast his eye
And perceived clearly
Where they had been set.
And when they were gone to church,
Then Sir Amis, truly,
Was left alone.
He took a candle, fair and bright,
And went straightaway to the keys
And took each one of them away.
Alone himself, with no more delay,[101]
He went into the chamber
Where his children were,
And beheld the both of them,
How beautifully they lay together
And slept beside each other.
Then he said to himself, "By Saint John,
It would be heartbreaking to slay you,
Who God has bought so dearly!"
He had drawn his knife out at that moment
But for sorrow he laid it away nearby
And wept with a remorseful heart.
When he had wept, he immediately
Regained his composure where he stood
And said without delay,
"My brother was so kind and good.
With horrible wounds he shed his blood
For my love one day.
Why should I spare my children then
To bring my friend out of peril?"
"Oh, surely, no!" he said.
"To help my brother now in his need,
May God grant me all success,
Along with Mary, that blessed maid!"
He did not waver a moment longer,
But gripped his knife with a heavy heart
And took his children then.
Because he would not spill their blood,
He cut their throats in two

---

101 *Alon him self, withouten mo*: The withouten mo may mean "with no more ado" or also "without anyone else". ME rhetoric is fond of piling on synonyms, as well as double or triple negatives, for added emphasis.

Her þrotes he schar atwo.	Over a basin, good and strong.
And when he hadde hem boþe slain	And when he had slain both of them,
He laid hem in her bed ogain	He laid them in their bed again—
No wonder þei him wer wo!	It was no wonder he was in anguish!—
And hilde hem þat no wiȝt schuld se	And covered them, so no one would see
As noman hadde at hem be.	That anyone had been at them.
Out of chaumber he gan go.	He made his way out of the chamber.
And when he was out of chaumber gon	And when he was outside the room,
Þe dore he steked stille anon	He fastened the door closed at once,
2320 As fast as it was biforn.	As locked tight as it was before.
Þe kays he hidde under a ston	He hid the keys under a stone
And þouȝt þai schuld wene ichon	And thought that everyone would believe
Þat þai hadde ben forlorn.	That they had been murdered.
To his broþer he went him þan	He then went to his brother
And seyd to þat careful man	And said to that troubled man
Swiche time as God was born,	At the same time as God was born,
"Ich have þe brouȝt mi childer blod	"I have brought you my children's blood.
Ich hope it schal do þe gode	I hope it will do you good
As þe angel seyd biforn".	As the angel said before".
2330 "Broþer", Sir Amiloun gan to say	"Brother", Sir Amiloun cried out,
"Hastow slayn þine children tway?	"Have you killed your two children?
Allas whi destow so?"	Alas, why did you do it?"
He wepe and seyd, "Waileway!"	He wept and wailed, "Woe is us!"
"Ich had lever til Domesday	"I would have preferred to live
Have lived in care and wo!"	In pain and misery until Doomsday!"
Þan seyd Sir Amis, "Be now stille!"	Then Sir Amis said, "Be still now!"
"Jhesu when it is His wille	"Jesus, when it is His will,
May send me childer mo.	May send me more children.
For me of blis þou art al bare.	Because of me you are barren of joys.
2340 Ywis mi liif wil y nouȝt spare	In truth, I would not spare my own life
To help þe now þerfro".	If it would help you now".
He tok þat blode þat was so briȝt	He took that blood, which was so bright,
And alied þat gentil kniȝt	And anointed that noble knight,
Þat er was hende in hale	Who was once so strong in health,
And seþþen in a bed him diȝt	And afterward he put him in bed
And wreiȝe him wel warm apliȝt	And covered him warmly, indeed,
Wiþ cloþes riche and fale.	With blankets that were rich and plentiful.
"Broþer", he seyd, "ly now stille	"Brother", he said, "lie still now
And falle on slepe þurth Godes wille	And fall asleep through God's will,
2350 As þe angel told in tale.	As the angel told in the tale.
And ich hope wele wiþouten lesing	And I fully believe, without falsehood,
Jhesu þat is Heven-king	That Jesus, who is Heaven's king,
Schal bote þe of þi bale".	Will relieve you of your suffering".
Sir Amis let him ly alon	Sir Amis let him lie alone
And into his chapel he went anon	And went at once into his chapel,
In gest as ȝe may here	In the story as you may hear,

And for his childer þat he hadde slon
To God of Heven he made his mon
And preyd wiþ rewely chere
2360 Schuld save him fram schame þat day
And Mari His Moder þat best may
Þat was him leve and dere.
And Jhesu Crist in þat stede
Ful wele he herd þat kniȝtes bede
And graunt him his praiere.
Amorwe astite as it was day
Þe leuedi com home al wiþ play
Wiþ kniȝtes ten and five.
Þai souȝt þe kays þer þai lay.
2370 Þai founde hem nouȝt þai were oway.
Wel wo was hem olive!
Þe douk bad al þat þer wes
Þai schuld hold hem still in pes
And stint of her strive
And seyd he hadde þe keys nome
Schuld noman in þe chaumber come
Bot him self and his wive.
Anon he tok his leuedi þan
And seyd to hir, "Leve leman
2380 Be bliþe and glad of mode.
For bi Him þat þis warld wan
Boþe mi childer ich have slan
Þat were so hende and gode.
For me þouȝt in mi sweven
Þat an angel com fram Heven
And seyd me þurth her blode
Mi broþer schuld passe out of his wo.
Þerfore y slouȝ hem boþe to
To hele þat frely fode".
2390 Þan was þe leuedi ferly wo
And seiȝe hir lord was also.
Sche comfort him ful ȝare.
"O lef liif", sche seyd þo
"God may sende ous childer mo.
Of hem have þou no care!
ȝif it ware at min hert rote
For to bring þi broþer bote
My lyf y wold not spare.
For noman shal oure children see

And for his children that he had slain,
He made his plea to God in Heaven,
And prayed with a remorseful heart that
He would save him from shame that day,
And to Mary, His Mother, that blessed
Maid, who was beloved and dear to him.
And Jesus Christ, in that place,
Heard in full that knight's petition
And granted him his prayer.
In the morning, as soon as it was day,
The lady came home in high spirits
With ten knights and five more. They
Looked for the keys where they laid them.
They could not find them; they were gone.
It was torment to be alive!
The duke asked all who were there
That they would keep themselves quiet
And stop being fretful,
And he said he had taken the keys
And that no man should go into the
Chamber except himself and his wife.
Then at once he took his lady
And said to her, "My dear heart,
Be content and glad in mood.
For by Him who saved this world,
I have slain both my children,
Who were so gentle and good.
For I had a vision in my sleep
That an angel came from Heaven
And informed me that through their blood
My brother would pass out of his troubles.
Therefore I killed the both of them
To heal that noble man".
Then the lady was grief-stricken
And saw that her lord was also.
She was eager to comfort him.
"Oh, dear heart!" she said,
"God may send us more children.
Do not be troubled for them![102]
If it were at the point of my heart,
To bring your brother a remedy
I would not spare my own life.
No one will see our children;

---

102 Belisaunt's placid acceptance of her children's deaths here seems outrageous, but the poet perhaps intends to stress the faithfulness and maturity she has gained from Amis's overflowing goodness, in comparison to her earlier coquettishness and impiety.

2400 To morow shal þey beryed be	Tomorrow they shall be buried
Right as þey faire ded ware!"	As if they died naturally!"
Al þus þe lady faire and bry3t	Thus the lady, fair and beautiful,
Comfort hur lord wiþ al hur myg3t	Comforted her lord with all her might,
As 3e mow understonde.	As you may understand.
And seth þey went boþ ful ry3t	And later they both went straight
To Sir Amylion þat gentyl kny3t	To Sir Amiloun, that gentle knight,
Þat ere was free to fonde.	Who had been so valiant in trial.
And whan Sir Amylion wakyd þoo	When Sir Amiloun woke up then,
Al his fowlehed was agoo	All his foulness was gone
2410 Þurch grace of Goddes sonde.	Through the grace of God's command.
And þan was he as feire a man	He was as fair a man then
As ever he was 3et or þan	As he ever was before,
Seþ he was born in londe.	Since he was born on the earth.
Þan were þey al bliþ;	Then they were all happy;
Her joy couþ noman kyþ	They could not express all their joy
And þonked God þat day.	And they thanked God that day.
And þan as 3e mow listen and lyþ	And then, as you may listen and learn,
To a chamber þey went swyþ	They went quickly into the chamber
Þere þe children lay.	Where the children were laying.
2420 And wiþ out wemme and wound	They found the children safe and sound,
Al hool and sound þe children found	Without blemish or wound,
And layen to geder and play.	And sitting together playing.
For joye þey wept þere þey stood	They wept for joy where they stood,
And þonked God wiþ myld mood	And thanked God with grateful hearts
Her care was al away.	That their troubles were all gone. And
And when Sir Amylion was hool and fere	When Sir Amiloun was healthy and whole
And wax was strong of powere	And had grown vigorous in strength
And mighte boþ goo and ryde	And could both walk and ride,
Amoraunt was a bold squyer.	Amoraunt was made a brave squire.[103]
2430 Bliþe and glad he was of chere	He was glad and content at heart
To serve his lord beside.	To serve beside his lord.
Þan saide þe kny3t uppon a day	Then one day the knight said
He wolde hoom to his contray	He would travel home to his country,
To speke wiþ his wyf þat tyde.	To speak with his wife at that time.
And for she halp him so at nede	For the help she had given him in his need,
Wel he þought to quyte hur mede!	He fully intended to give her what she
No lenger wold he abyde.	Deserved![104] He would delay no longer.
Sir Amys ful hastely	Sir Amis hastily sent
Sent after mony kny3t hardy	For many hardy knights
2440 Þat dou3ty were of dede	Who were valiant in deeds—

---

103 *Squyer:* Formally in feudal practice a child progressed from page to squire to knight. In later centuries the title of squire was divorced from knighthood and referred more broadly to nobility in official or professional positions.

104 *Quyte hur mede*: Other than the Anglo-Saxon *litote*, a sort of humorous understatement, irony and sarcasm is rare in medieval English literature. Here the sense of Sir Amis paying his traitorous wife her *mede*, 'reward', seems close to PDE 'just desserts'.

Wele fyve hundred kene and try

. . . .

E   And oþer barons by and by
On palfray and on steede.
He preked boþ nyght and day
Til he com to his contray
Þere he was lord in lede.
Þan had a knyȝt of þat contre
Spoused his lady bryȝt of ble
In geste as we rede.
2450 But þus in geste as y ȝow say
Þey com hoom þat silf day
Þat þe bridal was hold.
To þe ȝates þey preked wiþ out delay.
Anon þer began a soory play
Among þe barouns bold.
A messengere to þe hal com
And seide her lord was com hom
As man meriest on molde.
Þan wox þe lady blew and wan;
2460 Þer was mony a sory man
Boþ ȝong and olde!
Sir Amys and Sir Amylion
And wiþ hem mony a stout baron
Wiþ knyȝtes and squyers fale
Wiþ helmes and wiþ haberyon
Wiþ swerd bryȝt and broun
Þey went in to þe hale.
Al þat þey þere arauȝt
Grete strokes þere þey cauȝt
2470 Boþ grete and smale.
Glad and blyþ were þey þat day
Who so myȝt skape away
And fle fro þat bredale.
When þei had wiþ wrake
Drove oute boþ broun and blake
Out of þat worþy woon
Sir Amylyon for his lady sake
A grete logge he let make

A good five hundred, tried and keen–

. . . .

And other barons by and by,
On palfreys and on steeds.[105]
They spurred both day and night
Until he came to his country
Where he was lord of the land.
A knight of that country had
Married his lady with the face so bright,
In the romance as we read it. But as
It happened, in the story as I tell you,
They came home the same day
That the wedding celebration was held.
They galloped to the gates without delay.
Soon there began a grim play
Among the bold barons.
A messenger came to the hall
And said that her lord had come home,
As the merriest man on earth.
Then the lady turned pale and ashen;
There was many a sorry man,
Both young and old!
Sir Amis and Sir Amiloun,
And with them many a stout baron
With knights and squires in plenty,
With helmets and with mailcoats,
With swords bright and gleaming,
Went into the hall.
All who they confronted there,
Both great and small,
Were caught by fierce strokes.
It was a glad and thankful man
Who was able to escape that day
And flee from that bridal feast.
When they had in vengeance
Driven out both high and low[106]
Out of that stately hall,
Sir Amiloun, for the sake of his lady,
Had a large cabin made

---

105 *On palfray and on steede*: Neither term refers to a breed. Steed suggests a warhorse, but a palfrey is a small horse used for riding or hunting. They were prized as fast and comfortable horses, but unsuited for battle. Sir Thopas riding out to war in full armor on a palfrey would have been humorous. A real knight would be humiliated.

106 *Both broun and blake*: See *Havelok*, 1015, and *Athelston*, 291. A ME idiom here likely meaning 'all different types of ordinary people', based on the colors of their clothing.

Boþ of lym and stoon.

Of both mortar-lime and stone.[107]

2480 Þere yn was þe lady led
And wiþ bred and water was she fed
Tyl her lyve dayes were goon.
Þus was þe lady brouȝt to dede.
Who þerof rouȝt he was a queede
As ȝe have herd echoon!
Þen Sir Amylion sent his sond
To erles barouns fre and bond
Boþ feire and hende.
When þey com he sesed in hond
2490 Child Oweys in al his lond
Þat was trew and kynde.
And when he had do þus ywys
Wiþ his broþer Sir Amys
Agen þen gan he wende.
In muche joy wiþ out stryf
To geder ladde þey her lyf
Tel God after hem dide sende.
Anoon þe hend barons tway
Þey let reyse a feire abbay
2500 And feffet it ryȝt wel þoo
In Lumbardy in þat contray
To senge for hem tyl Domesday
And for hor eldres also.
Boþ on oo day were þey dede
And in o grave were þey leide
Þe knyyȝtes boþ twoo.
And for her trewþ and her godhede
Þe blisse of Hevyn þey have to mede
Þat lasteþ ever moo.

2510 Amen.

The lady was placed there in it,
And she was fed with bread and water
Until her life's days were over.
Thus the lady was brought to death.
Whoever cared about it was worthless,
As each one of you has heard!
Then Sir Amiloun sent his summons
To earls and barons, free and bound,
Both fair and noble.
When they came, he placed all of his land
In Child Amoraunt's hand,[108]
Who had been faithful and kind.
And when he had done this, in truth,
Then he made his way on again
With his brother, Sir Amis.
They led their lives together
In great joy without strife
Until God sent for their souls.
At once a fair abbey was established
For the two noble barons,
And they endowed it generously
In Lombardy, in that country,
To sing for them until Judgment Day
And for their parents also.[109]
They both died on the same day
And they were laid in one grave,
Both of the two knights.
And for their loyalty and their godliness,
They have the bliss of Heaven as a reward,
Which lasts forevermore.

Amen.

---

107 *Lym and stoon:* The equivalent of cement and brick. Unlike Sir Amiloun's lodge made from wood, lime and stone is more expensive but can last centuries. Sir Amiloun may be being more generous with his lady, or he may be making the point that it is a true and much more permanent prison, along with the 'bread and water' diet.

108 *Child Oweys:* Line 1635 indicates that this is Amoraunt's childhood name, and some MSS prefer this usage.

109 One employment for clerics was to sing prayers for the dead in order to shorten their time in purgatory. In Shakespeare's *Henry V* Henry founds chapels for priests to sing for Richard II (V.i.281-3). Abbeys could also be founded for this purpose, as was All Soul's College, Oxford.

Athelston

Athelston (c. 1380-1400), at least in its surviving textual form, is one the later Middle English romances and has an uncharacteristic pessimism perhaps reflecting the decline of social, religious, and political order in the latter fourteenth century, a time troubled by both the Black Death and the Peasants' Revolt of 1381. Proclaiming itself a poem about "falsnesse, hou it wil ende" (8), the story begins with four messengers who swear themselves as brothers. Subsequently, one becomes king (Athelston), one is archbishop (Alyric), and two are earls (Wymonde, Egelond). As the shortest text in this collection, the poem has a ballad-like feel.

The narrative is driven by Wymonde's false accusation that Egelond plans to usurp him, whereupon Athelston orders a summary execution and is opposed by Alyric and others. In the climax Egelond and family are vindicated in a trial by ordeal and Wymonde is exposed and punished. Though Athelston may be reminiscent of the historical King Athelstan (927-39), here he is gullible and impetuous and more like Henry II in dealing with Thomas Becket, or perhaps more delicately like the temperamental young Richard II, who ruled during the manuscript's probable writing. Reflecting this crisis of faith in government, the most prudent characters in the poem are the wives and the lowly messenger.

Nevertheless, true to its essential nature as an English romance, through the bishop's loyalty to his brothers all is saved, treachery is justly punished, and aristocratic order is restored. In response to the negative example of brotherhood given by Wymonde, Athelston is given a positive example by Alyric. Some critics see the poem as a didactic lesson on good kingship, and Athelston does act as structural protagonist; he is the

From Cambridge, Corpus Christi College MS 183, f.1v. Source: Wikipedia

first character of the story and undergoes the most change as he transforms from implementing a rule based on mercurial autocracy into one of responsible concern. As well, as a romantic English folk-hero, the hard-working messenger connects all of these threads by interceding and escorting the bishop to Athelston, providing an earthy and good-natured response to the cynicism of the world around him.

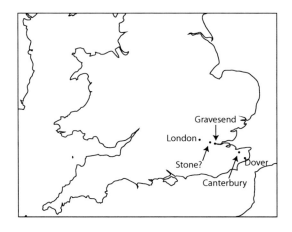

Athelston survives in one late manuscript: Caius College Library, MS 175 (c. 1500). As my basic textual source I use Thomas Wright and James O. Halliwell, *Reliquiae Antique*, Vol. 2 (London: John Russell Smith, 1845), and Julius Zupitza, "Die Romanze von *Athelston*", *Englische Studien* 13 (1883): 331-414.

C: Caius

Main characters:

Athelston, king of England
The queen
Egelond, earl of Stone
Edith, countess to Egelond and sister to Athelston
Alaric, bishop of Canterbury
Wymonde, earl of Dover
Athelston the messenger

1 C Lord that is of myghtys most,	Lord, who is of the highest might,[110]
Fadyr and Sone and Holy Gost,	Father, Son, and Holy Ghost,
Bryng us out of synne	Deliver us from sin and grant
And lene us grace so for to wyrke	Us the grace to renew ourselves
To love bothe God and Holy Kyrke	To love both God and holy church
That we may hevene wynne.	So that we may win Heaven.
Lystnes, lordyngys, that ben hende,	Hear, lordings, in your graciousness,
Of falsnesse, hou it wil ende	About falseness and how it will end
A man that ledes hym therin.	A man who is led into it.
10 Of foure weddyd brethryn I wole yow itel	I will tell you about four sworn brothers[111]
That wolden yn Yngelond go dwel,	Who wished to dwell in England,
That sybbe were nouȝt of kyn.	Who were related, but not by family.
And all foure messangeres they were,	All four of them were messengers
That wolden yn Yngelond lettrys bere,	Who used to carry letters in England,
As it wes here kynde.	As it was their trade.
By a forest gan they mete	They met in a forest
With a cros, stoode in a strete	Near a cross standing on a road
Be lef undyr a lynde,	By the leaves under a linden tree.
And, as the story telles me,	And, as the story tells me,
20 Ylke man was of dyvers cuntré,	Each man was from a different country,
In book iwreten we fynde–	As we find it written in the book.
For love of here metyng thare,	For the fellowship of their meeting,
They swoor hem weddyd bretheryn	They swore themselves
/ for evermare,	Brothers forever,
In trewthe trewely dede hem bynde.	Binding themselves earnestly in oaths.
The eldeste of hem ylkon,	The oldest one of them
He was hyȝt Athelston,	Was called Athelston,[112]
The kyngys cosyn dere;	The king's dear cousin.
He was of the kyngys blood,	He was of the king's blood,
Hys eemes sone, I undyrstood;	His maternal uncle's son, as I understand.
30 Therefore he neyȝyd hym nere.	Therefore he stayed near to him.
And at the laste, weel and fayr,	And at the end, fair and clear,[113]
The kyng him dyyd withouten ayr.	The king died without an heir.

---

110 The MS transcription has *off*, doubling most *f*s and some vowels. As the doublings are confusing (*ffalsnesse, wyff*) and are a period typographical usage probably not in earlier texts of the poem I have used single letters.

111 *Of foure weddyd bretheryn*: The four men are not married, but like Sirs Amis and Amiloun, they have taken an oath of brotherhood to be loyal to each other until death. In pagan Nordic culture men cut themselves and literally intermingled blood to become 'blood brothers'. This pledge was seen as nobler than marriage vows: in 306-7 the queen realizes that the bishop will honor the king before he does her. A. Mcintyre Trounce, ed., *Athelston: A Middle English Romance*, Early English Text Society [EETS] O.S. 224 (London: Oxford University Press, 1951), 13, quoted in *Athelston*, ed. Roland B. Herzman, Graham Drake, and Eve Salisbury, *Four Romances of England* (Kalamazoo, MI: Medieval Institute Publications, 1999), http://www.lib.rochester.edu/camelot/teams/athelfrm.htm.

112 There were several ruling Athelstans before the Norman conquest and the poet may not mean any of them, but see Treharne, who believes that King Athelstan (c. 894-939) is meant. Athelstan also had a sister named Edith, but never married. Elaine M. Treharne, "Romanticizing the Past in the Middle English *Athelston*", *Review of English Studies* 50:197 (1999): 1-21. There was no bishop Alaric of Canterbury and Wymonde ("Evil mind") was probably a stock villain's name.

113 *Weel and fayr*: This may simply be a formula saying that the king had a graceful passing, but it may also be emphasizing that there was no foul play in the king's death and thus a peaceful succession took place, which was certainly not always the case for an English king.

Thenne was ther non hys pere	There was at the time no one his peer
But Athelston, hys eemes sone;	Except Athelston, his uncle's son.
To make hym kyng wolde they nouȝt schone,	They did not refuse to make him king,
To corowne hym with gold so clere.	To crown him with shining gold.
Now was he kyng semely to se:	Now he was king, a fitting sight.
He sendes aftyr his bretheryn thre	He sent for his three friends
And gaf hem here warysoun.	And gave them their reward. He made
40 The eldest brothir he made Eerl of Dovere	The oldest brother Earl of Dover,
And thus the pore man gan covere	And thus the poor man was elevated,
Lord of tour and toun.	A lord of town and tower. The other
That other brothyr he made Eerl of Stane	Brother he made Earl of Stone—[114]
Egeland was hys name,	Egelond was his name,
A man of gret renoun–	A man of great renown–
And gaf him tyl hys weddyd wyf	And he gave him as his wedded wife
Hys owne sustyr, Dame Edyf,	His own sister, Dame Edith,
With gret devocyoun.	With great devotion.
The ferthe brothir was a clerk,	The fourth brother was a cleric
50 Mekyl he cowde of Godys werk.	Who knew much about God's work.
Hys name it was Alryke.	His name was Alaric.
Cauntyrbury was vacant	Canterbury was vacant,
And fel into that kyngys hand;	And fell into that king's hand.
He gaf it hym that wyke,	He gave him that posting
And made hym byschop of that stede,	And made him bishop of that place,
That noble clerk, on book cowde rede–	That noble cleric, who could read a book;
In the world was non hym lyche.	There were none like him in the world.
Thus avaunsyd he hys brother thorwȝ	Thus through God's grace
/ Goddys gras,	He advanced his friends,
And Athelstone hymselven was	And Athelston himself became
60 A good kyng and ryche.	A good and prosperous king.
And he that was Eerl of Stane–	And he who became Earl of Stone,
Sere Egeland was hys name–	Sir Egelond was his name,
Was trewe, as ye schal here.	Was faithful, as you will hear.
Thorwȝ the myȝt of Goddys gras,	Through the might of God's blessings,
He gat upon the countas	With the countess the earl fathered
Two knave-chyldren dere.	Two dear boys.
That on was fyftene wyntyr old,	One of them was fifteen years old,
That other thrytene, as men me told:	The other thirteen, as men have told me.
In the world was non here pere–	In the world they had no peer.
70 Also whyt so lylye-flour,	They were as white as a lily,
Red as rose of here colour,	Red as a rose in color,
As bryȝt as blosme on brere.	As bright as a blossom on a briar.
Bothe the Eerl and hys wyf,	The king loved both the earl and his wife
The kyng hem lovede as hys lyf,	As much as his own life,

---

114 *Stane*: There are many English Stones. Perhaps this is the Stone near Dartford or the one near Faversham, both on the road between London and Canterbury. It seems odd that Athelston would give a close friend an unimportant earldom, but this is not likely Maidstone, which is called as such in the Domesday Book.

And here sones two;
And oftensythe he gan hem calle
Bothe to boure and to halle,
To counsayl whenne they scholde goo.
Therat Sere Wymound hadde gret envye,
80 That Eerle of Dovere, wytyrlye.
In herte he was ful woo.
He thou3te al for here sake
False lesyngys on hem to make,
To don hem brenne and sloo.
And thanne Sere Wymound hym bethou3t
"Here love thus endure may nou3te;
Thorw3 wurd oure werk may sprynge".
He bad hys men maken hem 3are;
Unto Londone wolde he fare
90 To speke with the kynge.
Whenne that he to Londone come,
He mette with the kyng ful sone.
He sayde, "Welcome, my derelyng".
The kyng hym fraynyd seone anon,
By what way he hadde igon,
Withouten ony dwellyng.
"Come thou ou3t by Cauntyrbury,
There the clerkys syngen mery
Bothe erly and late?
100 Hou faryth that noble clerk,
That mekyl can on Goddys werk?
Knowest thou ou3t hys state?
And come thou ou3t be the Eerl of Stane,
That wurthy lord in hys wane?
Wente thou ou3t that gate?
Hou fares that noble kny3t,
And hys sones fayr and bry3t
My sustyr, yif that thou wate?"
"Sere", thanne he sayde, "withouten les,
110 Be Cauntyrbery my way I ches;
There spak I with that dere.
Ry3t weel gretes thee that noble clerk,
That mykyl can of Goddys werk;
In the world is non hys pere.
And also be Stane my way I drow3;
With Egelond I spak inow3,
And with the countesse so clere.
They fare weel, is nou3t to layne,
And bothe here sones". The king was fayne
120 And in his herte made glad chere.

Along with their two sons.
And often he would call them
Both to his chamber and to the hall,
For counsel when they were there.
For that, the Earl of Dover,
Sir Wymonde, had great jealousy
For sure. He was tormented at heart.
He wished on their account
To impugn false lies on them, to have
Them burned and slain. And then
Sir Wymonde thought to himself,
"Their love will not endure as it is!
The job might be done through words".
He ordered his men to get themselves
Ready. He would go to London
To speak with the king.
When he arrived in London,
He met with the king immediately,
Saying, "Welcome, dear friend!"
The king asked him soon after
By what way he had come,
Without any stopover.
"Did you pass near Canterbury,
Where the monks sing merrily,
Both early and late?
How does that noble cleric fare,
Who knows so much of God's work?
Do you know anything of his condition?
And did you pass by the Earl of Stone,
To the home of that admirable lord?
Were you anywhere near their gate?
How does that noble knight fare,
And his sons, fair and bright,
Or my sister, if you know?"
"Sire", he said, "without a lie,
I chose to go by Canterbury.
There I spoke with that dear person.
That noble priest, who knows so much
About God's work, greeted you courteously.
There are none his peer in the world.
And I also took my way past Stone.
I talked enough with Egelond, and
With the beautiful countess. They are
Doing well—there's nothing to hide—
Along with both their sons". The king
Was pleased and was cheered at heart.

"Sere kyng", he saide, "ʒif it be thi wille
To chaumbyr that thou woldest wenden tylle
Consayl for to here,
I schal thee telle a swete tydande,
There comen nevere non swyche in this lande
Of all this hundryd ʒere".
The kyngys herte than was ful woo
With that traytour for to go;
They wente bothe forth in fere;
130   And whenne that they were the
/ chaumbyr withinne,
False lesyngys he gan begynne
On hys weddyd brother dere.
"Sere kyng", he saide, "woo were me,
Ded that I scholde see thee,
So moot I have my lyf!
For by Hym that al this worl wan,
Thou has makyd me a man,
And iholpe me for to thryf.
For in thy land, sere, is a fals traytour.
140   He wole doo thee mykyl dyshonour
And brynge thee of lyve.
He wole deposen thee slyly,
Sodaynly than schalt thou dy
By Chrystys woundys fyve!"
Thenne sayde the kyng, "So moot thou the,
Knowe I that man, and I hym see?
His name thou me telle".
"Nay", says that traytour, "that wole I nouʒt
For al the gold that evere was wrouʒt—
150   Be masse-book and belle—
But yiff thou me thy trowthe will plyʒt
That thou schalt nevere bewreye the knyʒt
That thee the tale schal telle".
Thanne the kyng his hand up rauʒte,
That false man his trowthe betauʒte,
He was a devyl of helle!
"Sere kyng", he sayde, "thou madyst me kniʒt
And now thou hast thy trowthe me plyʒt
Oure counsayl for to layne:
160   Sertaynly, it is non othir
But Egelane, thy weddyd brothir—

"Sire king", he said, "If it is your will
That you would go to your chamber
To hear private counsel,
I will give you some interesting news.
Nothing like it has come to this land
In a hundred years".
The king's heart was distraught
In going forth with that traitor.
Both of them went in together.
And when they were within
The chamber,
He began to ply falsehoods
On his dear sworn brother. "Sire king",
He said, "it would be dreadful
If I were to see you dead,
So long as I am alive!
For by Him who redeemed all this world,
You have made me a man
And helped me to prosper.
But in this land, sir, there is a false traitor.
He will do you great dishonor
And will take away your life.
He will depose you slyly,
And then you will suddenly die,
By Christ's five wounds!"[115] Then the king
Said, "As you live and breathe,
Would I know the man if I see him?
Tell me his name".
"No", said the traitor, "I will not do that
For all the gold that was ever made,
By mass-book or bell,[116]
Unless you pledge your vow
That you will never betray the knight
Who has told you the story".
Then the king raised up his hand,
Giving his promise to that false man.
He was a devil from Hell! "Sire King",
He said, "you made me a knight,
And now you have pledged your word
To conceal our conversation.
Certainly, it is no other
Than Egelond, your brother.

---

115 *By Chrystys woundys fyve*: Like lines 135 and 145, simply an oath for emphasis. Scripture reports that Christ received five wounds during crucifixion, four by nails through his limbs and one by a spear in his side.

116 *Masse-book and belle*: Similarly, church hymnals, bibles, and bells and all of the implements of service were also used for oaths, whether in seriousness or in profanity. Here their use emphasizes Wymound's hypocrisy.

He wolde that thou were slayne;
He dos thy sustyr to undyrstand
He wole be kyng of thy lande,
And thus he begynnes here trayne.
He wole thee poysoun ryȝt slyly;
Sodaynly thanne schalt thou dy,
By Him that suffryd payne".
Thanne swoor the kyng be Cros and Roode:
170 "Meete ne drynk schal do me goode
Tyl that he be dede;
Bothe he and hys wyf, hys sones two,
Schole they nevere be no mo
In Yngelond on that stede".
"Nay", says the traytour, "so moot I the,
Ded wole I nouȝt my brother se;
But do thy beste rede".
No lengere there then wolde he lende;
He takes hys leve, to Dovere gan wende.
180 God geve hym schame and dede!
Now is that traytour hom iwent.
A messanger was aftyr sent
To speke with the kyng.
I wene he bar his owne name:
He was hoten Athelstane;
He was foundelyng.
The lettrys were imad fullyche thare,
Unto Stane for to fare
Withouten ony dwellyng,
190 To fette the eerl and his sones two,
And the countasse also,
Dame Edyve, that swete thyng.
And in the lettre yit was it tolde,
That the kyng the eerlys sones wolde
Make hem bothe knyȝt;
And therto his seel he sette.
The messanger wolde nouȝt lette;
The way he rydes ful ryȝt.
The messanger, the noble man,
200 Takes hys hors and forth he wan,
And hyes a ful good spede.
The eerl in hys halle he fande;
He took hym the lettre in his hande
Anon he bad hym rede:

He wishes that you were dead.
He has your sister under the impression
That he will be king of this land,
And so he leads her astray.
He intends to poison you cunningly.
You will then suddenly die,
By Him who suffered pain!" Then the
King swore, by the wooden Cross,
"Neither food or drink will do me good
Until he is dead,
Both him and his wife, and his two sons!
They will no longer be in England
In that place".
"No", said the traitor, "so help me God,
I will not see my brother dead.
But follow your best advice".
Then he would not stay any longer.
He said his goodbyes and left for Dover.
May God give him shame and death!
When the traitor had gone home,
A messenger was afterwards summoned
To speak with the king.
I believe he had his own name;
He was also called Athelstan.[117]
He was an orphaned child.
The letters were made out in full there,
For him to go to Stone
Without any delay
To fetch the earl and his two sons
And the countess also,
Dame Edith, that sweet lady.
It was also stated in the letter
That the king would make
Both of the earl's sons knights,
And to this he set his seal.
The messenger did not delay;
He rode the way swiftly.
The noble man, this messenger,
Took his horse and went forth
And hastened at top speed.
He found the earl in his hall.
He gave him the letter into his hand
And asked him to read it straightaway.

117 *Athelstane*: This is a different person. There may be a poetic significance or it may simply reflect the popularity of the name. Dickerson argues that the youth is "the alter ego of the arrogant King Athelston, who was once a messenger". A. Inskip Dickerson, "The Subplot of the Messenger in *Athelston*", *Papers on Language & Literature* 12 (1976): 124.

"Sere", he sayde also swythe,
"This lettre ouȝte to make thee blythe:
Thertoo thou take good hede.
The kyng wole for the cuntas sake
Bothe thy sones knyȝtes make–
210 To London I rede thee spede.
The kyng wole for the cuntas sake
Bothe thy sones knyȝtes make,
The blythere thou may be.
Thy fayre wyf with thee thou bryng
And ther be ryght no lettyng
That syȝte that sche may see".
Thenne sayde that eerl with herte mylde,
"My wyf goth ryȝt gret with chylde,
And forthynkes me,
220 Sche may nouȝt out of chaumbyr wyn,
To speke with non ende of here kyn
Tyl sche delyveryd be".
But into chaumbyr they gunne wende,
To rede the lettrys before that hende
And tydingys tolde here soone.
Thanne sayde the cuntasse, "So moot I the,
I wil nouȝt lette tyl I there be,
Tomorwen or it be noone.
To see hem knyȝtes, my sones fre,
230 I wole nouȝt lette tyl I there be;
I schal no lengere dwelle.
Cryst forȝelde my lord the kyng,
That has grauntyd hem here dubbyng.
Myn herte is gladyd welle".
The eerl hys men bad make hem ȝare;
He and hys wyf forth gunne they fare,
To London faste they wente.
At Westemynstyr was the kyngys wone;
There they mette with Athelstone,
240 That aftyr hem hadde sente.
The goode eerl soone was hent
And feteryd faste, verrayment,
And hys sones two.
Ful lowde the countasse gan to crye,
And sayde, "Goode brothyr, mercy!
Why wole ȝe us sloo?
What have we aȝens ȝow done,
That ȝe wole have us ded so soone?
Me thynkith ȝe arn ourn foo".
250 The kyng as wood ferde in that stede;

"Sir", he said as quickly,
"This letter ought to make you glad.
Therefore pay attention to it.
The king will, for the countess' sake,
Make both your sons knights.
I advise you to hurry to London.
The king will, for the countess' sake,
Make both your sons knights,
To make you all the happier.
Bring your fair wife with you,
And let there be no delay,
So that she may see that sight".
Then the earl said with a tender heart,
"My wife is very late in her pregnancy,
And so it seems to me that
She cannot go out from her chamber
To speak with anyone of her kin
Until she has given birth".
But they made their way to the chamber
To read the letter before that noble lady
And soon told her the news. Then the
Countess said, "As I live and breathe,
I will not rest until I am there
Tomorrow, before it is noon!
To see my noble sons knighted,
I will not delay until I am there.
I will not linger any longer.
May Christ reward my lord the king
Who has granted them their dubbing!
My heart is very glad".
The earl had his men ready themselves.
He and his wife set out,
Traveling quickly to London.
The king's home was at Westminster.
There they met with Athelston,
Who had sent for them.
The good earl was at once seized
And tightly chained, in truth,
And his two sons as well.
The countess began to cry loudly,
And said, "Good brother, have mercy!
Why do you want to execute us?
What have we done against you,
That you will have us dead so soon?
I feel like I am your enemy!" In the
Moment the king behaved as if mad.

He garte hys sustyr to prysoun lede–
In herte he was ful woo.
Thenne a squyer, was the countasses frende,
To the qwene he gan wende,
And tydyngys tolde here soone.
Gerlondes of chyryes off sche caste,
Into the halle sche come at the laste,
Longe or it were noone.
"Sere kyng, I am before thee come
260 With a child, douȝtyr or a sone.
Graunte me my bone,
My brothir and sustyr that I may borwe
Tyl the nexte day at morwe,
Out of here paynys stronge;
That we mowe wete by comoun sent
In the playne parlement".
"Dame", he saide, "goo fro me!
Thy bone shall nouȝt igraunted be,
I doo thee to undyrstande.
270 For, be Hym that weres the corowne of thorn,
They schole be drawen and hangyd tomorn,
Ȝyff I be kyng of lande!"
And whenne the qwene these wurdes herde,
As sche hadde be beten with ȝerde,
The teeres sche leet doun falle.
Sertaynly, as I ȝow telle,
On here bare knees doun she felle,
And prayde yit for hem alle.
"A, dame", he sayde, "verrayment
280 Hast thou broke my comaundement
Abyyd ful dere thou schalle".
With hys foot– he wolde nouȝt wonde–
He slowȝ the chyld ryȝt in here wombe;
She swownyd amonges hem alle.
Ladyys and maydenys that there were,
The qwene to here chaumbyr bere,

He ordered his sister sent to prison;
He was distressed at heart. Then a
Squire who was the countess' friend
Made his way to the queen
And soon gave her the news.
She threw off her garlands of cherries,[118]
Finally coming into the hall
Well before it was noon.
"Sire king, I have come before you
With a child, a daughter or a son.
Grant me my plea, that I might act
As guarantor to my brother and sister
Until tomorrow morning when they
Can be released from their strong pains,
So that we may decide this by common
Assent in the open parliament".[119]
"My lady", he replied, "get away from
Me! Your request will not be granted,
I will have you understand! For by Him
Who wore a crown of thorns, they will
Be drawn and hanged tomorrow,
If I am the king of this land!"
And when the queen heard these words,
She let her tears fall down
As if she had been beaten with a stick.
For certain, as I tell you,
She fell down on her bare knees
And begged for them all.
"Well, madam!" he said, "Truly you have
Defied my commandment!
You will pay for it dearly". With his
Foot–he would not hold back–
He killed the child right in her womb.[120]
She fainted before them all.
The ladies and maidens who were there
Bore the queen to her chamber,

---

118 *Gerlondes of chyryes off sche caste*: A mysterious line, perhaps only meaning that the queen is snacking on cherries to emphasize her innocence of what is happening. Wright notes that cherries were very popular in medieval England. T. Wright and J. O. Halliwell, *Reliquiae Antiquae*, Vol. 2 (London: J. R. Smith, 1845), 85-103.

119 As with *Amis and Amiloun*, the queen asks if she can be a guarantor to her brother and sister so that they can be freed. The queen, who is also heavily pregnant, is evidently worried about her sister's condition in prison, making the king's response even more callous.

120 *He slowgh the chyld ryȝt in here wombe*: Herzman et al. note a little dryly that "many critics have commented on the cruelty in this passage". Although the poet's tone clearly disapproves strongly, Rowe notes that this act would not have been seen as a crime in the time period. Elizabeth A. Rowe, "The Female Body Politic and the Miscarriage of Justice in *Athelston*", *Studies in the Age of Chaucer* 17 (1995), 87. Alternatively, Loomis states that ballad-form stories still conventionally retained scenes of violence that were no longer usual in romance. Laura A. Hibbard Loomis, "Athelston, a Westminster Legend", *PMLA* 36:2 (1921): 232.

And there was dool inowȝ.
Soone withinne a lytyl spase
A knave-chyld iborn ther wase,
290 As bryȝt as blosme on bowȝ.
He was bothe whyt and red;
Of that dynt was he ded—
His owne fadyr hym slowȝ!
Thus may a traytour baret rayse
And make manye men ful evele at ayse;
Hymself nouȝt aftyr it lowȝ.
But ȝit the qwene, as ȝe schole here,
Sche callyd upon a messangere,
Bad hym a lettre fonge.
300 And bad hym wende to Cauntyrbery,
There the clerkys syngen mery
Bothe masse and evensonge.
"This lettre thou the byschop take,
And praye hym for Goddys sake,
Come borewe hem out off here bande.
He wole doo more for hym, I wene,
Thanne for me, thouȝ I be qwene.
I doo thee to undyrstande
An eerldom in Spayne I have of land;
310 Al I sese into thyn hand,
Trewely, as I thee hyȝt,
And hundryd besauntys of gold red.
Thou may save hem from the ded,
ȝyff that thyn hors be wyȝt".
"Madame, brouke weel thy moregeve,
Also longe as thou may leve.
Therto have I no ryȝt.
But of thy gold and of thy fee,
Cryst in hevene forȝelde it thee;
320 I wole be there to nyȝt.
Madame, thryty myles of hard way
I have reden syth it was day.
Ful sore I gan me swynke;
And for to ryde now fyve and twenti thertoo
An hard thyng it were to doo,

And there was commotion enough.
Soon, within a short time
A baby boy was delivered,
As bright as a blossom on the bough.
He was both white and red;[121]
From that blow he was dead.
His own father had killed him!
Thus may a traitor raise havoc and
Make many men ill at ease. He would
Have nothing to laugh about later.
But still the queen, as you will hear,
Called for a messenger,[122]
Asking him to deliver a letter,
And had him go to Canterbury,
Where the priests sing merrily,
Both for mass and evensong.
"Take this letter to the bishop,
And petition him for God's sake,
To come rescue them out of their bonds.
He will do more for his brother, I think,
Than for me, even though I am queen.
I will have you understand
That I have as land an earldom in Spain;
I give it all into your hand,
Truly, as I promise you,
And a hundred coins of red gold.
You may save them from death
If your horse is strong".
"Madam, enjoy your wedding gifts,
As long as you may live.
I have no right to them,
To your gold or to your property.
Christ in Heaven has given it to you.
I will be there tonight.
Madam, I have ridden thirty miles
Of rough road since it was sundown.
I have done hard work.
And to ride now another twenty-five
Would be a hard thing to do,

---

121 *Whyt and red*: This is not a macabre description of the stillborn boy's bruises but the colors of aristocratic breeding, used approvingly by romance poets. French and Hale argue that the "brown and black" of *Amis and Amiloun* and of *Havelok* alternatively suggest the common people, although the idiom is disputed (Herzman et al.). Walter H. French and Charles B. Hale, ed., *Middle English Metrical Romances* (New York: Prentice Hall, 1930).

122 *A messangere*: The poet uses the indefinite article a, but this is evidently the same Athelstan (not the king) who rides to Stone to fetch Egelond and his wife. The messenger complains that he has ridden thirty miles (321). London to Stone near Faversham is forty-six miles, but to Stone near Dartford is fifteen–a return journey? For further discussion see Dickerson, 115-16.

Forsothe, ryȝt as me thynke.
Madame, it is ner hande passyd prime,
And me behoves al for to dyne,
Bothe wyn and ale to drynke.

330 Whenne I have dynyd, thenne wole I fare.
God may covere hem of here care,
Or that I slepe a wynke".
Whenne he hadde dynyd, he wente his way,
Also faste as that he may,
He rod be Charynge-cross
And entryd into Flete-strete
And sithen thorwȝ Londone, I ȝow hete,
Upon a noble hors.
The messanger, that noble man,

340 On Loundone brygge sone he wan–
For his travayle he hadde no los–
From Stone into Steppyngebourne,
Forsothe, his way nolde he nouȝt tourne;
Sparyd he nouȝt for myre ne mos.
And thus hys way wendes he
Fro Osprynge to the Blee.
Thenne myȝte he see the toun
Of Cauntyrbery, that noble wyke,
Therin lay that byschop ryke,

350 That lord of gret renoun.
And whenne they rungen undernbelle,
He rod in Londone, as I ȝow telle:
He was non er redy;
And ȝit to Cauntyrbery he wan,
Longe or evensong began;
He rod mylys fyfty.
The messanger nothing abod;
Into the palays forth he rod,
There that the byschop was inne.

360 Ryght welcome was the messanger,
That was come from the qwene so cleer,
Was of so noble kynne.

In truth, so far as I can see.
My lady, it is nearly six in the morning,[123]
And it is right for me to eat,
And to drink both wine and ale.
When I have eaten, then I will set out.
May God relieve them from their cares
Before I sleep a wink".
When he had finished, he went his way,
As fast as he could.
He rode by Charing Cross
And entered into Fleet Street
And then through London, I assure you,
Upon a splendid horse.
The messenger, that noble man,
Soon reached London Bridge.
For his labors he had no praise.[124]
From Stone into Sittingbourne,
In truth, he did not alter his course.
He did not stop for mud or bog.
And in this way he traveled
From Ospringe to the Blean forest.
Then he could see the town
Of Canterbury, that noble village,[125]
Where that powerful bishop lived,
That lord of great renown.
When they had rung the morning bell,
He was still riding in London, I tell you.
He was not ready earlier.
And yet he reached Canterbury
Long before the six o'clock songs;
He rode fifty miles.
The messenger did not linger.
He rode forth into the palace
Where the bishop was inside. There was
A warm welcome for the messenger,
Who had come from the radiant queen,
Who was of such a noble family.

---

123 *Prime* is about 6 AM, according to the monastic prayer divisions of the day: matins, prime, terce, sext, nones, vespers, and compline. Medieval time was much less clock-bound and was often reckoned by the canonical hours or by movements of the tides (such as *undertide*). *Nona hora*, the ninth hour of the day, was originally 3 PM, only shifting to 12 and becoming modern noon in the twelfth to fourteenth centuries. *Bevis of Hampton* seems to have the modern meaning when the barons believe that Miles has slept through mid-morning until noon (3237).

124 *He hadde no los*: Some commentators read this as 'loss', as in "he lost no time". I agree with Herzman et al. that the sense is that the poet is extolling the the unsung messengers throughout the story, describing their labors in detail and complaining that it is thankless work, without *los*, praise.

125 *Wyke*: Perhaps a village, borrowing from Latin *vicus*; or the clerical meaning of a church seat or jurisdiction may also be intended (PDE *bailiwick*).

He took hym a lettre ful good speed
And saide, "Sere byschop, have this and reed"
And bad hym come with hym.
Or he the lettre hadde half iredde,
For dool, hym thoughte hys herte bledde;
The teeres fyl ovyr hys chyn.
The byschop bad sadele hys palfray:
370 "Also faste as thay may,
Bydde my men make hem ȝare;
And wendes before", the byschop dede say,
"To my maneres in the way;
For nothyng that ȝe spare,
And loke at ylke fyve mylys ende
A fresch hors that I fynde,
Schod and nothing bare;
Blythe schal I nevere be,
Tyl I my weddyd brother see,
380 To kevere hym out of care".
On nyne palfrays the bysschop sprong,
Ar it was day, from evensong,
In romaunce as we rede.
Sertaynly, as I ȝow telle,
On Londone brygge ded doun felle
The messangeres stede.
"Allas", he sayde, "that I was born!
Now is my goode hors forlorn,
Was good at ylke a nede;
390 Ȝistyrday upon the grounde,
He was wurth an hundryd pounde,
Ony kyng to lede".
Thenne bespak the erchebyschop.
Oure gostly fadyr undyr God,
Unto the messangere:
"Lat be thy menyng of thy stede,
And thynk upon oure mykyl nede,
The whylys that we ben here;
For ȝif that I may my brother borwe
400 And bryngen hym out off mekyl sorwe,
Thou may make glad chere;
And thy warysoun I schal thee geve,
And God have grauntyd thee to leve
Unto an hundryd ȝere".
The byschop thenne nought ne bod:
He took hys hors, and forth he rod

He gave him a letter with urgency
And said, "Sir Bishop, take this and read",
And asked that he come with him.
Before he had read half the letter,
He thought his heart had been pierced
For sorrow. The tears fell from his chin.
The bishop ordered his palfrey saddled.
"As fast as they can,
Have my men make themselves ready.
And go on ahead", the bishop stressed,
"To my manors along the way.
Spare no difficulty,
And see that at every five miles' space
I find a fresh horse,
Shod and never barehooved.
I will never be at peace
Until I see my blood brother,
To deliver him from trouble".
The bishop rode nine palfreys
Before it was daylight, from evensong,[126]
In the romance as we read.
For certain, as I tell you,
The messenger's horse fell down dead
On London Bridge.
"Alas!" he cried, "that I was ever born!
Now I have lost my good horse,
Who was ready in every need!
Yesterday on the ground
He was worth a hundred pounds,
Fit for any king to ride!"
Then the archbishop,
Our spiritual father under God,
Spoke to the messenger.
"Forget your moaning for your horse,
And concentrate on our great need,
The reason that we are here.
For if I can rescue my brother
And bring him out of his great sorrow,
You will be of good cheer.
And I will reward you with an income,
Even if God grants you to live
For a hundred years".
The bishop did not stay any longer.
He took his horse, and rode

---

126 *Evensong*: Early evening and the sixth of the seven canonical hours, also known as vespers. The poem betrays a rather working-class concern with time.

Into Westemynstyr so ly3t;	Quickly into Westminster,[127]
The messanger on his foot also:	With the messenger on foot as well.
With the byschop come no mo,	No more came with the bishop,
410 Nether squyer ne kny3t.	Neither squire nor knight.
Upon the morwen the kyng aros,	In the morning the king rose
And takes the way, to the kyrke he gos,	And made his way to the chapel,
As man of mekyl my3t.	As a man of great authority.
With hym wente bothe preest and clerk,	With him went both priest and cleric,
That mykyl cowde of Goddys werk,	Who knew much about God's work,
To praye God for the ry3t.	To pray to God for the right direction.
Whenne that he to the kyrke com;	When he arrived in the chapel,
Tofore the Rode he knelyd anon,	He kneeled at once before the Cross
And on hys knees he felle:	And fell on his knees.
420 "God, that syt in Trynyté	"God, who sits in Trinity,
A bone that thou graunte me,	Grant me a plea, Lord,
Lord, as Thou harewyd helle–	Just as you conquered Hell.
Gyltless men 3if thay be,	If they are guiltless men
That are in my presoun free,	Who are in my strong prison,
Forcursyd there to 3elle,	Condemned there to yell,
Of the gylt and thay be clene,	If they are innocent of their guilt,
Leve it moot on hem be sene,	Grant that it may be seen by them
That garte hem there to dwelle".	Who caused them to be there".
And whenne he hadde maad his prayer,	And when he had made his prayer,
430 He lokyd up into the qweer;	He looked up into the choir loft
The erchebysschop sawe he stande.	And saw the archbishop standing there.
He was forwondryd of that caas,	He was astonished by the sight
And to hym he wente apas,	And went to him quickly,
And took hym be the hande.	And took him by the hand.
"Welcome", he sayde, "thou erchebyschop,	"Welcome", he said, "My archbishop,
Oure gostly fadyr undyr God".	Our saintly father under God".
He swoor be God levande,	The archbishop swore by the living God,
"Weddyd brother, weel moot thou spede,	"Sworn brother, may you prosper long,
For I hadde nevere so mekyl nede,	For I never had such an urgent need
440 Sith I took cros on hande.	Since I took the cross in my hand.
Goode weddyd brother, now turne thy rede;	Good brother, now change your mind.
Doo nought thyn owne blood to dede	Do not put your own blood to death
But 3if it wurthy were.	Unless it were justified. For Him
For Hym that weres the corowne of thorn,	That wore the crown of thorns, let me
Lat me borwe hem tyl tomorn,	Be surety for them until tomorrow,
That we mowe enquere,	So that we may have an inquiry
And weten alle be comoun asent	And decide by common assent
In the playne parlement	In the full parliament
Who is wurthy be schent.	Who is worthy to be punished.
450 And, but 3if ye wole graunte my bone,	And if you will not grant my plea,

---

127 *So ly3t*: Or, "he rode into Westminster, which was so bright".

It schal us rewe bothe or none,
Be God that alle thyng lent".
Thanne the kyng wax wrothe as wynde,
A wodere man myȝte no man fynde
Than he began to bee:
He swoor othis be sunne and mone:
"They scholen be drawen and hongyd or none
With eyen thou schalt see!
Lay doun thy cros and thy staff,
460 Thy mytyr and thy ryng that I thee gaff;
Out of my land thou flee!
Hyȝe thee faste out of my syȝt!
Wher I thee mete, thy deth is dyȝt;
Non othir then schal it bee!"
Thenne bespak that erchebysschop,
Oure gostly fadyr undyr God,
Smertly to the kyng,
"Weel I wot that thou me gaf
Bothe the cros and the staff,
470 The mytyr and eke the ryng;
My byschopryche thou reves me,
And Crystyndom forbede I thee!
Preest schal ther non syngge;
Neyther maydynchyld ne knave
Crystyndom schal ther non have;
To care I schal thee brynge.
I schal gare crye thorwȝ ylke a toun
That kyrkys schole be broken doun
And stoken agayn with thorn.
480 And thou schalt lygge in an old dyke,
As it were an heretyke,
Allas that thou were born!
ȝif thou be ded, that I may see,
Assoylyd schalt thou nevere bee;
Thanne is thy soule in sorwe.
And I schal wende in uncouthe lond,
And gete me stronge men of hond;
My brothir ȝit schal I borwe.
I schal brynge upon thy lond
490 Hungyr and thyrst ful strong,
Cold, drouȝhe, and sorwe;
I schal nouȝt leve on thy lond
Wurth the gloves on thy hond

We will both regret it before noon,
By God, who gave all things". Then the
King grew as furious as the winds.
No one might find a man more enraged
Than he became.
He swore oaths by the sun and moon:
"They shall be hanged and drawn before
Noon! You will see it with your own eyes!
Lay down your cross and your staff,
Your miter and your ring that I gave you.
Flee out of my land!
Get yourself quickly out of my sight!
If I ever meet you, your death is decided.
It will not be any other way!"
Then the archbishop,
Our devout father under God,
Spoke sharply to the king,
"I know very well that you gave me
Both the cross and the staff,
The miter and the ring as well.
You rob me of my bishop's office,
And in turn I excommunicate you!
No priest shall sing;
No one shall have church or sacrament,
Neither maiden-child nor boy.
I will bring you to grief!
I will go proclaiming through each town
That churches shall be broken down
And struck at with thorns.
And your body will lie in an old ditch,
As if you were a heretic.[128]
Alas that you were born!
If you are dead, I will see to it
That you will never be absolved.
Then your soul will be in torment.
And I will travel to faraway lands
And gather strong men of might.
I will save my brother yet!
I will bring upon your land
Fierce hunger and thirst,
Cold, drought, and misery.
I will leave nothing on your land
Worth the gloves on your hand,

---

128 *As it were an heretyke*: This is a very serious matter. The archbishop is not only excommunicating the king and his realm but denying him a Christian burial, which was also refused to heretics, criminals, and suicides. King John was forced to submit to Innocent III in 1213 after interdiction had threatened his rule.

To begge ne to borwe".
The bysschop has his leve tan.
By that his men were comen ylkan:
They sayden, "Sere, have good day".
He entryd into Flete strete;
With lordys of Yngelond gan he mete
500 Upon a noble aray.
On here knees they kneleden adoun,
And prayden hym of hys benysoun,
He nykkyd hem with nay.
Neyther of cros neyther of ryng
Hadde they non kyns wetyng;
And thanne a knyght gan say.
A knyȝt thanne spak with mylde voys:
"Sere, where is thy ryng? Where is thy croys?
Is it fro thee tan?"
510 Thanne he sayde, "ȝoure cursyd kyng
Hath me reft of al my thyng,
And of al my worldly wan;
And I have entyrdytyd Yngelond:
Ther schal no preest synge Masse with hond,
Chyld schal be crystenyd non,
But ȝif he graunte me that knyȝt,
His wyf and chyldryn fayr and bryȝt:
He wolde with wrong hem slon".
The knyȝt sayde, "Bysschop, turne agayn;
520 Of thy body we are ful fayn;
Thy brothir ȝit schole we borwe.
And, but he graunte us oure bone,
Hys presoun schal be broken soone,
Hymself to mekyl sorwe.
We schole drawe doun both halle and boures,
Bothe hys castelles and hys toures,
They schole lygge lowe and holewe.
Thouȝ he be kyng and were the corowun,
We scholen hym sette in a deep dunjoun:
530 Oure Crystyndom we wole folewe".
Thanne, as they spoken of this thyng,
Ther comen twoo knyȝtes from the kyng,
And sayden, "Byschop, abyde,
And have thy cros and thy ryng,
And welcome whyl that thou wylt lyng,
It is nouȝt for to hyde.
Here he grauntys thee the knyȝt,
Hys wyf and chyldryn fayr and bryȝt;
Again I rede thou ryde.

To beg or to borrow".
The bishop took his leave.
By then all of his men had arrived.
They said, "Sire, good day".
He entered into Fleet Street;
He started to meet the lords of England,
All in a noble array.
They stooped down on their knees
And beseeched him for his blessing.
He refused them with 'no'.
They had no idea at all where
Either his cross or his ring were.
And then a knight spoke up.
The knight said in a low voice, "Sir,
Where is your ring? Where is your cross?
Have they been taken from you?"
The bishop replied, "Your accursed king
Has left me without all of my things
And all of my worldly goods,
And I have excommunicated England.
There will be no priests singing mass by
Hand, and no child will be christened,
Unless he releases to me that knight with
His wife and children, fair and innocent.
He wrongly wishes to slay them". The
Knight answered, "Bishop, change your
Mind! We are very glad of your presence.
We will secure your brother yet.
And unless he grants us our demand,
His prison will soon be broken into,
And himself driven to great sorrow.
We will pull down both halls and rooms,
Both his castles and his towers.
They will lay low and razed.
Even if he is king and wears a crown,
We will throw him in a deep dungeon.
We will follow our Christian faith".
Then, as they spoke about this matter
Two knights came from the king
And said, "Bishop, wait,
And have your cross and your ring,
And be welcome while you wish to stay.
There is no need to hide! The king
Grants you here the knight with his
Wife and children, fair and innocent.
Again I advise you to come back.

540 He prayes thee pur charyté	He petitions you for charity's sake
That he my3te asoylyd be,	That he might be forgiven,
And Yngelond long and wyde".	Along with England near and far".
Hereof the byschop was ful fayn,	For this the bishop was gladdened
And turnys hys brydyl and wendes agayn	And turned his bridle and went back,
Barouns gunne with hym ryde	With the barons riding alongside him,
Unto the Brokene cros of ston.	To the Chester Cross of stone.[129]
Thedyr com the kyng ful soone anon,	The king came there immediately after
And there he gan abyde.	And there he waited.
Upon hys knees he knelyd adoun,	He kneeled down upon his knees
550 And prayde the byschop of benysoun,	And implored the bishop for his blessing.
And he gaf hym that tyde.	This time he gave it to him
With holy watyr and orysoun,	With holy water and prayer.
He asoylyd the kyng that weryd the coroun,	He absolved the king who wore the crown,
And Yngelond long and wyde.	And England far and wide.
Than sayde the kyng anon ry3t:	Then the king at once said,
"Here I graunte thee that kny3t,	"Here I grant you that knight,
And hys sones free,	And his noble sons,
And my sustyr hende in halle.	And my sister, so gracious in the hall.
Thou hast savyd here lyvys alle:	You have saved all of their lives.
560 Iblessyd moot thou bee".	May you be blessed".
Thenne sayde the bysschop also soone:	The bishop replied just as promptly,
"And I schal geven swylke a dome	"And I will render such a judgment
With eyen that thou schalt see!	That you will see it with your eyes!
3if thay be gylty off that dede,	If they are guilty of that deed,
Sorrere the doome thay may drede,	They will dread an even sorrier doom.
Thanne schewe here schame to me".	Present their crimes to me".[130]
Whanne the byschop hadde sayd soo,	When the bishop had spoken so,
A gret fyr was maad ry3t thoo,	At once a great fire was made,
In romaunce as we rede–	In the romance as we read it.
570 It was set, that men my3te knawe,	It was raised, so that men might see it,
Nyne plow3-lengthe on rawe,	As long as nine plow lengths in a row,
As red as ony glede.	As red as any glowing coal.
Thanne sayde the kyng "What may this mene?"	Then the king said, "What is this for?"
"Sere, of gylt and thay be clene,	"Sire, if they are innocent of guilt,
This doom hem thar nou3t drede".	They need not fear this ordeal".
Thanne sayde the good Kyng Athelstone:	Then the good king Athelston said,

---

129 *The Broken cros of stone*: Zupitza identifies this as the Chester Cross in the Strand in Westminster, near present-day Charing Cross. Among other functions, the cross marked the limits of Westminster. J. Zupitza, "Die Romanze von *Athelston*", *Englische Studien* 13 (1883): 331-414. Trounce (123) and other scholars believe the line refers to the Broken Cross near St. Paul's Cathedral, which existed by 1379 and until 1390, supplying a possible dating for the poem. See also the discussion in Rowe, 94.

130 The bishop is invoking trial by ordeal, a legal process by which innocence or guilt would be determined by healing from (or surviving) a painful or dangerous test. Priests were forbidden to participate by the Fourth Lateran Council (1215) but trial by ordeal took centuries to be fully replaced by the modern trial system. American economist Peter Leeson asserts that what appears to be a highly questionable legal method could actually be psychologically effective, as innocent parties tended to consent to ordeal, expecting divine protection, and the guilty would confess, fearing mortal punishment. Peter T. Leeson, "Ordeals", accessed at http://www.peterleeson.com/Ordeals.pdf.

"An hard doome now is this on:	"This judgment is a hard one.
God graunte us alle weel to spede".	God grant that we all fare well".
580 They fetten forth Sere Egelan–	They brought forth Sir Egelond–
A trewere eerl was ther nan–	There was no truer earl–
Before the fyr so bryʒt.	Before the fire so bright.
From hym they token the rede scarlet,	From him they took the red scarlet,
Bothe hosyn and schoon that weren hym met,	Both the hose and shoes fitting for him
That fel al for a knyʒt.	Which were permitted for a knight.
Nyne sythe the bysschop halewid the way	Nine times the bishop sanctified the path
That his weddyd brother scholde go that day,	That his brother would go that day,
To praye God for the ryght.	To beseech God for justice.
He was unblemeschyd foot and hand;	He was unharmed in hand and foot.
590 That sawʒ the lordes of the land,	This was seen by the lords of the land,
And thankyd God of Hys myght.	Who thanked God for His might.
They offeryd him with mylde chere	They offered him with gentle hands
Unto Saint Powlys heyʒe awtere,	Unto Saint Paul's high altar,
That mekyl was of myʒt.	Which was of great authority.
Doun upon hys knees he felle,	He fell down on his knees
And thankyd God that harewede helle	And thanked God, who conquered Hell,
And Hys modyr so bryʒt.	And His mother so fair.
And ʒit the byschop tho gan say:	And still the bishop continued on,
"Now schal the chyldryn gon the way	"Now the children shall go the way
600 That the fadyr ʒede".	That the father went".[131]
Fro hem they tooke the rede scarlete,	From them they took the red scarlet,
The hosen and schoon that weren hem mete,	And the hose and shoes fit for them,
And al here worldly wede.	And all their worldly clothes.
The fyr was bothe hydous and rede,	The fire was both hideous and red,
The chyldryn swownyd as they were ded;	And the children fainted as if they were
The byschop tyl hem yede;	Dead. The bishop went to them
With careful herte on hem gan look;	And looked on them with attentive heart.
Be hys hand he hem up took:	He took them up by his hand and said,
"Chyldryn, have ʒe no drede".	"Children, have no fear".
610 Thanne the chyldryn stood and lowʒ:	Then the children stood and laughed,
"Sere, the fyr is cold inowʒ".	"Sir, the fire is cold enough!"
Thorwʒout they wente apase.	They passed through it quickly
They weren unblemeschyd foot and hand:	And were unharmed in hand and foot.
That sawʒ the lordys of the land,	That was seen by the lords of the land,
And thankyd God of His grace.	Who thanked God for His grace.
They offeryd hem with mylde chere	They offered them with kind hands
To Seynt Poulys hyghe awtere	To Saint Paul's high altar

---

131 Why do the children and the countess need to undergo the ordeal? The three tests form a narrative triplet, but Bellamy also argues that in Anglo-Saxon law "the crime of treason was so horrible that the traitor's offspring were contaminated by his misdeed and ought to be destroyed with him". The bishop evidently wishes to clear the entire family from any such stain and believes the children will be unharmed, in contrast to the doubting Athelstan. J. Bellamy, *The Law of Treason in England in the Later Middle Ages* (Cambridge, 1970), 4, quoted in Treharne, 15. The punishment of family members also serves as a chilling disincentive to treason and is still done in absolutist regimes such as North Korea.

This myracle schewyd was there. / Where this miracle was displayed.

And ʒit the byschop eft gan say: / And yet the bishop again continued,

620 "Now schal the countasse goo the way / "Now the countess will go the way

There that the chyldryn were". / That the children went there".

They fetten forth the lady mylde; / They brought forth the gentle lady.

Sche was ful gret igon with chylde / She was very much with child,

In romaunce as we rede– / As we read in the romance.

Before the fyr whan that sche come, / When she came before the fire,

To Jesu Cryst he prayde a bone, / She prayed a plea to Jesus Christ,

That leet His woundys blede: / Who let His wounds bleed:

"Now, God lat nevere the kyngys foo / "Now, may God never let the king's enemy

Quyk out of the fyr goo". / Walk out of the fire alive".

630 Therof hadde sche no drede. / Because of that she had no dread.

Whenne sche hadde maad here prayer, / When she had made her prayer,

Sche was brought before the feer, / She was brought before the fire,

That brennyd bothe fayr and lyght. / Which burned both strong and bright.

Sche wente fro the lengthe / / She went from the start

/ into the thrydde; / Into the third part.[132]

Stylle sche stood the fyr amydde, / She stood still in the middle of the fire

And callyd it merye and bryʒt. / And called it merry and bright.

Hard schourys thenne took here stronge / Then she was taken by the pains of labor,

Bothe in bak and eke in wombe; / Both in her back as well as in womb,

And sithen it fell at syʒt. / Which came to everyone's notice.[133]

640 Whenne that here paynys slakyd was, / When her pains had lessened,

And sche hadde passyd that hydous pas, / And she had passed that hideous stage,

Here nose barst on bloode. / Her nose began to bleed.

Sche was unblemeschyd foot and hand: / She was unharmed in hand and foot.

That sawʒ the lordys of the land, / That was seen by the lords of the land,

And thankyd God on Rode. / Who thanked God on the Cross.

They comaundyd men here away to drawe, / They ordered men to move away

As it was the landys lawe; / As it was the custom of the land,

And ladyys thanne tyl here yode. / And then ladies went to her.

She knelyd doun upon the ground / She kneeled down on the ground

650 And there was born Seynt Edemound: / And there was born Saint Edmund.[134]

Iblessed be that foode! / Blessed be that child!

And whanne this chyld iborn was, / And when the boy was born,

---

132 *Into the thrydde*: Trounce posits that the countess walks over the third of nine burning plowhares, explaining why the bishop sanctifies the path nine times in line 586 (p. 17). The scene would also remind the audience of the popular legend of Emma (c. 985-1052), mother of Edward the Confessor, who also walks across nine plowshares to vindicate herself from false charges of adultery.

133 *And sithen it fell at syʒt*: No one seems to have come up with a clear idea of what this line means. Some suggest a scribal error, that the lady sighed in pain. Herzman et al. posit that "the baby has dropped into the birthing position". I am suggesting simply that 'it' is the onset of labor which the crowd notices. Another possibility is that this is a period euphemism for a woman's water breaking.

134 Likely this is St. Edmund of East Anglia, king of the East Angles (c. 840-869) and famously martyred by the Vikings. However, the historical Edmund had different parents and was born in Nuremburg. Some of the poem's place names do not exist in the ninth century. Either a different Edmund is meant, or else these are anachronisms which would not have troubled the poet or audience, which did not have Wikipedia.

It was brouȝt into the plas;
It was bothe hool and sound
Bothe the kyng and bysschop free
They crystnyd the chyld, that men myȝt see,
And callyd it Edemound.
"Half my land", he sayde, "I thee geve,
Also longe as I may leve,
660 With markys and with pounde;
And al aftyr my dede–
Yngelond to wysse and rede".
Now iblessyd be that stounde!
Thanne sayde the byschop to the Kyng:
"Sere, who made this grete lesyng,
And who wrouȝte al this bale?"
Thanne sayde the kyng, "So moot I thee,
That schalt thou nevere wete for me,
In burgh neyther in sale;
670 For I have sworn be Seynt Anne
That I schal nevere bewreye that manne,
That me gan telle that tale.
They arn savyd thorwȝ thy red;
Now lat al this be ded,
And kepe this counseyl hale".
Thenne swoor the byschop, "So moot I the,
Now I have power and dignyté
For to asoyle thee as clene
As thou were hoven off the fount-ston.
680 Trustly trowe thou therupon,
And holde it for no wene:
I swere bothe be book and belle,
But ȝif thou me his name telle,
The ryȝt doom schal I deme:
Thyself schalt goo the ryghte way
That thy brother wente today,
Thouȝ it thee evele beseme".
Thenne sayde the kyng, "So moot I the,
Be schryfte of mouthe telle I it thee;
690 Therto I am unblyve.
Sertaynly, it is non othir
But Wymound, oure weddyd brother;

It was brought into the open.
It was both whole and sound.
Both the king and the noble bishop
Baptized the child, so that men might
See it, and named it Edmund.
"Half my land", he said, "I give you,
As long as I may live,
With pennies and with pounds,
And all else after my death,
To guide and rule England.
Now blessed be that moment!"
Then the bishop said to the king,
"Sire, who made this great lie,
And who brought about all this evil?"
The king answered, "So help me God,
You will never learn that from me,
Neither in town nor in the hall.
For I have sworn by Saint Anne[135]
That I will never betray that man
Who told me that tale.
They are saved through your counsel;
Now let all this be finished,
And keep such matters private".
The bishop then swore, "As I live and
Breathe, I have the power and authority
To absolve you as clean as if
You were lifted from the baptismal font!
Believe in what I say truly,
And do not think of it as just talk:
I swear both by the book and bell,[136]
That unless you tell me his name,
I will pronounce justice!
You yourself will walk the same way
That your brother went today,
Even if it ill suits you".[137]
The king answered, "For better or worse,
I will tell you by confession of mouth,
Though I am reluctant to do it.
For sure, it is no other
But Wymonde, our sworn brother.

135 *Seynt Anne*: Believed to be the mother of the Virgin Mary, and the patron saint of childbirth (Herzman et al.).

136 *Book and belle*: Swearing by a book in medieval romance means, of course, the Bible. Here the oath may refer to the Catholic rite of excommunication, where a Bible is closed, bells are rung, and a candle is snuffed. See also Stanzaic *Guy of Warwick*, 735.

137 There is some speculation on what exactly the king needs absolution for. At worst, he has caused the entire debacle by betraying his brother and has killed his son. At minimum, the bishop is irritated by the king's flippant speech to let sleeping dogs lie and is offering a face-saving way for him to reveal Wymound and receive forgiveness for breaking his promise.

He wole nevere thryve".	He will never prosper".
"Allas", sayde the byschop than,	"Alas", said the bishop in return,
I wende he were the treweste man,	"I thought he was the truest man
That evere ȝit levyd on lyve.	Who has ever yet lived his life.
And he with this ateynt may bee,	If he is guilty of this,
He schal be hongyd on trees three,	He will be hanged on three beams
And drawen with hors fyve".	And dragged with five horses!"
700 And whenne that the byschop the sothe hade	And when the bishop knew the truth
That that traytour that lesyng made,	That the traitor had made such lies,
He callyd a messangere,	He called the messenger,[138]
Bad hym to Dovere that he scholde founde,	Ordering him to hasten to Dover
For to fette that Eerl Wymounde.	To seize Earl Wymonde.
That traytour has no pere!	That scoundrel had no equal!
"Sey Egelane and hys sones be slawe,	"Tell him Egelond and his sons are dead,
Bothe ihangyd and to-drawe.	Both hanged and drawn.
Doo as I thee lere!	Do as I tell you![139]
The countasse is in presoun done;	The countess is clapped in prison.
710 Schal sche nevere out of presoun come,	She will never come out of jail
But ȝif it be on bere".	Unless it is on a funeral bier". Now
Now with the messanger was no badde;	There was no delay for the messenger.
He took his hors, as the byschop radde,	He rode his horse, as the bishop ordered,
To Dovere tyl that he come.	Until he had come to Dover.
The eerl in hys halle he fand:	He found the earl in his hall.
He took hym the lettre in his hand	He gave him the letter into his hand,
On hyȝ, wolde he nought wone:	And swiftly; he did not dally.
"Sere Egelane and his sones be slawe,	"Sir Egelond and his sons are slain,
Bothe ihangyd and to-drawe:	Both hanged and drawn.
720 Thou getyst that eerldome.	You have received that earldom.
The countasse is in presoun done;	The countess is shut into prison.
Schal sche nevere more out come,	She will never again come out,
Ne see neyther sunne ne mone".	Nor see either the moon or sun".
Thanne that eerl made hym glade,	Then the earl was very pleased, and
And thankyd God that lesyng was made:	Thanked God that the lie had worked.
"It hath gete me this eerldome".	"It has gotten me the earldom!"
He sayde, "Felawe, ryȝt weel thou be!	He said, "Fellow, may all be well with you!
Have here besauntys good plenté	Take a good plenty of coins
For thyn hedyr come".	For your travel here".
730 Thanne the messanger made his mon:	Then the messenger made his request:
"Sere, of ȝoure goode hors lende me on:	"Sire, from your good horses give me one.
Now graunte me my bone;	Now grant me my reward!
For ȝstyrday deyde my nobyl stede,	For yesterday my noble steed died,
On ȝoure arende as I ȝede,	On your errand as I went,
Be the way as I come".	On the way as I came".

---

138 *A messangere*: Evidently this is the same messenger, as he complains in line 733 about his horse dying the day before.

139 *Doo as I thee lere!*: The messenger might plausibly be puzzled in seeing that Egelond is alive. As well, the poet may be emphasizing that the messenger acts under orders and is innocent of the deceptive message he is conveying.

"Myn hors be fatte and cornfed,
And of thy lyff I am adred",
That eerl sayde to him than.
"Thanne ʒif min hors sholde thee sloo,
740 My lord the kyng wolde be ful woo
To lese swylk a man".
The messanger ʒit he brouʒte a stede,
On of the beste at ylke a nede
That evere on grounde dede gange,
Sadelyd and brydelyd at the beste.
The messanger was ful preste,
Wyʒtly on hym he sprange.
"Sere", he sayde, "have good day;
Thou schalt come whan thou may;
750 I schal make the kyng at hande".
With sporys faste he strook the stede;
To Gravysende he come good spede,
Is fourty myle to fande.
There the messanger the traytour abood,
And sethyn bothe insame they rod
To Westemynstyr wone.
In the palays there thay lyʒt;
Into the halle they come ful ryʒt,
And mette with Athelstone.
760 He wolde have kyssyd his lord swete.
He sayde: "Traytour, nouʒt ʒit! lete!
Be God and be Seynt Jhon!
For thy falsnesse and thy lesyng
I slowʒ myn heyr, scholde have ben kyng,
When my lyf hadde ben gon!"
There he denyd faste the kyng,
That he made nevere that lesyng,
Among hys peres alle.
The byschop has hym be the hand tan;
770 Forth in same they are gan
Into the wyde halle.
Myʒte he nevere with craft ne gynne,
Gare hym shryven of hys synne,
For nouʒt that myʒte befalle.
Thenne sayde the goode Kyng Athelston,
"Lat hym to the fyr gon,
To preve the trewthe with alle".
Whenne the kyng hadde sayd soo,

"My own horse is fat and corn-fed,
And I am anxious for your safety",[140]
The earl said to him then.
"Then if my horse should throw you,
My lord the king would be very
Saddened to lose such a man".
He brought to the messenger a steed,
One of the best in such a need
That ever went on the ground,
Saddled and bridled in the finest way.
The messenger was ready in full,
And sprang on him nimbly.
"Sir", he said, "good day to you.
You may come when you will.
I will make the king aware".
With firm spurs he struck the steed.
He reached Gravesend with good speed,
A journey of forty miles.
There the messenger awaited the traitor,
And afterwards they both rode together
To the town of Westminster.
They dismounted there in the palace.
They came right away into the hall
And met with Athelston.
Wymonde tried to kiss his sweet lord.
The king shouted, "Traitor, not so fast!
Stop! By God and by Saint John!
For your falseness and your lying
I killed my heir who should have been king
After my life was finished!"
He strongly denied to the king
That he ever made such a deception,
In front of all his peers.
The bishop seized him by the hand;
They went forth together
Into the wide hall.
He would never, with any trick or excuse,
Have himself absolved of his sin,
For anything that might happen.
Then the good king Athelston
Pronounced, "Let him go to the fire
To prove the truth before all".
When the king had spoken so,

---

140 These are presumably Wymonde's words, who feels that his own horse is too spoiled for hard riding and might throw the
messenger, and thus he gives him a steed. The act is inexplicably kind for Wymonde, although the fat, useless horse may
echo his own moral slackness and dissolution.

A gret fyr was maad thoo,
780 In romaunce as we rede.
It was set, that men myȝten knawe,
Nyne plowȝ-lenge on rawe,
As red as ony glede.
Nyne sythis the bysschop halewes the way
That that traytour schole goo that day:
The wers him gan to spede.
He wente fro the lengthe into the thrydde,
And doun he fell the fyr amydde:
Hys eyen wolde hym nouȝht lede.
790 Than the eerlys chyldryn were war ful smerte,
And wyȝtly to the traytour sterte,
And out of the fyr him hade;
And sworen bothe be book and belle:
"Or that thou deye, thou schalt telle
Why thou that lesyng made".
"Certayn, I can non other red,
Now I wot I am but ded:
I telle ȝow nothyng gladde–
Certayn, ther was non other wyte:
800 He lovyd him to mekyl and me to lyte;
Therfore envye I hadde".
Whenne that traytour so hadde sayde,
Fyve good hors to hym were tayde,
Alle men myȝten see with yȝe–
They drowen him thorwȝ ylke a strete,
And sethyn to the Elmes, I ȝow hete,
And hongyd him ful hyȝe.
Was ther nevere man so hardy,
That durste felle hys false body:
810 This hadde he for hys lye.
Now Jesu, that is Hevene-kyng,
Leve nevere traytour have betere endyng,
But swych dome for to dye.

814 Explicit

A great fire was then raised,
In the romance as we read it.
It was set, that men might see,
As long as nine plow-lengths in a row,
As red as any glowing coal. The bishop
Blessed the path nine times where the
Traitor would walk that day. As for him,
His fortunes would turn for the worse.
He went from the start to the third part,
And down he fell in the middle of the
Fire. His eyes could not guide him.
Then the earl's children were fully aware,
And boldly ran to the traitor,
And pulled him out of the fire.
They swore both by the book and bell,
"Before you die, you will confess
Why you told that lie".
"For sure, I have no other course.
Now I know I am almost dead.
I tell you no good news– For sure,
There was no other cause: He loved
Egelond too much and me too little,
And because of that I was jealous".
When the criminal had spoken so,
Five strong horses were tied to him,[141]
Which all men could see with their eyes.
They dragged him through each street
And after to the Elms, I assure you,
And hanged him very high.
There was no man so brave
Who dared take down his sinful body.
This was what he got for his lies!
Now may Jesus, who is Heaven's king,
Allow no traitor to have a better ending,
But such a sentence to die.

The End.

---

141 As in *Amis and Amiloun*, Wymonde's sentence is to be hanged and drawn, i.e. dragged through unpaved streets behind horses. Here the hanging follows. Bodies might be left hanging for weeks as a public example, and thus the lines that no man dared take him down (808-9).

Floris and Blancheflor

As Gertrude Stein said of Oakland, the Middle English romance *Floris and Blancheflor* seemingly has little "there" there. The story lacks any distinct hagiographic meaning, and the main characters are not particularly saintly; both histrionically threaten suicide over lost love, and its protagonist is a non-Christian. The poem has little interest in Saracen-Christian issues or martial heroism, and Floris's perfunctory conversion at the end receives one line. Despite the exotic and mysterious "wonders of the east" setting, the poem's characters and sentimental plot border on banal, as no believable peril ever seriously threatens Floris or Blancheflor's lives. Worse, the poem also forestalls any possible tension by revealing the denouement in the introduction: in brief, a narrative with no conflict, suspense, climax, or resolution is not much of a narrative.

Yet in the medieval mind the faraway east of Arabia and Asia both suggested fantastic adventures and recalled the failure of the crusades. Its popularity as a romance theme possibly also reflected both the desire to create a more comforting fictional history where Christians acted more honorably and succeeded in their aim of redeeming the Holy Lands, as well as the fact that many romance narratives originally had eastern sources. The verbal wordplay between Floris and his hosts or between Clarice and Blancheflor, the tricks and gags of Floris gambling with the porter or being carried in a flower-basket, and the lush, sexual imagery of the emir's garden all provide festive entertainment.

From Flore und Blancheflur, Cod. Pal. Germ. 362, f.173v (Konrad Fleck), Heidelberg University Library

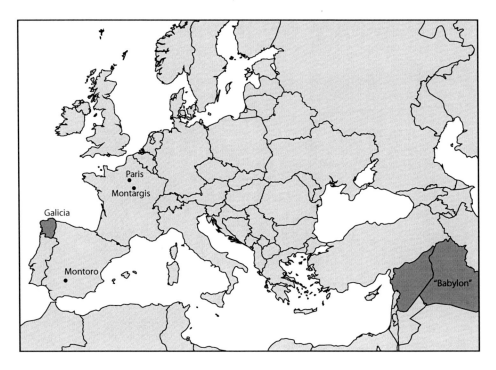

Moreover, from the time of *Floris and Blancheflor* well into that of *Romeo and Juliet* and after, young love, particularly for an audience which historically did not generally marry as it wished, would have been an attractive theme. This wish-fulfillment is enacted in Floris's transition from childishness to adult love as he progresses toward self-actualization. The text might be usefully read as exploring deeper themes of emotional, moral, and sexual development which might have appealed to a younger audience.

The English *Floris and Blancheflor* survives in four incomplete manuscripts: Auchinleck, Adv. MS 19.2.1 (c. 1330), Cambridge University Library, MS Gg.iv.27.2 (c. 1300), Egerton 2862 (c. 1400), and MS Cotton Vitellius D.iii. (c. 1275). As my basic textual source I use George H. McKnight, *King Horn, Floriz and Blancheflur, The Assumption of Our Lady* (London: EETS, 1866, 1901), and David Laing, *A Penni Worth of Witte: Florice and Blauncheflour: And Other Pieces of Ancient English Poetry* (Edinburgh: Abbotsford Club, 1857), checking against the Auchinleck images where necessary. McKnight refers to Egerton by its former name, Trentham-Sutherland, Staffordshire.

As no English MS preserves the beginning, I use excerpts from *Floire et Blanceflor*, supplied by Édélestand Du Méril, ed., *Floire et Blanceflor, Poèmes du 13è Siècle* (Paris: 1856), http://www.archive.org/details/floireetblancefl00floiuoft, who uses National Library of France (Fonds Français) MS 375, 1447, and 12562 (c. 1200). For the French section I give a separate lineation as I have used text selectively to comform to the English narrative. Following that are lines 1-383 from Egerton with some lines from Cotton and Auchinleck.

F: French (Fonds)   A: Auchinleck
E: Egerton 2862   C: Cambridge Gg.iv.27.2
V: Cotton Vitellius

F1	Oyez signor tout li amant	Listen, lords, and all the lovers
	Cil qui d'amors se vont penant	Whose hearts have felt suffering,
	Li chevalier et les puceles	The knights and the women,
	Li damoisel les demoiselles.	The young maids, and noble ladies.
	Se mon conte volez entendre	Whoever wishes to hear my tale
	Moult i porrez d'amors aprendre.	Will be able to learn much about love!
	Cou est du roi Floire l'enfant	The story is about the royal child Floris
	Et de Blanceflor la vaillant	And of Blancheflor the brave
	De qui Berte as-grans-piés fu née.	To whom Berta Goosefeet was later born,[142]
10	Puis fu mere Charlemaine	Herself the mother of Charlemagne,
	Qui puis tint et France et le Maine.	Who later held France and the Maine.
	Floire son pere que vous di	Floris, their forefather whom I speak about,
	Uns rois payens l'engenuï.	Was fathered by a pagan king,
	Et Blanceflor que tant ama	And Blancheflor, who was loved by many,
	Uns cuens crestïens l'engendra.	Was fathered by a Christian earl.[143]
	Floire fut tout nés de payens	And so Floris was born to heathens,
	Et Blancheflor de crestïens.	And Blancheflor to Christians.
	Bauptizier se fist en sa vie	Floris had himself baptized during his life
	Floire por Blanceflor s'amie	Because of the love he had for Blancheflor,
20	Car en un biau jor furent né	For on one joyful day they were born,
	Et en une nuit engender.	And on the same night conceived.
	Puisque Floire fu crestïens	Because Floris was later a Christian,
	Li avint grans honors et biens.	He became a king of great honor and
30	Or sivrai mon proposement	Riches. Now to continue with our story,
	Si parlerai avenanment.	If I might come to speak about it.
	En une chambre entrai l'autr'ier	Not long ago on a Friday
	Un venredi apres mangier	I entered a room after supper
	Por deporter as demoiselles	To have conversation with some ladies
	Don't en la chambre avoit de beles.	Who were having a chat there.
43	Illoec m'assis por escouter	There I seated myself to listen
	Deus puceles qu'oï parler.	To what the two women were saying.
	Eles estoient doi serors.	They were two sisters;
	Ensamble parloient d'amors.	They spoke together about love.
	L'aisnée d'une amor contoit	The older one told a story
	A sa seror que moult amoit	Which the younger one enjoyed very much,
	Qui fa ja entre deus enfans	And it was about two children who had
50	Bien avoit passé deus cens ans.	Lived well over two centuries ago.
	Mais a un clerc dire l'oït	But they had heard it recited by a clerk
	Qui l'avoit léu en escrit.	Who had written it down.
	El commenca avenanment:	The story is pleasant,

---

142 *Berte as-grans-piés*: Bertrada of Laon (720-783), wife of Pepin the Short and Charlemagne's mother, whose unfortunate nickname possibly refers to misshapen feet. One of the earliest manuscripts of the poem, Paris BN 1447, also has Adenot le Roi's Berte aus Grans Piés (c. 1270). For a discussion of the French sources, see Patricia E. Grieve, *Floire and Blancheflor and the European Romance* (Cambridge: University Press, 1997), chapter 1.

143 The ostensibly historical Blanche Fleur de Laon (died c. 720) was the daughter of the Merovingian king Dagobert III (699-715) and a Saxon princess.

	Or oyez son commencement.	And so now listen to its beginning.
	Uns rois estoit issus d'Espaigne.	A king came from Spain
	De chevaliers ot grant compaigne.	With a large company of knights.
	En sa nef ot la mer passée.	He passed over the sea in his ship
	En Galisse fu arivée.	And arrived in Galicia.
	Felis ot non si fu payens;	Felix had no faith and so he was pagan;
60	Mer ot passé sor crestïens	He passed over the sea to Christendom.
	Por ou païs la praie prendre	Wherever he went, he ravaged the land
	Et la viles torner en cendre.	And turned the villages into ashes.
	Un mois entier et quinze dis	For an entire month and a half
	Sejorna li rois ou païs.	The king stayed in that country.
	Ains ne fu jors qu'o sa maisniée	There was no day in that time when the
	Ne féist li rois chevauciée.	King did not campaign with his army.
	Viles reuboit avoirs praoit	He despoiled villages, preying on them,
	Et a ses nes tout conduisoit:	And had everyone driven away.
	De quinze liues el rivache	Within the limit of fifteen miles
70	Ne remanoit ne bués ne vache	No cattle or oxen remained;
	Ne castel ne vile en estant:	No castle or village was standing.
	Vilains n'i va son boef querant.	Peasants could find no meat.
	Es-vos le païs tout destruit.	The countryside was totally destroyed,
	Payen en ont joie et deduit.	While the pagans rejoiced and celebrated.
91	En la compaigne ot un Francois.	Among the locals was a Frenchman.
	Chevaliers ert preu et cortois	He was a knight, virtuous and courteous,
	Qui au baron saint Jaque aloit.	On pilgrimage to the shrine of Saint
	Une soie fille i menoit	James.[144] He was escorting a woman
	Qui a l'Apostle s'ert vouée	Who had devoted herself to the apostle
	Ains qu'ele issist de sa contrée	And who was from that country.
	Por son mari qui mors estoit	For her husband had died, the man
	De qui remise enceinte estoit.	Whose baby she was pregnant with.
	Li chevaliers se veut deffendre.	The knight resolved to defend them,
100	Ne chaut a aus de lui vif prendre	But he was not able to save his life,
	Ains l'ocient. s'el laissent mort	And the plunderers left him for dead
	Et sa fille mainent au port.	And took his lady to the port.
	Au roi Felis l'ont presentée	They presented her to King Felix
	Et il l'a forment esgardée:	And he carefully observed her,
	Bien apercoit a son visage	Closely perceiving her appearance
	Que ele estoit de haut parage	And that she was of noble peerage.
	Et dist s'il puet qu'a la roïne	He said, if it would please the queen,
	Fera present de la meschine	He would make her a slave as a present
	Car de tel chose li préa	Since he valued such things
110	Quant il por reuber mer passa.	When he crossed the sea from plundering.
	Atant s'en-entrent tout es nes	Then all of them boarded,

144 The French version relates that a group of pilgrims en route to the shrine of Santiago de Compostela in Galicia, northern Spain, is attacked and robbed by Felix, a pagan Spanish king. The path, "The Way of Saint James", was one of the most important Christian pilgrimage routes of the Middle Ages. Pilgrimages could be dangerous and Chaucer's entourage to Canterbury is armed with weapons for protection as well as decoration.

	Amont traient tres-tout lor tres.	And they traveled upstream expertly.
	Or ont boin vent et bien portent.	They were carried well by the wind
	Si repairent lié et joiant.	So that they returned safely and easily.
	Il n'orent pas deus jor erré.	They had not sailed two days
	Qu'en lor païs sont arrive.	When they arrived in their country.
127	Es-vos le roi en la cite	Then the king was in the city
	Son barnage a tres-tout mandé.	And all of his baronage was summoned.
	Son eschec lor depart li rois	The king divided up the booty,
130	Bien largement comme cortois	Very generously and with courtesy,
	Et por sa part a la roïne	And as for the queen,
	Donc de gaaing la meschine.	She was rewarded with the slave.
	La roïne s'en fait moult liée.	The queen herself was very happy.
	En sa chambre l'a envoyée.	The slave was sent to her chamber.
	Sa loi li laisse bien garder.	She obeyed the queen's rules well,
	Servir la fait et honorer.	And served and honored her;
	O li sovent jue et parole	They often amused themselves and talked
	Et francois aprent de s'escole.	And schooled themselves in French.
	La meschine ert cortoise et prous.	The slave was courteous and virtuous;
140	Moult se faisoit amer a tous:	She was loved by all
	La roïne moult bien servoit	And was of good service to the queen,
	Comme cele cui ele estoit.	Who was also expecting a child.
161	Le jor de le la Pasque-florie	On the day of Palm Sunday,
	Si com le reconte lor vie	As the story of their life is told,
	Vint li terme qu'eles devoient	The term came to a close
	Enfanter cou que pris avoient.	Of this child who was so priceless.
	Travail orent et paine grant	Great labor pains came to the mothers
	Ains que né fussent li enfant:	And later the children were born:
	Valles fu nés de la payene	The pagan gave birth to a boy,
	Et meschine ot la crestïene.	And the slave had a Christian girl.
	Li doi enfant quant furent né	When the two children were born,
170	De la feste furent nomé:	They were named for the festival:
	La crestïene por l'honor	The Christian, to honor the day,
	De la feste ot nom Blancheflor.	Was named Blancheflor;
	Li rois noma son chier fil Floire.	The king named his dear son Floris;[145]
	Aprende le fist a Montoire.	His schooling was taken at Montargis.[146]
	Li pere ama moult son enfant.	The father had great love for his child;
	La mere plus ou autretant.	The mother loved him equally or more.
	Livré l'ont a la damoisele	They were entrusted to the slave,
	Por cou qu'ele estoit sage et bele	For she was wise and beautiful,
	A norrir et a maistroier	To raise and to teach,

---

145 The two children are given "flowery" names–Floris ("Belonging to the flower") and Blancheflor ("White flower")–as they are both born on Palm Sunday, also called *Paske Flourie*.

146 *Montoire*: The French MS has Montoro, Spain, near Cordoba. The English MSS have Montargis, France, near Orleans instead. Kooper states that Montargis derives from Odysseus' faithful dog Argos, and suggests that the choice of place name may symbolize Floris' loyalty. *Floris and Blancheflour*, ed. Erik Kooper, *Sentimental and Humorous Romances* (Kalamazoo, MI: Medieval Institute Publications, 2006), http://www.lib.rochester.edu/camelot/teams/ekfbfrm.htm.

180 Fors seulement de l'alaitier.	Excepting only their nursing.
Une payene l'alaitoit	A pagan woman nursed them
Si com lor lois le commandoit.	As was commanded by their laws.[147]
Moult le norrissoit doucement	She cared for him with kindness
Et gardoit ententivement	And guarded him attentively just as
Plus que sa fille et ne savoit	Much as her daughter, and no one knew
Lequel des deus plus chier avoit:	Which of the two were dearer to her.
Onques ne lor sevra mangier	They never ate or drank separately,
Ne boire fors seul l'alaitier.	Only excepting their nursing.
En un lit tout seul les couchoit.	They slept only in one bed;
190 Andeus passoit et abevroit.	Together they grew and were raised.[148]
Quant cinq ans orent li enfant	When the children were five years old,
Moult furent bel et gent et grant.	They were very tall, beautiful, and noble.
. . . .	. . . .
1 E Ne thurst men never in londe	No one in the land would ever need
After feirer children fonde.	To try to find fairer children.
Þe Cristen woman fedde hem þoo	The Christian woman cared for them then
Ful wel she louyd hem boþ twoo.	And loved the two of them very deeply.
So longe sche fedde hem in feere	She raised them together
þat þey were of elde of seven ʒere.	Until they were seven years of age.
Þe kyng behelde his sone dere	The king beheld his dear son
And seyde to him on this manere	And said to him on the subject
Þat harme it were muche more	That it would be a great loss
10 But his sone were sette to lore	Unless his son were sent
On þe book letters to know	To study books and to know letters,
As men done both hye and lowe.	As men do, both high and low.
"Feire sone", she seide "þou shalt lerne	"Fair son", he said, "you will learn,
Lo þat þou do ful ʒerne".	Now see that you do it very intently".
Florys answerd with wepyng	Floris answered in tears,
As he stood byfore þe kyng.	As he stood before the king.
Al wepyng seide he	As he wept he said,
"Ne schal not Blancheflour lerne with me?	"Blancheflor will not learn with me?
Ne can y noʒt to scole goone	I can't go to school
20 With-out Blanchefloure", he seide þane.	Without Blancheflour", he said.
"Ne can y in no scole syng ne rede	I can't read or recite in any school
With-out Blancheflour", he seide.	Without Blancheflour", he pleaded.
Þe king seide to his soone	The king said to his son,
"She shal lerne for þy love".	"Because of your love, she will learn".
To scole þey were put	They were sent to school,
Boþ þey were good of wytte.	And both of them had good wits.
Wonder it was of hur lore	It was a wonder to see their studies
And of her love wel þe more.	And their love even more so.
Þe children louyd to-geder soo	The children were so devoted to each other

---

147 One Spanish version of the story states that the mother's milk transferred the spirit of Christianity to Floris, perhaps explaining such a prohibition (Grieve, 162).

148 *Passoit*: Some MSS seem to have *pessoit*, which suggests "they drank and ate", rather than passing time.

30	Þey myȝt never parte a twoo.
	When þey had v ȝere to scoole goone
	So wel þey had lerned þoo
	Inowȝ þey couþ of Latyne
	And wel wryte on parchemyne.
	Þe kyng understod þe grete amoure
	Bytwene his sone and Blanchefloure
	And þouȝt when þey were of age
	Þat her love wolde noȝt swage.
	Nor he myȝt noȝt her love withdrawe
40	When Florys shuld wyfe after þe lawe.
	Þe king to þe queene seide þoo
	And tolde hur of his woo
	Of his þouȝt and of his care
	How it wolde of Floreys fare.
	"Dame", he seide, "y tel þe my reede.
	I wyl þat Blaunchefloure be do to deede.
	When þat maide is y-slawe
	And brouȝt of her lyf dawe
	As sone as Florys may it under ȝete
50	Rathe he wylle hur forȝete.
	Þan may he wyfe after reede".
	Þe queene answerde þen and seide
	And þouȝt with hur reede
	Save þe mayde fro þe deede.
	"Sir", she seide, "we auȝt to fonde
	Þat Florens lyf wit menske in londe
	And þat he lese not his honour
	For þe mayden Blaunchefloure.
	Who so myȝt þat mayde clene
60	Þat she nere brouȝt to deþ bydene
	Hit were muche more honour
	Þan slee þat mayde Blanchefloure".
	Unneþes þe king graunt þat it be soo.
	"Dame rede us what is to doo".
	"Sir we shul oure soone Florys
	Sende into þe londe of Mountargis.
	Blythe wyl my suster be
	Þat is lady of þat contree.
	And when she woot for whoom
70	Þat we have sent him us froom
	She wyl doo al hur myȝt

That they could never be parted.
When they had gone to school five years,
They had learned so well
That they knew Latin fluently enough
And could write finely on parchment.
The king perceived the great affection
Between his son and Blancheflour,
And worried that when they were of age
Their love might not weaken.
Nor might he prevent their wishes when
Floris could marry according to law.[149]
The king spoke to the queen then,
And told her of his distress,
Of his thoughts and of his worries
About how things might go with Floris.
"My lady", he said, "I will tell you my
Plans. I want Blancheflour to be put to
Death. When that maid is executed,
And her life's days brought to an end,
As soon as Floris might discover it
He will soon forget her.
Then he may marry more advisedly".
The queen answered and spoke,
And hoped with her counsel
To save the maiden from death,
"Sir", she said, "we ought to ensure
That Floris lives with honor in the land,
And that he not lose his reputation
Because of the maiden Blancheflour.
If someone were to take that girl away
So that she was not put to death,[150]
It would be much more respectable
Than to slay that innocent virgin".
Reluctantly, the king granted that it be so.
"Madam, advise me what is to be done".
"Sir, we will send our son Floris
Into the land of Montargis.
My sister, the lady of that country,
Will be very pleased.
And when she knows the reason
We have sent him away from us,
She will do all her might,

---

149 Felix likely worries that his son will take a wife who is not only socially disadvantaged but a Christian, and that when Floris becomes of age the king will have difficulty preventing their marriage.

150 *Nere*: Egerton has were, but some editors believe this should be nere, i.e. Blancheflor should not be put to death, which makes more contextual sense if the queen is pleading for her (54).

Boþ by day and by nyȝt,
To make hur love so undoo
As it had never ben soo.
And sir", she seide, "y rede eke
Þat þe maydens moder make hur seek.
Þat may be þat other resoun
For þat ylk enchesoun
Þat she may not fro hur moder goo".
80 Now ben þese children swyþ woo
Now þey may not goo in fere.
Drewryer þinges never noone were!
Florys wept byfore þe kyng
And seide, "Sir with-out lesyng
For my harme out ȝe me sende
Now she ne myȝt with me wende.
Now we ne mot to-geder goo
Al my wele is turned to woo".
Þe king seide to his soone aplyȝt
90 "Sone withynne þis fourtenyȝt
Be her moder quykke or deede
Sekerly", he him seide
"Þat mayde shal come þe too".
"Ȝe sir", he seid, "y pray ȝow it be soo.
Ȝif þat ȝe me hur sende
I rekke never wheder y wende".
Þat þe child graunted þe kyng was fayne
And him betauȝt his chamburlayne.
With muche honoure þey þeder coome
100 As fel to a ryche kynges soone.
Wel feire him receyvyd þe Duke Orgas
Þat king of þat castel was
And his aunt wiþ muche honour.
But ever he þouȝt on Blanchefloure.
Glad and blythe þey ben him withe
But for no joy þat he seith
Ne myȝt him glade game ne gle
For he myȝt not his lyf see.
His aunt set him to lore
110 Þere as other children wore
Boþ maydons and grome
To lerne mony þeder coome.
Inowȝ he sykes but noȝt he lernes;
For Blaunchefour ever he mornes.
Yf enyman to him speke
Love is on his hert steke.
Love is at his hert roote

Both by day and by night,
To make their love so distant
As if it had never been.
And sir", she continued, "I also advise
That the maiden's mother feign illness.
That can be another reason
For the same action,
That she may not leave her mother".
Now these children were in great sorrow,
For they could not go together.
There was never a sadder sight!
Floris wept before the king
And said, "Sir, without a lie,
You send me away to my doom
If she may not go with me.
Now that we cannot be together,
All my happiness is turned to despair".
The king said to his son in earnest,
"Son, within this fortnight,
Whether her mother is alive or dead,
For sure", he said to him,
"That maid will come to you".
"Yes, sire", he answered, "I beg of you
That it be so. If you send her to me,
I don't care at all where I go".
With the child's consent, the king was eased
And entrusted him to his chamberlain.
With much grandeur they traveled forth,
As was fitting for a rich king's son.
The duke, Orgas, who was lord of that
Castle, received him graciously,
As did his aunt, with great honor.
But he only thought about Blancheflour.
They were glad and merry with him,
But he could find no joy, nor could games
Or entertainments cheer him,
For he could not see his sweetheart.
His aunt set him to study
Where the other children were,
Where many came to learn,
Both maidens and young men.
He sighed enough, but learned nothing;
He continually mourned for Blancheflour.
If any man spoke to him,
Only love stuck to his heart.
Love was at his heart's root,

	Þat no þing is so soote;	And nothing was so sweet;
	Galyngale ne lycorys	Neither spice nor licorice[151]
120	Is not so soote as hur love is	Was as sweet as her love was,
	Ne nothing ne none other.	Nor anything of any other flower.
	So much he þenkeþ on Blancheflour	He thought so much about Blancheflour
	Of oo day him þynkeþ þre	That one day seemed like three,
	For he ne may his love see.	For he could not see his love.
	Þus he abydeth with muche woo	Thus he waited with great sadness
	Tyl þe fourtenyȝt were goo.	Until the fourteenth night had passed.
	When he saw she was nouȝt ycoome	When he saw she had not come,
	So muche sorow he haþ noome	He was taken by so much grief
	Þat he loveth mete ne drynke	That he wanted neither food nor drink,
130	Ne may noone in his body synke.	And neither would go into his body.
	Þe chamberleyne sent þe king to wete	The chamberlain sent word to tell the king
	His sones state al y-wrete.	Of his son's state in writing.
	Þe king ful sone þe waxe to-brake	The king hurriedly broke the wax,
	For to wete what it spake.	In order to know what the letter said.
	He begynneth to chaunge his moode	His mood began to darken,
	And wel sone he understode	And very soon he understood,
	And with wreth he cleped þe queene	And with anger he called the queen,
	And tolde hur alle his teene	And told her all his vexation,
	And with wraþ spake and sayde	And spoke in wrath and said,
140	"Let do bryng forþ þat mayde!	"Have that maid sent for!
	Fro þe body þe heued shal goo!"	Her head will go from her body!"
	Þenne was þe quene ful woo.	The queen was very distraught then.
	Þan spake þe quene þat good lady	The queen, that good lady, answered,
	"For Goddes love sir mercy!	"For God's love, sir, have mercy!
	At þe next haven þat here is	At the nearest harbor
	Þer ben chapmen ryche y-wys	There are rich traders, for sure,
	Marchaundes of Babyloyne ful ryche	Wealthy merchants from Persia,[152]
	Þat wol hur bye blethelyche.	Who will gladly buy her.
	Than may ȝe for þat lovely foode	Then you will have for that lovely girl
150	Have muche catell and goode.	A great deal of property and goods.
	And soo she may fro us be brouȝt	And so she will be gotten rid of
	Soo þat we slee hur nouȝt".	In such a way that we do not slay her".
	Unneþes þe king graunted þis.	Reluctantly, the king granted this.
	But forsoþ so it is	But truly, it happened in that way.
	Þe king let sende after þe burgeise	The king sent for the agent,
	Þat was hende and curtayse	Who was able and well-mannered,
	And welle selle and bygge couth	And knew how to buy and sell well,

---

151 *Galyngale*: Galingal is an Asian spice related to ginger which would have been very exotic to a medieval English audience. It is commonly used in Thai tom yum soup. *Flower* is not in Egerton, but again makes contextual sense.

152 *Babyloyn*: The ancient city of Babylon was south of Baghdad, but the poet may simply mean a romantic idea of the Middle East in what is now Iraq and Iran. The French MS also has *Babiloine*. Reiss argues that this is *Bab-al-yun*, a district of old Cairo. E. Reiss, "Symbolic Detail in Medieval Narrative: *Floris & Blancheflour*", *Papers on Language & Literature* 7 (1971): 346. But the land area of the emir's palace complex seems too massive to fit inside a suburb.

And moony langages had in his mouth.
Wel sone þat mayde was him betauȝt
160 An to þe havene was she brouȝt.
Þer have þey for þat maide ȝolde
XX mark of reed golde
And a coupe good and ryche;
In al þe world was none it lyche.
Þer was never noone so wel grave.
He þat it made was no knave.
Þer was purtrayd on y weene
How Paryse ledde awey þe queene.
And on þe couercle a-bove
170 Purtrayde was þer both her love.
And in þe pomel þerone
Stood a charbuncle stoone.
In þe world was not so depe soler
Þat it nold lyȝt þe botelere
To fylle boþ ale and wyne
Of sylver and golde boþ good and fyne.
Enneas þe king þat nobel man
At Troye in batayle he it wan
And brouȝt it in-to Lumbardy
180 And gaf it his lemman his amy.
Þe coupe was stoole fro king Cesar;
A þeef out of his tresour hous it bar.
And sethe þat ilke same þeef
For Blaunchefloure he it ȝeef
For he wyst to wynne suche þree
Myȝt he hur bryng to his contree.
Now þese marchaundes saylen over þe see
With þis mayde to her contree.
So longe þey han undernome
190 Þat to Babyloyne þey ben coome.
To þe amyral of Babyloyne
Þey solde þat mayde swythe soone.
Rath and soone þey were at oone.
Þe amyral hur bouȝt anoone
And gafe for hur as she stood upryȝt
Sevyne sythes of golde her wyȝt
For he þouȝt without weene
Þat faire mayde have to queene.

And had many languages at his tongue.
Very soon the maid was given to him,
And she was brought to the harbor.
There the traders paid for that maiden
Twenty marks of red gold,[153]
And a cup, splendid and costly;
In all the world there was none like it.
There was never one so finely engraved.
He who crafted it was no fool.
There was a depiction on it, as I am told,
Of how Paris led away Queen Helen,
And on the lid above it
Their love for each other was portrayed.
And on the round knob on top
Stood a carbuncle stone.
In all the world there was no cellar so deep
That it would not give light to a butler
To pour either ale or wine
Into the silver and gold, good and fine.
Aeneas the king, that valiant man,
Won it at Troy in battle,
And brought it to Lombardy,
And gave it to his beloved, his Lavinia.[154]
The cup was stolen from the caesar;
A thief carried it out of his treasure house.
And afterward that same thief
Gave it in trade for Blancheflour,
For he expected to gain such a profit
If he could bring her to his country.
Now these merchants sailed over the sea
With this maid to their land.
They journeyed so far
Until they arrived in Babylon.
Very quickly, they sold the girl
To the emir of Babylon.
Hastily, they soon agreed on the sale.
The emir bought her at once,
And paid for her, as she stood upright,
Seven times her weight in gold,
For he thought, without a doubt,
To have that fair maid as queen.

---

153 *XX mark*: A mark was 2/3 of a pound in England, or 13s 4p. According to the UK National Archives website, 20 marks in today's money would be about US$10,000 (http://www.nationalarchives.gov.uk/currency/). As with many romances, this may be as fanciful as paying seven times her weight in gold (196). Arabic numerals were not common in English texts until the spread of printing presses.

154 *Amy*: Lavinia, Aeneas' love and Latinus' daughter in Virgil's *Aeneid*.

Among his maydons in his bour
200 He hur dide with muche honour.
Now þese merchaundes þat may belete
And ben glad of hur byȝete.
Now let we of Blauncheflour be
And speke of Florys in his contree.
Now is þe burgays to þe king coome
With þe golde and his garysone
And haþ take þe king to wolde
Þe selver and þe coupe of golde.
They lete make in a chirche
210 As swithe feire grave wyrche.
And lete ley þer-uppone
A new feire peynted stone,
With letters al aboute wryte
With ful muche worshippe.
Who-so couth þe letters rede
Þus þey spoken and þus þey seide
"Here lyth swete Blaunchefloure
Þat Florys lovyd paramoure".
Now Florys haþ undernome
220 And to his fader he is coome.
In his fader halle he is lyȝt.
His fader him grette anoone ryȝt
And his moder þe queene also.
But unneþes myȝt he þat doo
Þat he ne asked where his lemman bee.
Nonskyns answere chargeþ hee.
So longe he is forth noome
In to chamber he is coome.
Þe maydenys moder he asked ryȝt
230 "Where is Blauncheflour my swete wyȝt?"
"Sir", she seide, "forsothe ywys
I ne woot where she is".
She beþouȝt hur on þat lesyng
Þat was ordeyned byfoore þe king.
"Þou gabbest me", he seyde þoo.
"Þy gabbyng doþ me muche woo.
Tel me where my leman be!"
Al wepyng seide þenne shee
"Sir", shee seide, "deede". "Deed?" seide he.
240 "Sir", sche seide, "for sothe ȝee".
"Allas when died þat swete wyȝt?"
"Sir withynne þis fourtenyȝt

He had her placed, with great honor,
Among the maidens in his harem.
Now the merchants left the maid behind,
And were pleased with their earnings.
Now we will let Blancheflour be,
And speak of Floris in his country.
The agent returned to the king
With the gold and the payment,
And remitted the silver and cup of gold
For the king to keep.
They had a very beautiful grave made
In a small chapel,
And placed on there
A new and finely painted stone,
With letters written all about
With reverent piety.
For whoever could read the letters
They spoke thus and read,
"Here lies sweet Blancheflour,
Who loved Floris with passion".[155]
Now Floris had undertaken his journey,
And he came to his father.
He dismounted in his father's hall.
He greeted the king right away,
And his mother, the queen, as well.
But he had scarcely done so
When he asked where his beloved was,
Not even waiting for any kind of answer.
And so he was brought forth
Until he arrived in a chamber.
He asked the maiden's mother at once,
"Where is Blancheflour, my sweet lass?"
"Sir", she said, "in truth, the fact is that
I don't know where she is".
She was mindful of the deception
Which had been ordered by the king.
"You're teasing me", he replied.
"Your gabbing hurts me deeply.
Tell me where my sweetheart is!"
She then replied, in heavy tears,
"Sir", she said, "she is dead". "Dead?",
He cried. "Sir", she said, "in truth, yes".
"Alas! When did that sweet creature die?"
"Sir, within this fortnight

---

155 *That Florys lovyd par amoure*: Kooper notes that who loved who is not clear in the ME line, and perhaps the ambiguity intentionally emphasizes that their feelings were mutual.

Þe erth was leide hur aboute
And deed she was for thy love".
Flores þat was so feire and gent
Sownyd þere verament.
Þe Cristen woman began to crye
To Jhesu Crist and seynt Marye.
Þe king and þe queene herde þat crye.
250 In to þe chamber þey ronne on hye.
And þe queene herde her byforne
On sowne þe childe þat she had borne.
Þe kinges hert was al in care
Þat sawe his sone for love so fare.
When he a-wooke and speke moзt
Sore he wept and sore he syзt
And seide to his moder ywys
"Lede me þere þat mayde is".
Þeder þey him brouзt on hyзe
260 For care and sorow he wolde dyзe.
As sone as he to þe grave com
Sone þere behelde he þen
And þe letters began to rede
Þat þus speke and þus seide
"Here lyth swete Blaunchefour
Þat Florys lovyd paramoure".
Þre sithes Florys sownydde nouth
Ne speke he myзt not with mouth.
As sone as he awoke and speke myзt
270 Sore he wept and sore he syзt.
"Blaunchefour!", he seide "Blaunchefour!
So swete a þing was never in boure.
Of Blaunchefour is þat y meene
For she was come of good kyne".

. . . .

V   "Vor in worle nes nere non
Þine imake of no wimmon.
Inouз þou cuþest of clergie
And of alle curteysie".

. . . .

E   "Lytel and muche loveden þe
280 For þy goodnesse and þy beaute.
Зif deþ were dalt aryзt
We shuld be deed boþ on oo nyзt.
On oo day borne we were;
We shul be ded boþ in feere".

The earth was laid above her,
And she was dead for your love".
Floris, who was so fair and gentle,
Was overcome there, in truth.
The Christian woman began to call
On Jesus Christ and sainted Mary.
The king and queen heard that cry.
They ran into the chamber in haste,
And the queen saw before her
The child that she had bore in a faint.
The king's heart was all distraught at
Seeing what had happened to his son
For love. When he awoke and could speak,
He wept and sighed bitterly,
And said to his mother in earnest,
"Take me to where that maid is".
They brought him there in haste,
For he was dying of anguish and sorrow.
As soon as he came to the grave,
He beheld it at once
And began to read the letters,
So that he spoke and said thus,[156]
"Here lies sweet Blanchefour,
Who loved Floris with passion".
Floris swooned three times
Before he could he speak with his mouth.
As soon as he awoke and could talk,
He wept and sighed bitterly.
"Blanchefour!" he said, "Blanchefour!
There was never so sweet a thing in any
Bower. I mourn for Blanchefour,
For she came from the noblest family".

. . . .

"There was no one in the world
Your equal among women!
You were well-learned in faith
And in all courtesies".

. . . .

"High and low loved you
For your goodness and your beauty.
If death were dealt out fairly,
We would both be dead the same night.
We were born on one day;
We will both be dead together".

---

156 *That thus spake*: Floris is reading out loud. It was considered unusual to read silently until the modern era. There is a famous
story of St. Augustine's curiosity at seeing Ambrose, Bishop of Milan (d. 397), reading without vocalizing.

"Deeþ!" he seide, "Ful of envye
And of alle trechorye
Refte þou hast me my lemman!"
"For soth", he seide, "þou art to blame.
She wolde have levyd and þu noldest
290 And fayne wolde y dye and þu woldest".
. . . .
V "Þilke þat buste best to libbe
Hem þou stikest under þe ribbe!
And ȝif þer is eni forlived wrecche
Þat of is live nouȝt ne recche
Þat fawe wolde deie for sorewe and elde
On hem neltou nouȝht bi helde!
No lengore ich nelle mi lef bileve
I shulle be mid hyre ere eve!"
. . . .
E "After deeþ clepe nomore y nylle
300 But slee my self now y wille!"
His knyf he braide out of his sheth.
Him self he wolde have doo to deth
And to hert he had it smetene
Ne had his moder it under ȝetene.
Þen þe queene fel him uppone
And þe knyf fro him noome.
She reft him of his lytel knyf
And savyd þere þe childes lyf.
Forþ þe queene ranne al wepyng
310 Tyl she come to þe kyng.
Þan seide þe good lady
"For Goddes love sir mercy!
Of xii children have we noone
On lyve now but þis oone!
And better it were she were his make
Þan he were deed for hur sake".
"Dame þou seist soþ", seide he.
"Sen it may noone other be
Lever me were she were his wyf
320 Þan y lost my sonnes lyf".
Of þis word þe quene was fayne
And to her soone she ran agayne.
"Floryes soone glad make the.
Þy lef þou schalt on lyve see.
Florys sone þrouȝ engynne
Of þy faders reed and myne
Þis grave let we make
Leve sone for þy sake.

"Death!" he cried, "Full of envy
And of all treachery!
You have robbed me of my beloved!
Truly", he said, "you are to blame.
She would have lived had you not denied it,
And I would gladly die had you let me!"
. . . .
"Those who struggle the most to live,
Them you stab under the rib!
And if there is any degenerate wretch
Who cares nothing for his life,
Who would gladly die for sorrow and age,
On him you take no hold!
No longer will I linger in life!
I shall be beside her before evening!"
. . . .
"I will no longer call after death
But will slay myself right now!"
He drew his knife out of its sheath.
He would have put himself to death
And struck at his own heart
Had his mother not realized it.
Then the queen fell upon him
And seized the knife from him.
She took away his little knife,
And there she saved the child's life.
The queen ran away in tears
Until she came to the king.
Then the good lady cried,
"For God's love, sir, have mercy!
From twelve children we have
None alive now but this one!
It would be better if she were his wife
Than for him to be dead for her sake".
"Madam, you speak the truth", he sighed.
"Since it cannot not be otherwise,
I would rather she were his wife
Than to lose my son's life".
With these words the queen was calmed,
And she ran back to her son.
"Floris, my son, cheer yourself.
You will see your sweetheart alive.
Floris, son, through a trick
Of your father's and my design,
We had this grave made,
Dear son, for your own sake.

	Ȝif þou þat maide forgete woldest
330	After oure reed wyf þou sholdest".
	Now every worde she haþ him tolde
	How þat þey þat mayden solde.
	"Is þis soth my moder dere?"
	"For soth", she seide, "she is not here".
	Þe rowȝ stoone adoune þey leyde
	And sawe þat was not þe mayde.
	"Now moder y þink þat y leve may.
	Ne shal y rest nyȝt ne day
	Nyȝt ne day ne no stounde
340	Tyl y have my lemmon founde.
	Hur to seken y woll wende
	Þauȝ it were to þe worldes ende!"
	To þe king he goþ to take his leve
	And his fader bade him byleve.
	"Sir y wyl let for no wynne.
	Me to bydden it it were grete synne".
	Þan seid þe king, "Seth it is soo
	Seþ þou wylt noone other doo
	Al þat þe nedeþ we shul þe fynde.
350	Jhesu þe of care unbynde".
	"Leve fader", he seide, "y telle þe
	Al þat þou shalt fynde me.
	Þou mast me fynde at my devyse
	Seven horses al of prys
	And twoo y-charged uppon þe molde
	Boþ with selver and wyþ golde
	And two ycharged with monay
	For to spenden by þe way
	And þree with clothes ryche
360	Þe best of al þe kyngryche.
	Seven horses and sevyn men
	And þre knaves without hem
	And þyne owne chamburlayne.
	Þat is a wel nobel swayne;
	He can us wyssth and reede.
	As marchaundes we shull us lede".
	His fader was an hynde king.
	Þe coupe of golde he dide him bryng

If you had forgotten that girl,
You would marry according to our wishes".
She told him every word[157]
About how they sold that maiden.
"Is this the truth, my dear mother?"
"In truth", she answered, "she is not here".
They laid aside the rough stone
And saw that the maid was not there.
"Now, mother, I think that I can live.
I will not rest night or day,
Night, day, or one moment,
Until I have found my beloved.
I will go to seek her,
Even to the ends of the earth!"
He went to the king to take his leave,
And his father asked him to stay.
"Sir, I won't desist for any gain. To
Demand that of me would be a great sin".
Then the king answered, "Since it is so,
Since you will not have it any other way,
We will provide you with all you need.
May Christ deliver you from distress".[158]
"Dear father", he said, "I will tell you
All that you will supply me with.
You may equip me, at my request,
With seven horses, all of prized value,
With two loaded, to the earth,
With both silver and gold,
And two laden with money
To spend along the way,
And three loaded with rich clothes,
The best in all the kingdom.
Seven horses and seven men,
And three attendants besides them,
And your own chamberlain.
He is a very dedicated servant;
He can both guide and advise us.
We will conduct ourselves as merchants".
His father was a gracious king.
He brought him the cup of gold,

---

157 *She haþ*: ME narratives often feature narratorial interjections, but the *Floris* poet has an unusual (and confusing) fondness for present and present continuous phrasings, perhaps to build immediacy and energy in the story.

158 *Jhesu thee of care unbynde:* To have the king entrust his son to Christ is either a mistake or another example of the period slipshod depiction of non-Christians. Felix's faith is ambiguous as the text never explicitly says that he is Muslim and the descriptor 'pagan' (French line 59) could mean any non-Christian or pre-Christian belief. The parents show particular respect for Blancheflor in placing her mock-burial in a *chirche* (209).

Þat ilke self coupe of golde
370 Þat was Blauncheflour for ȝolde.
"Have þis soone", seide þe king
"Herewith þou may þat swete þing
Wynne so may betyde
Blauncheflour with þe white syde
Blauncheflour þat faire may".
Þe king let sadel a palfray
Þe oone half so white so mylke
And þat other reed so sylk.
. . . .

A   I ne kan telle you nowt
380 How richeliche þe sadel was wrout.
Þe arsouns were gold pur and fin
Stones of vertu set þerin
Bigon abouten wiȝ orfreis.
Þe quen was hende and curteis.
Ȝhe cast her hond to hire fingre
And drouȝ þerof a riche ringe.
"Have nou sone here þis ring.
While þou hit hast doute þe no þing
Ne fir þe brenne ne drenchen in se;
390 Ne iren ne stel schal derie þe.
And be hit erli and be hit late
To þi wille þou schalt have whate".
Weping þai departed nouþe
And kiste hem wiȝ softe mouþe.
Þai made for him non oþer chere
Þan þai seȝe him ligge on bere.
Nou forht þai nime wiȝ alle main
Himself and his chaumberlain.
So longe þai han undernome
400 To þe havene þai beȝ icome
Þer Blauncheflour lai aniȝt.
Richeliche þai were idiȝt.
Þe louerd of þe hous was wel hende;
Þe child he sette next his hende
In þe alþrest fairest sete.
Gladliche þai dronke and ete
Al þat þerinne were.
Al þai made glade chere
And ete and dronke echon wiȝ oþer

The same golden cup itself
That had been traded for Blancheflour.
"Take this, son", said the king,
"With it you might win back
That sweet girl, if it may so happen,
Blancheflour with the light complexion,[159]
Blancheflour, that fair maid".
The king had a palfrey saddled,
With one side as white as milk,
And the other as red as silk.
. . . .

I cannot begin to describe
How richly the saddle was made.
The saddlebows were gold, pure and fine,
With stones of quality set inside,
Surrounded about with gold embroidery.
The queen was graceful and courteous.
She put her hand to her finger
And drew off a magnificent ring.
"Take this ring here now, son.
While you have it, fear nothing. You will
Not burn in fire, or drown in the sea;
Neither iron nor steel will harm you.
Whether it be sooner or later,
You will have what is your will".
They parted then in tears,
And kissed each other softly.
They behaved for him no differently than
If they saw him lying on a funeral bier.
Now he and his chamberlain
Went forth with all their strength.
They traveled for a long time
Until they came to the harbor
Where Blancheflour had slept at night.
They were provided for lavishly.
The lord of the house was very hospitable;
He sat the young man next to him,
In the finest of all seats.
All those who were in there
Ate and drank happily.
They all made a cheerful mood
And ate and drank with each other,

---

159 *White syde:* A puzzling line. Kooper has *side*, suggesting a light aspect, where Bennett and Smithers render *syde* as long or flowing, i.e. blonde hair. The medieval sense that light hair or skin complexion was purer or more beautiful is evidently operant here, as Blancheflor is the daughter of a Saxon noble. See also Walter C. Curry, *The Middle English Ideal of Personal Beauty* (Baltimore: J.H. Furst, 1916), 11-21 and 80-86.

410	Ac Florice þou3te al anoþer.
	Ete ne drinke mi3te he nou3t
	On Blauncheflour was al his þou3t.
	Þe leuedi of þe hous under3at
	Hou þis child mourning sat
	And seide here louerd wi3 stille dreme
	"Sire", 3e saide, "nimstou no 3eme
	How þis child mourning sit?
	Mete and drink he for3it.
	Litel he ete3 and lasse he drinke3.
420	He nis no marchaunt as me þinke3".
	To Florice þan spak 3he
	"Child ful of mourning I þe se
	Þus far herinne þis ender dai
	Blauncheflour þat faire mai.
	Herinne was þat maiden bow3t
	And over þe se 3he was ibrow3t.
	Herinne þai bou3te þat maden swete
	And wille here eft selle to bi3ete.
	To Babiloyne þai wille hire bring
430	And selle hire to kaiser oþer to king.
	Þou art ilich here of alle þinge
	Of semblant and of mourning
	But þou art a man and 3he is a maide"!
	Þous þe wif to Florice saide.
	Þo Florice herde his lemman nevene
	So bliþe he was of þat stevene
	Þat his herte bigan al li3t.
	A coupe of gold he let fulle ri3t.
	"Dame", he saide, "þis hail is þin
440	Boþe þe gold and þe win
	Boþe þe gold and þe win eke
	For þou of mi lemman speke!
	On hir I þout for here I si3t.
	And wist ich wher hire finde mi3t
	Ne scholde no weder me assoine
	Þat I ne schal here seche at Babiloine".
	Florice rest him þere al ni3t.
	Amorewe whanne hit was dai-li3t
	He dide him in þe salte flod.
450	Wind and weder he hadde ful god.
	To þe mariners he 3af largeliche
	Þat brou3ten him over bleþeliche

	But Floris' thoughts were all elsewhere.
	He could not eat or drink,
	For all his thoughts were on Blancheflour.
	The lady of the house noticed
	How this child sat mourning,
	And said to her lord in a low voice,
	"Sir", she said, "haven't you noticed
	How this boy sits so gloomily?
	He takes no notice of food and drink.
	He eats little and drinks less.
	It seems to me he is no merchant".
	She then said to Floris,
	"Child, I see you are full of mourning,[160]
	The same way that Blancheflour,
	That fair maid, sat here the other day.
	That girl was delivered here
	And was sold over the sea.
	Here they bought that sweet maiden,
	And they will trade her again for a profit.
	They will take her to Babylon,
	And will sell her to a caesar or a king.
	How alike you are to her in every way,
	In your appearance and mood, except
	That you are a man and she is a maid"!
	This is what the wife spoke to Floris.
	When Floris heard his lover's name,
	He was so glad to hear that sound
	That his heart was all lit up.
	He had the cup of gold filled straightaway.
	"Madam", he said, "this toast is yours,
	Both the gold and the wine–
	Both the gold and the wine as well,
	For you spoke of my beloved!
	For her I thought, for her I sighed.
	And now I know where I might find her.
	No bad weather will hinder me
	From seeking her in Babylon!"
	Floris rested there all night.
	In the morning, when it was daylight,
	He set out on the salty sea.
	He had favorable wind and weather.
	He paid the sailors liberally,
	Who gladly brought him across

---

160 *Child* may formally denote a knight-in-training, but Floris is an eastern prince and is nowhere mentioned as becoming a knight. The poet is likely sentimentally emphasizing his youth.

To þe londe þar he wold lende	To the land where he wished to go,
For þai founden him so hende.	For they found him so gracious.
Sone so Florice com to londe	As soon as Floris came ashore,
Wel yerne he þankede Godes sonde	He fervently thanked God for bringing him
To þe lond þer his lemman is;	To the land where his beloved was;
Him þouȝte he was in Paradis.	It seemed to him he was in Paradise.
Wel sone men Florice tidingges told	Very soon men told Floris the news that
460 Þe amerail wolde feste hold	The emir planned to hold a feast, and all
And kinges an dukes to him come scholde	The kings and dukes were to come to him,
Al þat of him holde wolde	All that held land from him,
For to honure his heȝhe feste	To honor his high feast
And also for to heren his heste.	And also to hear his commands.
Þo Florice herde þis tiding	When Floris heard this report,
Þan gan him glade in alle þing	He was cheered in every way,
And in his herte þouȝte he	And in his heart he resolved
Þat he wolde at þat feste be	That he would be at that feast,
For wel he hopede in þe halle	For he was confident he would see
470 His leman sen among hem alle.	His lover among them all in the hall.
So longe Florice haþ undernome	Floris undertook his journey
To a fair cite he is icome.	Until he came to a fair city.
Wel faire men haþ his in inome	Men lodged him comfortably,
Ase men scholde to a kinges sone	As one should for a king's son,
At a palais was non him iliche.	In a palatial house–there were none like it.
Þe louerd of þe hous was wel riche	The master of the inn was prosperous,
And god inow him com to honde	And gold in plenty came into his hand,
Boþe bi water and be londe.	Both by water and by land.
Florice ne sparede for no fe	Floris did not spare any expense,
480 Inow þat þere ne scholde be	Lest there should not be enough
Of fissc of flessch of tendre bred	Of fish, of meat, of soft bread,
Boþe of whit win and of red.	Or of wine, both white and red.
Þe louerd hadde ben wel wide;	The lord was wise in the world's ways;
Þe child he sette bi his side	He set the youth by his side,
In þe alþerferste sete.	In the best seat of all.
Gladliche þai dronke and ete.	They ate and drank happily.
Ac Florice et an drank riȝt nowt	But Floris ate and drank almost nothing;
On Blauncheflour was al his þouȝt.	All of his thoughts were on Blancheflour.
Þan bispak þe bourgeis	Then the master, a gracious man,
490 Þat hende was fre and curteys	Noble and courteous, spoke,
"Child me þinkkeȝ swiþe wel	"Young man, it seems clear to me
Þi þout is mochel on þi catel".	Your mind is very much on your goods".
"Nai on mi catel is hit nowt	"No, not at all on my property.
On oþer þink is al my þouȝt.	My thoughts are all on something else.
Mi þouȝt is on alle wise	My mind in every way
Mochel on mi marchaundise	Is on recovering my merchandise.[161]

---

161 Egerton 2862 MS has *For to fynde my marchaundise* (464).

And 3it þat is mi meste wo	And it will be my greatest sorrow
3if ich hit finde and schal forgo".	If I find it and must lose it".
Þanne spak þe louerd of þat inne	Then the master of that inn mused,
500 "Þous sat þis oþer dai herinne	"It's the same way that Blancheflour,
Þat faire maide Blauncheflour.	That fair maid, sat here the other day
Boþe in halle and ek in bour	Both in the hall and in her room.
Evere 3he made mourning chere	She always had a look of mourning and
And biment Florice here leve fere.	Grieved for 'Floris,' her dear companion.[162]
Joie ne blisse ne hadde 3he none	She had no joy or ease,
Ac on Florice was al here mone".	But all her pining was for Floris".
Florice het nime a coppe of silver whi3t	Floris ordered a cup of white silver brought,
And a mantel of scarlet	And a cloak of scarlet,
Ipaned al wi3 meniuer	All lined with fur,
510 And 3af his hostesse þer.	And gave it to his host there.
"Have þis", he saide, "to þine honour	"Have this", he said, "for your honor,
And þou hit mi3te þonke Blauncheflour!	And you may thank Blancheflour for it!
Stolen 3he was out mine countreie	She was stolen from my country,
Here ich here seche bi þe waie.	And I seek her here by these roads.
He mi3te make min herte glad	The man would make my heart glad
Þat couþe me telle whider 3he was lad".	Who could tell me where she was taken".
"Child to Babiloyne 3he his ibrou3t	"Child, she has been brought to Babylon,
And ameral hire had ibou3t.	And the emir has bought her.
He 3af for hire ase 3he stod upri3t	He paid for her, as she stood upright,
520 Seven sithes of gold here wi3t!	Seven times her weight in gold!
For hire faired and for hire schere	For her beauty and her bearing
Þe ameral hire bou3te so dere	The emir has paid so dearly for her,
For he þenke3 wi3outen wene	For he thinks, beyond a doubt,
Þat faire mai to haven to quene.	To have that fair maid as queen.
Amang oþer maidenes in his tour	He has placed her with great honor
He haþ hire ido wi3 mochel honour".	Among the other maidens in his tower".
Nou Florice rest him þere al ni3t.	Then Floris rested there all night.
On morewe whan hit was dai-li3t	In the morning when it was daylight,
He aros up in þe moreweninge	He rose up early
530 And 3af his hoste an hondred schillinge	And gave his host a hundred shillings,[163]
To his hoste and to hes hostesse	To him and to his hostess,
And nam his leve and gan hem kesse.	And took his leave and kissed them.
And 3erne he haþ his ostesse bisou3t	And he earnestly asked his hostess
Þat 3he him helpe 3if 3he mou3t	If she would help him, if she could,[164]
Hou he mi3te wi3 sum ginne	How he might with some ruse
Þe faire maiden to him awinne.	Win the fair maiden for himself.

---

162 The innkeeper may not know Floris's name until he reveals himself, as he refers to Blancheflor's lover in third person.

163 *An hondred schillinge*: about £2590 or $US4000 in modern money (UK National Archives), rather an expensive hotel bill but in keeping with Floris' aristocratic refinement. The sentiment also emphasizes by extension Blancheflor's value to Floris. See also line 744.

164 Auchinleck seems to use feminine pronouns here, but the following dialogue refers to a sworn brother. Possibly the master of the house answers for the lady.

. . . .	. . . .

C   Þann sede þe burgeis   Then the master spoke,

      Þat was hende and curtais   Who was so gracious and courteous,

      At Babilloine atte frume   Right at the limits of Babylon,

540   To one brigge þu schalt cume.   You will come to a bridge,

. . . .	. . . .

E   A burgeis þou findest ate frome.   And you will see a townsman right away.[165]

      His paleis is ate brigges ende.   His mansion is at the bridge's end.

      Curteis man he his and hende.   He is a gracious and gentle man.

      We beþ wed-breþren and trewþe ipliȝt   We are sworn brothers pledged by oath,

      He þe can wissen and reden ariȝt.   And he can advise and guide you rightly.

      Þou schalt beren him a ring   You will give him a ring,

      Fram miselve to tokning   From myself as a token,

      Þat he þe helpe in eche helve   And he will help you in every way

      So hit were bifalle miselve".   As if it had happened to me".

550   Florice tok þe ring and nam his leve   Floris took the ring and made his goodbye,

      For þere no leng wolde he bileve.   For he would not stay any longer.

      Bi þat hit was undren heghȝ   By the time it was high noon

      Þe brigge he was swiþe negȝ.   He was very near the bridge.

      When he was to þe brigge icome   When he came to the bridge,

      Þe burges he fond ate frome   The first thing he saw was the townsman,

      Stondend on a marbel ston.   Standing on a marble stone.

      Fair man and hende he was on.   He was a fair and gracious man.

      Þe burgeis was ihote Darye;   The burgess was named Dary;

      Florice him grette swiþe faire   Floris greeted him courteously

560   And haþ him þe ring irawt   And handed him the ring

      And wel faire him bitawt.   And entrusted it to him in good faith.

      Þourgh tokning of þat ilke ring   Through the token of that ring

      Florice hadde þer god gestning   Floris had a good welcome there

      Of fichss of flessch of tendre bred   Of fish, of meat, of soft bread,

      Boþe of whit win and of red.   And wine, both white and red.

      Ac evere Florice siȝte ful cold   But Floris continually sighed distractedly,

      And Darys gan him bihold.   And Dary looked on him.

      "Leve child what mai þe be   "Dear boy, what is the matter,

      Þous carfoul ase I þe se?   To be as sorrowful as I see you?

570   I wene þou nart nowt al fer   I guess you are not feeling well

      Þat þou makest þous doelful cher   So that you have such a doleful look,

      Oþer þe likeȝ nowt þin in?"   Or do you not like your lodgings?"

      Nou Florice answered him   Then Floris answered him,

      "Ȝis sire bi Godes hore   "Not so, sir, by God's mercy,[166]

      So god I ne hadde ȝore!   I never had so good a one before!

      God late me bide þilke dai   May God let me see the day

---

165 *Burgeis*: Technically a burgess was a citizen with full rights, but the nuance is that of a successful middle-class businessman or tradesman in a town (thus the modern *bourgeois*).

166 *Ȝis, sire*: The tendency of PDE with negative questions, so frustrating for many learners of English, is to say 'no', i.e. I disagree with what you said, rather than 'yes', i.e. I do like the lodgings. At least here, ME does the latter.

	Þat ich þe ȝelde mai.	That I may repay you.
	Ac I þenke in alle wise	But I am thinking in every way
	Upon min owen marchaundise	About my own property,
580	Wherfore ich am hider come	Which is why I have come here,
	Lest I ne finde hit nowt ate frome.	Lest I not find it at all.
	And ȝit is þat mi meste wo	And yet it will be my greatest sorrow
	Ȝif ich hit finde and sschal forgo".	If I find it and must lose it".
	"Child woldest þou tel me þi gref	"Child, if you would tell me your heart,
	To helpe þe me were ful lef".	I would be very pleased to help you".
	Nou everich word he haþ him told	Then he told him every word,
	Hou þe maide was fram him sold	How the maid was sold from him
	And hou he was of Speyne a kinges sone	And how he was a king's son from Spain,
	And for hir love þider icome	Who had come here for love of her,
590	For to fonde wiȝ som ginne	In order to devise some stratagem
	Þat faire maide to biwinne.	To win that fair maid.
	Daris now þat child bihalt	Dary looked on the boy then
	And for a fol he him halt.	And took him for a fool.
	"Child", he seiȝ, "I se hou goȝ.	"Boy", he said, "I know how it will go.
	Iwis þou ȝernest þin owen deȝ!	For sure, you seek your own death!
	Þ'ameral haþ to his justening	The emir's invited to his tournament
	Oþer half hondred of riche king.	Over fifty rich kings.[167]
	Þat alþerrichest kyng	The most powerful king among them
	Ne dorste biginne swich a þing.	Would not dare attempt such a thing.
600	For miȝte þe ameral hit underȝete	For if the emir discovered it,
	Sone þou were of live quite.	You would soon lose your life.
	Abouten Babiloine wiȝouten wene	Around Babylon, without a doubt,
	Dureþ sexti longe milen and tene!	It's sixty long miles and ten more!
	And ate walle þar beþ ate	And on the walls there are gates–
	Seven siþe twenti ȝate!	Seven times twenty!
	Twenti tours þer beȝ inne	There are twenty towers inside
	Þat everich dai cheping is inne.	Where there is trading every day.
	Nis no dai þourg þe ȝer	There isn't a day throughout the year
	Þat scheping nis þerinne plener.	That the markets aren't going strong.
610	An hondred toures also þerto	There's a hundred towers to go with them
	Beȝ in þe borewe and somdel mo.	In the district, and several more.
	Þat alderest feblest tour	The weakest tower of them
	Wolde kepe an emperour	Would keep an emperor
	To comen al þer wiȝinne	From coming inside there,
	Noiþer wiȝ strengȝe ne wiȝ ginne!	Whatever strength or ingenuity they had!
	And þei alle þe men þat beþ ibore	Even if all the men who've been born
	Adden hit up here deth iswhore	Swore to fight to their death,
	Þai scholde winne þe mai so sone	They would just as soon win the maid
	As fram þe hevene heȝ þe sonne and mone!	As win the sun and moon from the heavens!
620	And in þe bourh amide þeriȝt	And in the castle, right in the middle,

---

167 *Other half hondred*: Another confusing expression which Kooper interprets as "half of a second hundred", 150 in total.

Þer stant a riche tour I þe aplytȝ;	There is a splendid tower, I assure you;
A ȝousang taisen he his heiȝe	Its height is a thousand fathoms tall
Wo so it bihalt wit fer and negȝene.	To whoever beholds it, near or far.
And an hondres taises he is wid	And it is a hundred fathoms wide,
And imaked wiȝ mochel prid	And built with extravagant pride,
Of lim and of marbel ston.	Of lime and marble stone.
In Cristiente nis swich non.	There is nothing like it in Christendom.
And þe morter is maked so wel	And the mortar is so well-built
Ne mai no mail hit breke wiȝ no stel.	That no man could break it with any steel.
630 And þe pomel above þe led	And the globe on top of the roof
Is iwrout wiȝ so moche red	Was created with so much skill
Þat men ne þorfen aniȝt berne	That men do not need to burn at night
Neiþer torche ne lanterne.	Either a torch or a lantern.
Swich a pomel was never bigonne!	Such a globe was never made before!
Hit schineȝ aniȝt so adai doþ þe sonne.	It shines at night like the sun by day.
Nou beþ þer inne þat riche toure	Inside that rich tower there is
Four and twenty maidenes boure.	A chamber for twenty-four maidens.
So wel were þat ilke man	The man would be doing well
Þat miȝte wonen in þat an!	Who could live in that place!
640 Now þourt him nevere ful iwis	He would never need, for sure,
Willen after more blisse.	To ask for more bliss.
Nou beþ þe seriaunts in þe stage	There are servants on the upper floor
To serven þe maidenes of parage.	To serve the maidens of high birth.
Ne mai no seriaunt be þerinne	No servant may go in there
Þat in his brech bereþ þet ginne	Who has his manhood in his pants,[168]
Neiþer bi dai ne bi niȝt	Neither by day or by night,
But he be ase capoun diȝt!	Unless he is fixed like a rooster!
And at þe gate is a gateward.	And at the entrance is a gatekeeper.
He nis no fol ne no coward.	He is no fool or coward.
650 Ȝif þer comeȝ ani man	If any man enters
Wiȝinne þat ilche barbican	Within that same fortress
But hit be bi his leve	Unless by his permission,
He wille him boþe bete and reve.	He will both beat and emasculate him.
Þe porter is proud wiȝalle.	The porter is proud, to add.
Everich dai he goþ in palle.	Every day he walks in fine clothes.
And þe amerail is so wonder a gome	And the emir is so incredible a man
Þat everich ȝer hit is his wone	That every year it is his custom
To chesen him a newe wif.	To choose himself a new wife.[169]
And whan he a newe wif underfo	And when he takes a new wife,
660 He knaweȝ hou hit schal be do.	He knows how it will be done.
Þanne scholle men fechche doun of þe stage	Then men will fetch down from upstairs
Alle þe maidenes of parage	All the maidens of high birth

---

168 *That in his brech bereth the ginne*: An amusing euphemism: 'Who has the engine in his pants'. A *capon* (647) is a castrated rooster. Eunuchs were indispensable for guarding harems in fiction.

169 In the French version the emir repudiates and executes his ex-wives annually, making Blancheflor like Scheherezade in *One Thousand and One Nights*. But the English text does not state this clearly. See the note to 1223.

	And brenge hem into on orchard	And bring them into the orchard,
	Þe fairest of all middelhard.	The fairest one on all earth.
	Þer is foulen song;	There are the songs of birds;
	Men miȝte libben þer among!	A man might live long there!
	Aboute þe orchard goþ a wal.	Around the orchard there is a wall.
	Þe werste ston is cristal!	The cheapest stone is crystal!
	Þer man mai sen on þe ston	A man might read on the stone
670	Mochel of þis werldes wisdom.	Much of this world's wisdom.[170]
	And a welle þer springeȝ inne	And a well springs in there
	Þat is wrowt wiȝ mochel ginne.	Which was crafted with great ingenuity.
	Þe welle is of mochel pris;	The well is of great majesty;
	Þe strem com fram Paradis!	The stream comes from Paradise!
	Þe gravel in þe grounde of preciouse stone	The gravel in the ground is precious stones,
	And of vertu iwis echone	And each one has special virtues–
	Of saphires and of sardoines	Sapphires and sardonyx stone,
	Of oneches and of calsidoines.	Onyx and clear quartz.
	Nou is þe waie of so mochel eye	The well is held in such awe that
680	Ȝif þer comeȝ ani maiden þat is forleie	If any maid nears it who is not a virgin,
	And hi bowe to þe grounde	And she bows to the ground
	For to waschen here honde	In order to wash her hands,
	Þe water wille ȝelle als hit ware wod	The water will cry out as if it were mad
	And bicome on hire so red so blod.	And turn on her as red as blood.
	Wich maiden þe water fareȝ on so	Whichever maiden the water reacts so with
	Hi schal sone be fordo.	Will soon be put to death.
	And þilke þat beþ maidenes clene	But those maidens who are pure
	Þai mai hem wassche of þe rene.	May wash themselves from the stream.
	Þe water wille erne stille and cler	The water will run still and clear
690	Nelle hit hem make no daunger.	And will give them no danger.
	At þe welle-heued þer stant a tre	At the head of the well there is a tree,
	Þe fairest þat mai in erthe be.	The fairest that might be on earth.
	Hit is icleped þe tre of love,	They call it the Tree of Love,
	For floures and blosmes beþ ever above.	As flowers and blossoms are always about.
	. . . .	. . . .
C	So sone so þe olde beoþ idon	As soon as an old one falls down,
	Þer springeþ niwe riȝt anon	A new one springs up at once.
	. . . .	. . . .
A	And þilke þat clene maidenes be	And for those who are pure maidens,
	Men schal hem bringe under þat tre	Men will bring them under the tree,
	And wich-so falleȝ on þat ferste flour	And whoever the flower falls on
700	Hi schal ben chosen quen wiȝ honour.	Will be chosen queen with honor.
	And ȝif þer ani maiden is	And if there is any maiden
	Þat þamerail halt of mest pris	Whom the emir thinks the most worthy,
	Þe flour schal on here be went	The flower will be steered toward her
	Þourh art and þourgh enchantement.	Through artifice and enchantment.

---

170 The observer might see the mason's craftsmanship and attention, or as Kooper suggests, the lines are literal: sage texts are inscribed on the stones.

	Þous he cheseþ þourȝ þe flour	Thus he chooses through the petal,
	. . . .	. . . .
C	Alle weneþ hit schulle beo Blancheflour	And all expect it will be Blancheflor".
	. . . .	. . . .
A	Þre sithes Florice swouned nouþe	Floris fell faint three times then
	Er he miȝte speke wiȝ mouþe.	Before he could speak with his tongue.
	Sone he awok and speke miȝt	As soon as he came to and could talk,
710	Sore he wep and sore he siȝt.	He wept sorely, and sighed bitterly.
	"Darie", he saide, "ich worht ded	"Dary", he said, "I will be finished
	But ich have of þe help and red".	Unless I have your help and advice".
	"Leve child ful wel I se	"Dear child, I can see full well
	Þat þou wilt to deþe te.	That you are walking to your death.
	Þe beste red þat I can	The best guidance I know,
	Oþer red I ne can	For I know no other course!–
	Wende tomorewe to þe tour	Is to go tomorrow to the tower
	Ase þou were a god ginour	As though you were an expert engineer,
	And nim in þin hond squir and scantiloun	And carry in your hand a square and ruler,
720	Als þai þou were a masoun.	As though you were a stonemason.
	Bihold þe tour up and doun.	Examine the tower up and down.
	Þe porter is coluard and feloun.	The porter is a scoundrel and a criminal.
	Wel sone he wil come to þe	Very soon he will come up to you
	And aske what mister man þou be	And ask what kind of craftsman you are,
	And ber upon þe felonie	And accuse you of some offense
	And saie þou art comen þe tour aspie.	And claim you came to spy on the tower.
	Þou schalt answeren him swetelich	You will answer him pleasantly
	And speke to him wel mildelich	And speak to him gently,
	. . . .	. . . .
C	And seie þert icome fram ferren londe	And explain that you've come from a
730	For to seche and for to fonde,	Foreign land to seek and to learn,
	If mi lif so longe ilast,	If your life might last so long,
	To makie atur after þis cast,	How to make a tower like it
	In þine londe at frume	In your own land at once
	Whanne þu ert hom icume.	When you have come home.
	Whane he þe hireþ speke so hendeliche,	When he hears you talk so grandly,
	And ansuerie so sueteliche,	And answer so smoothly,
	. . . .	. . . .
A	Wel sone he wil com þe ner	Right away he will come near you
	And bidde þe plaien at þe scheker.	And invite you to play checkers.[171]
	To plaien he wil be wel fous	He will be very keen to play,
740	And to winnen of þin wel coveitous.	And greedily intent on beating you.
	When þou art to þe scheker brouȝt	When you are brought to the board,
	Wiȝouten pans ne plai þou nowt.	You can't play without any money.
	Þou schalt have redi mitte	You will have ready at hand

---

171 The medieval English played backgammon and other board games but checkers was not commonly played until later centuries. As with the chess match in Stanzaic *Guy of Warwick*, such games would have had an exotic eastern atmosphere to them.

Þritti mark under þi slitte.
And ȝif he winne ouȝt al þin
Al leve þou hit wiȝ him
And ȝif þou winne ouȝt of his
Þou lete þerof ful litel pris.
Wel ȝerne he wille þe bidde and praie
750 Þat þou come amorewe and plaie.
Þou schalt sigge þou wilt so
And nim wiȝ þe amorewe swich two.
And ever þou schalt in þin owen wolde
Þi gode cop wiȝ he atholde
Þat ilke self coppe of golde
Þat was for Blauncheflour iȝolde.
Þe þridde dai bere wiȝ þe an hondred pond
And þi coppe al hol and sond.
ȝif him markes and pans fale
760 Of þi mone tel þou no tale.
Wel ȝerne he þe wille bidde and praie
Þat þou legge þi coupe to plaie.
Þou schalt answeren him ate first
No lenger plaie þou ne list.
Wel moche he wil for þi coupe bede
ȝif he miȝte þe better spede.
Þou schalt bleþelich ȝiven hit him
Þai hit be gold pur and fin
And sai, "Me þinkeȝ hit wel bisemeȝ te
770 Þai hit were worȝ swiche þre".
Sai also þe ne faille non
Gold ne selver ne riche won.
And he wil þanne so mochel love þe
Þat þou hit schalt boþe ihere and see
Þat he wil falle to þi fot
And bicome þi man ȝif he mot.
His manred þou schalt afonge
And þe trewþe of his honde.
ȝif þou miȝt þous his love winne
780 He mai þe help wiȝ som ginne".
Nou also Florice haþ iwrowt
Also Darie him haþ itawt
Þat þourgh his gold and his garsome
Þe porter is his man bicome.
"Nou", quaþ Florice, "þou art mi man
And al mi trest is þe upan.
Nou þou miȝt wel eþe

Thirty marks in your pocket.
And if he wins anything from you,
Be sure to give it to him.
And if you win anything from him,
Do not make too much of it.
He will eagerly ask you and insist
That you come back the next day and play.
You will say that you will,
And take twice as much with you.
And you will always keep
At hand your fine cup,
That very same cup of gold
Which was given for Blancheflour.
On the third day take a hundred pounds[172]
With you, and your cup, safe and sound.
Give him marks and plenty of pennies,
And do not keep count of your money.
He will eagerly ask and insist
That you stake your cup in the game.
You will at first answer him
That you don't feel like playing any longer.
He will make a high offer for your cup,
If he might have more luck for doing so.
You will give it to him cheerfully,
Even if it is gold, pure and fine,
And say, "To me it suits you well,
Even if it were worth three times as much".
Say also that you are not short of anything,
Gold or silver or fine goods.
And then he will love you so much,
And you will both hear and see it,
That he will fall to your feet
And become your man, if he may.
You will receive his homage,
And an oath of loyalty from his hand.
If you might win him over so,
He might help you with some stratagem".
Then Floris arranged things
Just as Dary instructed him to,
So that through his gold and treasure
The porter became his man.
"Now", said Floris, "you are my man,
And all my trust is in you.
Now you can easily

---

172 *An hondred pond*: Enormous stakes, US$75,000 in modern money (UK National Archives), though Floris is 'gambling' for Blancheflor.

Arede me fram þe deþe".	Protect me from death".
And everich word he haþ him told	And he told him every word
790 Hou Blaunchefloúr was fram him sold	How Blanchefloúr was sold from him,
And hou he was of Spaine a kynges sone	And how he was a prince of Spain
And for hire love þider icome	Who had come here for her love,
To fonde wiʒ som ginne	To try with some ploy
Þe maiden aʒen to him winne.	To win the maiden back to him.
Þe porter þat herde and sore siʒte	The porter listened and sighed sorely,
"Ich am bitraied þourʒ riʒte.	"I have been tricked in full.
Þourʒ þi catel ich am bitraid	Through your possessions I am ensnared,
And of mi lif ich am desmaid!	And I am in despair for my life!
Nou ich wot child hou hit geþ.	Now I know, boy, how things stand.
800 For þe ich drede to þolie deþ!	For you I dread to suffer death!
And naþeles ich ne schal þe nevere faile mo	But nonetheless, I will never fail you,
Þer whiles I mai ride or go.	As long as I can ride or walk.
Þi foreward ich wil helden alle	I will hold your conditions in full,
Whatso wille bitide or falle.	Whatever happens or comes.
Wende þou hom into þin in	Go back home to your inn
Whiles I þink of som ginne.	While I think of some plan.
Bitwene þis and þe þridde dai	Between now and the third day
Don ich wille þat I mai".	I will do what I can".
Florice spak and wep among.	Floris at times spoke and wept,
810 Þat ilche terme him þouʒte wel long.	Thinking the time very long.
Þe porter þouʒte what to rede.	The porter decided what to do.
He let floures gaderen in þe mede.	He had flowers gathered from the meadow.
He wiste hit was þe maidenes wille	Thinking it would be to the maiden's liking,
Two coupen he let of floures fille.	He had two baskets of flowers filled.
Þat was þe rede þat he þouʒt þo:	And this was the ruse he thought of then:
Florice in þat o coupe do.	Floris was put into one basket.
Tweie gegges þe coupe bere	Two young women carried the basket,
So hevi charged þat wroþ þai were.	Who were annoyed by the heavy weight.
Þai bad God ʒif him evel fin	They asked God to give a nasty end
820 Þat so mani floures dede þerin!	To whoever put so many flowers in there!
Þider þat þai weren ibede	When they were ordered to go up,
Ne were þai nowt ariʒt birede	They were not directed correctly,
Acc þai turned in hire left hond	And so they turned to their left,
Blaunchefloures bour an hond.	Bypassing Blanchefloúr's room.
To Clarice bour þe coupe þai bere	They carried the basket to Clarice's bower
Wiʒ þe floures þat þerinne were.	With the flowers that were inside.
Þere þe couppe þai sette adoun	There they set the basket down
And ʒaf him here malisoun	And muttered their curses on him
Þat so fele floures hem brouʒte on honde.	Who put together so many flowers.
830 Þai wenten forht and leten þe coppe stonde.	They went out and left the basket standing.
Clarice to þe coppe com and wolde	Clarice went to the basket, wanting
Þe floures handleden and biholde.	To handle and look at the flowers.
Florisse wende hit hadde ben his swet wiʒt;	Floris thought it was his sweet lass;

In þe coupe he stod upriȝt	He stood upright in the basket,
And þe maide al for drede	And the maid, out of fright,
Bigan to schrichen an to grede.	Began to shriek and cry out.
Þo he seghȝ hit nas nowth he	When he saw that it was not his beloved,
Into þe coupe he stirte aȝe	He jumped back into the basket,
And held him bitraied al clene.	Thinking himself betrayed in full.

840	Of his deȝ he ne ȝaf nowt a bene.	He didn't count his life worth a bean.[173]
	Þer come to Clarice maidenes lepe	Maidens came rushing to Clarice,
	Bi ten be twenti in one hepe	By ten and twenty, in one crowd,
	And askede what here were	And asked her what was the matter
	Þat hi makede so loude bere.	That made her carry on so.
	Clarice hire understod anonriȝt	Clarice realized right away that it was
	Þat hit was Blauncheflour þat swete wiȝt	Meant for Blancheflour, that sweet girl,
	For here boures neȝ were	For their rooms were near each other
	And selden þat þai neren ifere	And they were seldom not together,
	And aiþer of oþer counseil þai wiste	So that they knew each other's secrets
850	And michel aiþer to oþer triste.	And had deep trust in each other.
	Hii ȝaf hire maidenes answere anon	After a moment she told the maidens
	Þat into boure þai sscholden gon.	That they should return to their rooms.
	"To þis coupe ich cam and wolde	"I came to this basket, wanting
	Þe floures handli and biholde.	To handle the flowers and look at them.
	Ac er ich hit ever wiste	But before I knew what was happening
	A boterfleȝe toȝain me fluste.	A butterfly darted out toward me.
	Ich was sor adrad of þan	I was so terribly startled by it
	Þat sschrichen and greden I bigan".	That I began to shriek and cry".
	Þe maidenes hadde þerof gle	The maidens had some laughter over it
860	And turnede aȝen and let Clarisse be.	And went back out, and left Clarice alone.
	So sone so þe madenes weren agon	As soon as the maidens were gone,
	To Blauncheflours bour Clarice wente anon	Clarice went at once to Blancheflour's room
	And saide leyende to Blauncheflour:	And said laughing to Blancheflour,
	"Wiltou sen a ful fair flour	"Would you like to see a very nice flower?
	Swiche a flour þat þe schal like	It's a flower that you will like,
	Have þou sen hit a lite?'	After you have seen it a little while".
	"Avoy dameisele", quaþ Blauncheflour	"Stop it, girl", said Blancheflour.
	"To scorne me is litel honour".	"There's little honor in teasing me".
	. . . .	. . . .

C	"Ho þat luveþ par amur	"She who marries for love and has joy for it
870	And haþ þerof joye mai luve flures".	Can take pleasure in flowers".
	. . . .	. . . .

A	"Iich ihere Clarice wiȝoute gabbe	I'm hearing, Clarice, it's no idle gab,
	Þe ameral wil me to wive habbe.	That the emir will take me as his wife.
	Ac þilke dai schal never be	But that day will never come

---

173 *Of his deth he ne gaf nowt a bene*: Egerton 2862 has *lyf*. ME often uses straw, berry, or oyster in such expressions to mean something almost worthless. PDE might use 'plugged nickel' or an obscenity. I take the translation from Taylor, who lists several related phrases. A.B. Taylor, *Floris and Blancheflor: A Middle English Romance* (Oxford: Clarendon, 1927), note to line 878.

Þat men schal atwite me
Þat ischal ben of love untrewe
Ne chaungi love for non newe
For no love ne for non eie
So doþ Floris in his contreie.
880 Nou I schal swete Florice misse
Schal non oþer of me have blisse".
Clarice stant and bihalt þat reuþe
And þe treunesse of þis treuþe.
Leiȝande sche saide to Blauncheflour
"Com nou se þat ilche flour!"
To þe coupe þai ȝeden þo.
Wel blisful was Florisse þo
For he had iherd al þis.
Out of þe coupe he stirte iwis.
Blauncheflour chaungede hewe;
890 Wel sone aiþer oþer knewe.
Wiȝouten speche togidere þai lepe
Þat clepte and keste and eke wepe.
Hire cussing laste a mile
And þat hem þouȝte litel while.
Clarice bihalt al þis
Here contenaunce and here bliss
And leiȝende saide to Blauncheflour
"Felawe knouestou ouȝt þis flour?
Litel er noldest þou hit se
900 And nou þou ne miȝt hit lete fro þe.
He moste conne wel mochel of art
Þat þou woldest ȝif þerof ani part!"
Boþe þise swete þinges for blis
Falleȝ doun here fet to kis
And crieȝ hire merci al weping
Þat ȝhe hem biwraie nowt to þe king
To þe king þat ȝhe hem nowt biwreie
Wherþourgh þai were siker to deye.
Þo spak Clarice to Blauncheflour
910 Wordes ful of fin amour
"Ne doute you nammore wiȝalle
Þan to miself hit hadde bifalle.
White ȝhe wel witerli
Þat hele ich wille youre boþer druri".
To on bedde ȝhe haþ hem ibrowt
Þat was of silk and sendal wrouȝt.
Þai sette hem þere wel softe adoun

When men will condemn me
For being untrue in love, nor will I
Change my heart for someone new,
For anyone's love, or for anyone else,
Just as Floris would not in his country.
Now that I will lose sweet Floris,
No one else will have joy from me".
Clarice stood and beheld that sorrow,
And the faithfulness of her pledge.
Then, laughing, she said to Blancheflour,
"Come now and see that same flower!"
They went to the basket.
Floris was overjoyed,
For he had overheard all this.
He sprang out of the basket, in truth.
Blancheflour changed her color;
At once they recognized each other.
Without words they leaped together
And embraced and kissed and wept as well.
Their kissing lasted the time to walk a mile,
Though it seemed to them too short
A while. Clarice saw all this,
Their emotions and their joy,
And said to Blancheflour laughing,
"Sister, do you know this flower?
A little earlier you would not see it,
And now you can't let it go from you.
He must know a lot of tricks
For you to give him any part of yourself!"
Both of these sweet things, in their joy,
Fell down to kiss her feet
And to beg for her mercy, in tears,
That she would say nothing to the king,
That she would not betray them to him,
For which they would be sure to die.
Clarice then spoke to Blancheflour
Words full of kind love,
"Have no more fear about all this
Than if it had happened to me.
You can be certain and be sure
That I will conceal your lovesickness".[174]
She brought them to a bed
Which was crafted of fine silk and linen.
They laid themselves down quietly,

---

174 *Hele ich wille youre bother druri:* Kooper suggests that heal here means, "I will cure your lovesickness", but also gives a
second meaning of heal as ME *helen*, hide or conceal, which is what Clarice does. The poet may mean another pun here.

And Clarice drowȝ þe courtyn roun.	And Clarice drew the curtain round.
Þo bigan þai to clippe and kisse	Then they began to embrace and kiss,
920 And made joie and mochele blisse.	And had joy and great pleasure.
Florice ferst speke bigan	Floris first began to speak
And saide, "Louerd þat madest man	And said, "Lord, who made man,
Þe I þanke Godes sone.	I thank you, God's son.
Nou al mi care ich have overcome.	For now I have overcome all my troubles.
And nou ich have mi lef ifounde	And now that I have found my beloved,
Of al mi kare ich am unbounde".	I am delivered from all my pains".
Nou haþ aiþer oþer itold	Then each told the other
Of mani a car foul cold	About many hardships, foul and cold,
And of mani pine stronge	And about many strong torments
930 Þat þai han ben atwo so longe.	Because they had been apart so long.
Clarice hem servede al to wille	Clarice served them to their liking,
Boþe dernelich and stille	Both discreetly and quietly,
But so ne miȝte ȝhe hem longe iwite	But she could not hide them for long
Þat hit ne sscholde ben underȝete.	Without it being discovered.
Nou hadde þe amerail swiche a wone	For the emir had such a custom
Þat everi dai þer scholde come	That every day two maidens
Þre maidenes ut of hire boure	Had to come out of their rooms[175]
To serven him up in þe toure	To serve him up in the tower,
Wiȝ water and cloþ and bacyn	With water and a cloth and basin
940 For to wasschen his hondes in.	For him to wash his hands in.
Þe þridde scholde bringge combe and mirour	The other was to bring a comb and mirror
To serven him wiȝ gret honour.	To serve him with great honor.
And þai þai servede him never so faire	And though he was never served so fairly,
Amorewen scholde anoþer paire.	The next morning another pair had to go.
And mest was woned into þe tour	And the two who went to the tower most
Þerto Clarice and Blauncheflour.	Often were Clarice and Blancheflour.
So long him servede þe maidenes route	The rest of the maidens had served him
Þat hire service was comen aboute.	So that their turn to serve was coming up.
On þe morewen þat þider com Florice	In the morning after Floris came
950 Hit fel to Blauncheflour and to Clarice.	It fell to Blancheflour and Clarice.
Clarice so wel hire mote bitide	Clarice, the best of fortune to her,
Aros up in þe morewentide	Rose up in the morning
And clepede after Blauncheflour	And called for Blancheflour
To wende wiȝ here into þe tour.	To go with her into the tower.
Blauncheflour saide, "Icham comende".	Blancheflour said, "I'm coming!"
Ac here answere was al slepende.	But her answer was half-asleep.
Clarice in þe wai is nome	Clarice made her way,
And wende þat Blauncheflour had come.	Thinking that Blancheflour was following.
Sone so Clarice com in þe tour	As soon as Clarice arrived in the tower
960 Þe ameral asked after Blauncheflour.	The emir asked about Blancheflour.
"Sire", ȝhe saide anonriȝt	"Sire", she answered at once,

---

175 Þre: But a third maiden is never mentioned. Egerton and Cambridge have *twoo/tuo*, which matches better with *paire* (944).

"Ʒhe had iwaked al þis niƷt
And ikneled and iloke
And irad upon hire boke
And bad to God here oreisoun
Þat He þe Ʒive His benisoun
And þe helde longe alive.
Nou sche slepeþ also swiþe
Blaunchefour þat maiden swete
970 Þat hii ne mai nowt comen Ʒhete".
"Certe", said þe kyng
"Nou is hi a swete þing.
Wel auƷte ich here Ʒerne to wive
Whenne Ʒhe bit so for mi live".
Anoþer dai Clarice arist
And haþ Blaunchefour atwist
Whi hi made so longe demoere.
"Aris up and go we ifere".
Blaunchefour saide, "I come anan".
980 And Florice he klippe bigan
And felle aslepe on þise wise.
And after hem gan sore agrise.
Clarice to þe piler cam.
Þe bacyn of gold Ʒhe nam
And had icleped after Blaunchefour
To wende wiƷ here into þe tour.
Ʒhe ne answerede nei ne yo
Þo wende Clarice Ʒhe ware ago.
Sone so Clarice com into þe tour
990 Þe ameral asked after Blaunchefour
Whi and wharfore Ʒhe ne come
As hi was woned to done.
"Ʒhe was arisen ar ich were.
Ich wende here haven ifonden here.
"What ne is Ʒhe nowt icomen Ʒit?"
"Nou Ʒhe me douteƷ al to lit!"
Forht he clepeþ his chaumberleyn
And bit him wende wiƷ alle main
And wite wi þat Ʒhe ne come
1000 As hi was wone bifore to done.
Þe chaumberleyn had undernome
Into hir bour he is icome.
And stant bifore hire bed
And find þar twai neb to neb

"She has been awake all the night,
And knelt, and watched,
And read her book,
And made her prayers to God
That He would give His blessing to you
And keep you alive long.
Now she is sleeping so soundly,
That sweet maid, Blanchefour,
That she is not able to come yet".
"For certain", said the king,
"She is a sweet thing!
I should very much want to marry her,
When she prays for my life so".
Another day came and Clarice arose
And asked Blanchefour scoldingly
Why she made such a long delay.
"Get up, and we will go together".
Blanchefour said, "I'm coming soon".
But Floris pulled her close
And they fell asleep in this way.
Afterwards it would bring them terror.
Clarice came to the doorway.
She took the basin of gold
And called for Blanchefour
To go with her into the tower.
She did not answer yes or no, and so
Clarice thought she had already gone.
As soon as Clarice arrived in the tower,
The emir asked about Blanchefour,
And why she did not come
As she used to do.
"What, she did not come yet?
She was up before I was.
I thought that I would find her here".
"Now she fears me all too little!"[176]
He called his chamberlain forth,
And ordered him to go with all his might
And find out why she did not come
As she was used to doing before.
The chamberlain made his way
And arrived in her bedroom.
He stood before her bed
To find two there, face to face,

---

176 It makes more sense that the emir is saying this. No ME romance MS has quotation punctuation, but in Egerton Clarice does not speak and the line is clearly the emir's.

Neb to neb an mouþ to mouþ.
Wel sone was þat sorewe couþ!
Into þe tour up he steiȝ
And saide his louerd þat he seiȝ.
Þe ameral het his swerd him bring;
1010 I-witen he wolde of þat þinge!
Forht he nimȝ wiȝ alle mayn
Himself and his chaumberlayn
Til þaie come þar þai two laie.
Ȝit was þe slep fast in hire eye.
Þe ameral het hire cloþes keste
A litel bineþen here breste.
Þan seȝ he wel sone anon
Þat on was a man þat oþer a womman.
He quok for anguisse þer he stod.
1020 Hem to quelle was his mod.
He him biþouȝte ar he wolde hem quelle
What þai were þai sscholde him telle
And siþen he þouȝte hem of dawe don.
Þe children awoken under þon.
Þai segh þe swerd over hem idrawe
Adrad þai ben to ben islawe.
Þo bispak þe ameral bold
Wordes þat scholde sone bi told
"Sai me now þou bel ami
1030 Who made þe so hardi
For to come into mi tour
To ligge þer bi Blauncheflour?
To wroþerhale ware ye bore
Ȝe schollen þolie deþ þerfore".
Þanne saide Florice to Blauncheflour
"Of oure lif nis non socour!"
And mercy þai cride on him so swithe
Þat he ȝaf hem respit of here live
Til he hadde after his barenage sent
1040 To awreken him þourgȝ jugement.
Up he bad hem sitte boþe
And don on oþer cloþes
And siþþe he let hem binde fast
And into prisoun hem he cast
Til he had after his barenage sent
To wreken him þourgh jugement.
What helpeȝ hit longe tale to sschewe?
Ich wille ȝou telle at wordes fewe.
Nou al his baronage had undernome
1050 And to þe amerail ȝhe beþ icome.

Body to body, and mouth to mouth.
Very soon the disaster was known!
He rushed into the tower
And told his lord all that he had seen.
The emir ordered him to bring his sword;
He would find out about this affair!
He came forth with all his might,
Himself and his chamberlain,
Until they arrived where the two lay,
With the sleep still in their eyes.
The emir had the covers thrown down
A little beneath their chests.
Then he saw very quickly that one
Was a man and the other a woman.
He quaked with anguish where he stood.
It was his urge to execute them. He
Thought to himself, before he killed them,
They should tell him who they were,
And later he would put them to death.
The couple awoke in the meantime.
They saw the sword drawn over them,
And were in terror of being slain.
Then the bold emir thundered
Words that demanded a prompt answer,
"Tell me now, my pretty lover,
Who made you so brave
To come into my tower
And lie there by Blancheflour?
You were born for ill fortune,
And you will suffer death for it".
Then Floris said to Blancheflour,
"There is no hope for our lives!"
They cried to him for mercy so intently
That he gave their lives reprieve
Until he could send for his barons
To avenge himself through judgment.
He ordered them both to sit up
And put on their clothes,
And then he had them bound fast
And cast them into prison
Until he could send for his baronage
To avenge himself through a verdict.
What good is it to tell a long tale?
I will tell you in a few words.
Now all his barons had arrived,
And came to the emir.

His halle þat was heiȝe ibult
Of kynges and dukes was ifult.
He stod up among hem alle
Bi semblaunt swiþe wroþt wiȝalle.
He saide, "Lordingges of mochel honour
Ȝe han herd speken of Blauncheflour
Hou ich hire bouȝt dere apliȝt
For seven sithes hire wiȝt of gold.
For hire faired and hire chere
1060 Iich hire bouȝte allinge so dere
For ich þouȝte wiȝouten wene
Hire have ihad to mi quene.
Bifore hire bed miself I com
And fond bi hire an naked grom.
Þo þai were me so wroþe
I þouȝte to han iqueld hem boþe!
Iich was so wroȝ and so wod
And ȝit ich wiȝdrouȝ mi mod.
Fort ich have after ȝou isent
1070 To awreke me þourȝ jugement.
Nou ye witen hou hit is agon
Awreke me swiþe of mi fon!"
Þo spak a king of on lond
"We han iherd þis schame and schonde
Ac er we hem to deye wreke
We scholle heren þo children speke
What þai wil speke and sigge
Ȝif þai ouȝt aȝein wil allegge.
Hit ner nowt riȝt jugement
1080 Wiȝouten answere to acoupement".
. . . .

C   Þe king of Nubie sede þo,
"For soþ, ne schal hit noȝt go so.
Hit is riȝt þurez alle þing
Felons inome hond habbing,
For to suffre jugement
Biþute ansuere oþer acupement".
. . . .

A   After þe children nou men sendeȝ
Hem to brenne fur men tendeȝ.
Twaie Sarazins forþ hem bringeȝ
1090 Toward here deþ sore wepinge.
Dreri were þis schildren two

His hall, which was built high,
Was filled with kings and dukes.
He stood up among them all,
With his expression one of great anger.
He said, "High honorable lords,
You have heard Blanchefloir spoken about,
How I bought her dearly and rightfully
For seven times her weight in gold.
For her fairness and her beauty,
I bought her in full at such expense,
For I thought, without a doubt,
To have her as my queen.
I stood myself in front of her bed
And found with her a naked youth.
At the time they were so hateful to me
That I wanted to kill them both!
I was so enraged and so crazed,
And yet I held back my emotions.
On that basis I have sent for you,
To avenge me through your decision.
Now that you know how it happened,
Avenge me swiftly on my foes!"
Then a king of one land spoke up,
"We have heard this shame and disgrace.
But before we condemn them to death,
We will hear the children speak
Whatever they wish to say, to see
If they have anything as a defense.
It would not be a just deliberation
Without an answer to the accusation".
. . . .

The King of Nubia spoke up then,[177]
"In truth, it should not go that way.
It is right, in all cases,
That felons caught red-handed in theft
Should suffer their judgment without
Defense against the accusation".
. . . .

After this, men sent for the children,
Intending for them to burn in fire.
Two Saracens brought them forth
Toward their death, as they wept bitterly.
The two lovers were inconsolable,

177 *Þe king of Nubie*: The king of Egypt's objection in Cambridge MS that the two forfeit their right to a defense because they are caught in the act explains why Floris and Blancheflor are not permitted to speak, though it does not conform to Islamic legal codes, which require that defendants have a right to answer to accusations.

Nou aiþer biwepeʒ oþeres wo.
Florice saide to Blauncheflour
"Of oure lif nis non socour.
ʒif manken hit þoli miʒt
Twies ischolde die wiʒ riʒt
One for miself anoþer for þe
For þis deþ þou hast for me".
Blaunchflour saide aʒen þo
1100 "Þe gelt is min of oure boþer wo!"
Florice drow forþ þe ring
Þat his moder him ʒaf at his parting.
"Have nou þis ring lemman min.
Þou ne schalt nowt die whiles hit is þin".
Blaunchflour saide þo
"So ne schal hit never go
Þat þis ring schal ared me.
Ne mai ihc no deþ on þe se".
Florice þe ring here arauʒt
1110 And hi him aʒein hit bitauʒt.
On hire he had þe ring iþrast
And hi hit haueʒ awai ikast.
A duk hit seʒ and beʒgh to grounde
An was glad þat ring he founde.
On þis maner þe children come
Weping to þe fur and to hire dome
Bifore al þat folk þai ware ibrowt.
Dreri was hire boþer þouʒt
Þer nas non so sterne man
1120 Þat þise children loked upan
Þat þai ne wolde alle ful fawe
Here jugement have wiʒdrawe
And wiʒ grete garisoun hem begge
ʒif þai dorste speke oþer sigge.
For Florice was so fair a yongling
And Blaunchflour so swete a þing.
Of men and wimmen þat beþ nouþe
Þat gon and riden and spekeþ wiʒ mouþe
Beþ non so fair in hire gladnesse
1130 Als þai ware in hire sorewenesse.
No man ne knewe hem þat hem was wo
Bi semblaunt þat þai made þo
But bi þe teres þat þai schadde
And fillen adoun bi here nebbe.
Þe ameral was so wroþ and wod
Þat he ne miʒt wiʒdraw his mod.
He bad binde þe children faste

As each wept for the other's grief.
Floris said to Blanchefour,
"For our lives there is no hope.
If it were possible for a human being,
I would rightfully die twice,
Once for myself, a second time for you,
For your death is because of me".
Blanchflour then answered,
"The guilt is mine for both our woe!"
Floris drew off the ring
That his mother gave him at their parting.
"Take this ring, my beloved.
You will not die while it is yours".
Blanchflour replied,
"It will never happen so
That this ring will save me.
I will not see you put to death".
Floris handed the ring to her,
And she passed it back to him.
He thrust the ring on her,
And she flung it away.
A duke saw it and bent to the ground,
And was glad to find that ring.
In this manner the children came weeping,
To the fire and to their doom,
As they were brought before all the people.
Both of them seemed so pitiable
That there was no man so stern
Who looked upon these children
Who did not wish fervently
To see their judgment withdrawn,
And to buy them with a great ransom if
They might only dare speak out or protest.
For Floris was so fair a young man,
And Blanchflour was so sweet a thing.
Of men and women who live now,
That walk and ride and speak with mouths,
None are so fair in their happiness
As those two were in their sorrow.
No man could see that they were full of
Grief by the bearing that they had
Except by the tears that they shed
Which fell down their faces.
The emir was so furious and livid
That he could not control his temper.
He ordered the couple bound fast

Into þe fir he bad hem caste.
Þilke duk þat þe gold ryng hadde
1140 Nou to speke rewþe he hadde.
Fain he wolde hem helpe to live
And tolde hou þai for þe ring strive.
Þe ameral het hem aȝen clepe
For he wolde þo schildren speke.
He askede Florice what he hete
And he told him swiȝe skete
"Sire", he saide, "ȝif hit were þi wille
Þou ne auȝtest nowt þis maiden spille
Ac sire let aquelle me
1150 And lat þat maiden alive be".
Blaunchefloor saide þo
"Þe gilt is min of oure boþer wo".
And þe ameral saide þo
"Iwis ye schulle die bo!
Wiȝ wreche ich wille me awreke.
Ȝe ne scholle nevere go no speke!"
His swerd he braid out of his sscheþe
Þe children for to do to deþe
And Blaunchefloor pult forþ hire swire
1160 And Florice gan hire aȝein tire.
"Ich am a man ich schal go bifore.
Þou ne auȝtest nouȝt mi deȝ acore".
Florice forht his swire pulte
And Blaunchefloor aȝein hit brutte.
Al þat iseȝen þis
Þerfore sori weren iwis
And saide "dreri may we be
Bi swiche children swich rewþe se!"
Þ'ameral wroþ þai he were
1170 Boþe him chaungege mod and chere
For aiþer for oþer wolde die
And he segh so mani a weping eȝe.
And for he hadde so mochel loved þe mai
Weping he turned his heued awai
And his swerd hit fil to grounde.
He ne miȝte hit helde in þat stounde.
Þilke duk þat þe ring found
Wiȝ þameral spak and round
And ful wel þerwiȝ he spedde
1180 Þe children þerwiȝ fram deþe he redde.
"Sire", he saide, "hit is litel pris
Þise children to slen iwis.
Hit is þe wel more worsschipe

And thrown into the fire.
The same duke who found the gold ring
Was now moved by compassion to speak.
He was eager to help them to live and
Explained how they argued over the ring.
The emir had them called back,
For he wanted the two to speak.
He asked Floris what his name was,
And he told him very promptly,
"Sire", he said, "if it should be your will,
You ought not to let this maiden die
But, sire, to let me be executed,
And let the maiden go alive".
Blancheflour then protested,
"The guilt is mine for both of our troubles".
The emir then thundered,
"For certain, both of you will die!
I will avenge myself with anger.
You will never walk or speak again!"
He drew his sword out of its sheath
To put the couple to death,
And Blancheflour thrust forth her neck,
And Floris pulled her back.
"I am a man, I will go before you.
You should not suffer my death".
Floris presented his neck forth
And Blancheflour drew it back.
All who saw this
Were remorseful for it, I know,
And said, "It is too much sadness
To see these youngsters in such anguish!"
The emir, as angry as he was,
Changed both his mood and his expression,
For each was ready to die for the other,
And he saw so many weeping eyes. And
Because he had loved the maid so much,
He turned his head away in tears
And let his sword fell to the ground.
He could not hold it at that moment.
The duke who had found the ring
Spoke and whispered with the emir,
And fared successfully for it,
For he saved the couple from death.
"Sire", he said, "there is little praise
In slaying these children, for sure.
It would be much more admirable

Florice conseile þat þou wite	For you to know Floris' confidante,
Who him tauȝte þilke gin	Who showed him the trick
For to come þi tour wiȝin	To come inside your tower,
And who þat him brouȝte þar	And who brought him there,
Þe bet of oþer þou miȝt be war".	So that you might be more aware of others".
Þan saide þameraile to Florice þo	Then the emir said to Floris,
1190 "Tel me who þe tauȝte herto".	"Tell me who taught you to do this".
"Þat", quaþ Florice, "ne schal I nevere do	"That", replied Floris, "I will never do,
But ȝif hit ben forȝiven also	Unless there is also forgiveness
Þat þe gin me tauȝte þerto.	For him who taught me the trick.
Arst ne schal hit never be do".	Before that it will never be done".
Alle þai praied þerfore iwis;	All there pleaded for this, for sure;
Þe ameral graunted þis.	The emir granted it.
Nou everi word Florice haþ him told	Then Floris told him every detail,
Hou þe made was fram him sold	How the maid was sold from him,
And hou he was of Speyne a kyngges sone	And how he was a king's son from Spain,
1200 For hire love þider icome	Who had come for the sake of her love
To fonden wiȝ som gin	To try with some plan
Þat faire maiden for to win;	To win that fair maiden;
And hou þourgh his gold and his garisoun	And how through his gold and treasures,
Þe porter was his man bicom	The porter had become his man,
And hou he was in þe coupe ibore.	And how he was carried in the basket.
And alle þis oþer lowen þerfore.	All the others laughed over this.
Nou þe amerail wel him mote bitide	Now the emir, may he fare well,
Florice he sette next his side	Set Floris by his side
And made him stonde þer upriȝt	And made him stand there upright,
1210 And haþ idubbed him to kniȝt	And dubbed him a knight,
And bad he scholde wiȝ him be	And asked if he would stay with him
Wiȝ þe formast of his mene.	With the leaders of his retinue.
Florice fallet to his fet	Floris fell to his feet and begged him
And bit him ȝif him his lef so swet.	To give him his love so sweet.
Þe ameral ȝaf him his lemman.	The emir granted him his beloved.
Alle þe oþere him þanked þan.	All the others thanked the emir.
To one chirche he let hem bringge	He had them ushered to a temple,[178]
And wedde here wiȝ here owene ringge.	And they were wedded with their own ring.
Nou boþe þis children alle for bliss	Now both of these children, all for bliss,
1220 Fil þe amerales fet to kis.	Fell at the emir's feet to kiss them,
And þourgh conseil of Blauncheflour	And through Blancheflour's counsel,
Clarice was fet doun of þe tour	Clarice was fetched down from the tower,
And þe amerale here wedded to quene.	And the emir wedded her as his queen.[179]
Þere was feste swiþe breme	There was a feast so sumptuous

---

178 *Chirche*: the Saracens are unlikely to have churches for just such an occasion. OF had variations on *moschea*, but the MED gives the first recorded use of musket/moseak in ME only much later in Mandeville's *Travels*, around 1400. The poet likely means 'place of worship' generically.

179 The French poet stresses that the emir gives up his practice of annually repudiating his wives for Clarice (Taylor, note to 1279, his lineation).

I ne can nowt tellen þe sonde	That I cannot describe all the courses,
Ac þe richest feste in londe.	But it was the richest feast in the land.
Nas hit nowt longe after þan	It was not long after then
Þat Florice tidingge ne cam	That the news came to Floris
Þat his fader þe kyng was ded.	That his father the king was dead.

1230	And al þe barnage ȝaf him red	All of the baronage gave him advice
	Þat he scholde wenden hom	That he should go home
	And underfongen his kyndom.	And take charge of his kingdom.
	At ameral he nom his leve	He took his leave of the emir,
	And he him bad wiȝ him bileve.	Who asked him to stay with him.
	Þanne bispak þe ameral	Then the emir said,
	"Ȝif þou wilt do Florice bi mi conseil	"Floris, if you will follow my wishes,
	Dwelle here and wend nowt hom.	Stay here, and do not go home.
	Ich wille þe ȝiven a kyngdom	I will give you a kingdom
	Also longe and also brod	As long and broad as well
1240	Als evere ȝit þi fader bod".	As anything your father offered".
	"I nel bileve for no winne.	"I won't stay for any such joys.
	To bidde me hit were sinne".	To require me to would be a sin".

. . . .

C	And to hire he haþ iȝolde	To Clarice he gave in thanks
	Twenti pond of ride golde.	Twenty pounds of red gold,
	And to Daris þat him so taȝte,	And to Dary, who had helped him,
	Twenti pund he araȝte.	He also bestowed twenty pounds.
	And alle þat for him duden eidel,	And anyone who did anything for him
	He ȝeld here while suþe wel.	He also rewarded well after.

. . . .

A	Þai bitauȝt þe amerail oure Driȝt	They commended the emir to our Lord,
1250	And þai com hom whan þai miȝt;	And they came home as soon as they could;
	And let croune him to king	And Floris was crowned king,
	And hire to quene þat swete þing	And she as queen, that sweet creature.
	And underfeng Cristendom of prestes honde	And he received baptism by priests' hands,
	And þonkede God of alle His sonde.	And thanked God for all His works.
	Nou ben þai boþe ded	Now they are both dead,
	Crist of Hevene houre soules led.	Their souls led by Christ to Heaven.
	Nou is þis tale browt to þ'ende	Now this tale is brought to the end,
	Of Florice and of his lemman hende	Of Floris and his fair sweetheart,
	How after bale hem com bote.	How after their troubles came relief.
1260	So wil oure Louerd þat ous mote	So that our Lord may do the same for us,
	Amen siggeȝ also	Say 'Amen' as well,
	And ich schal helpe ȝou þerto.	And I will join you in it.

1263	Explicit	The End

Havelok the Dane

Havelok the Dane is one of the older extant English romances, dating to approximately 1285. Analogues of the story date back to Geoffrey Gaimar's *Estorie des Engles* (1140) and the twelfth-century *Lai d'Havelok*. The story is the 'male Cinderella' type where Havelok's father, king of Denmark, dies and a disloyal steward attempts to eliminate Havelok, who is rescued by a fisherman and raised in England. In the double-plot structure, the English king also dies and his daughter Goldeboru is disinherited. Havelok is raised a peasant but distinguishes himself, avenging himself on both traitors and winning Goldeboru as queen.

Like *Guy of Warwick*, the poem has supposed quasi-historical content, but *Havelok*'s currency for the Anglo-Danish communities of northeastern England gives its setting a unusual realism; unlike the usual generic locations, Lincoln and Grimsby are real places, and claims were made until well into the nineteenth century about the rock that Havelok throws in the games, identifying it in various places in the region. The medieval seal of the town of Grimsby has the figures of Havelok, Grim, and Goldeboru on it.

Much criticism of the poem has dealt with its supposedly low-class milieu or audience– the story emphasizes the simple joys of feasting, wrestling, and children rather than aristocratic values of *treupe* or penitential vows. Yet a focus on class locks the poem within a later medieval timeframe it does not belong to. Dominique Battles argues in her recent *Cultural Difference and Material Culture in Middle English Romance* that many romances perform a coded defiance of Norman culture, and in *Havelok* the idealized virtues of the warrior-king reflect earthier Anglo-Saxon and Germanic norms more than Anglo-Norman ones. Similarities have been seen between *Havelok* and *Beowulf*: both are narrated by a minstrel, with the call to attention "herkneth to me" (1) sounding much like "Hwaet!" There is a curious absence of the middle barony in the poem and the courtly mores they aspired to. Most of the action takes

From Harriet B. Barbour, Old English Tales Retold, 1924; illustration by Rodney Thomson

place outdoors, and often in mud. With Ubbe Havelok drinks *pyment* (1549), a mix of mead and grape juice, and the minstrel narrator is also evidently a man of the people who requests "ful god ale" (14) rather than wine.

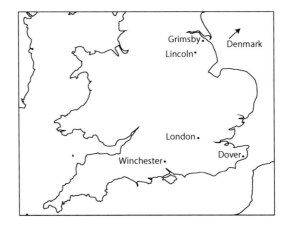

Another interesting reading is provided by Julie Couch in "The Vulnerable Hero: *Havelok* and the Revision of Romance", who sees a poetic stress on Havelok's vulnerability at the hands of others, sentimentalizing and intensifying his later victories. The reading is further support for *Havelok*'s rather natively English roots, in that the text betrays a sympathy for childlike weakness different from more continental protagonists such as Horn, who has the command of a king even as a boy. Moreover, Havelok's innocence works to redeem other characters, helping to explain both Grim's and Ubbe's oddly rapid character changes.

Havelok the Dane survives in one unique manuscript: Bodleian MS Laud Misc. 108 (c. 1300), with fragments in Cambridge University Library, Add. 4407. I take as my text source Walter W. Skeat, ed. *The Lay of Havelok the Dane* (1868). Skeat modernizes the text's thorn and yogh letters. One leaf is missing from Laud after fol. 211 of about 180 lines, and so as an editorial supposition I give some lines from the Anglo-Norman *Lai D'Havelok* (c. 1200), supplied from M. Francisque Michel, ed., *Lai D'Havelok Le Danois* (Paris: Silvestre, 1834). As the *Lai* is shorter and somewhat dissimilar only a brief and tentative reconstruction is possible.

L: Laud Misc. 108
C: Cambridge Add. 4407
A: Anglo-Norman *Lai*

1 L	Herknet to me gode men	Listen to me, good men,
	Wives maydnes and alle men	Wives, maidens, and everyone else
	Of a tale þat ich you wile telle	To a tale that I will tell you
	Wo so it wile here and þer-to dwelle.	For whoever wants to stay and hear it.
	Þe tale is of Havelok i-maked	The story is about Havelok,
	Wil he was litel he yede ful naked.	Who when he was little went half-naked.
	Havelok was a ful god gome	Havelok was the finest of men,
	He was ful god in everi trome.	The best in every company.
	He was þe wicteste man at nede	He was the best man in need
10	Þat þurte riden on ani stede!	Who might ride on any steed!
	Þat ye mowen nou y-here	So that you may hear me,
	And þe tale ye mowen y-lere	And so that you might know the tale,
	At the beginning of ure tale	At the beginning of our story,
	Fil me a cuppe of ful god ale.	Fill me a cup of your best ale.
	And wile drinken her y spelle	And while drinking, while I tell it,
	Þat Crist us shilde alle fro Helle!	May Christ shield us all from Hell!
	Krist late us hevere so for to do	May Christ protect us forever
	Þat we moten comen Him to	So that we might come to Him,
	And wit þat it mote ben so	And so that it may be so,[180]
20	*Benedicamus Domino*!	Let us praise the Lord!
	Here y schal biginnen a rym	Here I will begin the rhyme,
	Krist us yeve wel god fyn!	And may Christ give us a good end!
	The rym is maked of Havelok	The rhyme is about Havelok,
	A stalworþi man in a flok.	A steady man to have in a crowd.
	He was þe stalworþeste man at nede	He was the sturdiest man in need
	Þat may riden on ani stede.	Who might ride on any steed.
	It was a king bi are dawes	There was a king in days of old,
	That in his time were gode lawes	Who in his time made good laws
	He dede maken an ful wel holden.	That were well and fully obeyed.
30	Hym lovede yung him lovede holde	He was loved by young, loved by old,
	Erl and barun dreng and kayn	By earl and baron, vassal and retainer,[181]
	Knict bondeman and swain	Knight, bondsman, and servant,
	Wydues maydnes prestes and clerkes	Widows, maidens, priests, and clerks,
	And al for hise gode werkes.	And all for his good works.
	He lovede God with al his micth	He loved God with all his might,
	And holi kirke and soth ant ricth.	And the holy church, and truth and justice.
	Ricth-wise man he lovede alle	He loved all righteous men,
	And overal made hem forto calle.	And everywhere had them at his call.
	Wreieres and wrobberes made he falle	He made traitors and robbers fail,

---

180 *And, witthat it mote ben so*: Herzman et al. connect line 19 to 20, whereas Skeat feels that 19 continues 18. Skeat gives the word division as *and wit that it mote ben so*, "and see that it may be so". *Havelok the Dane*, ed. Ronald B. Herzman, Graham Drake, and Eve Salisbury, *Four Romances of England* (Kalamazoo, MI: Medieval Institute Publications, 1999), http://www.lib.rochester.edu/camelot/teams/danefrm.htm; Walter W. Skeat, ed., *The Lay of Havelok the Dane* (London: EETS, 1868).

181 *Dreng and thayn*: The list seems to be in decreasing level of social rank from nobility (earl and baron), to non-noble landholders, down to non-free peasants (bondsmen). The food chain is complicated and evolves between Anglo-Saxon and Norman England, but Skeat states that a dreng held land in exchange for military service and a thane provided lesser services (note for line 31, page 88).

40 And hated hem so man doth galle.	And hated them like men hate bitter drink.
Utlawes and theves made he bynde	Outlaws and thieves were bound,
Alle that he micthe fynde	All that he might find,
And heye hengen on galwe-tre.	And hung high on the gallows tree.
For hem ne yede gold ne fe.	From them he took neither gold nor bribe.
In that time a man þat bore	In that time a man who bore
Wel fyfty pund y woth or more	Upwards of fifty pounds, I know, or more,
Of red gold up-on hijs bac	Of red gold on his back,
In a male with or blac	In a pouch, white or black, would not
Ne funde he non that him misseyde	Meet anyone who would harm him,
50 Ne with ivele on hond leyde.	Or lay hands on him with evil intent.
Þanne micthe chapmen fare	Merchants could travel then
Þuruth Englond wit here ware	Throughout England with their wares,
And baldelike beye and sellen	And boldly buy and sell, anywhere they
Overal þer he wilen dwellen	Wanted to stay, in fine towns and in
In gode burwes and þer-fram.	The countryside. They would not meet
Ne funden he non þat dede hem sham	Anyone to cause them trouble
Þat he ne weren sone to sorwe brouth	Who would not soon be brought to sorrow,
An pouere maked and browt to nouth.	Made poor, and reduced to nothing.
Þanne was Engelond at hayse!	England was at ease then!
60 Michel was swich a king to preyse	There was much to praise about such a king
Þat held so Englond in grith.	Who held England in such peace.
Krist of Hevene was him with;	Christ in Heaven was with him;
He was Engelondes blome!	He was England's bloom!
Was non so bold lond to Rome	There was no lord as far as Rome
Þat durste upon his bringhe	Who dared to bring to his people
Hunger ne here wicke þinghe.	Hunger, invasion, or wicked causes.
Hwan he felede hise foos	When the king defeated his enemies,
He made hem lurken and crepen in wros.	He made them lurk and creep in corners.
Þe hidden hem alle and helden hem stille	They all hid and kept themselves quiet,
70 And diden al his herte wille.	And did all his heart's bidding.
Ricth he lovede of alle þinge.	But he loved justice above all things.
To wronge micht him no man bringe	No man could corrupt him into wrong,
Ne for silver ne for gold	Not for silver or for gold,
So was he his soule hold.	So faithful was he to his soul.
To þe faderles was he rath;	To the orphaned he was their protector;
Wo so dede hem wrong or lath	Whoever did them wrong or harm,
Were it clerc or were it knicth	No matter if they were a cleric or knight,
He dede hem sone to haven ricth.	Was soon brought to justice by him.
And wo diden widuen wrong	And for anyone who did widows wrong,
80 Were he nevre knicth so strong	There was no knight so strong
Þat he ne made him sone kesten	That he wouldn't soon have him thrown
And in feteres ful faste festen.	Into fetters and fasten them tightly.
And wo so dide maydne shame	And as for whoever shamed a maiden
Of hire bodi or brouth in blame	By her body, or brought her into blame,
Bute it were bi hire wille	Unless it was by her will,

He made him sone of limes spille.　　　He made him lose some of his limbs.[182]
He was te beste knith at nede　　　　The king was the best knight in need
Þat hevere micthe riden on stede　　　Who might ever ride on a steed,
Or wepne wagge or folc ut lede.　　　Or hold a weapon, or lead out an army.

90　Of knith ne hauede he nevere drede　He was never so afraid of any knight that
Þat he ne sprong forth so sparke　　He would not spring forth
/ of glede　　　　　　　　　　　　Like sparks from a fire, and let them
And lete him knawe of hise hand-dede　Know by the deeds of his hand how
Hw he couþe with wepne spede.　　　He could triumph with a weapon. With
And oþer he refte him hors or wede　　Others he took their horses or clothes,[183]
Or made him sone handes sprede　　　Or made them quickly spread their hands,
And, "Louerd merci" loude grede.　　And cry loudly, "Mercy, Lord!"
He was large and no wicth gnede.　　He was generous and by no means miserly.
Hauede he non so god brede　　　　He never had bread so good
Ne on his bord non so god shrede　　On his table or a morsel so fine

100　Þat he ne wolde þorwit fede　　　That he would not give it to feed
Poure þat on fote yede　　　　　　The poor who went on foot,
Forto haven of Him þe mede　　　In order to receive from Him the reward
Þat for us wolde on rode blede　　That He bled on the cross for us to have–
Crist that al kan wisse and rede　　Christ, who can guide and protect all
Þat evere woneth in ani þede.　　Who ever live in any land.
Þe king was hoten Aþelwold.　　The king was called Athelwold.
Of word of wepne he was bold.　With speech and weapons he was bold.
In Engeland was nevre knicth　In England there was never a knight
Þat betere hel þe lond to ricth.　Who better held the land in justice.

110　Of his bodi ne hauede he eyr　But he had fathered no heir
Bute a mayden swiþe fayr　　Except for a very fair maiden
Þat was so yung þat sho ne couþe　Who was so young that she could not
Gon on fote ne speke wit mouþe.　Walk on foot or speak with her mouth.
Þan him tok an ivel strong　　Then he was taken by a violent illness,[184]
Þat he wel wiste and under-fong　So that he knew well and understood
Þat his deth was comen him on　That his death was approaching.
And seyde, "Crist wat shal y don?　And he said, "Christ, what should I do?
Louerd wat shal me to rede?　Lord, how should I be advised?
I woth ful wel ich have mi mede　I know full well I will have my reward,

120　Hw shal nou mi douhter fare?　But how will my daughter fare?
Of hire have ich michel kare　I have great worries about her
Sho is mikel in mi þouth;　And she is much in my thoughts;
Of me self is me rith nowt.　I have no concerns about myself.

---

182 Although the Wife of Bath's knight is initially condemned to death for rape, sexual assault in Anglo-Saxon England was seen more as a property crime against the woman's family and would usually have resulted in a stiff fine. Here Athelwold's untypical strictness is lauded by the poet.

183 *Other he refte him hors or wede*: A victorious army despoiled the defeated. French and Hale note, "The practice was deplored by moralists as unchristian, but is a matter of course in the romances". Here Athelwold receives no censure. Walter H. French and Charles B. Hale, eds., *Middle English Metrical Romances* (New York: Prentice-Hall, 1930), 78.

184 *Him tok an ivel strong*: ME romance seems to regularly use such poetic formulas for illness. See also *Bevis of Hampton*, 179 where the queen fakes her oncoming death. Yet in *Amis and Amiloun*, 504 Amis suffers from a *malady*.

No selcouth is þouh me be wo!

Sho ne kan speke ne sho kan go.

Yif scho couþe on horse ride

And a thousande men bi hire syde

And sho were comen intil helde

And Engelond sho couþe welde

130 And don hem of þar hire were queme

An hire bodi couþe yeme.

No wolde me nevere ivele like

Me þou ich were in Hevene-riche!"

Quanne he hauede þis pleinte maked

Þer-after stronglike quaked.

He sende writes sone on-on

After his erles evere-ich on

And after hise baruns riche and poure

Fro Rokesburw al into Dovere

140 That he shulden comen swiþe

Til him that was ful unbliþe.

To þat stede þer he lay

In harde bondes nicth and day.

He was so faste wit yvel fest

Þat he ne mouthe haven no rest.

He ne mouthe no mete hete

Ne he ne mouchte no lyþe gete.

Ne non of his ivel þat couþe red

Of him ne was nouth buten ded.

150 Alle þat the writes herden

Sorful an sori til him ferden.

He wrungen hondes and wepen sore

And yerne preyden Cristes hore

Þat He wolde turnen him

Ut of þat yvel þat was so grim.

Þanne he weren comen alle

Bifor þe king into the halle

At Winchestre þer he lay,

"Welcome", he seyde, "be ye ay!

160 Ful michel þank kan y yow

That ye aren comen to me now".

Quanne he weren alle set

It is no wonder that I am anxious!

She cannot speak, nor can she walk.

If she knew how to ride a horse,

With a thousand men by her side,

And she came to age,

She could rule England

And do to others as she pleased

And would know how to rule herself.

I would have no worries, even if I

Were far away in Heaven's realm!"[185]

When he had made this plea,

He shivered strongly after.[186]

Straightaway he sent out writs

To his earls, each one of them,

And to his barons, rich and poor,

From Roxburgh through to Dover,[187]

That they should come quickly

To him, as he was very unwell,

To the place where he lay

In hard bonds by night and day.

He was so trapped in death's grip

That he could have no rest.

He could take no food,

Nor might he have any comfort.

No one could advise him in his gloom,

For he was little more than dead.

All who obeyed the writs

Journeyed to him in sorrow and grief.

They wrung their hands and wept bitterly,

And earnestly prayed for Christ's grace,

That He would release him

From his illness which was so grim.

When they had all come

Before the king in the hall

Where he lay at Winchester,

He said, "You are forever welcome!

I give you great thanks

That you have come to me now".

When they were all seated

---

185 The poet's predilection for extended negative constructions, combined with ME's tendency to pile on multiple negatives, sometimes results in confusing lines such as this. The poet may intend the *yif* in 126 to be more like unless, which would make the entire clause from 126 to 131 a conditional: "Unless she could rule England I would be unhappy even if I were in Heaven". Skeat has "It would never displease me, not even if I were in Heaven" (106), but the reading is a strange one.

186 The poet tends to omit pronouns. Again, combined with early ME's weak distinction between single and plural pronouns, at times referents are less than clear.

187 *Rokesburw*: Roxburgh, about 70 km south of Edinburgh, was an often-disputed fort on the Scottish border, and some have tried to date the poem based on its possession at the time. The expression suggests totality: "from sea to shining sea".

And þe king aueden i-gret
He greten and gouleden and gouen
/ hem ille
And he bad hem alle ben stille
And seyde, "Þat greting helpeth nouth
For al to dede am ich brouth.
Bute now ye sen þat i shal deye
Nou ich wille you alle preye
170 Of mi douther þat shal be
Yure leuedi after me.
Wo may yemen hire so longe
Boþen hire and Engelonde
Til þat she mowe winan of helde
And þa she mowe yemen and welde?"
He answereden and seyden an-on
Bi Crist and bi seint Jon
That þerl Godrigh of Cornwayle
Was trewe man wit-uten faile
180 Wis man of red wis man of dede
And men haueden of him mikel drede.
"He may hire alþer-best yeme
Til þat she mowe wel ben quene".
Þe king was payed of that rede.
A wol fair cloth bringen he dede
And þer-on leyde þe messebok
Þe caliz and þe pateyn ok
Þe corporaus þe messe-gere.
Þer-on he garte þe erl suere
190 Þat he sholde yemen hire wel
With-uten lac wit-uten tel
Til þat she were twelf winter hold
And of speche were bold
And þat she couþe of curteysye
Gon and speken of luue-drurye
And til þat she loven þoucte
Wom so hire to gode thoucte;
And þat he shulde hire yeve
Þe beste man that micthe live
200 Þe beste fayreste the strangest ok.
Þat dede he him sweren on þe bok.

And the king had greeted them,
They wept and wailed and carried on
Mournfully, until the king
Asked that they all be quiet, and said
"This crying does nothing to help,
For I am brought to death.
But now that you see I am dying,
I will ask you all at this time
About my daughter, who will be
Your sovereign lady after me.
Who will guard her for the time,
Both her and England,
Until she is a woman of age,[188]
And she can guide and care for herself?"
They answered and said at once,
By Christ and by Saint John,
That Earl Godrich of Cornwall
Was a faithful man, without doubt,
A wise man in counsel, a wise man in deed,
And men had great deference for him.
"He can best take care of her,
Until she may be queen in full".
The king was pleased with that advice.
He had a beautiful woolen cloth brought,
And laid the mass-book on it,
The chalice, and the Eucharist plate as well,
And the communion cloth and vestments.
Thereupon he made the earl swear
That he would protect her well,
Without fail, without reproach,
Until she was twelve years old[189]
And she was confident in speech
And could understand court etiquette
And the manners and speech of courtship,
And until she might love
Whoever she felt seemed best to her;
And that he would give to her
The highest man who might ever live,
The best, fairest, and the strongest as well.
All this the king had him swear on the

---

188 *Wman*: The MED has no other text with this spelling of woman, and it is used again in 281. The scribe tends to omit letters. Skeat has *winan*, used here.

189 *Twelf winter hold*: Middle English poetically counts years as winters. A noble woman might have been eligible for marriage after first menstruation, between 12 and 15, although non-noble women would have married later. Shakespeare's Juliet is similarly fourteen and her nurse is concerned that she is still unmarried. But note line 259 where Godrich cynically delays her advancement until age 20.

And þanne shulde he Engelond	Book. And then he would bestow
Al bitechen in-to hire hond.	All of England into her hand.
Quanne þat was sworn on his wise	When that was sworn in this way,
Þe king dede þe mayden arise	The king had the maiden rise,
And þe erl hire bitaucte	And committed her to the earl
And al the lond he evere awcte	Along with all the land he ever owned,
Engelonde everi del	Every part of England,
And preide he shulde yeme hire wel.	And prayed that he would keep her well.
210 Þe king ne mowcte don no more	The king could do no more,
But yerne preyede godes ore	But earnestly prayed for God's grace
And dede him hoslen wel and shrive	And took communion and confession,
I woth fif hundred siþes and five	Five hundred and five times, I know,
An ofte dede him sore swinge	And repeatedly scourged himself severely,
And wit hondes smerte dinge	And beat himself painfully with his own
So þat þe blod ran of his fleys	Hands so that the blood ran from his flesh,
Þat tendre was and swiþe neys.	Which had been so tender and soft.
And sone gaf it evere-il del	He made his will out carefully,
He made his quiste swiþe wel.	And soon after had every part affirmed.
220 Wan it was gouen ne micte men finde	When it was executed, no man could find
So mikel men micte him in winde	So much as a burial sheet to wrap him in
Of his in arke ne in chiste	Of his in any coffer or chest
In Engelond þat noman wiste	That anyone knew of in England, for
For al was youen faire and wel	Everything was disposed of, fair and clear,
Þat him was leved no catel.	So that no possessions were left to him.
Þanne he hauede ben ofte swngen	When he had been repeatedly scourged,
Ofte shriven and ofte dungen	Confessed, and beaten,
"In manus tuas Louerde", he seyde	He said, "Into your hands, O Lord",[190]
Her þat he þe speche leyde.	And set aside his words then.
230 To Jhesu Crist bigan to calle	He called on Jesus Christ
And deyede biforn his heymen alle.	And died before all of his noblemen.
Þan he was ded þere micte men se	When he was dead, men could see
Þe meste sorwe that micte be.	The greatest sorrow that might be.
Þer was sobbing siking and sor	There was sobbing, sighing, and grief,
Handes wringing and drawing bi hor.	Hands wringing, and clutching of hair.
Alle greten swiþe sore	Everyone there wept bitterly,
Riche and poure þat þere wore	All the rich and poor that were there,
An mikel sorwe haueden alle	And all had great sorrow,
Leuedyes in boure knictes in halle.	Ladies in chambers, and knights in the hall.
240 Quan þat sorwe was somdel laten	When the mourning had subsided
And he haueden longe graten	Somewhat, and they had wept a long time,
Belles deden he sone ringen	They soon had bells rung,

---

190 *In manus tuas, Louerde*: Christ's last words before death, in Luke 23:46: "Into your hands, O Lord, I commit my spirit".
The poet emphasizes Athelwold's Christian saintliness with the reference and with his final acts of charity, although unlike
Christ, Athelwold's penitential scourging is voluntary. Self-flagellation for mortification of the flesh was practiced in some
austere monasteries until it grew into extremes such as the Flagellants lay movement of the fourteenth century. The church
largely suppressed the practice afterward.

Monkes and prestes messe singen
And sauteres deden he manie reden
Þat God self shulde his soule leden
Into Hevene biforn His sone
And þer wit-uten hende wone.
Þan he was to þe erþe brouth
Þe riche erl ne foryat nouth
250 Þat he ne dede al Engelond
Sone sayse intil his hond.
And in þe castels leth he do
Þe knictes he micte tristen to
And alle þe Englis dede he swere
Þat he shulden him ghod fey baren.
He yaf alle men þat god þoucte
Liven and deyen til þat him moucte
Til þat þe kinges dowter wore
Twenti winter hold and more.
260 Þanne he hauede taken þis oth
Of erles baruns lef and loth
Of knictes cherles fre and þewe
Justises dede he maken newe
Al Engelond to faren þorw
Fro Dovere into Rokesborw.
Schireves he sette bedels and greyves
Grith-sergeans wit longe gleyves
To yemen wilde wodes and paþes
Fro wicke men that wolde don scaþes
270 And forto haven alle at his cri
At his wille at his merci
Þat non durste ben him ageyn
Erl ne baron knict ne sweyn.
Wislike for soth was him wel
Of folc of wepne of catel.
Soþlike in a lite þrawe
Al Engelond of him stod awe.
Al Engelond was of him adrad
So his þe beste fro þe gad.
280 Þe kinges douther bigan þrive
And wex þe fayrest wman on live.
Of alle þewes was she wis
Þat gode weren and of pris.
Þe mayden Goldeboru was hoten.
For hire was mani a ter igroten.

Monks and priests sang mass,
And they read out many psalm books,
Praying that God Himself would lead his
Soul into Heaven before His Son
To live there without end. After the
King was committed to the earth,
The powerful earl overlooked nothing
Until he soon had all of England
Seized into his hand.
He placed in the castles
The knights which he could trust,
And he forced all the English to swear
That they would act in good faith to him.
He gave men what seemed right to him,
To live and die as he saw fit
Until the king's daughter was
Twenty years old or more.
When the earl had received this oath
From earls and barons, fair and foul,
From knights and laborers, free and bound,
He had new justices appointed
To travel through all England
From Dover into Roxburgh.[191] He made
Sheriffs, church officers, and reeves,
And peace sergeants with long lances,
To guard the wild woods and paths
From wicked men who would commit
Harm, and to have all at his beck and call,
At his will, and at his mercy,
So that no one would dare oppose him,
Not earl, baron, knight, or peasant.
In this way, in truth, he had people,
Weapons, and possessions in plenty.
In a short while, truly,
All of England stood in awe of him.
All of England was afraid of him,
Like the cattle fears the prod.
The king's daughter began to flower
And grew into the fairest woman alive.
She was wise in all manners
That were good and were worthy.
The maiden was called Goldeboro;
For her many a tear would be wept.

---

191 The *Havelok* poet writes before the expansion of justices in the fourteenth century, but throughout the medieval period the English citizenry had mixed feelings about such appointments as they brought both order and venal oppression, a theme informing much of *Gamelyn*.

Quanne the Erl Godrich him herde	When the earl heard about the maiden,
Of þat mayden hw wel she ferde	How well she was faring,
Hw wis sho was w chaste hw fayr	How wise she was, how chaste, how fair,
And þat sho was þe rithe eyr	And how she was the rightful heir
290 Of Engelond of al þe rike	Of England, of all the kingdom,
Þo bigan Godrich to sike	Then Godrich began to complain,
And seyde, "Weþer she sholde be	And griped, "Why should she be
Quen and leuedi over me?	Queen and lady over me?
Hweþer sho sholde al Engelond	Why should she have all England,
And me and mine haven in hire hond?	And me and what's mine, in her hand?
Daþeit hwo it hire thaue!	Damn whoever lets her have it![192]
Shal sho it nevere more have!	She will never see it happen!
Sholde ic yeve a fol a þerne	Should I give a fool, some serving wench,
Engelond þou sho it yerne?	England, just because she wants it?
300 Daþeit hwo it hire yeve	Damn whoever hands it to her
Evere more hwil i live!	While I'm still alive!
Sho is waxen al to prud	She has grown all too proud
For gode metes and noble shrud	With the good food and fine clothes
Þat hic have youen hire to offte.	That I have too often given her.
Hic have yemed hire to softe!	I have spoiled her too much!
Shal it nouth ben als sho þenkes:	It is not going to end as she plans:
'Hope maketh fol man ofte blenkes'.	'Hope often makes a foolish man blind'.
Ich have a sone a ful fayr knave;	I have a son, a handsome boy;
He shal Engelond al have.	He shall have all England.
310 He shal king he shal ben sire	He shall be king, he will be sire,
So brouke i evere mi blake swire!"	So long as I have a head on my shoulders!"
Hwan þis trayson was al þouth	When this treason was all thought out,
Of his oth ne was him nouth.	His oath no longer meant anything to him.
He let his oth al over-ga	He let his promise go entirely,
Þerof ne yaf he nouth a stra.	And afterward did not care a straw for it.
But sone dede hire fete	But before he would eat another thing,
Er he wolde heten ani mete	He ordered for her to be fetched
Fro Winchestre þer sho was	From where she was at Winchester,
Also a wicke traytur Judas	And just like a wicked traitor Judas,
320 And dede leden hire to Dovre	He had her sent to Dover,
Þat standeth on þe seis oure.	Which stands on the seashore,
And þerhinne dede hire fede	And had her kept there
Pourelike in feble wede.	In poverty in ragged clothes.
Þe castel dede he yemen so	He had the castle guarded
Þat non ne micte comen hire to	So that none of her friends
Of hire frend with to speken	Might come to speak with her,
Þat hevere micte hire bale wreken.	Who might ever avenge her wrong.

---

192 *Datheit*: The poet repeatedly uses this epithet, which is perhaps a corruption of *odium Dei habet*, "May he have the hate of God", or Deu hat, "God's hate", from Old French. Thomas J. Garbaty, *Havelok the Dane, Medieval English Literature* (Long Grove, Il: Waveland, 1984), his note to line 296. See also Denise Battaglia, Esther Kaufmann, et al., "You Can Say You to Me: English Politeness from the Middle Ages up to Now", conference paper, *eHistLing* 1 (2004).

	Of Goldeboru shul we nou laten	We will now leave Goldboro for a while,
	Þat nouth ne blinneth forto graten	Who laments without ceasing,
330	Þet sho liggeth in prisoun.	Where she lies in prison.
	Jhesu Crist that Lazarun	May Jesus Christ, who brought Lazarus
	To live broucte fro dede bondes	To life from the bonds of death,
	He lese hire wit Hise hondes!	Release her with His hands!
	And leve sho mo him y-se	And grant that she might see him
	Heye hangen on galwe tre	Hanging high on the gallows tree,
	Þat hire haued in sorwe brouth	The man who brought her into sorrow,
	So as sho ne misdede nouth!	Though she had done nothing wrong!
	Sawe nou forth in hure spelle.	Let us continue forth in our story.
	In þat time so it bifelle	In that time, as it so happened,
340	Was in þe lon of Denmark	In the land of Denmark there was
	A riche king and swyþe stark.	A rich and very powerful king.
	Þe name of him was Birkabeyn	His name was Birkabeyn.
	He hauede mani knict and sweyn;	He had many knights and attendants;
	He was fayr man and wicth	He was a handsome and valiant man.
	Of bodi he was þe beste knicth	He was the best knight in body
	Þat evere micte leden uth here	Who ever might command an army,
	Or stede onne ride or handlen spere.	Or ride a horse, or handle a spear.
	Þre children he hauede bi his wif	He had three children by his wife,
	He hem lovede so his lif.	And he loved them as much as his life.
350	He hauede a sone douhtres two	He had a son and two daughters
	Swiþe fayre as fel it so.	Who were, as it happened, very fair.
	He þat wile non forbere	But death, who spares no one,
	Riche ne poure king ne kaysere	Neither rich nor poor, king nor caesar,
	Deth him tok þan he best wolde	Took him when he would rather live;
	Liven but hyse dayes were fulde	But his days were complete,
	Þat he ne moucte no more live	So that he could no longer remain,
	For gol ne silver ne for no gyve.	Not for gold, silver, or any gift.
	Hwan he þat wiste raþe he sende	When the king realized this he swiftly sent
	After prestes fer an hende	For priests from near and far,
360	Chanounes gode and monkes beþe	Canon priests and monks as well,[193]
	Him for to wisse and to rede	To counsel and advise him,
	Him for to hoslon an forto shrive	And to confess and absolve him
	Hwil his bodi were on live.	While his body was still alive. When he
	Hwan he was hosled and shriven	Was forgiven and given communion,
	His quiste maked and for him gyven	With his will made and given for him,
	His knictes dede he alle site	He had all his knights seated,
	For þorw hem he wolde wite	For through them he would know
	Hwo micte yeme hise children yunge	Who might take care of his young children
	Til þat he kouþen speken wit tunge	Until they could speak with their tongues,
370	Speken and gangen on horse riden	Walk and talk, and rise horses,
	Knictes an sweynes bi here siden.	With knights and attendants by their sides.

193 *Chanounes gode*: A canon was "a priest of a cathedral church or a member of a particular religious community" (Herzman et al.). Here they are regular clergy of enough authority to give confession to the king.

	He spoken þer-offe and chosen sone	He spoke of this matter and soon chose
	A riche man was under mone	A powerful man who was the truest
	Was þe trewest þat he wende	Under the moon that he knew,
	Godard þe kinges oune frende	Godard, the king's own friend,
	And seyden he moucthe hem best loke	And said he might care for them best[194]
	Yif þat he hem undertoke	If he took them to himself,
	Til hise sone mouthe bere	Until his son could bear
	Helm on heued and leden ut here	A helmet on his head and lead an army,
380	In his hand a spere stark	With a strong spear in his hand,
	And king ben maked of Denmark.	And be made king of Denmark.
	He wel trowede þat he seyde	The king believed what Godard said
	And on Godard handes leyde	And laid hands on him
	And seyde, "Here bi-teche i þe	And said, "I hereby entrust to you
	Mine children alle þre	All of my three children,
	Al Denmark and al mi fe	All Denmark, and all my properties,
	Til þat mi sone of helde be.	Until my son is of age.
	But þat ich wille þat þou suere	But I want you to swear
	On auter and on messe-gere	On the altar and the church vestments,
390	On þe belles þat men ringes	On the bells that men ring,
	On messe-bok þe prest on singes	And on the hymnal the priests sing from,
	Þat þou mine children shalt wel yeme	That you will protect my children well,
	Þat hire kin be ful wel queme	So that their family will be satisfied,
	Til mi sone mowe ben knicth.	Until my son can be a knight.
	Þanne biteche him þo his ricth:	Then endow him with his rights:
	Denemark and þat þertil longes	Denmark and all that belongs to it,
	Casteles and tunes wodes and wonges".	Castles and towns, woods and fields".
	Godard stirt up an swor al þat	Godard rose and swore everything
	Þe king him bad and siþen sat	That the king asked him, and then sat
400	Bi the knictes þat þer ware	With the knights who were there,
	Þat wepen alle swiþe sare	Who were all weeping very bitterly
	For þe king þat deide sone.	For the king, who soon died.
	Jhesu Crist that makede mone	May Jesus Christ, who makes the moon
	On þe mirke nith to shine	Shine on the darkest night,
	Wite his soule fro Helle pine.	Protect his soul from Hell's pains,
	And leve þat it mote wone	And grant that it may dwell
	In Hevene-riche with Godes Sone!	In Heaven with God's Son!
	Hwan Birkabeyn was leyd in grave	When Birkabeyn was laid in his grave,
	Þe erl dede sone take þe knave	The earl immediately took the boy,
410	Havelok þat was þe eir	Havelok, who was the heir,
	Swanborow his sister helfled þe toþer	Swanboro, his sister, and Hefled, the other,
	And in þe castel dede he hem do.	And had them put in the castle.
	Þer non ne micte hem comen to	None of their kin might come to them
	Of here kyn þer þei sperd wore.	There where they were kept.

---

194 *He moucthe hem best loke*: Who is speaking here is not clear, as the pronouns do not indicate. Likely the king is addressing Godard, referring back to the clause beginning on 372. But in 382, "He [the king] believed what he said", although this may refer to Godard's implied response.

Þer he greten ofte sore
Boþe for hunger and for kold
Or he weren þre winter hold.
Feblelike he gaf hem cloþes;
He ne yaf a note of hise oþes.
420 He hem cloþede rith ne fedde
Ne hem ne dede richelike be-bedde.
Þanne Godard was sikerlike
Under God þe moste swike
Þat evre in erþe shaped was
With-uten on þe wike Judas.
Have he þe malisun to-day
Of alle þat evre speken may
Of patriark and of pope
And of prest with loken kope
430 Of monekes and hermites boþe
And of þe leve holi rode
Þat God Him-selve ran on blode!
Crist warie him with His mouth!
Waried wrthe he of norþ and suth
Offe alle man þat speken kunne
Of Crist þat made mone and sunne!
Þanne he hauede of al þe lond
Al þe folk tilled in-til his hond
And alle haueden sworen him oth
440 Riche and poure lef and loth
Þat he sholden hise wille freme
And þat he shulde him nouth greme.
He þouthe a ful strong trechery
A trayson and a felony
Of þe children forto make.
Þe devel of Helle him sone take!
Hwan þat was þouth onon he ferde
To þe tour þer he woren sperde
Þer he greten for hunger and cold.
450 Þe knave þat was sumdel bold
Kam him ageyn on knes him sette
And Godard ful feyre he fer grette.
And Godard seyde, "Wat is yw?
Hwi grete ye and goulen nou?"
"For us hungreth swiþe sore"
Seyden he wolden more.
"We ne have to hete ne we ne have
Herinne neyther knith ne knave
Þat yeveth us drinken ne no mete
460 Halvendel þat we moun ete.

They cried there miserably,
Both from hunger and the cold,
Before they were even three years old.
He gave them clothes grudgingly;
He didn't care a nut about his oaths!
He didn't clothe or feed them properly,
Or provide them with a rich bed.
At that time Godard was surely
The worst traitor under God
Who was ever created on earth,
Except for one, the wicked Judas.
May he have the curse this day
Of all who will ever pronounce them,
Of patriarchs and popes,
And of priests with buttoned cloaks,
Of both monks and hermits,
And by the beloved holy cross
That God Himself bled upon!
May Christ condemn him by His mouth!
He deserves to be reviled from north to
South, by all men who can speak,
By Christ, who made the moon and sun!
For after that he had all the land
And all the folk tilled into his hand,
And all had to swear him oaths,
Rich and poor, fair and foul,
That they would perform his will,
And that they would never anger him.
He worked up a villainous treachery,
A treason and a felony,
To carry out on the children.
May the devil soon take him to Hell!
When that was planned, he went on
To the tower where they were kept,
Where they wept for hunger and cold.
The boy, who had more boldness,
Came to him and set himself on his knees,
And greeted Godard courteously.
Godard said, "What's the matter with you?
Why are you all bawling and yowling?"
"Because we are bitterly hungry", he said,
Saying they needed more to eat.
"We have no heat, nor do we have
Either a knight or a servant in here
Who gives us half the amount of food
Or drink that we could eat.

Wo is us þat we weren born!
Weilawei! Nis it no korn
Þat men micte maken of bred?
Us hungreth we aren ney ded!"
Godard herde here wa
Ther-offe yaf he nouth a stra
But tok þe maydnes bothe samen
Al-so it were up-on hiis gamen
Al-so he wolde with hem leyke
470   Þat weren for hunger grene and bleike.
Of boþen he karf on two here þrotes
And siþen hem alto grotes.
Þer was sorwe we so it sawe!
Hwan þe children bi þe wawe
Leyen and sprauleden in þe blod
Havelok it saw and þer bi stod.
Ful sori was þat seli knave.
Mikel dred he mouthe have
For at hise herte he saw a knif
480   For to reven him hise lyf.
But þe knave þat litel was
He knelede bifor þat Judas
And seyde, "Louerd merci nou!
Manrede louerd biddi you.
Al Denmark i wile you yeve
To þat forward þu late me live.
Here hi wile on boke swere
Þat nevre more ne shal i bere
Ayen þe louerd shel ne spere
490   Ne oþer wepne that may you dere.
Louerd have merci of me!
To-day i wile fro Denmark fle
Ne nevere more comen ageyn.
Sweren y wole þat Bircabein
Nevere yete me ne gat".
Hwan þe devel herde that
Sumdel bigan him forto rewe.
With-drow þe knif þat was lewe
Of þe seli children blod.
500   Þer was miracle fair and god
Þat he þe knave nouth ne slou
But for rewnesse him witdrow.
Of Avelok rewede him ful sore

Woe is us that we were born!
Alas! Is there not even some grain
That someone could make bread from?
We are hungry and we are nearly dead!"
Godard heard their plea,
And did not care a straw about it,
But lifted up both of the girls together,
Who were green and pale from hunger,
As if it were a game,
As if he were playing with them.
He slashed both of their throats in two,
And then cut them to pieces.
There was sorrow in whoever saw it!
When the children lay by the wall,
Sprawled in the blood,
Havelok saw it and stood there.
The innocent boy was full of grief.
He must have had great terror,
For he saw a knife pointed at his heart
To rob him of his life.
But the boy, as small as he was,
Kneeled before that Judas,
And said, "Lord, have mercy now!
Lord, I offer you homage.
I will give you all of Denmark,
On the promise that you let me live.
I will swear on the Bible right here
That I will never bear against you
Shield or spear, Lord, nor any
Other weapon that might harm you.
Lord, have mercy on me!
Today I will flee from Denmark
And never come back again.
I will swear that Birkabeyn
Never fathered me".
When the devil Godard heard that,
He felt a slight twinge of guilt.
He drew back the knife, which was warm
From the innocent children's blood.
It was a miracle, fair and bright,
That he did not slay the boy,
But out of pity he held back.
He felt strong regret over Havelok,

And þoucte he wolde þat he ded wore
But on þat he nouth wit his hend
Ne drepe him nouth þat fule fend!
Þoucte he als he him bi stod
Starinde als he were wod
"Yif y late him lives go
510 He micte me wirchen michel wo.
Grith ne get y nevere mo
He may me waiten for to slo.
And yf he were brouct of live
And mine children wolden thrive
Louerdinges after me
Of al Denmark micten he be!
God it wite he shal ben ded.
Wile i taken non oþer red!
I shal do casten him in þe se
520 Þer i wile þat he drench be
Abouten his hals an anker god
Þat he ne flete in the flod".
Þer anon he dede sende
After a fishere þat he wende
Þat wolde al his wille do
And sone anon he seyde him to
"Grim þou wost þu art mi þral;
Wilte don mi wille al
Þat i wile bidden þe?
530 To-morwen shal maken þe fre
And aucte þe yeven and riche make
With þan þu wilt þis child take
And leden him with þe to-nicht.
Þan þou sest se mone lith
In-to þe se and don him þer-inne.
Al wile i taken on me þe sinne".
Grim tok þe child and bond him faste
Hwil þe bondes micte laste
Þat weren of ful strong line.
540 Þo was Havelok in ful strong pine.
Wiste he nevere her wat was wo!
Jhesu Crist þat makede to go
Þe halte and þe doumbe speken

And in his mind he wished he were dead,[195]
But Godard not could bring himself to
Kill him with his own hand, the foul fiend!
Godard thought as he stood by him,
Staring into space as if he were mad,
"If I let him go alive,
He might bring me great trouble.
I will never have peace,
For he may bide his time to kill me.
And if his life were taken away,
And my children were to thrive,
After my time they might be
Lords of all Denmark!
God knows, he must be killed.
I will take no other course!
I'll have him thrown into the sea,
And there I'll have him drowned,
With a solid anchor about his neck,
So that he can't float in the water".[196]
From there he immediately sent for
A fisherman that he believed
Would do all his will,
And he said to him at once,
"Grim, you know you are my servant;
Will you do all my will
That I order you to?
Tomorrow I will free you
And give you property, and make you rich,
Provided that you take this child
And bring him with you tonight.
When you see the moonlight,
Go into the sea and throw him in it.
I will take on myself all the sin".
Grim took the boy and tied him up tightly,
While the bonds might last,
Which were made of strong rope.
Then Havelok was in great pain;
He never knew before what suffering was!
May Jesus Christ, who makes the lame walk
And the mute speak,

195 *And thoucte he wolde that he ded wore*: A difficult line as the pronouns are not clear. The context suggests that Godard wishes Havelok were dead but cannot bring himself to kill him. *Thoucte* is 'thought' (see 507) and probably not 'though' (ME *thagh, though*). The second *he* is probably Havelok.

196 Garbaty notes that Godard, like the pirates in *King Horn*, rationalizes that putting Havelok in the water removes his moral responsibility, as fate will be to blame if he dies. Godard still wants to give fate "a heavy helping hand" with an anchor (Garbaty, his note to 519-22).

Havelok þe of Godard wreken!

. . . .

C He was traitur in mani a kas
And he it aboute þat he swilc was
He broute þe child in mechel sorwen.
Yet wurth is soule nevere borwen;
He bad Grim don is comaundemet
550 And þerfore was he ate þe laste schent.

. . . .

L Hwan Grim him hauede faste bounden
And siþen in an eld cloth wnden

. . . .

C He thriste in his muth wel faste

. . . .

L A kevel of clutes ful un-wraste
Þat he ne mouthe speke ne fnaste
Hwere he wolde him bere or lede.
Hwan he hauede don þat dede
Hwan þe swike him hauede hethede
Þat he shulde him forth lede
560 And him drinchen in þe se
Þat forwarde makeden he
In a poke ful and blac
Sone he caste him on his bac
Ant bar him hom to hise cleve.
And bi-taucte him dame Leve
And seyde, "Wite þou þis knave
Also thou with mi lif have!
I shal dreinchen him in þe se.
For him shole we ben maked fre
570 Gold haven ynou and oþer fe;
Þat hauet mi louerd bihoten me".
Hwan dame Leve herde þat
Up she stirte and nouth ne sat
And caste þe knave adoun so harde
Þat hise croune he þer crakede
Ageyn a gret ston þer it lay.
Þo Havelok micte sei, "Weilawei
Þat evere was i kinges bern!

Wreak revenge on Godard for Havelok![197]

. . . .

He was a traitor at every opportunity
And it was because of this that
He brought the child into great sorrow.
Yet he would never save his own soul;
He ordered Grim to do his commands
And for that he was in the end lost.

. . . .

When Grim had tied him up fast,
And then bound him in an old cloth,

. . . .

He shoved tightly in his mouth

. . . .

A gag of filthy rags,
So that he could not speak or snort out
Wherever he might carry or lead him.
When he had done that deed
And heeded the traitor's orders
That he should take him forth
And drench him in the sea
In a bag, big and black,
Which was the agreement they made,
He threw him at once on his back
And took him home to his hut.
Grim entrusted him to his wife Leve,
And said, "Watch this boy[198]
As if you were protecting my life!
I will drown him in the sea.
For his sake we will be made free,
And have plenty of gold and other goods;
My lord has promised me this".
When Dame Leve heard this,
She did not sit but jumped up,
And dropped the boy down so hard
That he banged his head
Against a great rock laying there.[199]
Then Havelok might have said,
"Alas, that I was ever a king's son!

---

197 Significantly, the poet does not condemn Grim, who is ostensibly "only following orders". The Cambridge fragment emphasizes the same point. For an alternative interpretation of Grim which sees him as suspiciously enthusiastic in seeking advancement, see Maldwyn Mills, "Havelok and the Brutal Fisherman", *Medium Aevum* 36 (1967): 219-30.

198 *Knave*: In early ME this simply meant 'boy'. Although the word had servile connotations, there was no pejorative nuance yet as there is later when Grim calls himself and Leve *cherles* in remorseful panic (627).

199 *Ageyn a gret ston*: Among other uses, rocks were heated in ovens and used to keep beds warm at night. In *The Miller's Tale*, Alison scolds Absolon from her bedside window, "Go forth thy wey, or I wol caste a ston" (*CT* I.3712), perhaps reflecting the same practice.

Þat him ne hauede grip or ern
580 Leoun or wlf wluine or bere
Or oþer best þat wolde him dere.
So lay þat child to middel nicth
Þat Grim bad Leve bringen lict
For to don on his cloþes:
"Ne thenkeste nowt of mine oþes
Þat ich have mi louerd sworen?
Ne wile i nouth be forloren!
I shal beren him to þe se
Þou wost þat bihoves me
590 And i shal drenchen him þer-inne.
Ris up swiþe an go þu binne
And blou þe fir and lith a kandel!"
Als she shulde hise cloþes handel
On forto don and blawe þe fir
She saw þer-inne a lith ful shir
Also brith so it were day
Aboute þe knave þer he lay.
Of hise mouth it stod a stem
Als it were a sunnebem.
600 Also lith was it þer-inne
So þer brenden cerges inne.
"Jhesu Crist!" wat dame Leve
"Hwat is þat lith in ure cleve?
Sir up Grim and loke wat it menes!
Hwat is þe lith as þou wenes?"
He stirten boþe up to the knave
For man shal god wille have
Unkeveleden him and swiþe unbounden
And sone anon him funden
610 Als he tirneden of his serk
On his rith shuldre a kyne merk.
A swiþe brith a swiþe fair.
"Goddot", quath Grim "þis ure eir
Þat shal louerd of Denmark!
He shal ben king strong and stark
He shal haven in his hand
Al Denmark and Engeland!
He shal do Godard ful wo;
He shal him hangen or quik flo
620 Or he shal him al quic grave.
Of him shal he no merci have".

If only he had fathered a vulture or eagle,
A lion or wolf, a she-wolf or bear, or some
Other beast to harm Godard back!"[200]
So the child lay there until midnight,
When Grim asked Leve to bring a light
In order to put on his clothes:
"Don't you think anything of my oaths
That I have sworn to my lord?[201]
I will not be ruined!
I will take him to the sea–
You know that's what I have to do!–
And I will drown him there in the water.
Get up quickly now and go in,
And stoke the fire and light a candle!"
But as she was about to handle his clothes
To put them on him, and kindle the fire,
She saw a shining light inside,
As bright as if it were day,
Around the boy where he lay.
From his mouth a gleam stood out
As if it were a sunbeam.
It was as light inside the hut
As if candles were burning there.
"Jesus Christ!" exclaimed Dame Leve,
"What is that light in our hut?
Get up, Grim, and see what it is!
What do you think the light is?"
They both hurried up to the boy,
For people are naturally goodwilled,
Ungagged him, and quickly untied him,
And as they pulled off the boy's shirt,
They immediately found on him
A royal birthmark on his right shoulder,
A mark so bright and so fair.
"God knows!" Grim said, "this is our heir
Who will be lord of Denmark!
He will be king, strong and mighty,
And he will have in his hand
All of Denmark and England!
He will bring Godard great grief;
He will have him hanged or flayed alive,
Or he will have him buried alive.
He will get no mercy from him".

200 This is again a surmisal taken from context, as the pronouns in early ME do not make it clear who Havelok is talking about.
201 Presumably Leve's conscience bothers her and Grim needs to argue with her to justify his actions. The sentiment dovetails with line 607 and helps humanize the couple.

Þus seide Grim and sore gret
And sone fel him to þe fet
And seide, "Louerd have merci
Of me and Leve that is me bi!
Louerd we aren boþe þine
Þine cherles þine hine.
Lowerd we sholen þe wel fede
Til þat þu cone riden on stede
630 Til þat þu cone ful wel bere
Helm on heued sheld and spere.
He ne shal nevere wite sikerlike
Godard þat fule swike.
Þoru oþer man louerd than þoru þe
Sal i nevere freman be.
Þou shalt me louerd fre maken
For i shal yemen þe and waken.
Þoru þe wile i fredom have".
Þo was Haveloc a bliþe knave.
640 He sat him up and cravede bred.
And seide, "Ich am ney ded
Hwat for hunger wat for bondes
Þat þu leidest on min hondes
And for kevel at þe laste
Þat in mi mouth was þrist faste.
Y was þer-with so harde prangled
Þat i was þer-with ney strangled".
"Wel is me þat þu mayth hete
Goddoth!" quath Leve, "y shal þe fete
650 Bred an chese butere and milk
Pastees and flaunes al with suilk.
Shole we sone þe wel fede
Louerd in þis mikel need.
Soth it is þat men seyt and swereth
'Þer God wile helpen nouth no dereth'".
Þanne sho hauede brouth þe mete
Haveloc anon bigan to ete
Grundlike and was ful bliþe.
Couþe he nouth his hunger miþe.
660 A lof he het y woth and more
For him hungrede swiþe sore.
Þre dayes þer-biforn i wene
Et he no mete þat was wel sene.
Hwan he hauede eten and was fed
Grim dede maken a ful fayr bed.

Grim said all this and cried bitterly,
And then fell at Havelok's feet
And said, "My lord, have mercy
On me and Leve, who is beside me!
Lord, we are both yours—
Your peasants, your servants.
Lord, we will raise you well
Until you know how to ride a steed,
Until you know well how to bear
A helmet on your head with shield and
Spear. Godard, that foul traitor,
Will never know, for sure.
I will never be a free man, Lord,
Except through you.
You, my lord, will release me,
For I will protect and watch over you.
Through you I will have freedom".
Then Havelok was a happy lad.
He sat up and asked for bread,
And said, "I am nearly dead,
What with hunger, what with the ropes
That you laid on my hands,
And at last because of the gag
That was stuck fast in my mouth.
With all that I was so tightly pressed
That I was nearly strangled".
Leve said, "God knows, I'm just pleased
That you can eat. I will fetch you
Bread and cheese, butter and milk,
And meat pies and desserts.
We'll soon feed you well with these things,
My lord, in your great need.
It's true what people say and swear, 'No one
Can harm whom God wishes to help'".[202]
When she had brought some food,
At once Havelok began to eat ravenously,
And was very pleased.
He could not hide his hunger.
He ate a loaf, I know, and more,
For he was half-starved.
For three days before then, I guess,
He had eaten nothing—that was easy to see.
When he had eaten and was content,
Grim made him a comfortable bed,

---

202 *Ther God wile helpen, nouth ne dereth*: Apparently proverbial. Compare Thomas a Kempis' *Imitation of Christ* (c. 1418), Book 2, *Humility*: "The malice of man cannot harm one whom God wishes to help". These may be the narrator's words.

Unclopede him and dede him þer-inne
And seyde, "Slep sone with michel winne
Slep wel faste and dred þe nouth
Fro sorwe to joie art þu brouth".

670 Sone so it was lith of day.
Grim it under-tok þe wey
To þe wicke traitour Godard
Þat was Denemak a stiward
And seyde, "Louerd don ich have
Þat þou me bede of þe knave.
He is drenched in þe flod
Abouten his hals an anker god.
He is witer-like ded.
Eteth he nevre more bred!

680 He liþ drenched in þe se.
Yif me gold and oþer fe
Þat y mowe riche be
And with þi chartre make fre
For þu ful wel bi-hetet me
Þanne i last spak with þe".
Godard stod and lokede on him
Þoruth-like with eyne grim
And seyde "Wiltu ben erl?
Go hom swiþe fule drit cherl!

690 Go heþen and be evere-more
Þral and cherl als þou er wore!
Shal have non oþer mede.
For litel i do þe lede
To þe galwes so God me rede
For þou haves don a wicke dede!
Þou mait stonden her to longe
Bute þou swiþe eþen gonge!"
Grim thoucte to late þat he ran
Fro þat traytour þa wicke man

700 And þoucte, "Wat shal me to rede?
Wite he him onlive he wile beþe
Heye hangen on galwe-tre.
Betere us is of londe to fle
And berwen boþen ure lives
And mine children and mine wives".
Grim solde sone al his corn
Shep wit wolle neth wit horn
Hors and swin gate wit berd
Þe gees þe hennes of þe yerd.

710 Al he solde þat outh douthe
That he evre selle moucte

Took his clothes off, and tucked him in,
And said, "Sleep, son, with much peace.
Sleep fast and do not be afraid of anything.
You are brought from sorrow to joy".

Soon it was the light of day.
Grim made his way
To the wicked traitor Godard,
Who was steward of Denmark,
And said, "My lord, I have done
What you ordered me to do with the boy.
He is drowned in the water,
With a firm anchor around his neck.
He is surely dead.
He will never eat any more bread!

He lies drowned in the sea.
Give me gold and other goods
So that I may be rich,
And make me free with your signature,
For you promised me these things in full
When I last spoke with you".
Godard stood and looked at him
Thoroughly with stern eyes
And said, "So you want to be an earl?
Go home fast, foul dirt-slave!

Get out of here and forever be
A slave and an oaf as you were before!
You will get no other reward.
So help me God, it would take little
For me to send you to the gallows,
For you've done a wicked deed!
You stay here too long for your own good
Unless you get out of here quick!"
Grim thought, too late, as he ran
From that traitor, that wicked man

And pondered, "What will I do?
If he knows he's alive, he will hang
Both of us high on the gallows tree.
It would be better for us to flee the land
And save both of our lives,
And my children's and my wife's".
Soon Grim sold all of his grain,
Sheep with wool, cattle with horns,
Horses and pigs, goats with beards,
The geese, and the hens of the yard.

He sold all that could be sold,
Everything that had value,

And al he to þe peni drou.	And he converted it all to money.
Hise ship he greyþede wel inow.	He outfitted his ship well enough.
He dede it tere an ful wel pike	He gave it tar and a full coat of pitch
Þat it ne doutede sond ne krike.	So that it would never fear inlet or creek.
Þer-inne dide a ful god mast	He placed a fine mast in it,
Stronge kables and ful fast	Fastened firmly with strong cables,
Ores god an ful god seyl.	Good oars, and a rugged sail.
Þer-inne wantede nouth a nayl	Nothing inside lacked even a nail
720 Þat evere he sholde þer-inne do.	That he should have put into it.
Hwan he hauedet greyþed so	When he had equipped it so,
Havelok þe yunge he dide þer-inne	He put young Havelok in it,
Him and his wif hise sones þrinne	Himself and his wife, his three sons,
And hise two doutres þat faire wore.	And his two daughters, who were so fair.
And sone dede he leyn in an ore	And then he laid in the oars
And drou him to þe heye se	And drew them out to the high sea
Þere he mith alþer-beste fle.	Where he might best flee.
Fro londe woren he bote a mile	He was only a mile from land,
Ne were nevere but ane hwile	And it was no more than a short while
730 Þat it ne bigan a wind to rise	When a breeze which men call
Out of þe north men calleth 'bise'	The North Wind began to rise[203]
And drof hem intil Engelond	And drove them on to England,
Þat al was siþen in his hond	Which would later all be in one man's hand,
His þat Havelok was þe name.	And that man's name would be Havelok.
But or he hauede michel shame	But before then he would endure
Michel sorwe and michel tene	Much shame, sorrow, and hardship,
And þrie he gat it al bidene	And yet he got it all in full,
Als ye shulen nou forthwar lere	As you will all soon learn
Yf that ye wilen þer-to here.	If you wish to hear about it.
740 In Humber Grim bigan to lende	Grim came to land along the Humber,
In Lindeseye rith at þe north ende.	In Lindsay, right at the north end.[204]
Þer sat is ship up-on þe sond	There his fishing boat sat on the sand.
But Grim it drou up to þe lond	But Grim drew it up onto the land,
And þere he made a litel cote	And built a little cottage there
To him and to hise flote.	For him and his family.
Bigan he þere for to erþe	He began to live and work there,
A litel hus to maken of erþe	In a little house made of earth,
So þat he wel þore were	So that in their harbor there
Of here herboru herborwed þere.	They were well-sheltered.
750 And for þat Grim þat place aute	And because Grim owned that place,
Þe stede of Grim þe name laute.	It took the name of Grim's stead,

---

203 *Bise*: Herzman et al. note that this Old French loanword for 'North Wind' is common in French literature but does not appear in any other English romance.

204 The poet knows his geography. The Humber River moves into an inlet northwest of Grimsby. Present-day East Lindsey is slightly further south, near Louth. This would have been a trip southwest from Denmark of upwards of 600-800 km, a very long voyage for a peasant fishing boat. A fast Viking longship traveling at 14 knots might have completed the trip in two days. Similarly, Grimsby to Lincoln (774) is a good day's walk at 50 km.

So þat Grimesbi calleth alle
Þat þer-offe speken alle.
And so shulen men callen it ay
Bituene þis and Domesday.
Grim was fishere swiþe god
And mikel couþe on the flod.
Mani god fish þer-inne he tok
Boþe with neth and with hok.

760 He tok þe sturgiun and þe qual
And þe turbut and lax with-al.
He tok þe sele and þe hwel
He spedde ofte swiþe wel.
Keling he tok and tumberel
Hering and þe makerel
Þe butte þe schulle þe þornebake.
Gode paniers dede he make
Ontil him and oþer þrinne
Til hise sones to beren fish inne

770 Up o-londe to selle and fonge.
Forbar he neyþer tun ne gronge
Þat he ne to-yede with his ware.
Kam he nevere hom hand-bare
Þat he ne broucte bred and sowel
In his shirte or in his covel
In his poke benes and korn.
Hise swink ne hauede he nowt forlorn.
And hwan he tok þe grete laumprei
Ful wel he couþe þe rithe wei

780 To Lincolne þe gode boru.
Ofte he yede it þoru and þoru
Til he hauede wol wel sold
And þer-fore þe penies told.
Þanne he com þenne he were bliþe
For hom he brouthe fele siþe
Wastels simenels with þe horn
Hise pokes fulle of mele an korn

So that everyone calls it Grimsby[205]
Who speaks about the town.
And so men will always call it
Between now and Judgment Day.
Grim was a skillful fisherman
And knew the waters well.
He caught plenty of good fish,
Both with a net and with a hook.
He took sturgeons and whales,
And turbot and salmon as well.
He caught seals and eels,
And often fared very well.
He took cod and porpoise,
Herring and mackerel,
Flounder, plaice, and skate.[206]
He made good bread baskets,
One for him and another three
For his sons to carry fish in
To sell and collect money for upland.
He missed neither town nor farm
Wherever he went with his wares.
He never came home empty-handed
Without bringing bread and sauce
In his shirt or in his hood,
And beans and grain in his bag.
He never wasted his efforts.
And when he caught a great lamprey,[207]
He knew the road very well
To Lincoln, the fine town.
He often crossed it through and through,
Until he sold everything as he wanted[208]
And had counted his pennies for it.
When he returned from there he was glad,
For many times he brought home
Cakes and horn-shaped breads,
With his bags full of flour and grain,

205 "Grim's By", reflecting the Old Danish word for *village*, still traditionally claims its origins from the story of Grim. Grimsby's medieval seal had images of Grim, Havelok, and Goldeboru, though findings suggest that a small number of Romans occupied the area near Cartergate centuries earlier.

206 Like lists of royalty in medieval romance, the fish here also seem to be ranked from highest to lowest. Sturgeon were a delicacy (as well as whales, curiously) whereas flounder and plaice were a staple now usually found in fish and chip dishes. Also see Skeat's note on fish as well as Luizza, who believes the fish symbolize an economy where goods and money have more value than "chivalric honor". Roy Michael Liuzza, "Representation and Readership in the ME *Havelok*", *Journal of English and Germanic Philology* 93 (1994): 510.

207 Lampreys are parasitic eels and are now seen as pests, but in the ancient and medieval world were expensive dainties. Henry I is recorded by contemporary historians as dying from eating too many lampreys in rich sauces. They are still eaten in Asia.

208 *Til he havede wol wel sold*: The MS suggests that Grim is selling wool (*wol*), which is never mentioned. Other editors read ful or al instead of wol, which makes more contextual sense.

	Netes flesh shepes and swines	Beef, lamb, and pork,
	And hemp to maken of gode lines	And hemp to make good fishing lines,
790	And stronge ropes to hise netes	And strong rope for his nets
	In þe se weren he ofte setes.	Where he set them in the sea.
	Þus-gate Grim him fayre ledde	Thus Grim lived comfortably,
	Him and his genge wel he fedde	And he fed himself and his household well
	Wel twelf winter oþer more.	For a good twelve years or more.
	Havelok was war þat Grim swank sore	Havelok knew that Grim worked hard
	For his mete and he lay at hom.	For his dinner while he lay at home.
	Thouthe, "Ich am nou no grom.	He thought, "I am no longer a boy.
	Ich am wel waxen and wel may eten	I am fully grown and can eat
	More þan evere Grim may geten.	More than Grim could ever get.
800	Ich ete more bi God on live	I eat more, by the living God,
	Þan Grim an hise children five.	Than Grim and his five children.
	It ne may nouth ben þus longe	God knows, it can't go on like this!
	Goddot! Y wile with þe gange	I will go with them
	For to leren sum god to gete	To learn some useful skill,
	Swinken ich wolde for mi mete.	And I will labor for my dinner.
	It is no shame forto swinken!	It is no shame to work!
	Þe man þat may wel eten and drinken	It is a foul thing for a man who eats
	Þat nouth ne have but on swink long	And drinks his fill, who has not
	To liggen at hom it is ful strong.	Worked hard for it, to lie at home.
810	God yelde him þer i ne may	God reward him more than I can
	Þat haueth me fed to þis day!	For having fed me to this day!
	Gladlike i wile þe paniers bere.	I will gladly carry the breadbaskets.
	Ich woth ne shal it me nouth dere	I know it won't do me any harm,
	Þey þer be inne a birþene gret	Even if they are a great burden,
	Al so hevi als a neth.	As heavy as an ox.
	Shal ich nevere lengere dwelle.	I will no longer linger here.
	To morwen shal ich forth pelle".	Tomorrow I will hustle forth".
	On þe morwen hwan it was day	In the morning when it was day
	He stirt up sone and nouth ne lay	He got up at once and did not lie down,
820	And cast a panier on his bac	And he threw a basket on his back
	With fish giveled als a stac.	With fish heaped up like a stack.
	Also michel he bar him one	He carried as much by himself
	So he foure bi mine mone!	As four men, by my word!
	Wel he it bar and solde it wel	He carried it firmly and sold it well,
	Þe silver he brouthe hom il del.	And he brought home every bit of silver.
	Al þat he þer-fore tok	With all that he got for it,
	With-held he nouth a ferþinges nok.	He did not hold back a penny's edge.[209]
	So yede he forth ilke day	He went out this way each day
	Þat he nevere at home lay	And was so eager to learn his trade
830	So wolde he his mester lere.	That he never idled at home again.

---

209 *A ferthinges nok*: i.e. he did not keep anything for himself. A farthing was a quarter of a penny and the smallest coin.
Herzman et al. explain that the idiom meant 'to the last penny' and referred to the illegal practice of clipping the edges of
coins to sell the silver as bullion. For this reason most modern coins have raised edges.

Bifel it so a strong dere
Bigan to rise of korn of bred
That Grim ne couþe no god red
Hw he sholde his meine fede.
Of Havelok hauede he michel drede
For he was strong and wel mouthe ete
More þanne hevere mouthe he gete.
Ne he ne mouthe on þe se take
Neyþer lenge ne þornbake
840 Ne non oþer fish þat douthe
His meyne feden with he mouthe.
Of Havelok he hauede kare
Hwilgat þat he micthe fare.
Of his children was him nouth;
On Havelok was al hise þouth
And seyde, "Havelok dere sone
I wene that we deye mone
For hunger þis dere is so strong
And hure mete is uten long.
850 Betere is þat þu henne gonge
Þan þu here dwelle longe.
Heþen þow mayt gangen to late.
Thou canst ful wel þe ricthe gate
To Lincolne þe gode borw
Þou havest it gon ful ofte þoru.
Of me ne is me nouth a slo
Betere is þat þu þider go
For þer is mani god man inne
Þer þou mayt þi mete winne.
860 But wo is me! þou art so naked
Of mi seyl y wolde þe were maked
A cloth þou mithest inne gongen
Sone no cold þat þu ne fonge".
He tok þe sheres of þe nayl
And made him a couel of þe sayl
And Havelok dide it sone on.
Hauede neyþer hosen ne shon
Ne none kines oþer wede.
To Lincolne barfot he yede.
870 Hwan he kam þer he was ful wil.
Ne hauede he no frend to gangen til.
Two dayes þer fastinde he yede
Þat non for his werk wolde him fede.
Þe þridde day herde he calle
"Bermen bermen hider forth alle!"
Poure þat on fote yede

But it so happened that a bad harvest
Brought a shortage of grain for bread,
So that Grim could find no good answer
To how he should feed his household.
He was very worried about Havelok,
For he was strong and could eat
More than every mouth there could get.
No longer could Grim catch on the sea
Either cod or skate,
Nor any other fish that would serve
To feed his family.
He was very anxious about Havelok
And how he might fare.
He did not think of his other children;
All of his thoughts were on Havelok,
And he said, "Havelok, dear son,
I fear that we must all die from hunger,
For this famine is so harsh
And our food is long gone.
It would be better if you go on
Than to stay here any longer.
You might leave here too late.
You know very well the right way
To Lincoln, the fine town,
For you have been there often enough.
As for me, I'm not worth a berry.
It's better that you go there,
For there are many good men in town
And you might earn your dinner there.
But woe is me! You are so poorly dressed,
I would rather take my sail and make
Some clothing you can go in, son,
So that you need not face the cold".
He took the scissors off the nail,
And made him a cloak from the sail,
And then put it on Havelok.
He had neither hose nor shoes,
Nor any other kind of clothing.
He walked barefoot to Lincoln.
When he arrived there, he was at a loss.
He had no friend to go to.
For two days he wandered there hungry,
For no one would feed him for his work.
The third day he heard a call,
"Porters, porters, come here, all!"
The poor who went on foot

Sprongen forth so sparke on glede.	Sprang forth like sparks from coals.
Havelok shof dun nyne or ten	Havelok shoved aside nine or ten,
Rith amidewarde þe fen	Right into the muddy swamp,
880 And stirte forth to þe kok.	And rushed forward to the cook.
Þer the herles mete he tok	There he took charge of the earl's food
Þat he bouthe at þe brigge.	Which he was given at the bridge.
Þe bermen let he alle ligge	He left the other porters lying there
And bar þe mete to þe castel	And delivered the food to the castle,
And gat him þere a ferþing wastel.	Where he was given a penny cake.[210]
Þet oþer day kepte he ok	The next day again he keenly kept
Swiþe yerne þe erles kok	A lookout for the earl's cook,
Til þat he say him on þe brigge	Until he saw him on the bridge
And bi him mani fishes ligge.	Where many fish lay beside him.
890 Þe herles mete hauede he bouth	He had bought the earl's provisions
Of Cornwalie and kalde oft	From Cornwall, and repeatedly called,
"Bermen bermen hider swiþe!"	"Porters, porters, come quickly!"
Havelok it herde and was ful bliþe	Havelok heard it and was glad
Þat he herde bermen calle.	That he heard the call for porters.
Alle made he hem dun falle	He made everyone fall down
Þat in his gate yeden and stode	Who walked or stood in his way,
Wel sixtene laddes gode.	A good sixteen strong lads.
Als he lep þe kok til	As he leaped up to the cook,
He shof hem alle upon an hyl	He shoved them down the hillside,
900 Astirte til him with his rippe	Hurrying to him with his basket,
And bigan þe fish to kippe.	And began to scoop up the fish.
He bar up wel a carte lode	He bore up a good cartload
Of segges laxes of playces brode	Of squid, salmon, and broad flatfish,
Of grete laumprees and of eles.	Of great lampreys, and of eels.
Sparede he neyþer tos ne heles	He did not spare heel or toe
Til þat he to þe castel cam	Until he came to the castle,
Þat men fro him his birþene nam.	Where men took his burden from him.
Þan men haueden holpen him doun	When men had helped take down
With þe birþene of his croun	The load off his shoulders,
910 Þe kok stod and on him low	The cook stood and smiled on him
And þoute him stalworþe man ynow	And decided he was a sturdy enough man
And seyde, "Wiltu ben wit me?	And said, "Will you stay with me?
Gladlike wile ich feden þe.	I will be glad to keep you.
Wel is set þe mete þu etes	The food you eat is well earned,
And þe hire þat þu getes!"	As well as the wages you get!"
"Goddot!" quoth he, "leve sire	"God knows!" Havelok said, "good sir,
Bidde ich you non oþer hire	I will ask you for no other pay

---

210 *Ferthing wastel*: A loaf of bread baked from the finest white flour, the same that Chaucer's Prioress extravagantly feeds her dogs with. During a food shortage it is a considerable treat. A farthing is a quarter of a penny (12d = 1 shilling; 20s = £1). English expressions which use coins to describe cheapness are much later, as in the thirteenth century a penny had much greater purchasing power (about £2.24 in today's money). Line 1179's mention of piles of pennies at Havelok's wedding would not have suggested parsimony to an audience.

But yeueþ me inow to ete.
Fir and water y wile yow fete

920 Þe fir blowe an ful wele maken.
Stickes kan ich breken and kraken
And kindlen ful wel a fyr
And maken it to brennen shir.
Ful wel kan ich cleuen shides
Eles to-turnen of here hides.
Ful wel kan ich dishes swilen
And don al þat ye evere wilen".
Quoth þe kok, "Wile i no more.
Go þu yunder and sit þore

930 And y shal yeve þe ful fair bred
And make þe broys in þe led.
Sit now doun and et ful yerne.
Daþeit hwo þe mete werne!"
Havelok sette him dun anon
Also stille als a ston
Til he hauede ful wel eten.
Þo hauede Havelok fayre geten!
Hwan he hauede eten inow
He kam to þe welle water up-drow

940 And filde þer a michel so.
Bad he non ageyn him go
But bi-twen his hondes he bar it in
Al him one to þe kichin.
Bad he non him water to fete
Ne fro brigge to bere þe mete.
He bar þe turues he bar þe star.
Þe wode fro the brigge he bar;
Al that evere shulden he nytte
Al he drow and al he citte.

950 Wolde he nevere haven rest
More þan he were a best.
Of alle men was he mest meke
Lauhwinde ay and bliþe of speke.
Evere he was glad and bliþe;
His sorwe he couþe ful wel miþe.

But that you give me enough to eat.[211]
I will fetch you firewood and water,
Raise the fire, and make it blaze.
I can break and crack sticks,
And kindle a fire expertly,
And make it burn brightly.
I know well how to split kindling
And how to skin eels from their hides.
I can wash dishes well,
And do all that you ever want".
The cook said, "I can't ask for more.
Go over there and sit,
And I will bring you some good bread,
And make you soup in the kettle.
Sit down now and eat your fill gladly.
Damn whoever begrudges you food!"
Havelok sat down at once,
As still as a stone,
Until he had fully eaten.
Havelok had done well then!
When he had eaten enough,
He came to the well, drew up the water,
And filled a large tub there.
He asked no one to go with him,
But he carried it in between his hands,
All by himself, to the kitchen. He asked
No one to fetch water for him, nor to
Bring provisions from the bridge. He bore
Turf for fuel, and grass for kindling.[212]
He carried wood from the bridge;
All that they might ever need,
He hauled and he cut everything.
He would never have any more rest
Than if he were a beast.
Of all men he was the most mild,
Always laughing and friendly in speech.
He was forever glad and pleasant;
He could fully hide his sorrows.[213]

---

211 Havelok asks only for enough to eat as his salary. The line has troubled some critics, with Delaney saying his humility marks the poem as a bourgeois fantasy, as it is admirable "only from the point of view of an employer". Nevertheless, Havelok demonstrates some well-bred discretion in not pushing his luck during a famine. Sheila Delaney, *Medieval Literary Politics* (Manchester: University Press, 1990), 69.

212 *He bar the turves, he bar the star*: Herzman et al. explain that turves were cuts of turf or peat moss which were dried and then burned for fuel. Star was wild grass (possibly genus *hypoxis* or *aletris*), used for kindling.

213 *His sorwe he couthe ful wel mithe*: Medieval England was not yet the time of the 'stiff upper lip', and so the comment that "he could hide his feelings well" is odd. Presumably the poet is praising Havelok for not burdening others with his tragic past while reminding the audience that he knows his true heritage.

It ne was non so litel knave
For to leyken ne forto plawe
Þat he ne wolde with him pleye.
Þe children that yeden in þe weie
960 Of him he deden al her wille
And with him leykeden here fille.
Him loveden alle stille and bolde
Knictes children yunge and holde.
Alle him loveden þat him sowen
Boþen heyemen and lowe.
Of him ful wide þe word sprong
Hw he was mike hw he was strong
Hw fayr man God him hauede maked
But on þat he was almest naked.
970 For he ne hauede nouth to shride
But a kovel ful unride
Þat was ful and swiþe wicke
Was it nouth worth a fir sticke.
Þe cok bigan of him to rewe
And bouthe him cloþes al spannewe.
He bouthe him boþe hosen and shon
And sone dide him dones on.
Hwan he was cloþed osed and shod
Was non so fayr under God
980 Þat evere yete in erþe were
Non þat evere moder bere.
It was nevere man þat yemede
In kinneriche þat so wel semede
King or cayser forto be
Þan he was shrid so semede he.
For þanne he weren alle samen
At Lincolne at þe gamen
And þe erles men woren al þore
Þan was Havelok bi þe shuldren more
990 Þan þe meste þat þer kam.
In armes him noman nam
Þat he doune sone ne caste.
Havelok stod over hem als a mast.
Als he was heie al he was long
He was boþe stark and strong.
In Engelond was non hise per
Of strengþe þat evere kam him ner.
Als he was strong so was he softe.
Þey a man him misdede ofte
1000 Nevere more he him misdede
Ne hond on him with yvele leyde.

There was no boy so little
Who wanted to sport or have fun
That he would not play with him.
For all the children who came his way,
He did everything they wanted,
And played with them to their fill.
He was loved by all, meek and bold,
Knights, children, young, and old.
All took to him who saw him,
Both high and low men.
Word spread far and wide of him,
How he was great, how he was strong,
How handsome a man God had made him,
Except for that he was almost naked.
For he had nothing to wear
Except a rough cloak,
Which was so dirty and foul
That it was not worth a stick of firewood.
The cook came to feel sorry for him
And bought him brand new clothes.
He bought him both hose and shoes,
And soon had him put them on.
When he was clothed, hosed, and in shoes
There was no one so handsome under God
Who was ever yet on earth,
No one that any mother ever bore.
There was never a man who ruled
A kingdom who looked so much
Like a king or a caesar
As he appeared when he was clothed.
For when they were all together
In Lincoln at the games,
And the earl's men were all there,
Havelok was taller by a head
Than the greatest who were there.
In wrestling no man grappled him
That he didn't soon throw down.
Havelok stood over them like a mast.
As high as he was, as tall as he was,
He was just as hardy and strong.
In England he had no equal in strength
Among whoever came near him.
As much as he was strong, he was gentle.
Though other men often mistreated him,
He never insulted them
Or laid a hand on them in malice.

Of bodi was he mayden clene;	His body was pure of maidens;
Nevere yete in game ne in grene	Never in fun or in lust would he
Þit hire ne wolde leyke ne lye	Flirt or lie with a loose woman,[214]
No more þan it were a strie.	No more than if she were an old witch.
In þat time al Hengelond	In that time Earl Godrich
Þerl Godrich hauede in his hond	Had all of England in his hand,
And he gart komen into þe tun	And he ordered into the town
Mani erl and mani barun	Many earls and many barons.
1010 And alle þat lives were	And all who were alive
In Englond þanne wer þere,	In England then were there,
Þat þey haueden after sent	For they had been sent for
To ben þer at þe parlement.	To be present at the parliament.[215]
With hem com mani chanbioun	With them came many champions,
Mani with ladde blac and brown.	With other lads of all sorts.[216]
An fel it so þat yunge men	And so it happened that young men,
Wel abouten nine or ten	Well around nine or ten,
Bigunnen þe for to layke.	Began to play sports there.
Þider komen bothe stronge and wayke.	Both the strong and weak came there.
1020 Þider komen lesse and more	Both the lesser and greater came
Þat in þe borw þanne weren þore:	Who were there in the town then:
Chaunpiouns and starke laddes	Athletes, and rugged fellows,
Bondemen with here gaddes	And bondsmen with their cattle prods
Als he comen fro þe plow.	Who had just come from the plow.
Þere was sembling i-now	The gathering was large enough,
For it ne was non horse-knave	For there was no stable boy
Þo þei sholden in honde have	Who did not come to see the games,
Þat he ne kam þider þe leyk to se.	Even if he should have been at work.
Biforn here fet þanne lay a tre	Before their feet they laid a tree trunk,
1030 And putten with a mikel ston	Where the strong lads, a good number,
Þe starke laddes ful god won.	Shot-put with a giant stone.
Þe ston was mikel and ek greth	The stone was solid and huge as well,
And al so hevi so a neth.	And as heavy as an ox.
Grund stalwrthe man he sholde be	It would have to be a very hardy man
Þat mouthe liften it to his kne.	Who might lift it to his knees.
Was þer neyþer clerc ne prest	There was neither clerk nor priest
Þat mithe liften it to his brest:	Who might bring it up to his chest.
Þerwit putten the chaunpiouns	With it the athletes shot-put,
Þat þider comen with þe barouns.	Those who had come with the barons.
1040 Hwo so mithe putten þore	Whoever there who could throw it
Biforn a-noþer an inch or more	Further than an inch or more,

214 *With hire ne wolde he leyke ne lye*: The *hire* is not clear and may simply be 'her', the *mayden* (1002). Herzman et al. suggest that the *hire* is a 'woman for hire', or at least a promiscuous woman who would frequent men's summer games. Some editors read 'whore', but there is no consensus that *hire* had this meaning or pronunciation in early ME.

215 Skeat remarks that a parliament was held in Lincoln in 1300 (note to 1006, his lineation). The poet mentions a summoned assembly in line 1013 and the barons (1039) whom the athletes accompany, but otherwise ignores any political deliberations. The point is likely that Godrich's cynical 'parliament' is also no more than a show of games. See also 1186.

216 *Blac and brown*: "Every type of ordinary person". See the note to *Amis and Amiloun* (2475) and *Athelston* (291).

Wore ye yung wore he hold	Whether he was young or old,
He was for a kempe told.	Was considered a hero.
Al-so þe stoden an ofte stareden	And so they stood and watched intently,
Þe chaunpiouns and ek the ladden	The athletes and the lads as well,
And he maden mikel strout	And made a heated dispute
Abouten þe alþerbeste but.	About who had made the greatest shot.
Havelok stod and lokede þer-til	Havelok stood and looked at it
And of puttingge he was ful wil	But he knew nothing about putting,
1050 For nevere yete ne saw he or	For he had never seen
Putten the stone or þanne þor.	Or thrown the stone before then.
Hise mayster bad him gon þer-to	His master told him to go try
Als he couþe þer-with do.	As he was best able to do.
Þo hise mayster it him bad	When his master asked him,
He was of him sore adrad	Because he was fearfully obedient to him,
Þerto he stirte sone anon	He therefore got up quickly
And kipte up þat heui ston	And plucked up that heavy stone
Þat he sholde puten wiþe.	Which he was supposed to put.
He putte at þe firste siþe	On the first try he threw it
1060 Over alle þat þer wore	Farther than anyone who was there,
Twel fote and sumdel more.	Twelve feet and somewhat more.
Þe chaunpiouns þat put sowen	When the champions saw that shot,
Shuldreden he ilc oþer and lowen.	They jostled each other and laughed.
Wolden he no more to putting gange	They would not put any more, only saying
But seyde, "We dwellen her to longe!"	"We've hung around here too long!"[217]
Þis selkouth mithe nouth ben hyd.	This marvel could not be hidden for long.
Ful sone it was ful loude kid	Very soon the news was loudly told
Of Havelok hw he warp þe ston	About Havelok, how he threw the stone
Over þe laddes everilkon;	Over each one of the lads;
1070 Hw he was fayr hw he was long	How he was handsome, how he was tall,
Hw he was with hw he was strong.	How he was manly, how he was strong.
Þoruth England yede þe speke	Throughout England the news spread,
Hw he was strong and ek meke.	How he was mighty and gentle as well.
In the castel up in þe halle	In the castle, up in the hall,
Þe knithes speken þer-of alle	The knights talked about it all
So that Godrich it herde wel.	So that Godrich heard it well.
Þe speken of Havelok everi del	They spoke of Havelok, every detail—
Hw he was strong man and hey	How he was a strong man, and high,
Hw he was strong and ek fri	How he was manly and generous too,
1080 And þouthte Godrich, "Þoru þis knave	And Godrich thought, "Through this
Shal ich Engelond al have	Peasant I will have all England
And mi sone after me	For myself and for my son after,
For so i wile þat it be.	For it's my will that it be so.

---

217 *We*: Some editors read *thee* in the manuscript here, as there is some textual confusion between *þe* and *þe*. Skeat's reading makes better contextual sense, as the good-natured camaraderie of the losing contestants contrasts with Godrich's solitary machinations, just as in *Gamelyn* where a wrestler who graciously concedes defeat underscores Gamelyn's brother's cynical plans.

The king Aþelwald me dide swere
Upon al þe messe-gere
Þat y shude his douther yeve
Þe hexte þat mithe live
Þe beste þe fairest þe strangest ok.
Þat gart he me sweren on þe bok.
1090 Hwere mithe i finden ani so hey
So Havelok is or so sley?
Þou y southe heþen in-to Ynde
So fayr so strong ne mithe y finde.
Havelok is þat ilke knave
Þat shal Goldeborw have!"
Þis þouthe with trechery
With traysoun and wit felony
For he wende þat Havelok wore
Sum cherles sone and no more.
1100 Ne shulde he haven of Engellond
Onlepi forw in his hond
With hire þat was þerof eyr
Þat boþe was god and swiþe fair.
He wende þat Havelok wer a þral.
Þer-þoru he wende haven al
In Engelond þat hire rith was.
He was werse þan Sathanas
Þat Jhesu Crist in erþe shop.
Hanged worþe he on an hok!
1110 After Goldeborw sone he sende
Þat was boþe fayr and hende
And dide hire to Lincolne bringe.
Belles dede he ageyn hire ringen
And joie he made hire swiþe mikel
But neþeles he was ful swikel.
He seyde þat he sholde hire yeve
Þe fayrest man þat mithe live.
She answerede and seyde anon
Bi Crist and bi seint Johan
1120 Þat hire sholde noman wedde
Ne noman bringen to hire bedde
But he were king or kinges eyr
Were he nevere man so fayr.
Godrich þe erl was swiþe wroth
Þat she swore swilk an oth
And seyde, "Hwor þou wilt be

King Athelwald made me swear
Upon all the mass finery
That I would give his daughter
The *highest* that might live, the best,
The fairest, and the strongest as well.
He made me swear that on the Bible.
Where could I find anyone so 'high'
As Havelok is, or so able?
If I searched from here to India,
I would not find someone so fair, so mighty.
Havelok is the very boy
That Goldeboro will have!"
He schemed this out with treachery,
With treason, and with felony,
For he surmised that Havelok was
Some commoner's son and no more.
Nor would he get a single furrow
Of England into his hand
With Godeboro, who was the rightful heir,
Who was both good and fair. He thought
That Havelok was some peasant.[218]
Therefore he planned to keep all
Of England, which was her right.
He was worse than Satan,
Who Jesus Christ locked in the earth!
He deserves to be hanged on an oak!
Soon after he sent for Goldeboro,
Who was both beautiful and courteous,
And had her brought to Lincoln.
He had bells for her rung alongside,
And made great celebration over her,
But nonetheless he was full of deceit.
He announced that he would give her
The fairest man that might live.
She answered straightaway and said,
By Christ and by Saint John,
That she would wed no man,
Nor would any man bring her to bed
Unless he were a king or king's heir,
No matter how fair he was.
Godrich the earl was furious
That she had sworn such an oath
And said, "Do you think that you'll be

---

218 *Þral*: Terms for peasant rank are not always clear or consistent in ME. Peasants could be literal slaves (the usual meaning of thrall), but could also be bound (serf) or free (churl) tenant-farmers with some rights of justice. Godrich hopes to prevent Goldeboru's accession by making a morganatic marriage between her and what he thinks is a commoner.

Quen and leuedi over me?	Queen and lady over me?
Þou shalt haven a gadeling!	You will have a beggar!
Ne shalt þou haven non oþer king.	You will not have any other king.
1130 Þe shal spusen mi cokes knave!	You will marry my cook's servant!
Ne shalt þou non oþer louerd have.	You will not have any other lord.
Daþeit þat þe oþer yeve	Damn whoever who gives you someone else
Evere more hwil i live!	While I am still alive!
To-morwe ye sholen ben weddeth	Tomorrow you will be married,
And maugre þin to-gidere beddeth!"	In spite of you, and bedded together!"
Goldeborw gret and was hire ille.	Goldeboro cried and was in distress.
She wolde ben ded bi hire wille.	She would have died if she had her will.
On the morwen hwan day was sprungen	In the morning, when day had sprung,
And day-belle at kirke rungen	And the early bells at the church were rung,
1140 After Havelok sente þat Judas	That Judas, who was worse than Satan,
Þat werse was þanne Sathanas	Sent for Havelok and said,
And seyde, "Mayster wilte wif?"	"Mister, would you like a wife?"
"Nay", quoth Havelok, "bi my lif!	"No", cried Havelok, "not on my life!
Hwat sholde ich with wif do?	What should I do with a wife?
I ne may hire fede ne cloþe ne sho.	I cannot give her food, clothes, or shoes.
Wider sholde ich wimman bringe?	Where could I bring a woman?
I ne have none kines þinge.	I have nothing to make a home with.
I ne have hws y ne have cote	I have no house, I have no cottage,
Ne i ne have stikke y ne have sprote	I have no sticks, I have no twigs for a fire,
1150 I ne have neyþer bred ne sowel	I have neither bread nor sauce,[219]
Ne cloth but of an hold with couel.	And no clothing except an old white cloak.
Þis cloþes þat ich onne have	These clothes that I have on
Aren þe kokes and ich his knave".	Are the cook's, and I am his boy".
Godrich stirt up and on him dong	Godrich jumped up and struck him
With dintes swiþe hard and strong	With hard and strong blows
And seyde, "But þou hire take	And said, "Unless you take the woman
Þat y wole yeven þe to make	That I give you as a mate,
I shal hangen þe ful heye	I will hang you from the highest heights,
Or y shal þristen uth þin heie!"	Or I will gouge out your eyes!"
1160 Havelok was one and was odrat	Havelok was alone and was afraid,
And grauntede him al þat he bad.	And agreed to all that he ordered.
Þo sende he after hire sone	Then Godrich sent for Goldeboro at once,
Þe fayrest wymman under mone	The fairest woman under the moon,
And seyde til hire false and slike	And said to her, false and slick,
Þat wicke þral þat foule swike	That wicked oaf, that foul traitor:
"But þu þis man under-stonde	"Unless you accept this man,
I shal flemen þe of londe	I will banish you from the land,
Or þou shal to þe galwes renne	Or you will be rushed to the gallows,
And þer þou shalt in a fir brenne".	And there you will burn in a fire".
1170 Sho was adrad for he so þrette	She was terrified, for he threatened her so,

---

219 *Bred ne sowel*: Literally, bread and sauce or anything eaten with bread, but the pairing could have the synecdochic sense of 'bread and butter', meaning that Havelok has no goods to make a household with.

And durste nouth þe spusing lette.

But þey hire likede swiþe ille

Þouthe it was godes wille–

God þat makes to growen þe korn

Formede hire wimman to be born.

Hwan he hauede don him for drede

Þat he sholde hire spusen and fede

And þat she sholde til him holde

Þer weren penies þicke tolde

1180 Mikel plente upon þe bok.

He ys hire yaf and she as tok.

He weren spused fayre and wel

Þe messe he deden everidel

Þat fel to spusing and god clek

Þe erchebishop uth of Yerk

Þat kam to þe parlement

Als God him hauede þider sent.

Hwan he weren togydere in godes lawe

Þat þe folc ful wel it sawe

1190 He ne wisten hwat he mouthen

Ne he ne wisten wat hem douthe

Þer to dwellen or þenne to gonge.

Þer ne wolden he dwellen longe

For he wisten and ful wel sawe

Þat Godrich hem hatede þe devel him hawe!

And yf he dwelleden þer outh

Þat fel Havelok ful wel on þouth.

Men sholde don his leman shame

Or elles bringen in wicke blame.

1200 Þat were him levere to ben ded.

For-þi he token anoþer red

Þat þei sholden þenne fle

Til Grim and til hise sones þre.

Þer wenden he alþer-best to spede

Hem forto cloþe and for to fede.

Þe lond he token under fote

Ne wisten he non oþer bote

And helden ay the riþe sti

And she dared not obstruct the marriage.

Though she was very unhappy,

She thought it was God's will–

God, who makes the grain grow

And who formed her to be born a woman.

When he had compelled them by fear

That he should marry and keep her,

And that she should hold to him,

There were thick piles of pennies counted,

A great plenty, upon the mass book.

He gave her tokens and she accepted his.[220]

They were wedded fair and clear.

The service was performed, every part

Pertaining to marriage, by a good cleric,

The archbishop of York,

Who came to the assembly

As God had sent him there.

When they were joined under God's law,

So that the people saw it fully,

Havelok did not know what to do,

Nor did he know where to turn for help,

Where to stay, or where to go.

They could not remain there long,

For he understood and saw plainly that

Godrich hated them– the Devil take him!

And if they stayed there unprotected,

Havelok worried about foul play.

Men might shame his beloved,

Or else disgrace her reputation.[221]

To him it would be better to be dead.

For this reason he took another course,

That they should flee from there

To Grim and his three sons.

He thought it best to hurry there

In order to clothe and feed themselves.

They took to the land on foot,

For he knew no other remedy,

And they kept the right route

---

220 *He ys hire yaf and she is tok*: This opaque line has numerous explanations. Skeat posits that *he* is Godard, who has given Goldeboru the 'thick pile of pennies' to send her off (his note to 1174). Garbaty suggests it is a holdover of the Anglo-Saxon *morgengifu*, a present made by the husband to the bride as a sign of trust, as in the OE *Apollonius of Tyre* (Garbaty's note to 1173-4, his lineation). French and Hale's explanation is that the money is partly the clerk's payment and partly the bride's dowry (p. 118). The *ys* may simply be Havelok's public vows of promise. The Wife of Bath is married at the "chirche dore" (*CT* III.6), and medieval weddings were community events, normally appended to the church service.

221 Garbaty explains that Havelok is perhaps worried about Godrich exercising the *jus primae noctis*, the lord's legal right to spend the first night with a vassal's bride (his note to 1192). Despite little historical evidence that the practice ever existed in Europe, it is a recurring theme in literature from the *Epic of Gilgamesh* to *The Marriage of Figaro*.

Til he komen to Grimesby.	Until they came to Grimsby.
1210 Þanne he komen þere þanne was Grim ded	When they arrived there Grim was dead.
Of him ne haueden he no red.	Havelok had had no word about him.
But hise children alle fyve	But of his five children,
Alle weren yet on live.	All were still alive.
Þat ful fayre ayen hem neme	They took them in very courteously
Hwan he wisten þat he keme	When they learned that he had come,
And maden joie swiþe mikel.	And made a great celebration.
Ne weren he nevere ayen hem fikel.	They were never fickle to them.
On knes ful fayre he hem setten	They set themselves on their knees
And Havelok swiþe fayre gretten	And greeted Havelok elegantly,
1220 And seyden, "Welkome louerd dere!	And said, "Welcome, our dear lord!
And welkome be þi fayre fere!	And welcome to your fair companion!
Blessed be þat ilke þrawe	Blessed be that very moment
Þat þou hire toke in Godes lawe!	When you took her in God's law!
Wel is hus we sen þe on lyve.	It is good for us to see you alive.
Þou mithe us boþe selle and yeve.	We are yours to sell or give away.
Þou mayt us boþe yeve and selle	You may both give us or trade us,
With þat þou wilt here dwelle.	For as long as you stay here.
We haven louerd alle gode:	Lord, we have every good thing:
Hors and neth and ship on flode	Horses and oxen, and a ship on the sea,
1230 Gold and silver and michel auchte	Gold and silver, and many things
Þat Grim ute fader us bitawchte.	That Grim our father left to us.
Gold and silver and oþer fe	He told us to pass on to you
Bad he us bi-taken þe.	Gold and silver and all other goods.
We haven shep we haven swin;	We have sheep, we have pigs;
Bi-leve her louerd and al be þin.	Remain here, lord, and all will be yours.
Þo shalt ben louerd þou shalt ben syre	You will be lord, you will be sire,
And we sholen serven þe and hire	And we will serve you and her,
And hure sistres sholen do	And our sisters will do
Al that evere biddes sho.	All that she ever bids.
1240 He sholen hire cloþen washen and wringen	They will wash and dry her clothes,
And to hondes water bringen.	And bring water to her hands.
He sholen bedden hire and þe	They will make a bed for you and her,
For leuedi wile we þat she be".	If it is the lady's will that they do it".
Hwan he þis joie haueden maked	When they had begun the celebration,
Sithen stikes broken and kraked	Kindling was cracked and split,
And þe fir brouth on brenne.	And the fire was stoked into flames.
Ne was þer spared gos ne henne	There was no goose or hen spared,
Ne þe hende ne þe drake.	Neither duck nor drake.
Mete he deden plente make	They prepared plenty of meat
1250 Ne wantede þere no god mete.	And did not lack for any good food.
Wyn and ale deden he fete	They fetched wine and ale,
And made hem ful glade and bliþe	And made the couple glad and at ease,

Wesseyl ledden he fele siþe.
On þe nith als Goldeborw lay
Sory and sorwful was she ay
For she wende she were bi-swike
Þat she were yeven un-kyndelike.
O nith saw she þer-inne a lith
A swiþe fayr a swiþe bryth
1260 Al so brith al so shir
So it were a blase of fir.
She lokede norþ and ek south
And saw it comen ut of his mouth
Þat lay bi hire in þe bed.
No ferlike þou she were adred!
Þouthe she, "Wat may this bi-mene!
He beth heyman yet als y wene.
He beth heyman er he be ded!"
On hise shuldre of gold red
1270 She saw a swiþe noble croiz
Of an angel she herde a voyz
"Goldeborw lat þi sorwe be!
For Havelok þat haueþ spuset þe
He kinges sone and kinges eyr.
Þat bikenneth þat croiz so fayr.
It bikenneth more þat he shal
Denemark haven and Englond al.
He shal ben king strong and stark
Of Engelond and Denmark.
1280 Þat shal þu wit þin eyne sen
And þo shalt quen and leuedi ben!"
Þanne she hauede herd the stevene
Of þe angel uth of Hevene
She was so fele siþes blithe
Þat she ne mithe hire joie mythe
But Havelok sone anon she kiste
And he slep and nouth ne wiste
Hwan þat aungel hauede seyd.
Of his slep a-non he brayd
1290 And seide "Lemman slepes þou?
A selkuth drem dremede me nou;
Herkne nou hwat me haueth met.
Me þouthe y was in Denmark set
But on on þe moste hil
Þat evere yete kam i til.

And drank to their health many times.[222]
Yet that night as Goldeboro lay in bed,
She continually felt sorry and miserable,
For she thought she had been wronged,
That she was married out of her kind.
But in the night she saw a light in there,
So fair, and so clear,
As bright, as shining,
As if it were a blaze of fire.
She looked north and south as well
And saw it coming out of his mouth
As he lay by her in the bed.
It is no wonder that she was afraid!
She thought, "What does this mean?
He will be a nobleman yet, I believe.
He will be a lord before he is dead!"
On his shoulder, in red gold,
She saw a majestic cross.
From an angel she heard a voice,
"Goldeboro, let your sorrows pass!
For Havelok, who has married you,
Is a king's son and a king's heir.
That is the meaning of his fair cross.
It means more, that he shall
Have Denmark and all England.
He will be a king, strong and bold,
Of England and Denmark.
You will see this with your own eyes,
And you will be a queen and lady!"
When she had heard the voice
Of the angel from Heaven,
She was glad so many times over
That she could not contain her joy,
But at once kissed Havelok,
Who slept and knew nothing
Of what the angel had said.
In a moment he woke from his sleep
And said, "Dear, are you asleep?
I just dreamed a wondrous dream;
Listen now to what happened.
It seemed as though I was in Denmark,
But on one of the highest hills
That I ever came to yet.

---

222 *Wesseyl*: 'Wassail' derives from Old Norse *ves heill* and perhaps OE *wes þu hal*, both meaning 'May you be healthy'. Although the Romans placed bits of toast into wine to flavor it or mellow the acidity of cheap wines, 'toast' was not used in this sense until early Modern English.

It was so hey þat y wel mouthe | It was so high that it seemed to me
Al þe werd se als me þouthe. | I could see all the world.
Als i sat up-on þat lowe | As I sat upon that summit,
I bigan Denmark for to awe | I began to embrace Denmark,
1300 Þe borwes and þe castles stronge | The towns and the strong castles,
And mine armes weren so longe | And my arms were so long
That i fadmede al at ones | That I held everything in Denmark
Denmark with mine longe bones! | At once with my long limbs!
And þanne y wolde mine armes drawe | And then I drew my arms back
Til me and hom for to have | Toward myself and lifted up
Al that evere in Denmark liveden | Everyone who ever lived in Denmark,
On mine armes faste clyveden. | Holding them fast within my arms.
And þe stronge castles alle | And all the strong castles
On knes bigunnen for to falle | Began to fall to their knees,
1310 Þe keyes fellen at mine fet. | And their keys fell at my feet.
Anoþer drem dremede me ek | I dreamed another dream too,
Þat ich fley over þe salte se | That I flew over the salty sea to England,
Til Engeland and al with me | And everyone came with me
Þat evere was in Denmark lyves | Who was ever alive in Denmark,
But bondemen and here wives. | Except for bondsmen and their wives.
And þat ich kom til Engelond | And when I came to England
Al closede it intil min hond | I enclosed it all in my hand,
And Goldeborw y gaf þe. | And Goldeboro, I gave it to you.
Deus! Lemman hwat may þis be?" | My God! Dear heart, what does this mean?"
Sho answerede and seyde sone | She answered and soon explained,
1320 "Jhesu Crist þat made mone | "Jesus Christ, who made the moon,
Þine dremes turne to joye". | Will turn your dreams to joy".
. . . . [223]

"Þat wite þw that sittes in trone. | "He who sits on the throne will lead you.
Ne non strong king ne caysere | There are none so mighty, king or caesar,
So þou shalt be fo þou shalt bere | As you will be, for you will wear
In Engelond corune yet! | A crown in England yet!
Denemark shal knele to þi fet | Denmark shall kneel at your feet,
Alle þe castles þat aren þer-inne | And you will win in full
Shal-tow lemman ful wel winne. | All the castles that are in it, my love.
1330 I woth so wel so ich it sowe. | I know it as well as if I had seen it.
To þe shole comen heye and lowe | High and low shall come to you,
And alle þat in Denmark wone: | And all who live in Denmark:
Em and broþer fader and sone | Uncle and brother, father and son,
Erl and baroun dreng an kayn | Earl and baron, vassal and retainer,
Knithes and burgeys and sweyn. | Knights, and townspeople, and workers,[224]
And mad king heyelike and wel. | Will make you king with great honor.
Denemark shal be þin evere-ilc del. | Denmark will be yours, every bit.

---

223 A few lines are likely missing or defective here, as there is no rhyme for *joye* or *trone*. The referent in 1322 is likely Christ.
224 *Burgeys*: A burgess could be a town magistrate, but often simply meant an urban citizen with a trade (such as Dary in *Floris*). As a member of the nascent middle class the word also led to PDE bourgeois (from Old French *borjois*, 'town-dweller').

Have þou nouth þer-offe douthe
Nouth þe worth of one nouthe!
1340 Þer-offe with-inne þe firste yer
Shalt þou ben king of evere-il del.
But do nou als y wile rathe:
Nim in with þe to Denmark baþe
And do þou nouth onfrest þis fare.
Lith and selthe felawes are!
For shal ich nevere bliþe be
Til i with eyen Denmark se
For ich woth þat al þe lond
Shalt þou haven in þin hond.
1350 Prey Grimes sones alle þre
That he wenden forþ with þe.
I wot he wilen þe nouth werne.
With þe wende shulen he yerne
For he loven þe herte-like.
Þou maght til he aren quike
Hwore so he o worde aren.
Þere ship þou do hem swithe yaren
And loke þat þou dwellen nouth:
'Dwelling haveth ofte scaþe wrouth!'"
1360 Hwan Havelok herde þat she radde
Sone it was day sone he him cladde
And sone to þe kirke yede
Or he dide ani oþer dede.
And bifor þe rode bigan falle
Croiz and Crist bigan to kalle
And seyde, "Louerd þat al weldes
Wind and water wodes and feldes
For the holi milce of You
Have merci of me Louerd nou!
1370 And wreke me yet on mi fo
Þat ich saw biforn min eyne slo
Mine sistres with a knif
And siþen wolde me mi lyf
Have reft for in the se
Bad he Grim have drenched me.
He hath mi lond with mikel un-rith
With michel wrong with mikel plith
For i ne misdede him nevere nouth
And haued me to sorwe brouth!
1380 He haueth me do mi mete to þigge
And ofte in sorwe and pine ligge.
Louerd have merci of me
And late me wel passe þe se

Do not have any doubt about it,
Not the value of a nut!
For within one year
You will be ruler of every part.
But now do as I will advise you:
Let's both go to Denmark together
And don't put off this task.
'Ambition and success are partners!'
For I will never be at peace
Until I see Denmark with my own eyes,
Because I know that all the land
Will be yours in your hand.
Insist to all three of Grim's sons
That they journey forth with you.
I know they will not refuse.
They will go eagerly with the wind,
For they love you with all their hearts.
You can tell that they are quick to act,
Wherever in the world they might go.
Have them prepare the ship quickly,
And see that you don't delay:
'Delaying often brings damage!'"
When Havelok heard what she counseled,
It was soon day, soon he dressed himself,
And at once he went to the church
Before he did any other thing.
He fell before the cross and began to
Call upon cross and Christ,
And said, "Lord, who rules all,
Wind and water, woods and fields,
For the sake of Your holy kindness,
Have mercy on me now, Lord!
And avenge me yet on my foe
Whom I saw slay my sisters
With a knife, before my own eyes,
And would have taken my life after,
For he ordered Grim
To drown me in the sea.
He holds my land with great wrong,
With great injustice, and with great harm,
For I never wronged him in any way
And he has brought me to sorrow!
He drove me to beg for my food
And to lie in constant sorrow and pain.
Lord, have mercy on me,
And let me cross the sea safely,

Þat ihc have ther-offe douthe and kare
With-uten stormes over-fare
Þat y ne drenched þer-ine
Ne forfaren for no sinne.
And bringge me wel to þe lond
Þat Godard haldes in his hond.
1390 Þat is mi rith everi del.
Jhesu Crist Þou wost it wel!"
Þanne he hauede his bede seyd
His offrende on þe auter leyd
His leve at Jhesu Crist he tok
And at His suete Moder ok
And at þe croiz þat he biforn lay.
Siþen yede sore grotinde awey.
Hwan he com hom he wore yare
Grimes sones forto fare
1400 In-to þe se fishes to gete
Þat Havelok mithe wel of ete.
But Avelok þouthe al anoþer.
First he kalde þe heldeste broþer
Roberd þe Rede bi his name
Wiliam Wenduth and Huwe Raven
Grimes sones alle þre
And seyde, "Liþes nou alle to me!
Louerdinges ich wile you shewe
A þing of me þat ye wel knewe.
1410 Mi fader was king of Denshe lond.
Denemark was al in his hond
Þe day þat he was quik and ded.
But þanne hauede he wicke red
Þat he me and Denmark al
And mine sistres bi-tawte a þral.
A develes lime he hus bitawte
And al his lond and al hise authe
For y saw that fule fend
Mine sistres slo with hise hend!
1420 First he shar a-two here þrotes
And siþen hem al to grotes
And siþen bad in þe se
Grim youre fader drenchen me.
Deplike dede he him swere
On bok þat he sholde me bere
Unto þe se an drenchen ine
And wolde taken on him þe sinne.

For which I am worried and afraid,
And sail over without storms
So that I will not be drowned in the water,
Nor shipwrecked for any sin.
And bring me safe and sound to the land
That Godard grips in his hand,
Which is my right, every bit.
Jesus Christ, You know it well!"
When he had said his prayer
And laid his offering on the altar,
He took his leave of Jesus Christ
And His sweet mother Mary also,
And of the cross that he lay before.
Then he went away, weeping bitterly.
When he came home they were ready,
All of Grim's sons, to set out
Into the sea to catch fish
So that Havelok might eat well.
But Havelok had something else in mind.
First he called the eldest brother,
Robert the Red, by his name,
And then William Wende and Hugh Raven,
All three of Grim's sons,
And said, "Listen now to me all!
Lordings, I will recount to you
Something about me you know well.[225]
My father was king of the Danes.
All of Denmark was in his hand
The day that he was alive and dead.
But then he followed wicked counsel,
So that I and all of Denmark
And my sisters were entrusted to a servant.
He trusted a tool of the devil with us
And all his land and all that he owned.
For I saw that foul fiend
Slay my sisters with his hand!
First he cut their throats in two,
And then hacked them into bits,
And then ordered Grim, your father,
To drown me in the sea.
He had him solemnly swear
On the Bible that he would take me
Into the water and sink me in it,
And he would take on himself the sin.

---

225 Critics have found Havelok's speech here problematic, as his brothers likely already know about his heritage. As it comes at
the midpoint of the story it may be a way of reminding the audience of previous events through a summary.

But Grim was wis and swiþe hende	But Grim was wise and kindly,
Wolde he nouth his soule shende.	And he would not stain his own soul.
1430 Levere was him to be for-sworen	He would rather be falsely sworn
Þan drenchen me and ben for-lorn.	Than drown me and be damned himself.
But sone bigan he forto fle	At once he prepared to flee
Fro Denmark forto berwen me	From Denmark in order to protect me,
For yif ich hauede þer ben funden	For if I had been found there,
Hauede ben slayn or harde bunden	He would have been slain or tightly bound,
And heye ben henged on a tre!	And hanged high on a tree! Neither
Hauede go for him gold ne fe.	Gold nor money would have helped him.
For-þi fro Denmark hider he fledde	For this he fled away from Denmark
And me ful fayre and ful wel fedde	And he kept me well and raised me,
1440 So þat un-to þis day	So that unto this day
Have ich ben fed and fostred ay.	I have always been fed and protected.
But nou ich am up to þat helde	But now I have come to the age
Cumen that ich may wepne welde	Where I may wield weapons,
And y may grete dintes yeve.	And where I may strike great strokes.
Shal i nevere hwil ich lyve	While I live, I will never be glad
Ben glad til that ich Denmark se!	Until I see Denmark!
I preie you þat ye wende with me	I ask of you that you will go with me
And ich may mak you riche men.	And I will make you rich men.
Ilk of you shal have castles ten	Each of you will have ten castles,
1450 And þe lond þat þor-til longes	And the land that belongs to it,
Borwes tunes wodes and wonges!”	Cities, towns, fields, and villages!”

. . . .

[Havelok's sister advises that he make an alliance with an official in Denmark who has opposed Godard's seizure of power.][226]

A	“L'autr'er en vint, n'ad mie un mois	“Someone came lately, not a month ago,
	Assez oït qe li Danois.	Who had heard enough from the Danes.
	Vus voudroient entr'eus tenir,	They will welcome your reign,
	Car mult se fet li rois haïr.	For Godard causes many to hate him.
	Un prodome ad en la terre	There is a powerful man in that land
	Qui touz jors ad vers li guerre.	Who has always been opposed to him.
	Sigar l'Estal est appellez.	Ubbe is his name.
	A lui looms qe vus alez.”	It's to him that you should go.”

[Havelok and his stepbrothers sell their possessions and fit out their fishing boat to sail to Denmark.]

1460 Lur nief tost aprestèrent	They quickly readied their boat,
Vers Danemarche mer passèrent.	And crossed the sea to Denmark.

---

226 One entire leaf is missing from the MS here of probably 180 lines. As earlier versions of the narrative are briefer and substantially different, only a speculative summary of the action is possible. Some editors resume lineation including the missing lines. English Ubbe is substituted for AN Sigar Estal.

Quant il sont el païs venu
Et de la nief à terre issu
Li marcheant qi's amena
De bons draz les atourna.
Puis lur enseigne q'il feront
Et à quiel ville il turneront
A la cité del seneschal
Qe l'om appelle Sigar l'Estal.

When they arrived in that country
And had disembarked from their ship,
The merchant who had guided them
Dressed them in good clothing.
Then he instructed them what to do
And where they should go:
To the place of the high justice,
Who was called Ubbe.

[They disguise themselves as merchants. Havelok meets Ubbe along the coast and offers him an expensive gold ring as a gift to gain permission to trade.]

. . . .

1470L "With swilk als ich byen shal
þer-of bi-seche you nou leve.
Wile ich speke with non oþer reve
But with þe þat justise are
Þat y mithe seken mi ware
In gode borwes up and doun
And faren ich wile fro tun to tun".
A gold ring drow he forth anon
An hundred pund was worth þe ston
And yaf it Ubbe for to spede.
1480 He was ful wis þat first yaf mede
And so was Havelok ful wis here.
He solde his gold ring ful dere
Was nevere non so dere sold
For chapmen neyþer yung ne old.
Þat sholen ye forthward ful wel heren.
Yif þat ye wile þe storie heren.
Hwan Ubbe hauede þe gold ring
Hauede he youenet for no þing
Nouth for þe borw evere-il del.
1490 Havelok bi-hel he swiþe wel
Hw he was wel of bones maked
Brod in þe sholdres ful wel schaped
Þicke in þe brest of bodi long
He semede wel to ben wel strong.

Havelok said, "I will trade such things as
This, and so I ask your permission now.
I will deal with no other official but you,
For you are a magistrate,
So that I might search for my wares[227]
In good boroughs up and down,
As I travel from town to town".
He then drew out a gold ring–
The stone was worth a hundred pounds–[228]
And gave it to Ubbe for good luck.
He is a wise man who gives a gift first,
And thus Havelok was shrewd there.[229]
He gave his gold ring very dearly;
There was never anything so precious given
By a merchant, neither young nor old.
That you will hear more about,
If you wish to listen to the story.
When Ubbe had the gold ring, he
Wouldn't have parted with it for anything,
Not for every bit of his county.
He looked over Havelok carefully,
How he was powerfully built,
Broad in the shoulders, well-shaped,
With a thick chest and a tall body;
He appeared to be very strong. "My God!"

227 *I mithe seken mi ware*: Like Floris in *Floris & Blancheflor*, Havelok perhaps intends a double meaning here, for merchants usually *sell* wares and he is really 'seeking' his lost heritage (Garbaty, his note to 1450).

228 *An hundred pund*: Like the gold cups Amis and Amiloun exchange, this extravagance for a fisherman's family is outlandish. According to the UK National Archives website, £100 in 1300 is roughly £50,000 / US$77,000 in modern money. Hodges gives a laborer's yearly wage as £2 in 1300. Kenneth Hodges, "Medieval Sourcebook: Medieval Prices", *Fordham University Center for Medieval Studies*, mirrored at http://faculty.goucher.edu/eng240/medieval_prices.html.

229 The line is obscure but feels proverbial. Far from censuring Havelok's bribery of an official, the poet praises his shrewdness. Smithers explains that "a soi-disant merchant might get himself, as an alien, exemption from the payment of local tolls" through such candid palm-greasing. G.V. Smithers, ed., *Havelok* (Oxford: Clarendon, 1987), xlviii.

"Deus" hwat Ubbe "qui ne were he knith?"
I woth þat he is swiþe with!
Betere semede him to bere
Helm on heued sheld and spere
Þanne to beye and selle ware.
1500 Allas þat he shal þer-with fare!
Goddot wile he trowe me
Chaffare shal he late be".
Neþeles he seyde sone
"Havelok have þi bone
And y ful wel rede þe
Þat þou come and ete with me
To-day þou and þi fayre wif
Þat þou louest also þi lif.
And have þou of hire no drede.
1510 Shal hire no man shame bede.
Bi þe fey that y owe to þe
Þerof shal i me serf-borw be".
Havelok herde þat he bad
And thow was he ful sore drad
With him to ete for hise wif
For him wore levere þat his lif
Him wore reft þan she in blame
Felle or lauthe ani shame.
Hwanne he hauede his wille wat
1520 Þe stede þat he onne sat
Smot Ubbe with spures faste.
And forth awey but at þe laste
Or he fro him ferde
Seyde he þat his folk herde
"Loke þat ye comen beþe
For ich it wile and ich it rede!"
Havelok ne durste þe he were adrad
Nouth with-sitten þat Ubbe bad.
His wif he dide with him lede
1530 Un-to þe heye curt he yede.
Roberd hire ledde þat was red
Þat hauede þarned for hire þe ded
Or ani hauede hire misseyd
Or hand with jvele onne leyd.
Willam Wendut was þat oþer
Þat hire ledde Roberdes broþer
Þat was with at alle nedes.

Marveled Ubbe, "Why isn't he a knight?
I can tell that he is very manly!
It would be more fitting for him to wear
A helmet on his head with a shield and
Spear, than to buy and sell wares.
A shame that he should succeed at that!
God knows if he heeded my advice
He would give up trading".
Nevertheless, he at once replied,
"Havelok, you have your request,
And I strongly advise
That you come and dine with me today,
You and your lovely wife
That you love as much as your life.
And have no fear for her.
No man will attempt to shame her.
By the faith that I owe to you,
I will myself be your guarantor".[230]
Havelok followed what Ubbe directed,
Though he was sorely afraid
To eat with him because of his wife,
For he would have rather had his life
Taken away than see her name ruined
Or have her suffer any shame.
When Havelok had given his consent,
Ubbe spurred the steed that he sat on
With taut spurs and he departed.
But at the last moment,
Before he had traveled far
He called so that Havelok's people heard,
"See that you both come,
For it's both my will and my advice!"
Though he was anxious, Havelok did not
Dare oppose what Ubbe asked.
He had his wife follow with him,
And they went into the high court.
Robert escorted her, who was wise
And who would suffer death for her
Before anyone shamed her
Or laid a hand on her in evil.
William Wendut, Robert's brother,
Was the other who accompanied her,
Who was bold in all times of need.

---

230 Why Havelok needs repeated guarantees of protection is not clear, although it emphasizes both Goldeboru's beauty and Denmark's general lawlessness under Godard. Skeat claims that Ubbe was a close friend of Birkabeyn based on other traditions (his note to 1444), and if Ubbe recognizes his lost son, Havelok is taking a dangerous gamble by trusting him.

Wel is him þat god man fedes!	Fortunate is he who keeps good men!
Þan he weren comen to þe halle	When they had come to the hall
1540 Biforen Ubbe and hise men alle	Before Ubbe and all his men,
Ubbe stirte hem ageyn	Ubbe went up to them,
And mani a knith and mani a sweyn	Along with many a knight and retainer,
Hem for to se and forto shewe.	In order to see and to show them.
Þo stod Havelok als a lowe	Havelok stood like a hill then
Aboven þo þat þer-inne wore	Above those who were present,
Rith al bi þe heued more	A good head above
Þanne ani þat þer-inne stod.	Any others who stood inside there.
Þo was Ubbe bliþe of mod	Then Ubbe was in a glad mood
Þat he saw him so fayr and hende.	When he saw him so handsome and noble.
1550 Fro him ne mithe his herte wende	He could not turn his heart away,
Ne fro him ne fro his wif	Not from him, nor from his wife;
He lovede hem sone so his lif.	He loved them as much as his life.
Weren non in Denmark þat him þouthe	There was no one in Denmark he thought
Þat he so mikel love mouthe.	He might have so much love for.
More he lovede Havelok one	He had more affection for Havelok alone
Þan al Denmark bi mine wone!	Than for all Denmark, by my word!
Loke nou hw God helpen kan	See now how God can help
O mani wise wif and man!	Many a wise woman and man!
Hwan it was comen time to ete	When the time to eat had come,
1560 Hise wif dede Ubbe sone in fete	Ubbe fetched his own wife inside,
And til hire seyde al on gamen	And said to her playfully, "My lady",
"Dame þou and Havelok shulen ete samen	"You and Havelok will eat together,
And Goldeboru shal ete wit me	And I will dine with Goldeboro,
Þat is so fayr so flour on tre.	Who is as beautiful as a flower on a tree.
In al Denmark nis wimman	In all of Denmark there's no woman
So fayr so sche bi seint Johan!"	As pretty as her, by Saint John!"
Þanne were set and bord leyd	When the table was laid and set,
And þe beneysun was seyd	And the blessing was said,
Biforn hem com þe beste mete	Before them came the best dinner
1570 Þat king or cayser wolde ete	That a king or caesar could eat—
Kranes swannes ueneysun	Cranes, swans, venison,
Lax lampreys and god sturgun	Salmon, lamprey, and fine sturgeon,
Pyment to drinke and god clare	Spiced wine, and wine with honey,[231]
Win hwit and red ful god plente.	And white and red wine in plenty.
Was þer-inne no page so lite	There was no servant there so low
Þat evere wolde ale bite.	That he ever had to bite down ale.[232]
Of þe mete forto tel	But as for the food served,
Ne of þe metes bidde i nout dwelle	Or the wine offered, I won't dwell on it;
Þat is þe storie for to lenge	That would make the story far too long

---

231 *Pyment*: Herzman et al. explain that medieval *claré* is not modern claret, red wine, but spiced wine with honey.

232 Swanton comments that Havelok's rise in status matches his diet. Curiously, ale is here treated as unworthy of the earl's court, whereas the narrator begins by asking for a cup of it (14). Michael Swanton, *English Literature Before Chaucer* (New York: Longman Group, 1987), 202.

1580 It wolde anuye þis fayre genge.	And would annoy this fine gathering.
But hwan he haueden þe kiwing deyled	But when they had shared the feast,[233]
And fele siþes haueden wosseyled	And had made toasts many times,
And with gode drinkes seten longe	Sitting a long time with fine drinks,
And it was time for to gonge	It was time for each man
Il man to þer he cam fro.	To go back where he came from.
Þouthe Ubbe, "Yf I late hem go	Ubbe thought, "If I let these four and one
Þus one foure with-uten mo	Go on their own, with no more,
So mote ich brouke finger or to	As sure as I have fingers and toes
For þis wimman bes mike wo!	This woman will cause great trouble!
1590 For hire shal men hire louerd slo".	For her men will slay her lords".
He tok sone knithes ten	At once he gathered ten knights,
And wel sixti oþer men	And a good sixty other men
Wit gode bowes and with gleives	With strong bows and with spears,
And sende him unto þe greyves	And sent them to the watchman's place
Þe beste man of al þe toun	With the best man of all the town,
Þat was named Bernard Brun.	Who was named Bernard Brown.
And bad him als he lovede his lif	And he ordered him, as he loved his life,
Havelok wel yemen and his wif	To guard Havelok and his wife well,
And wel do wayten al þe nith	And to keep watch all the night
1600 Til þe oþer day þat it were lith.	Until the next day when it was light.
Bernard was trewe and swiþe with	Bernard was loyal and powerfully strong.
In al þe borw ne was no knith	In all the town there was no knight
Þat betere couþe on stede riden	Who could better ride a steed,
Helm on heued ne swerd bi side.	Helmet on head, with a sword by his side.
Havelok he gladlike under-stod	He gladly took charge of Havelok
With mike love and herte god	With great affection and a kind heart,
And dide greyþe a super riche	And prepared a lavish supper,
Also he was no with chinche	As he was in no way stingy
To his bihoue ever-il del	In taking care of Havelok's every need
1610 Þat he mithe supe swiþe wel.	So that they might dine finely.
Also he seten and sholde soupe	As they were sitting down to eat,
So comes a ladde in a joupe	Along came a lad in an outlaw's jacket,
And with him sixti oþer stronge	And with him sixty others strong,[234]
With swerdes drawen and knives longe	With swords drawn and long knives,
Ilkan in hande a ful god gleive.	Each one with a firm lance in hand.
And seyde, "Undo Bernard þe greyve!	And he said, "Open up, watchman Bernard!
Undo swiþe and lat us in	Open up quick and let us in,

---

233 *Kiwing/kilthing* (?): Herzman et al. define this word as 'tippling', but it is not in the MED and even Skeat gives up on a definition. Some editors have *ilk þing*, 'each thing', which makes more sense as the next line deals with drinking toasts. Smithers (132) sees a possible link between *kil-* and ON *kyla*, "fill one's belly with".

234 In the French *Lai d'Aveloc* Havelok's assailants are motivated by lust for his wife, but in the English they are murderous thieves. The number of attackers is also pumped up considerably from six to sixty to emphasize Havelok's valor. The scene has puzzled scholars as evidently they are the same sixty men that Ubbe sends to protect Havelok (1592), though the poet gives no implication that Ubbe is complicit. They may also simply be different people, as *sixty* was often used to mean an indefinite number. Susie I. Tucker, "'Sixty' as an Indefinite Number in Middle English", *Review of English Studies* 25:98 (1949): 152-153. See also the note to line 1774.

Or þu art ded bi seint Austin!"
Bernard stirt up þat was ful big
1620 And caste a brinie up-on his rig
And grop an ax þat was ful god.
Lep to þe dore so he wore wod
And seyde, "Hwat are ye þat are þer-oute
Þat þus biginnen forto stroute?
Goth henne swiþe fule þeves!
For bi þe Louerd þat man on leves
Shol ich casten þe dore open
Summe of you shal ich drepen
And þe oþre shal ich kesten
1630 In feteres and ful faste festen!"
"Hwat have ye seid", quoth a ladde.
"Wenestu þat we ben adradde?
We shole at þis dore gonge
Maugre þin carl or outh longe!"
He gripen sone a bulder ston
And let it fleye ful god won
Agen þe dore þat it to-rof.
Avelok it saw and þider drof
And þe barre sone ut-drow
1640 Þat was unride and gret ynow
And caste þe dore open wide
And seide, "Her shal y now abide!
Comes swiþe un-to me!
Datheyt hwo you henne fle!"
"No", quodh on, "þat shaltou coupe!"
And bigan til him to loupe
In his hond is swerd ut-drawe
Havelok he wende þore have slawe.
And with him comen oþer two
1650 That him wolde of live have do.
Havelok lifte up þe dore-tre
And at a dint he slow hem þre.
Was non of hem þat his hernes
Ne lay þer-ute ageyn þe sternes.
Þe ferþe þat he siþen mette
Wit þe barre so he him grette
Bifor þe heued þat þe rith eye
Ut of þe hole made he fleye
And siþe clapte him on þe crune
1660 So þat he stan-ded fel þor dune.
Þe fifte þat he over-tok
Gaf he a ful sor dint ok
Bitwen þe sholdres þer he stod

Or by Saint Augustine, you're dead!"
Bernard, who was very big, jumped up
And threw a coat of mail on his back
And grabbed a good, strong ax.
He leaped to the door as if he were mad,
And shouted, "Who are you out there,
Who are trying to start trouble?
Get out of here fast, you dirty thieves!
For by the Lord who men believe in,
If I have to throw this door open,
Some of you I will kill,
And the rest I will throw
In fetters and bind them tightly!"
"What did you say?" said one lad.
"Do you think that we're afraid?
We will go through this door
Before long, you big oaf, in spite of you!"
At once he gripped a giant stone
And let it fly with great force
Against the door, breaking it apart.
Havelok saw that, and ran up
And in an instant drew out the door bar,
Which was huge and rough enough,
And flung the door open wide
And said, "Here I stand now waiting!
Come to me fast!
Damn any of you who runs away!"
"No!" said one, "you will pay for that!"
And he began to run toward Havelok,
And drew out his sword in his hand,
Thinking to slay him there.
And with him came two others
Who would have ended his life.
Havelok lifted up the door bar,
And with one blow he killed all three.
There were none of them whose brains
Did not lie there under the stars.
The fourth one that he met next
He greeted with the bar against his head,
So that he made the right eye
Fly out of the socket,
And then clapped him on the head
So that he fell down stone dead.
The fifth that he overtook
He gave a painful blow as well
Between the shoulders where he stood,

Þat he spen his herte blod.	So that his heart's blood was spent.
Þe sixte wende for to fle	The sixth turned to run away,
And he clapte him with þe tre	And he slapped him with the bar
Rith in þe fule necke so	Right on the full shoulder,
Þat he smot hise necke on to.	So that he broke his neck in two.
Þanne þe sixe weren doun feld	When the sixth was brought down,
1670 Þe sevenþe brayd ut his swerd	The seventh whipped out his sword,
And wolde Havelok riht in the eye	Wanting to stab Havelok right in the eye,
And Havelok let þe barre fleye	And Havelok sent the bar flying
And smot him sone ageyn þe brest.	And hit him at once against the chest.
Þat hauede he nevere schrifte of prest	He had no time for a priest's rites,
For he was ded on lesse hwile	For he was dead in less time
Þan men mouthe renne a mile.	Than men might run a mile.
Alle þe oþere weren ful kene.	All the others were eager to fight.
A red þei taken hem bi-twene	They made a plan among themselves
þat he sholde him bi-halve	That they would surround him
1680 And brisen so þat wit no salve	And batter him, so that no salve
Ne sholde him helen leche non.	Of a doctor's would heal him.
Þey drowen ut swerdes ful god won	They drew out swords, a good number,
And shoten on him so don on bere	And rushed on him just like dogs
Dogges þat wolden him to-tere	That intend to tear apart a bear
Þanne men doth þe bere beyte.	When men watch bear-baiting.[235]
Þe laddes were kaske and teyte	The thugs were keen and quick,
And un-bi-yeden him ilkon.	And each one surrounded him. Some
Sum smot with tre and sum wit ston.	Struck with clubs and some with stones.
Summe putten with gleyve in bac and side	Some threw knives in his back and sides
1690 And yeven wundes longe and wide	And inflicted wounds long and wide
In twenti stedes and wel mo	In twenty places and many more,
Fro þe croune til the to.	From the head to the toe.
Hwan he saw þat he was wod	When Havelok saw that he was maddened,
And was it ferlik hw he stod!	And it was a miracle how he stood!
For the blod ran of his sides	For the blood ran down his sides
So water þat fro þe welle glides.	Like water flowing from a well.
But þanne bigan he for to mowe	But then he began to cut them down
With the barre and let hem shewe	With the bar, and to show them
Hw he cowþe sore smite.	How he could strike painfully.
1700 For was þer non long ne lite	For there were none, tall or short,
Þat he mouthe ouer-take	That he might overtake
Þat he ne garte his croune krake	Who did not have their heads cracked,
So þat on a litel stund	So that within a little while
Felde he twenti to þe grund.	He dropped twenty to the ground.
Þo bigan gret dine to rise	Then a great din began to rise,

---

235 *Bere beyte*: Bear baiting was a savagely violent 'sport' in which a bear would be chained to a stake and trained dogs would be set on. Bets would be taken and dogs would be replaced as they were mauled until the bear succumbed (Garbaty, note to 1659-61 [his lineation]). Henry VIII was not surprisingly a fan and the games were popular until their prohibition in 1835. Cockfighting, a similar blood-sport, still enjoys popularity in parts of the world. See also line 2176.

For þe laddes on ilke wise	For the lads attacked him
Him asayleden wit grete dintes.	In every way with great blows.
Fro fer he stoden him with flintes	From a distance they stood and flung
And gleyves schoten him fro ferne	Flintstones and knives at him,
1710 For drepen him he wolden yerne	For they were eager to kill him.
But dursten he newhen him no more	But they dared not get any nearer him
Þanne he bor or leun wore.	Than if he were a boar or a lion.
Huwe Rauen þat dine herde	Hugh Raven heard that clamor
And þowthe wel þat men mis-ferde	And knew full well that men were
With his louerd for his wif.	Acting wrongly against his lord for his wife.
And grop an ore and a long knif	He grabbed an oar and a long knife,
And þider drof al so an hert	And leaped out like a stag deer
And cham þer on a litel stert	And arrived there in a short moment,
And saw how þe laddes wode	And saw how the crazed outlaws
1720 Havelok his louerd umbistode	Surrounded his lord Havelok
And beten on him so doth þe smith	And beat on him like the smith
With þe hamer on þe stith.	Does with the hammer on the anvil.
"Allas!" hwat Hwe, "þat y was boren!	"Alas", cried Hugh, "that I was ever born
Þat evere et ich bred of koren	And ever ate bread from grain,
Þat ich here þis sorwe se!	To see this sorrow here!
Roberd! Willam! Hware ar ye?	Robert, William, where are you?
Gripeth eþer unker a god tre	Both of you, grab a good club
And late we nouth þise doges fle	And we will not let these dogs escape
Til ure louerd wreke we!	Until our lord is avenged!
1730 Cometh swiþe and folwes me!	Come quickly, and follow me!
Ich have in honde a ful god ore	I have a good strong oar in my hand;
Datheit wo ne smite sore!"	Damn anyone who isn't hit hard!"
"Ya leve ya!" quod Roberd sone	"Here, brother, here!" said Robert quickly,
"We haven ful god lith of þe mone".	"We have a good light from the moon".
Roberd grop a staf strong and gret	Robert seized a staff, strong and huge,
Þat mouthe ful wel bere a net	Which might well have carried an ox,
And Willam Wendut grop a tre	And William Wendut grabbed a club
Mikel grettere þan his þe	Much thicker than his own thigh,
And Bernard held his ax ful faste.	And Bernard held his ax firmly.–
1740 I seye was he nouth þe laste!	I say, he wasn't the last out!– And they
And lopen forth so he weren wode	Leaped forth as if they were berserk,
To þe laddes þer he stode	Toward the attackers where they stood,
And yaf hem wundes swiþe grete.	And gave them harsh wounds.
Þer mithe men wel se boyes bete	There one could see the thieves beaten,[236]
And ribbes in here sides breke	And the ribs in their sides broken,
And Havelok on hem wel wreke.	And Havelok avenged on them well.

236 *Men wel se*: OE *man* is an indefinite pronoun meaning both sexes, but by the fifteenth century it is replaced by *one*. Here the word appears to have a loose intermediate meaning as even plural *men* has an indefinite sense within the context. See Bettelou Los, "The Loss of the Indefinite Pronoun Man: Syntactic Change and Information Structure", in *English Historical Syntax and Morphology,* ed. Teresa Fanego, María J. López-Couso, & Javier Pérez-Guerra (Amsterdam: John Benjamins, 2002), 181-202.

He broken armes he broken knes
He broken shankes he broken thes.
He dide þe blode þere renne dune
1750 To þe fet rith fro the crune
For was þer spared heued non:
He leyden on heuedes ful god won
And made croune breke and crake
Of þe broune and of þe blake.
He maden here backes al so bloute
Als here wombes and made hem rowte
Als he weren kradelbarnes
So dos þe child þat moder þarnes.
Daþeit wo recke! For he it served!
1760 Hwat dide he þore weren he werewed!
So longe haueden he but and bet
With neves under hernes set
Þat of þo sixti men and on
Ne wente þer awey lives non.
On þe morwen hwan it was day
Ilc on other wirwed lay
Als it were dogges þat weren henged.
And summe leye in dikes slenget
And summe in gripes bi þe her
1770 Drawen ware and laten ther.
Sket cam tiding intil Ubbe
Þat Havelok hauede with a clubbe
Of hise slawen sixti and on
Sergaunz þe beste þat mithen gon.
"Deus!" quoth Ubbe, "hwat may þis be!
Betere his i nime miself and se
Þat þis baret on hwat is wold
Þanne i sende yunge or old.
For yif i sende him un-to
1780 I wene men sholde him shame do
And þat ne wolde ich for no þing.
I love him wel bi Hevene king!
Me wore levere i wore lame
Þanne men dide him ani shame
Or tok or onne handes leyde
Un-ornelike or same seyde".
He lep up on a stede lith
And with him mani a noble knith
And ferde forth un-to þe tun.
1790 And dide calle Bernard brun

They broke arms, they broke knees,
They broke legs, they broke thighs;
They made the blood run down
Right from their foreheads to their feet,
For not one head was spared.
They laid on a great number of men,
And made skulls break and crack
On every kind of fighter.
They beat their backs as soft
As their bellies and made them roar
Like they were babies in cradles,
Like the child that loses its mother.
Damn whoever cares! They deserved it!
What business had they there being mauled!
They battered and beat them,
With fists set on their brains,
For so long that of the sixty-one men,
None went their way alive.
In the morning, when it was day,
Each lay mangled on the other
As if they were dogs that were hanged.
And some lay slung in ditches,
And some in trenches,
Dragged by their hair and left there.
The news came fast to Ubbe
That Havelok had, with a club,
Slain sixty-one of his retinue–
Sergeants, the best that might be.[237]
"My God", said Ubbe, "what is this about?
It would be better to go myself,
And see what this trouble is about,
Than to send someone, young or old.
For if I send him to Havelok,
I expect men would take revenge,
And I would not have that for anything.
I love him well, by Heaven's king!
I would rather be crippled
Than have men do him any shame,
Or seize or lay hands on him roughly,
Or speak abuse to him".
He leaped upon a nimble horse,
Along with many a noble knight,
And journeyed forth into the town.
He called Bernard Brown

---

237 *Sergaunz:* In medieval usage a sergeant was any armed attendant or officer with a protective or guarding function. The line again suggests that the outlaws who attack Bernard Brun and Ubbe's retinue are the same men.

Ut of his hus wan he þer cam	Out of his house when he came there,
And Bernard sone ageyn nam.	And Bernard appeared at once.
Al to-tused and al to-torn	He was all cut up and torn to pieces,
Ner also naked so he was born	Nearly as naked as when he was born,
And al to-brised bac and þe.	And all bruised on the back and thighs.
Quoth Ubbe, "Bernard hwat is þe?	Ubbe said, "Bernard, what's wrong with
Hwo haues þe þus ille maked	You? Who has treated you so foully,
Þus to-riuen and al mad naked?"	To be ripped apart and almost naked?"
"Louerd merci!" quot he sone.	"Mercy, my lord!" he answered at once.
1800 "To-nicht also ros þe mone	"Last night, as the moon rose,
Comen her mo þan sixti þeves	More than sixty thieves showed up here,
With lokene copes and wide sleves	With fastened cloaks and wide sleeves,
Me forto robben and to pine	To rob and torment me,
And for to drepe me and mine!	And to slay me and all that's mine!
Mi dore he broken up ful sket	They broke down my door in a rush,
And wolde me binden hond and fet.	And would have bound me hand and foot.
Wan þe godemen þat sawe	When those gentlemen saw that,
Havelok and he þat bi þe wowe	Havelok, and those lying by the wall,
Leye he stirten up sone on-on	They got up right away, and some
1810 And summe grop tre and sum grop ston	Grabbed trees, and some took stones,
And drive hem ut þei he weren crus	And though they were fierce, they drove
So dogges ut of milne-hous.	Them out like dogs out of a mill-house.
Havelok grop þe dore-tre	Havelok gripped the door bar,
And a dint he slow hem thre.	And with one blow he killed three of them.
He is þe beste man at nede	He is the best man in need
Þat evere mar shal ride stede!	Who will ever ride a steed!
Als helpe God bi mine wone	So help me God, by my word,
A þhousend of men his he worth one!	He is as good as a thousand men!
Yif he ne were ich were nou ded	If not for him I would be dead now,
1820 So have ich don mi soule red.	As sure as I trust my own soul.
But it is hof him mikel sinne.	But as for him, it is a great sin.
He maden him swilke woundes þrinne	They gave him three wounds so harsh
Þat of þe alþer-leste wounde	That the very least of them
Were a stede brouht to grunde.	Would bring a horse to the ground.
He haues a wunde in the side	He has an ugly gash in his side
With a gleyve ful un-ride	From a lance,
And he haues on þoru his arum	And he has a wound through the arm
Þer-of is ful mikel harum	Which is a very dangerous one,
And he haues on þoru his þhe	And he has one through his thigh,
1830 Þe un-rideste þat men may se.	The most horrible that men might see.
And oþe wundes haues he stronge	And he has other serious wounds,
Mo than twenti swiþe longe.	More than twenty, just as deep.
But siþen he hauede lauth þe sor	But after he felt the pain of the wounds,
Of þe wundes was nevere bor	There was never a wild boar
Þat so fauth so he fauth þanne!	That fought as he fought then!
Was non þat hauede þe hern-panne	There was none who heaved on skulls

So hard þat he ne dede alto-cruhsse	So hard as he completely crushed,
And alto-shivere and alto-frusshe.	Shattered, and smashed them!
He folwede hem so hund dos hare	To Hell with anyone he might spare!
1840 Daþeyt on he wolde spare!	He chased them like a hound does a hare,
Þat ne made hem everilk on	So that he made each one of them
Ligge stille so doth þe ston.	Lie still like a stone.
And þer nis he nouth to frie	And there is nothing to blame him for,
For oþer sholde he make hem lye	For they either had to lie dead by his hand
Ded or þei him hauede slawen	Or they would have slain him,
Or alto-hewen or al-to-drawen!	Or totally hacked or ripped him apart!
Louerd havi no more plith	My lord, I have no more trouble
Of þat ich was þus greþed to-nith.	From what threatened me last night.
Þus wolde þe theves me have reft	The thieves would have robbed me,
1850 But God-þank he havenet sure keft!	But, thank God, they surely paid for it!
But it is of him mikel scaþe.	But it is a great pity about Havelok.
I woth þat he bes ded ful raþe".	I believe he will soon be dead". Ubbe said,
Quoth Ubbe, "Bernard seyst þou soth?"	"Bernard, are you telling the truth?"
"Ya sire that i ne lepe oth!	"Yes, sire, I do not make false oaths![238]
Yif y louerd a word leye	If I lie one word, my lord,
To-morwen do me hengen heye!"	Tomorrow have me hanged high!"
Þe burgeys þat þer-bi stode þore	The town elders who stood nearby,
Grundlike and grete oþes swore	Low and great, young and old,
Litle and mikle yunge and holde	Swore great and solemn oaths
1860 Þat was soth þat Bernard tolde.	That it was true what Bernard said.
Soth was þat he wolden him bynde	It was true that they wanted to tie him up
And trusse al þat he mithen fynde	And carry off all they might find of his
Of hise in arke or in kiste	In coffers or in chests,
Þat he mouthe in seckes þriste.	That they would jam it into sacks.
"Louerd he haueden al awey born	"My lord, they would have taken
His þing and him-self alto-torn	All he had, with himself torn apart.
But als God self barw him wel	But God Himself has preserved him well
Þat he ne tinte no catel.	So that he has not lost any goods.
Hwo mithe so mani stonde ageyn	Who could stand against so many men
1870 Bi nither-tale knith or swein?	In the night time, knight or peasant?
He weren bi tale sixti and ten	They were sixty and ten more in count,
Starke laddes stalworþi men	Strong men, rugged men,
And on þe mayster of hem alle	And one was the master of them all,
Þat was þe name Giffin Galle.	Who had the name Griffin Galle.
Hwo mouthe ageyn so mani stonde	Who could stand against so many,
But als þis man of ferne londe	Except this man from faraway lands,
Haueth hem slawen with a tre?	Who has killed them with a door bar?
Mikel joie have he!	May he have great joy!
God yeve him mikel god to welde	May God give him wealth to wield,

---

238 *That I ne leye o tooth*: Word division in the MS is unclear. Herzman et al. suggest the idiom 'I do not lie through my teeth', but this spelling of tooth is not in the MED. Skeat has *that ine lepe oth* but the phrase makes no sense. Some give *leye othe*, 'lie' + 'oath', which seems to work here.

1880 Boþe in tun and ek in felde.	Both in town and in the fields as well.
Wel is set he etes mete!"	The food he eats is well spent!"
Quoth Ubbe, "Doth him swiþe fete	Ubbe said, "Have him brought quickly,
Þat y mouthe his woundes se	So that I may see his wounds,
Yf that he mouthen heled be.	If he may be healed.
For yf he mouthe couere yet	For if he might still recover,
And gangen wel up-on hise fet	And walk firmly on his feet,
Mi-self shal dubbe him to knith	I myself will dub him a knight
For-þi þat he is so with.	Because of his bravery.
And yif he livede þo foule theves	And if any are alive, those foul thieves
1890 Þat weren of Kaym kin and Eves	Who came from Cain and Eve's kin,[239]
He sholden hange bi þe necke!	They will hang by the neck!
Of here ded daþeit wo recke	Curse whoever cares about their death,
Hwan he yeden þus on nithes	Since they ran about at night
To binde boþe burgmen and knithes.	To tie up both townsmen and knights.
For bynderes love ich nevere mo	I have no love for outlaws;
Of hem ne yeve ich nouht a slo!"	I wouldn't give a berry for them!"
Havelok was bifore Ubbe browth	Havelok was brought before Ubbe,
Þat hauede for him ful mikel þouth	Who had great concern for him
And mikel sorwe in his herte	And much sorrow in his heart
1900 For hise wundes þat we so smerte.	For his wounds, which were so painful.
But hwan his wundes weren shewed	But when his injuries were examined
And a leche hauede knawed	And a doctor had determined
Þat he hem mouthe ful wel hele	That he would be able to heal them,
Wel make him gange and ful wel mele	To make him walk and talk with vigor,
And wel a palefrey bistride	And sit on a saddle-horse
And wel up-on a stede ride	And then ride a steed confidently,
Þo let Ubbe al his care	Then Ubbe let his worries go
And al his sorwe over-fare.	And all his sorrow passed away.
And seyde, "Cum now forth with me	He said, "Come back with me now,
1910 And Goldeboru þi wif with þe	With Goldeboro, your wife,
And þine seriaunz al þre.	And your men-at-arms, all three.
For nou wile y youre warant be.	For I will be your guarantor now.
Wile y non of here frend	I want none of the friends
Þat þu slowe with þin hend	Of those you killed with your hand
Moucte wayte þe to slo	To be able to wait for you in ambush
Also þou gange to and fro.	As you go to and fro.
I shal lene þe a bowr	I will lend you a bedroom
Þat is up in þe heye tour	Which is up in the high tower
Til þou mowe ful wel go	Until you can get around
1920 And wel ben hol of al þi wo.	And be fully healed from all your woes.
It ne shal no þing ben bitwene	There will be nothing between

239 The descendants of Cain were considered evil, just as Grendel is in *Beowulf* (108). Eve was viewed with similar opprobrium, as she was seen as responsible for the fall of man into sin. The antifeminist literature that Janekyn reads and which vexes the Wife of Bath has a typical excoriation of Eve: "that for hir wikkednesse / was al mankynde broght to wrecchednesse" (*CT* III.715-16).

Þi bour and min also y wene
But a fayr firrene wowe.
Speke y loude or spek y lowe
Þou shalt ful wel heren me.
And þan þu wilt þou shalt me se.
A rof shal hile us boþe o-nith
Þat none of mine clerk ne knith
Ne sholen þi wif no shame bede
1930 No more þan min so God me rede!"
He dide un-to þe borw bringe
Sone anon al with joynge
His wif and his serganz þre
Þe beste men þat mouthe be.
Þe firste nith he lay þer-inne
Hise wif and his serganz þrinne
Aboute þe middel of þe nith
Wok Ubbe and saw a mikel lith
In þe bour þat Havelok lay
1940 Also brith so it were day.
"Deus!" quoth Ubbe, "hwat may þis be?
Betere is i go miself and se
Hweþer he sitten nou and wesseylen
Or of ani shotshipe to-deyle
Þis tid nithes also foles.
Þan birþe men casten hem in poles
Or in a grip or in þe fen.
Nou ne sitten none but wicke men
Glotuns reveres or wicke þeves
1950 Bi Crist þat alle folk onne leves!"
He stod and totede in at a bord
Her he spak anilepi word
And saw hem slepen faste ilkon
And lye stille so þe ston.
And saw al þat mikel lith
Fro Havelok cam þat was so brith.
Of his mouth it com il del
Þat was he war ful swiþe wel.
"Deus!" quoth he, "hwat may þis mene?"
1960 He calde boþe arwe men and kene
Knithes and serganz swiþe sleie
Mo þan an hundred with-uten leye
And bad hem alle comen and se
Hwat þat selcuth mithe be.
Als þe knithes were comen alle
Þer Havelok lay ut of þe halle
So stod ut of his mouth a glem

Your room and mine, I know,
But a fine fir-wood wall.
If I speak loudly or speak quietly,
You will hear me well.
And whenever you want, you will see me.
A roof will cover us both at night,
So that no one of mine, priest or knight,
Will try to cause shame to your wife
Any more than mine, so help me God!"
He had Havelok brought into the room
Right after, with his wife and his
Three retainers all rejoicing,
The best men that might be.
The first night that he lay in there,
With his wife and three brothers,
About the middle of the night
Ubbe woke up and saw a great light
From the room where Havelok lay,
As bright as if it were day.
"Good lord!" said Ubbe, "what is this?
I had better go myself and see
Whether he is up now and drinking toasts,
Or taking part in some debauchery
Like fools do this time of night.
Men ought to throw them in pools,
Or in a ditch, or in the muddy swamp.
No one is up now but wicked men,
Gluttons, criminals, or foul thieves,
By Christ who all people believe in!"
He stood up and peered through a board
Before he spoke another word,
And saw each one of them fast asleep
And lying as still as a stone.
He saw all that great light coming
From Havelok, which was so bright.
Every bit of it came out of his mouth;
He could see that clearly.
"My God", he said, "what can this mean?"
He called for men, both timid and bold,
His wisest knights and officers,
More than a hundred, without a lie,
And he ordered them all to come and see
What this marvel might be.
As the knights were all arriving,
Havelok lay there outside the hall.
Out of his mouth streamed a gleam,

Rith al swilk so þe sunne-bem.	Exactly like a sunbeam.
Þat al so lith was þare bi Hevene	The light there, by Heaven,
1970 So þer brenden serges sevene	Was as if seven tapers were burning
And an hundred serges ok.	And a hundred more candles with it.
Þat durste hi sweren on a bok!	I would dare to swear it on a Bible!
He slepen faste alle five	They were fast asleep, all five,
So he weren brouth of live	As if they had departed from life,
And Havelok lay on his lift side	And Havelok lay on his left side,
In his armes his brithe bride.	With his shining bride in his arms.
Bi þe pappes he leyen naked	He lay naked down to the chest;[240]
So faire two weren nevere maked	So fair a two were never created
In a bed to lyen samen.	To lie together in a bed.
1980 Þe knithes þouth of hem god gamen	The knights thought it was good fun
Hem forto shewe and loken to.	To look at them and watch them.
Rith also he stoden alle so	But just as they all stood there
And his bac was toward hem wend	And his back shifted toward them,
So weren he war of a croiz ful gent	They were aware of a majestic cross
On his rith shuldre swiþe brith	On his right shoulder, so clear, and
Brithter þan gold ageyn þe lith.	Brighter than gold against the light,
So þat he wiste heye and lowe	So that they realized, high and low,
Þat it was kunrik þat he sawe.	It was a royal birthmark they saw.
It sparkede and ful brith shon	It sparkled and shone brightly
1990 So doth þe gode charbucle ston	Just as a good carbuncle stone does,
Þat men mouthe se by þe lith	So that men could pick out a penny
A peni chesen so was it brith.	By its light, it was so brilliant.
Þanne bihelden he him faste	Then they beheld him closely,
So þat he knewen at þe laste	So that they at last understood
Þat he was Birkabeynes sone	That he was the son of Birkabeyn,
Þat was here king þat was hem wone	The man who was their king, who used
Wel to yeme and wel were	To govern and protect them well
Ageynes uten-laddes here	Against foreign armies:
"For it was nevere yet a broþer	"For there has never been a brother
2000 In al Denmark so lich anoþer	In all Denmark so like another
So þis man þat is so fayr	As this man, who is so noble,
Als Birkabeyn he is hise eyr".	Is like Birkabeyn. He is his heir".
He fellen sone at hise fet	At once they fell at his feet;
Was non of hem þat he ne gret	There were none who did not hail him.
Of joie he weren alle so fawen	They were all as full of joy
So he him haueden of erþe drawen.	As if he had risen from the grave.
Hise fet he kisten an hundred syþes	They kissed his feet a hundred times,
Þe tos þe nayles and þe lithes	The toes, the nails, and the tips,
So þat he bigan to wakne	So that he began to wake up.

---

240 Skeat cites George Ellis's *Specimens of Early English Metrical Romances* (1811), who asserts that the medieval custom was to sleep naked. The emir in *Floris & Blancheflor* describes Floris as a naked boy in Blancheflor's bed (1064). Some critics see the scene as voyeuristic, but it is unlikely that the poet's statement that Havelok went *ful naked* (5, 860) means total nudity. More likely, in the heat of summer Havelok and Goldeboru are wearing minimal bedclothing.

2010 And wit hem ful sore to blakne	On seeing them he blanched painfully,
For he wende he wolden him slo	For he thought they would slay him,
Or elles binde him and do wo.	Or else tie him up and do woe.
Quoth Ubbe, "Louerd ne dred þe nowth!"	Ubbe said, "My lord, have no fear!
Me þinkes that I se þi þouth.	I think I know your thoughts.
Dere sone wel is me	Dear son, how fortunate I am
Þat y þe with eyn se.	To see you with my own eyes.
Man-red louerd bede y þe.	Lord, I offer you homage.
Þi man auht i ful wel to be	I wholly ought to be your man,
For þu art comen of Birkabeyn	For you are born from Birkabeyn,
2020 Þat hauede mani knith and sweyn	Who had many knights and servants,
And so shalt þou louerd have	And you, lord, shall have the same.
Þou þu be yet a ful yung knave.	Though you are still a young man,
Þou shalt be king of al Denmark!	You will be king of all Denmark!
Was þer-inne nevere non so stark.	There was never anyone so strong here.
To-morwen shaltu manrede take	Tomorrow you will receive pledges
Of þe brune and of þe blake	From every type of man,
Of alle þat aren in þis tun	From all who are in this town,
Boþe of erl and of barun	Both from earl and from baron,
And of dreng and of thayn	And from vassal and retainer,
2030 And of knith and of sweyn.	And from knight and bondsman.
And so shaltu ben mad knith	And so you will be made a knight
Wit blisse for þou art so with".	With gladness, for you are so valiant".
Þo was Havelok swiþe bliþe	Then Havelok was very joyful,
And þankede God ful fele siþe.	And thanked God many times.
On þe morwen wan it was lith	In the morning, when it was light,
And gon was þisternesse of þe nith	And the gloom of the night was gone,
Ubbe dide up-on a stede	Ubbe had a young messenger
A ladde lepe and þider bede	Leap on a steed, and go to summon
Erles barouns drenges theynes	Earls, barons, retainers, vassals,
2040 Klerkes knithes burgeys sweynes	Priests, knights, townspeople, and peasants,
Þat he sholden comen a-non	That they should come quickly
Biforen him sone everilkon	Before him soon, each of them,
Also he loven here lives	As much as they loved their lives
And here children and here wives.	And their children and their wives.
Hise bode ne durste he non at-sitte	No one dared ignore his command,
Þat he ne neme for to wite	So that all came immediately
Sone hwat wolde þe justice.	To find out what the justice wanted.
And bigan anon to rise	Ubbe at once rose
And seyde sone, "Liþes me	And said, "Listen to me,
2050 Alle samen þeu and fre!	All together, bound and free!
A þing ich wile you here shauwe	I will relate to you here a matter
Þat ye alle ful wel knawe.	That you all know clearly about.
Ye witen wel þat al þis lond	You know well that all this land
Was in Birkabeynes hond	Was in Birkabeyn's hand
Þe day þat he was quic and ded	The day that he was alive and dead,

And how þat he bi youre red
Bitauhte hise children þre
Godard to yeme and al his fe.
Havelok his sone he him tauhte
2060 And hise two douhtres and al his auhte.
Alle herden ye him swere
On bok and on messe-gere
Þat he shulde yeme hem wel
With-uten lac with-uten tel.
He let his oth al over-go!
Evere wurþe him yvel and wo!
For þe maydnes here lif
Refte he boþen with a knif
And him shulde ok have slawen.
2070 Þe knif was at his herte drawen
But God him wolde wel have save.
He hauede reunesse of þe knave
So þat he with his hend
Ne drop him nouth þat sori fend!
But sone dide he a fishere
Swiþe grete oþes swere
Þat he sholde drenchen him
In þe se þat was ful brim.
Hwan Grim saw þat he was so fayr
2080 And wiste he was þe rith eir
Fro Denmark ful sone he fledde
In-til Englond and þer him fedde.
Mani winter þat til þis day
Haues he ben fed and fostred ay.
Lokes hware he stondes her!
In al þis werd ne haues he per.
Non so fayr ne non so long
Ne non so mikel ne non so strong.
In þis middelerd nis no knith
2090 Half so strong ne half so with.
Bes of him ful glad and bliþe
And cometh alle hider swiþe
Manrede youre louerd forto make
Boþe brune and þe blake.
I shal mi-self do first þe gamen
And ye siþen alle samen".
Oknes ful fayre he him sette
Mouthe noþing him þer-fro lette.
And bi-cam is man rith þare

And how he, by your counsel,
Entrusted his three children, and all
His property, to Godard to protect.
He committed his son Havelok to him,
And his two daughters and his holdings.
All of you heard him swear
On the Bible and on the mass garments
That he would keep them well,
Without fault, without reproach.
He forget all about his oath!
He deserves eternal evil and woe!
For he deprived both of the maidens
Of their lives with a knife,
And he would have killed the boy also.
The knife was drawn at his heart,
But God wished to save him.
Godard felt sorry for the boy
So that he could not kill him
With his own hand, that miserable fiend!
But soon after he forced a fisherman
To swear solemn oaths
That he would drown him
In the sea that was so wild.
When Grim saw that he was so fair,
And realized he was the rightful heir,
They quickly fled from Denmark
Into England and took care of him there.
Many years until this day
He has been fed and raised up well.
Look where he stands here!
In all this world he has no peer,
None so handsome, none so tall,
Nor any so great, nor none so strong.
On this earth there is no knight
Half so mighty, nor half so valiant.
Be joyful and glad because of him,
And come forward quickly
To pledge loyalty to your lord,
Every rank of person.
I shall first do the honors myself,
And you will all follow together after".
Ubbe set himself courteously on his knees;
Nothing might delay him from it.
And he became Havelok's man right there,

2100 Þat alle sawen þat þere ware.	So that all who were there saw it.[241]
After him stirt up laddes ten	After him ten lads started up
And bi-comen hise men	And became his men,
And siþen everilk a baroun	And after then each baron
Þat evere weren in al that toun	Who was ever in that town,
And siþen drenges and siþen thaynes	And then servants, and then vassals,
And siþen knithes and siþen sweynes.	And then knights, and then peasants,
So þat or þat day was gon	So that before the day was gone,
In al þe tun ne was nouth on	In all the town there was not one
Þat it ne was his man bicomen.	Who had not become his man.
2110 Manrede of alle hauede he nomen.	They had all taken oaths of loyalty.
Hwan he hauede of hem alle	When he had accepted homage
Manrede taken in the halle	From all of them in the hall,
Grundlike dide he hem swere	He had them solemnly swear
Þat he sholden him god feyth bere	That they would bear him good faith
Ageynes alle þat woren on live	Against all who were alive,
Þer-yen ne wolde never on strive	That no one would ever strive against him
Þat he ne maden sone þat oth	Who made that oath at that time,
Riche and poure lef and loth.	Rich or poor, fair or foul.
Hwan þat was maked sone he sende	When that was done, at once he sent
2120 Ubbe writes fer and hende	Ubbe's summons far and wide
After alle þat castel yemede	To all who ruled a castle,
Burwes tunes sibbe an fremde	City, or town, friend or stranger,
Þat þider sholden comen swiþe	That they should come to him quickly
Til him and heren tiþandes bliþe	And hear the good news
Þat he hem alle shulde telle.	That he would tell them.
Of hem ne wolde nevere on dwelle	Of them, not a one delayed
Þat he ne come sone plattinde.	So that he did not come hurrying.
Hwo hors ne hauede com gangande	Whoever had no horse came on foot,
So þat with-inne a fourtenith	So that within a fortnight
2130 In al Denmark ne was no knith	In all of Denmark, there was no knight,
Ne conestable ne shireve	Constable, or sheriff[242]
Þat com of Adam and of Eve	Who came from Adam and Eve
Þat he ne com biforn sire Ubbe	Who did not appear before Sir Ubbe;
He dredden him so þhes doth clubbe.	They feared him as the thief does the club.
Hwan he haueden alle þe king gret	When they had all greeted the king
And he weren alle dun set	And they were all seated,
Þo seyde Ubbe, "Lokes here	Then Ubbe said, "Behold here
Ure louerd swiþe dere	Our lord so dear,
Þat shal ben king of al þe lond	Who will be king of all the land

---

241 Strohm notes that the swearing of fealty between vassal and lord, manrede, was becoming an increasingly practical and contractual matter by the fourteenth century, but in romance there is still the older Germanic ideal of a sacred and emotional bond of loyalty expressed in a public rite. Paul Strohm, *Social Chaucer* (Cambridge: Harvard Press, 1989), 14. Note the use of *riche and poure* (2118), sounding much like a wedding vow.

242 *Ne conestable, ne shireve*: Like *sergeant*, these are terms predating modern police forces. A constable or marshall (*mareschal*) was an officer of the stables. A sheriff was a *shire-reeve*, the lord's representative in maintaining order in the countryside, such as Gamelyn's brother.

2140 And have us alle under hond!	And have us all in his hand!
For he is Birkabeynes sone	For he is Birkabeyn's son,
Þe king þat was umbe stonde wone	The king who once used
For to yeme and wel were	To rule and protect us well
Wit sharp swerd and longe spere.	With a sharp sword and long spear.
Lokes nou hw he is fayr	Look now, how noble he is;
Sikerlike he is hise eyr!	Surely he is his heir!
Falles alle to hise fet	Everyone fall to his feet
Bicomes hise men ful sket".	And become his man in haste".
He weren for Ubbe swiþe adrad	They were so in awe of Ubbe
2150 And dide sone al þat he bad	That they did all he ordered at once,
And yet deden he sumdel more:	And yet they did something more:
O bok ful grundlike he swore	They gravely swore on the Bible
Þat he sholde with him halde	That they would stand with him
Boþe ageynes stille and bolde	Against both timid and bold,
Þat evere wolde his bodi dere.	Against whoever wished to harm his body.
Þat dide he hem o boke swere.	He had them swear it on the book.
Hwan he hauede manrede and oth	When he had taken homage and oaths
Taken of lef and of loth	From fair and foul,
Ubbe dubbede him to knith	Ubbe dubbed him a knight
2160 With a swerd ful swiþe brith	With a sword shining bright,
And þe folk of al þe lond	And the people of all the land
Bitauhte him al in his hond	Entrusted everything into his hand,
Þe cunnriche everil del	Every bit of the kingdom,
And made him king heylike and wel.	And made him king, fully and majestically.
Hwan he was king þer mouthe men se	When he was king, men might see there
Þe moste joie þat mouhte be.	The greatest joy that could be.
Buttinge with sharpe speres	There was jousting with sharp spears,
Skirming with taleuaces þat men beres	Fencing with shields that men bear,
Wrastling with laddes putting of ston	Wrestling with the lads, shot-putting,
2170 Harping and piping ful god won	Harping and piping in plenty,
Leyk of mine of hasard ok	Games of backgammon and dice as well,
Romanz reding on þe bok.	And readings from books of romances.
Þer mouthe men here þe gestes singe	There one could hear tales sung,
Þe gleymen on þe tabour dinge.	With minstrels beating on a drum.
Þer mouhte men se þe boles beyte	Men could see bulls baited,
And þe bores with hundes teyte.	And the boars with lively dogs.
Þo mouthe men se everil gleu	Men could see every kind of sport
Þer mouthe men se hw grim greu.	And enjoy the growing excitement.[243]
Was nevere yete joie more	There was never yet more joy
2180 In al þis werd þan þo was þore.	In all this world than there was there.

---

243 *Ther mouthe men se hw Grim grew*: Skeat asserts in his note to 2320 (his lineation) that this is early evidence of secular theatre, as the celebrants are reenacting the life of Havelok's stepfather, Grim. More likely the poet means ME *grim*, in this context 'excitement or action'.

Þer was so mike yeft of cloþes
Þat þou i swore you grete othes
I ne wore nouth þer-offe croud.
Þat may i ful wel swere bi God!
Þere was swiþe gode metes
And of wyn þat men fer fetes
Rith al so mik and gret plente
So it were water of þe se.
Þe feste fourti dawes sat
2190 So riche was nevere non so þat.
Þe king made Roberd þere knith
Þat was ful strong and ful with
And Willam Wendut het his broþer
And Huwe Raven þat was þat oþer.
And made hem barouns alle þre
And yaf hem lond and oþer fe
So mikel þat ilker twenti knihtes
Hauede of genge dayes and nithes.
Hwan þat feste was al don
2200 A thusand knihtes ful wel o bon
With-held þe king with him to lede.
Þat ilkan hauede ful god stede
Helm and sheld and brinie brith
And al þe wepne þat fel to knith.
With hem five thusand gode
Sergaunz þat weren to fyht wode
With-held he al of his genge.
Wile I na more þe storie lenge.
Yet hwan he hauede of al þe lond
2210 Þe casteles alle in his hond
And conestables don þer-inne
He swor he ne sholde never blinne
Til þat he were of Godard wreken
Þat ich have of ofte speken.
Hal hundred knithes dede he calle
And hise fif thusand sergaunz alle
And dide sweren on the bok
Sone and on þe auter ok
Þat he ne sholde nevere blinne
2220 Ne for love ne for sinne
Til þat he haueden Godard funde
And brouth biforn him faste bunde.
Þanne he haueden swor þis oth

There were so many gifts of clothes[244]
That even if I swore you great oaths
It would never be believed.
That I may swear in full, by God!
There were costly foods and wines
That men bring from distant lands,
Just as much and in such abundance
As if it were water from the sea.
The feast lasted forty days;
There was never one so lavish as that.
The king made Robert a knight there,
Who was strong and brave,
And William Wendut as well, his brother,
And Hugh Raven, who was the third.
He made all three of them barons,
And gave them land and other wealth,
So much that each had in his retinue
Twenty knights by day and night.
When the feast was all over,
A thousand knights, fully equipped,
Escorted the king with him leading them.
Each had a strong steed,
Helmet and shield, and bright mailcoat,
And all the weapons fitting for a knight.
With them were also five thousand men,
Good officers that were raring to fight,
Who filled out his company.
I will not make the story any longer.
And yet when he had, from all the land,
All the castles in his command,
And had placed constables in them,
He swore he would never rest
Until he had revenge on Godard,
Whom I have spoken often enough about.
He summoned half a hundred knights,
And all his five thousand officers,
And had them swear at once
On the Bible and on the altar as well,
That they would never cease,
Not for love, nor for sin,
Until they had found Godard
And brought him before him bound fast.
When they had sworn this oath,

---

244 *So mike yeft of clothes*: Lavish presents of clothing were common in wealthy households during holidays and celebrations. Chaucer and wife Philippa received many such gifts as recorded in royal account books of the period (Garbaty, his note to 2157-59).

Ne leten he nouth for lef ne loth
Þat he ne foren swiþe rathe
Þer he was unto þe paþe
Þer he yet on hunting for
With mikel genge and swiþe stor.
2230 Robert þat was of al þe ferd
Mayster was girt wit a swerd
And sat up-on a ful god stede
Þat under him rith wolde wede.
He was þe firste þat with Godard
Spak and seyde, "Hede cavenard!
Wat dos þu here at þis paþe?
Cum to þe king swiþe and raþe!
Þat sendes he þe word and bedes
Þat þu þenke hwat þu him dedes
Hwan þu reftes with a knif
2240 Hise sistres here lif
An siþen bede þu in þe se
Drenchen him þat herde he!
He is to þe swiþe grim.
Cum nu swiþe un-to him
Þat king is of þis kuneriche.
Þu fule man þu wicke swike!
And he shal yelde þe þi mede
Bi Crist þat wolde on rode blede!"
Hwan Godard herde þat þer þrette
2250 With þe neve he Robert sette
Biforn þe teth a dint ful strong
And Robert kipt ut a knif long
And smot him þoru þe rith arum.
Þer-of was ful litel harum.
Hwan his folk þat sau and herde
Hwou Robert with here louerd ferde
He haueden him wel ner browt of live
Ne weren his two breþren and oþre five
Slowen of here laddes ten
2260 Of Godardes alþer-beste men.
Hwan þe oþre sawen þat he fledden
And Godard swiþe loude gredde
"Mine knithes hwat do ye?
Sule ye þus-gate fro me fle?
Ich have you fed and yet shal fede!
Helpe me nu in þis nede
And late ye nouth mi bodi spille
Ne Havelok don of me hise wille!
Yif ye id do ye do you shame

They would not be delayed for love or hate,
So that they went forth in a hurry
To where Godard was, on the path
Where he went hunting,
With a retinue that was large and proud.
Robert, who was master of the militia,
Was equipped with a sword
And sat upon a mighty steed
That would gallop mightily under him.
He was the first to speak to Godard,
And shouted, "Stop right there, rogue!
What are you doing on this path?
Come to the king quickly in haste!
He sends you word and commands you
To think on what you did to him
When you took the lives of
His sisters with a knife
And then ordered him to be drowned
In the sea– he heard all about that!
He is very angry with you.
Now come to him immediately,
The sovereign of this kingdom,
You foul man, you wicked traitor!
And he will give you your reward,
By Christ who bled on the cross!"
When Godard heard what he threatened,
With his fist he struck Robert
In the teeth with a powerful blow,
And Robert pulled out a long knife
And stuck him through the right arm.
There was little harm done in that;
And when his retinue saw and heard
What Robert had done to their lord,
They nearly would have taken his life
If not for his two brothers and five others
Who killed ten lads
Out of Godard's very best men.
When the others saw that, they fled,
And Godard shouted loudly,
"My knights, what are you doing?
Will you abandon me this way?
I have kept you and will do so still!
Help me now in this need
And do not let my blood be spilled,
Or let Havelok do his will with me!
If you do so, you shame yourselves

2270 And bringeth you-self in mikel blame!"
Hwan he þat herden he wenten ageyn
And slowen a knit and a sweyn
Of þe kinges oune men
And woundeden abuten ten.
The kinges men hwan he þat sawe
Scuten on hem heye and lowe
And everilk fot of hem slowe
But Godard one þat he flowe
So þe þef men dos henge
2280 Or hund men shole in dike slenge.
He bunden him ful swiþe faste
Hwil þe bondes wolden laste
Þat he rorede als a bole
Þat he wore parred in an hole
With dogges forto bite and beite.
Were þe bondes nouth to leite.
He bounden him so fele sore
Þat he gan crien Godes ore
Þat he sholde of his hend plette.
2290 Wolden he nouht þer-fore lette
Þat he ne bounden hond and fet.
Daþeit þat on þat þer-fore let!
But dunten him so man doth bere
And keste him on a scabbed mere
Hise nese went un-to þe crice.
So ledden he þat fule swike
Til he was biforn Havelok brouth
Þat he hauede ful wo wrowht
Boþe with hungre and with cold
2300 Or he were twel winter old
And with mani hevi swink
With poure mete and feble drink
And swiþe wikke cloþes
For al hise manie grete othes.
Nu beyes he his holde blame:
'Old sinne makes newe shame!'
Wan he was so shamelike
Biforn þe king þe fule swike
Þe king dede Ubbe swiþe calle

And bring yourselves into dishonor!"
When they heard that, they came back,
And killed a knight and an attendant
Of the king's own men,
And wounded about ten others.
Havelok's troops, when they saw this,
Rushed on them, high and low,
And slaughtered every foot of them
Except for Godard alone, whom they would
Flay, like a thief that men hang,
Or a dog that men hurl into a ditch.
They tied him up tightly
While the bonds would last,
So that he roared like a bull
That was trapped in a pit
With dogs biting and goading.
The bonds were not light in weight.
They held him so painfully tight
That he began to cry for God's mercy,
That they would cut off his hands.
They did not stop for that,
Until he was bound hand and foot.
Cursed be the man who would stop it!
They beat him like men do a bear
And threw him on a mangy mare with
His nose turned back into its behind.[245]
They led that foul traitor in this way
Until he was brought before Havelok,
To whom he had caused so much woe,
Both with hunger and with cold
Before he was twelve years old,
With much heavy labor,
With poor food and little drink,
And with ragged clothing,
For all his many fine oaths.
Now he paid for his earlier crime:
'Old sin makes new shame!'[246]
When the foul traitor was so
Disgracefully brought before the king,
The king had Ubbe quickly call

---

245 *Hise nese went unto the crice*: It was a special humiliation to have a knight ride on a mare or ass, usually facing backwards (Garbaty, his note to 2298-99). Here the punishment is especially degrading with the criminal's nose pressed near the animal's anus. In the bawdy fabliau *Dame Sirith* the lady similarly fears this penalty if she is exposed as a procurer of prostitutes (247). See also *Havelok* 2688.

246 Evidently a known expression; see also Proverb 47 in Rawlinson MS D 328, "Wold' syne makyth new shame / Sepe nouum vetera faciunt peccata pudorem". Quoted in Sanford B. Meech, "A Collection of Proverbs in Rawlinson MS D 328", *Modern Philology* 38:2 (1940): 121.

2310 Hise erles and hise barouns alle	His earls and all his barons,
Dreng and thein burgeis and knith	Vassal and retainer, citizen and knight,
And bad he sholden demen him rith	And ordered that they should judge him,
For he kneu þe swike dam.	For they knew the criminal well.
Everildel God was him gram!	God was angry with him in every way!
He setten hem dun bi þe wawe	They seated themselves by the wall,
Riche and pouere heye and lowe	Rich and poor, high and low,
Þe helde men and ek þe grom	The old men and the young as well,
And made þer þe rithe dom.	And made their judgment there.
And seyden unto þe king anon	Soon they said to the king,
2320 Þat stille sat so þe ston	Who sat as still as a stone,
"We deme þat he be al quic slawen	"We order that he be flayed alive,
And siþen to þe galwes drawe	And then taken to the gallows,
At þis foule mere tayl	Facing this foul mare's tail, with a
Þoru is fet a ful strong nayl	Good strong harness through his feet,
And þore ben henged wit two feteres	And be hanged there on two chains,[247]
And þare be writen þise leteres:	With these words written there:
'Þis is þe swike þat wende wel	'This is the traitor who fully intended
Þe king have reft þe lond il del	To rob the king of every acre of land,
And hise sistres with a knif	And who took the lives of both
2330 Boþe refte here lif'.	His sisters with a knife'.
Þis writ shal henge bi him þare.	This writ will hang by him there. The
Þe dom is demd seye we na more".	Verdict is given. We have no more to say".
Hwan þe dom was demd and give	When the judgment was given and
And he was wit þe prestes shrive	Approved, and he received last rites from
And it ne mouhte ben non oþer	The priests, there was no other course,
Ne for fader ne for broþer	Not for father nor for brother,
Þat he sholde þarne lif.	But that he should lose his life.
Sket cam a ladde with a knif	A lad came swiftly with a knife
And bigan rith at þe to	And began right at the toe
2340 For to ritte and for to flo	To cut and to slice,
And he bigan for to rore	As if it were a gown or dress,[248]
So it were grim or gore	And Godard began to roar then
Þat men mithe þeþen a mile	So that men a mile away
Here him rore þat fule file!	Might hear him yell, that foul wretch!
Þe ladde ne let no with for-þi	The youth did not stop at all for that,
Þey he criede 'Merci merci!'	Even though he cried, "Mercy! Mercy!",
Þat ne flow him everil del	To skin every bit of him
With knif mad of grunden stel.	With a knife made of ground steel.
Þei garte bringe þe mere sone	Soon they had the mare brought,

---

247 Garbaty notes that because hanged criminals were left exposed as a public example, chains were preferred to rope as they would not deteriorate in bad weather (his note to 2301). French and Hale explain that the *nayl* (2324) probably attaches a harness to secure Godard to the horse (p. 158, in Herzman et al.).

248 *So it were grim or gore*: Garbaty has *so it were goun or gore*, 'gown or dress' i.e. tailored by the knife. Though the executioners drive the mare over a rough field, presumably to inflict further agony, Godard is probably dead long before his ride to the gallows. Levine criticizes the poet for his rather pornographic glee over Godard's suffering in this scene. Robert Levine, "Who Composed Havelok for Whom?", *Yearbook of English Studies* 22 (1992): 96.

2350 Skabbed and ful ivele o bone	Scabbed and sick to the bone,
And bunden him rith at hire tayl	And bound him right to the tail
With a rop of an old seyl.	With a rope from an old sail.
And drowen him un-to þe galwes	They dragged him to the gallows,
Nouth bi þe gate but over þe falwes	Not by the road but over the fields,
And henge him þore bi þe hals.	And hanged him there by the neck.
Daþeit hwo recke! He was fals!	Damn whoever cares! He was false!
Þanne he was ded þat Sathanas	When he was dead, that devil,
Sket was seysed al þat his was	All that was his was quickly seized
In þe kinges hand il del	Into the king's hand, every bit,
2360 Lond and lith and oþer catel.	Lands and tenants and other goods.
And þe king ful sone it yaf	And the king in turn gave it
Ubbe in þe hond wit a fayr staf	Into Ubbe's hand with a fine staff[249]
And seyde "her ich sayse þe	And said, "I hereby invest you
In al þe lond in al þe fe".	With all the land, and all the properties".
. . . .	. . . .
A Quant Haveloc est rois pussanz	Havelok was a mighty king then,[250]
Le règne tint plus de iiii anz	And he reigned more than four years
Merveillous trésor i auna.	And amassed marvelous treasures.
Argentille li comanda	But Goldeboro urged him
Que il passast en Engleterre	To journey back to England
2370 Pur son héritage conquerre	To conquer her heritage,
Dont son oncle l'out engettée	For which her guardian had exiled
Et à grant tort désheritée.	And very unjustly disinherited her.
Li rois li dist que il fera	The king told her he would do
Ceo q'ele li comandera.	As she had asked him.
Sa navie fet aturner	He had his fleet prepared
Ses genz et ses ostz mander.	And sent for his men and his host.
En mier se met quant orré a	After praying, he put to sea
Et la réyne od lui mena.	And took the queen with him.
Quatre vinz et quatre cenz	Havelok had four hundred
2380 Out Haveloc pleines de genz.	And eighty ships, full of men.
Tant oüt nagé et siglé	They sailed and steered
Q'en Carleflure est arivé.	Until they arrived at Saltfleet.[251]
Sur le havene se herbergèrent	They anchored near the harbor
Par le païs viande quierent.	And looked for provisions on land.
. . . .	. . . .
L Þo swor Havelok he sholde make	Then Havelok swore that
Al for Grim of monekes blake	He would establish a priory for Grim

---

249 *Wit a fayr staf*: Havelok likely gives Ubbe a staff of wood to symbolize his authority, just as King Edgar gives Bevis a *yerd* (*Bevis of Hampton*, 3509). The denotation of a "staff" of retainers and supporters is early modern and not in the MED.

250 Editors feel about twenty lines are missing from the English story explaining Havelok's return to England, although it is not a MS defect. An extract from the *Lai d'Aveloc* suggests a substitute for the lacuna. In the French version Goldeboru's name is Argentille.

251 Carleflure is near Saltfleet, 30 km south of Grimsby. Charles W. Whistler, preface to *Havelok the Dane: A Legend of Old Grimsby and Lincoln* (T. Nelson and Sons, 1899). The medieval capital of Denmark was Roskilde, but the poem nowhere indicates where in the country Havelok is.

A priorie to serven inne ay	Of Benedictine monks to serve
Jhesu Crist til domesday	Jesus Christ forever, until Judgment Day,
For þe god he haueden him don	For the kindness he had shown him
2390 Hwil he was pouere and ivel o bon.	When he was poor and weak.
And þer-of held he wel his oth	And he would keep his promise in full,
For he it made God it woth	For he had it built, God knows,
In þe tun þer Grim was graven	In the town where Grim was buried,
Þat of Grim yet haues þe name.	Which still has his name.[252]
Of Grim bidde ich na more spelle.	I have no more to say about Grim;
But wan Godrich herde telle	But when Godrich,
Of Cornwayle þat was erl	Who was earl of Cornwall–
Þat fule traytour that mixed cherl	That foul traitor, that filthy slave–
Þat Havelok was king of Denmark	Heard that Havelok was king of Denmark,
2400 And ferde with him strong and stark	And that an army, strong and bold,
Comen Engelond with-inne	Had come into England,
Engelond al for to winne	To win all of England;
And þat she þat was so fayr	And that the beautiful Goldeboro,
Þat was of Engelond rith eir	Who was England's rightful heir,
Þat was comen up at Grimesbi	Had arrived at Grimsby,
He was ful sorful and sori	He was distraught and miserable
And seyde "Hwat shal me to raþe?	And said, "What shall I do?
Goddoth i shal do slou hem baþe!	God knows, I will kill them both!
I shal don hengen hem ful heye	I will have them hanged high,
2410 So mote ich brouke mi rith eie	As sure as I see with my right eye,
But yif he of mi londe fle!	Unless they flee my land! What,
Hwat wenden he to desherite me?"	Do they think they'll disinherit me?"
He dide sone ferd ut bidde	At once he ordered his army out,
Þat al þat evere mouhte o stede	All who could ever ride a horse
Ride or helm on heued bere	Or bear a helmet on their head,
Brini on bac and sheld and spere	A mailcoat on their back, shield and spear,
Or ani oþer wepne bere	Or carry any other weapon,
Hand-ax syþe gisarm or spere	Battle-ax, scythe, halberd, or spear,
Or aunlaz and god long knif	Or dagger or a good long knife,
2420 Þat als he lovede leme or lif	So that if they loved life or limb,
Þat þey sholden comen him to	They should report to him,
With ful god wepne ye ber so	Bearing their finest weapons,
To Lincolne þer he lay	To Lincoln, where he waited,
Of Marz þe seventenþe day	On the seventeenth day of March,
So þat he couþe hem god þank.	So that he might thank them properly.
And yif þat ani were so rang	And if any were so haughty
That he þanne ne come anon	That they did not come speedily,
He swor bi Crist and bi seint Iohan	He swore by Christ and by Saint John,
That he sholde maken him þral	That he would make him a slave,

---

252 Skeat posits that this is either Wellow Abbey in Grimsby, established by Henry I in 1110, or the Grimsby Friary, founded around 1290 (his note to line 2521). Herzman et al. assert that the 'black monks' are Benedictine, but Skeat and Garbaty have Augustinians. See also Smithers' note, p.144.

2430 And al his of-spring forth with-al.	And all his offspring after the same.[253]
Þe Englishe þat herde þat	Of the English who heard that,
Was non þat evere his bode sat	There were none who refused his orders,
For he him dredde swiþe sore	For they dreaded him so sorely
So runci spore and mikle more.	Like the nag fears the spur, and much more.
At þe day he come sone	On the day that Godard set for them
Þat he hem sette ful wel o bone	They promptly came, fully equipped,
To Lincolne with gode stedes	To Lincoln, with good warhorses
And al þe wepne þat knith ledes.	And all the weapons that knights bear.
Hwan he wore come sket was þe erl yare	When they had arrived, the earl was eager
2440 Ageynes Denshe men to fare	To face against Danish men,
And seyde, "Lyþes me alle samen!	And he said, "Listen to me, all together!
Have ich gadred you for no gamen	I have not gathered you for fun and games,
But ich wile seyen you forþi:	But for what I am telling you now:
Lokes hware here at Grimesbi	Look where, there at Grimsby,
Hise uten-laddes here comen	These foreigners have come,
And haues nu þe priorie numen	And have now seized the priory
Al þat evere mithen he finde.	And all that they can find.
He brenne kirkes and prestes binde	They burn churches and tie up priests;
He strangleth monkes and nunnes boþe!	They strangle both monks and nuns!
2450 Wat wile ye frend her-offe rede?	What, friends, do you advise to be done?
Yif he regne þus-gate longe	If they reign free in this way for long,
He moun us alle ouer-gange.	They may overcome us all.
He moun us alle quic henge or slo	They may hang or slay us all alive,
Or þral maken and do ful wo	Or make us slaves and do us great woe,
Or elles reve us ure lives	Or else rob us of our lives,
And ure children and ure wives!	Along with our children and our wives!
But dos nu als ich wile you lere	But now do as I will instruct you,
Als ye wile be with me dere.	If you wish to be faithful to me.
Nimes nu swiþe forth and raþe	Let us go forth now, and in haste,
2460 And helpes me and yu-self baþe	And save both me and yourselves
And slos up-on þe dogges swiþe!	And strike at the dogs quickly!
For shal i nevere more be bliþe	For I will never be at peace,
Ne hoseled ben ne of prest shriven	Nor be confessed or absolved by a priest,
Til þat he ben of londe driven.	Until they are driven from our land.
Nime we swiþe and do hem fle	Let us go forth and make them flee,
And folwes alle faste me!	And everyone follow me closely!
For ich am he of al þe ferd	For in all the army, it is I
Þat first shal slo with drawen swerd.	Who will first kill with his sword drawn.
Daþeyt hwo ne stonde faste	Damn anyone who doesn't stand fast
2470 Bi me hwil hise armes laste!"	By me while his arms last!"
"Ye lef ye!" couth þe erl Gunter.	"Yes, my dear lord, yes!" said Earl Gunter.

---

253 Godard threatens to disinherit any knight if he will not fight, a "flagrant and unheard-of violation of custom and law" (68). Delaney, *Literary Politics*, 68. Similarly, in lines 2450 Godard asks for advice rhetorically, forestalling any answer, and then lies about the Danes to stir up anger. The poet intends to highlight Havelok's good rule, as he defers to the counsel of others and thus needs no coercion to inspire loyalty.

"Ya!" quoth þe erl of Cestre Reyner.	"Yes!" said the earl of Chester, Reyner.
And so dide alle þat þer stode	And who stood there did the same,
And stirte forth so he were wode.	And they rushed forth as if they were mad.
Þo mouthe men se þe brinies brihte	Then men could see bright mailcoats
On backes keste and late rithe	Thrown on backs and laced firmly,
Þe helmes heye on heued sette.	And helmets set high on heads.
To armes al so swiþe plette	All hurried so quickly to arms
Þat þei wore on a litel stunde	That they were ready in the time
2480 Grethet als men mithe telle a pund.	It takes to count out a pound.
And lopen on stedes sone anon	Straightaway they leaped on steeds,
And toward Grimesbi ful god won	And towards Grimsby, with full force,
He foren softe bi þe sti	They lumbered along the road
Til he come ney at Grimesbi.	Until they came near to Grimsby.
Havelok þat hauede spired wel	Havelok, who had inquired closely
Of here fare everil del	Into their movements, every detail,
With al his ferd cam hem a-geyn.	Came against them with all his forces.
For-bar he noþer knith ne sweyn.	He spared neither knight nor peasant.
Þe firste knith þat he þer mette	The first knight that he met there
2490 With þe swerd so he him grette	He charged so hard with his sword
For his heued of he plette.	That he sheared off his head.
Wolde he nouth for sinne lette.	He did not hesitate to inflict harm.
Roberd saw þat dint so hende	When Robert saw that skillful blow,
Wolde he nevere þeþen wende	He would not turn away
Til þat he hauede anoþer slawen	Until he had slain another
With þe swerd he held ut-drawen.	With the sword he held drawn out.
Willam Wendut his swerd ut-drow	William Wendut drew out his sword,
And þe þredde so sore he slow	And he struck a third so hard
Þat he made up-on the feld	That he made his left arm fly off
2500 His lift arm fleye with the swerd.	Onto the field with his sword.
Huwe Raven ne forgat nouth	Hugh Raven did not forget to use
Þe swerd he hauede þider brouth	The sword he had brought there.
He kipte it up and smot ful sore	He swung it up, and struck hard
An erl þat he saw priken þore	On an earl that he saw spurring there
Ful noblelike upon a stede	Nobly upon a steed,
Þat with him wolde al quic wede.	Who galloped quickly toward him.
He smot him on þe heued so	He struck him on the head so forcefully
Þat he þe heued clef a-two	That he cleft the skull in two,
And þat bi þe shudre-blade	And near the shoulder-blade
2510 Þe sharpe swerd let wade	He let the sharp sword pass
Þorw the brest unto þe herte.	Through the breast into the heart.
Þe dint bigan ful sore to smerte	The blow began to bite so painfully
Þat þe erl fel dun a-non	That the earl fell down at once,
Al so ded so ani ston.	As dead as any stone.
Quoth Ubbe, "Nu dwelle ich to longe!"	Ubbe said, "I stay back too long!",
And leth his stede sone gonge	And immediately charged his horse
To Godrich with a god spere	Toward Godrich, with a good spear

Þat he saw a-noþer bere
And smoth Godrich and Godrich him
2520 Hetelike with herte grim
So þat he boþe felle dune
To þe erþe first þe croune.
Þanne he woren fallen dun boþen
Grundlike here swerdes ut-drowen
Þat weren swiþe sharp and gode
And fouhten so þei woren wode
Þat þe swot ran fro þe crune
To the fet rith þere adune.
Þer mouthe men se to knithes bete
2530 Ayþer on oþer dintes grete
So þat with alþer-leste dint
Were al to-shivered a flint.
So was bi-twenen hem a fiht
Fro þe morwen ner to þe niht
So þat þei nouth ne blunne
Til þat to sette bigan þe sunne.
Þo yaf Godrich þorw þe side
Ubbe a wunde ful un-ride
So þat þorw þat ilke wounde
2540 Hauede ben brouth to þe grunde
And his heued al of-slawen
Yif God ne were and Huwe Raven
Þat drow him fro Godrich awey
And barw him so þat ilke day.
But er he were fro Godrich drawen
Þer were a þousind knihtes slawen
Bi boþe halve and mo y-nowe
Þer þe ferdes to-gidere slowe.
Þer was swilk dreping of þe folk
2550 Þat on þe feld was nevere a polk
Þat it ne stod of blod so ful
Þat þe strem ran intil þe hul.
Þo tarst bigan Godrich to go
Up-on þe Danshe and faste to slo
And forth rith also leuin fares
Þat nevere kines best ne spares
Þanne his gon for he garte alle
Þe Denshe men biforn him falle.
He felde browne he felde blake
2560 Þat he mouthe over-take.
Was nevere non þat mouhte þaue

That he saw another bear,
And he struck Godrich, and him back,
Hotly with fierce hearts,
So that they both fell headfirst
Down to the earth.
When they were both fallen,
They drew out their swords violently,
Which were so sharp and hard,
And fought like they were berserk,
So that the sweat and blood ran
From their heads down to their feet.
There men could see two knights
Beat on each other with great blows
So that the least strike
Would have shattered a stone to pieces.
There was a fight between them
From the morning nearly to night,
So that they did not let up
Until the sun began to set.
Godrich had given Ubbe
An ugly wound through the side,
So that with that same injury
He would have been brought to the earth
And his head hacked off
If God and Hugh Raven were not there,
Who drew him away from Godrich
And saved him that very day.
But before he was taken from Godrich
There were a thousand knights killed
And more enough on both sides.
Where the armies clashed together
There was such slaughter of the warriors
That on the field there was no puddle
That was not so full of blood
That the stream didn't run downhill.
Then Godrich began to strike quickly[254]
Upon the Danish again, killing swiftly
And relentlessly, as a lion pounces
Who spares no kind of prey
And then is gone, for he made all
The Danish men fall dead before him.
He dropped every type of warrior,
Any that he might overtake.
There was no one who might survive

---

254 *Tarst*: The word is unrecorded in the MED, and Skeat believes it may be an error for *faste*. The poet compares Godard to a lightning strike.

Hise dintes noyþer knith ne knave
Þat he felden so dos þe gres
Bi-forn þe syþe þat ful sharp is.
Hwan Havelok saw his folk so brittene
And his ferd so swiþe littene
He cam drivende up-on a stede
And bigan til him to grede
And seyde, "Godrich wat is þe
2570 Þat þou fare þus with me?
And mine gode knihtes slos
Siker-like þou mis-gos!
Þou wost ful wel yif þu wilt wite
Þat Aþelwold þe dide site
On knes and sweren on messe-bok
On caliz and on pateyn hok
Þat þou hise douhter sholdest yelde
Þan she were winnan of elde
Engelond everil del.
2580 Godrich þe erl þou wost it wel!
Do nu wel with-uten fiht
Yeld hire þe lond for þat is rith.
Wile ich forgive þe þe lathe
Al mi dede and al mi wrathe
For y se þu art so with
And of þi bodi so god knith".
"Þat ne wile ich nevere mo"
Quoth erl Godrich, "for ich shal slo
Þe and hire for-henge heye!
2590 I shal þrist ut þi rith eye
Þat þou lokes with on me
But þu swiþe heþen fle!"
He grop þe swerd ut sone anon
And hew on Havelok ful god won
So þat he clef his sheld on two.
Hwan Havelok saw þat shame do
His bodi þer bi-forn his ferd
He drow ut sone his gode swerd
And smot him so up-on þe crune
2600 Þat Godrich fel to þe erþe adune.
But Godrich stirt up swiþe sket.
Lay he nowth longe at hise fet
And smot him on þe sholdre so
Þat he dide þare undo
Of his brinie ringes mo
Þan þat ich kan tellen fro
And woundede him rith in þe flesh

His blows, neither knight nor serf,
That he cut down like the grass
Before a sharpened scythe.
When Havelok saw his men so shaken
And his forces so reduced,
He came driving up on a steed
And began to parley with him,
And said, "Godrich, what is with you
That you act this way with me
And slay my good knights?
Surely, you do wrong!
You know full well, if you remember,
That Athelwold had you swear
On your knees and on the missal,
On chalice and sacramental cloth as well,
That you would yield to his daughter,
When she was a woman of age,
Every bit of England.
Earl Godrich, you know it well!
Do it now without struggle.
Yield to her the land, for it is her right.
I will forgive you for your hate,
For all my dead, and all my wrath,
For I see you are valiant
And in body a good knight".
"That I will never do",
Answered Earl Godrich, "for I will
Slay you, and hang her high!
I will thrust out your right eye
That you look upon me with,
Unless you flee from here quickly!"
He straightaway gripped his sword,
And cut down on Havelok forcefully,
So that he split his shield in two.
When Havelok saw that shame done
To his own body in front of his host,
At once he drew out his best sword
And smashed him so hard upon the head
That Godrich fell to the earth.
But Godrich got up very quickly.
He did not lay long at his feet,
And struck Havelok on the shoulder
So that he took off more
Of his mailcoat rings
Than I can count,
And wounded him right in the flesh,

Þat tendre was and swiþe nesh
So þat þe blod ran til his to.
2610 Þo was Havelok swiþe wo
Þat he hauede of him drawen
Blod and so sore him slawen.
Hertelike til him he wente
And Godrich þer fulike shente
For his swerd he hof up heye
And þe hand he dide of fleye
Þat he smot him with so sore.
Hw mithe he don him shame more?
Hwan he hauede him so shamed
2620 His hand of plat and yvele lamed
He tok him sone bi þe necke
Als a traytour daþeyt wo recke!
And dide him binde and fetere wel
With gode feteres al of stel
And to þe quen he sende him.
Þat birde wel to him ben grim
And bad she sholde don him gete
And þat non ne sholde him bete
Ne shame do for he was knith
2630 Til knithes haueden demd him rith.
Þan þe Englishe men þat sawe
Þat þei wisten heye and lawe
Þat Goldeboru þat was so fayr
Was of Engeland rith eyr
And þat þe king hire hauede wedded
And haueden ben samen bedded
He comen alle to crie merci
Unto þe king at one cri.
And beden him sone manrede and oth
2640 Þat he ne sholden for lef ne loth
Nevere more ageyn him go
Ne ride for wel ne for wo.
Þe king ne wolde nouth for-sake
Þat he ne shulde of hem take
Manrede þat he beden and ok
Hold oþes sweren on þe bok.
But or bad he þat þider were brouth
Þe quen for hem swilk was his þouth
For to se and forto shawe
2650 Yif þat he hire wolde knawe.
Þoruth hem witen wolde he
Yif þat she aucte quen to be.
Sixe erles weren sone yare

Which was so tender and soft,
So that the blood ran down to his toe.
Havelok was distressed then
That Godrich had drawn blood
From him and wounded him so sorely.
With furious heart he went at him
And brought great shame to Godrich there,
For he heaved his sword up high
And struck him so harshly
That he made Godrich's hand fly off.
How could he dishonor him more?
When Havelok had disgraced him,
His hand cut off, and badly lame,
He seized him at once by the neck
As a traitor—damn whoever cares!—
And had him bound and fettered fast
With strong chains, all of steel,
And he sent him to the queen.
That lady had cause to be stern with him,
And she ordered that he be guarded,
But that no one should beat him
Or abuse him, for he was a knight, until
Other knights had rightfully judged him.
When the English men saw that,
When they realized, high and low,
That Goldeboro, who was so fair,
Was the rightful heir of England,
And that the king had married her,
And they had bedded together,
They all came to cry for mercy
Unto the king with one voice.
At once they offered him homage and vows
That they would never,
For love or hate, oppose him again,
Or rebel, for better or for worse.
The king did not forsake them
So that he should refuse
The homage that they offered, as well as
Other oaths of loyalty sworn on the Bible.
But before doing so he ordered the queen
To be brought, for such were his thoughts
To watch and to see
If they would recognize her.
Through them he would know
If she ought to be queen.
Six earls were soon ready

After hire for to fare. | To set out after her.
He nomen on-on and comen sone | They went at once and soon returned
And brouthen hire þat under mone | Bringing her, she who had no peer
In al þe werd ne hauede per | Under the moon in all the world
Of hende-leik fer ne ner. | In gentility, near or far.
Hwan she was come þider alle | As she was coming near,
2660 Þe Englishe men bi-gunne to falle | All the English men began to fall
O knes and greten swiþe sore | On their knees and cried out bitterly
And seyden, "Leuedi Kristes ore | And said, "Our lady, Christ's mercy,
And youres! We haven misdo mikel | And yours as well! We have done great evil
Þat we ayen you have be fikel | To be disloyal to you,
For Englond auhte forto ben youres | For England ought to be yours,
And we youre men and youres. | And we your men, and all yours.
Is non of us yung ne old | There is none of us, young or old,
Þat we ne wot þat Aþelwold | Who does not know that Athelwold
Was king of þis kunerike | Was sovereign of this kingdom
2670 And ye his eyr and þat þe swike | And you his heir, and that the traitor
Haues it halden with mikel wronge. | Has held it with great injustice.
God leve him sone to honge!" | May God soon grant for him to hang!"
Quot Havelok, "Hwan þat ye it wite. | Havelok said, "Now that you understand,
Nu wile ich þat ye doun site | I will have you all sit down,
And after Godrich haues wrouht | And for what Godrich has caused,
Þat haues in sorwe him-self brouht | Who has brought himself to calamity,
Lokes þat ye demen him rith | See that you judge him rightly,
For dom ne spared clerk ne knith. | For justice spares neither priest nor knight.
And siþen shal ich under-stonde | And after then I will accept from you,
2680 Of you after lawe of londe | Under the law of the land,
Manrede and holde oþes boþe | Both your homage and oaths of loyalty,
Yif ye it wilen and ek rothe". | If you want and advise it as well".[255]
Anon þer dune he hem sette | They seated themselves at once,
For non þe dom ne durste lette | For no one dared obstruct the verdict,
And demden him to binden faste | And they ordered the traitor bound tight
Up-on an asse swiþe un-wraste | Upon a filthy donkey,
Andelong nouht ouer-þwert | End to end, not across,
His nose went unto þe stert | His nose set toward its behind,
And so to Lincolne lede | And led to Lincoln in this manner,
2690 Shamelike in wicke wede | Shamefully in wretched rags;
And hwan he cam un-to þe borw | And, when he arrived in the town,
Shamelike ben led þer-þoru | To be dishonorably paraded through,
Bisouþe þe borw un-to a grene | To south of the town onto a green field–
Þat þare is yet als y wene | Which is still there, as far as I know–
And þere be bunden til a stake | And to be tied to a stake

255 The poet emphasizes that Havelok respects the rule of law as his father did by submitting both Godard and Godrich to a trial. While some commentators have objected that the trials are hardly impartial, period juries were chosen for their knowledge of the case and not for their objectivity. See Edgar F. Shannon, Jr., "Mediaeval Law in the *Tale of Gamelyn*", *Speculum* 26:3 (1951): 458-64.

Abouten him ful gret fir make	With a great fire set around him,
And al to dust be brend rith þere.	And all to be burned to dust right there.
And yet demden he þer more	And yet they ordered more,
Oþer swikes for to warne	In order to warn other traitors:
2700 Þat hise children sulde þarne	That his children should forever lose
Evere more þat eritage	Their heritage of what was his.
Þat his was for hise utrage.	This was his reward for his crimes.
Hwan þe dom was demd and seyd	When the verdict was given and approved,
Sket was þe swike on þe asse leyd	The traitor was quickly laid on the donkey
And led un-til þat ilke grene	And he was led to that same green
And brend til asken al bidene.	And burned to ashes right away.
Þo was Goldeboru ful bliþe.	Then Goldeboro was fully at ease.
She þanked God fele syþe	She thanked God many times
Þat þe fule swike was brend	That the foul traitor who had intended
2710 Þat wende wel hire bodi have shend	To disgrace her body was burned,
And seyde, "Nu is time to take	And she said, "Now is the time to take
Manrede of brune and of blake	Homage from every sort of people
Þat ich se ride and go	That I see riding and walking,
Nu ich am wreke of mi fo".	Now that I am avenged on my foe".
Havelok anon manrede tok	Havelok at once received pledges
Of alle Englishe on þe bok	On the Bible from all the English,
And dide hem grete oþes swere	And had them swear solemn oaths
Þat he sholden him god feyth bere	That they would bear him good faith
Ageyn alle þat woren lives	Against all who were alive
2720 And þat sholde ben born of wives.	And who were born of women.[256]
Þanne he hauede sikernesse	When he had taken guarantees
Taken of more and of lesse	From the great and the small,
Al at hise wille so dide he calle	With all at his will, he summoned
Þe erl of Cestre and hise men alle	The earl of Chester and all his men,[257]
Þat was yung knith wit-uten wif	Who was a young knight without a wife,
And seyde, "Sire erl bi mi lif	And said, "Sir Earl, by my life,
And þou wile mi conseyl tro	If you will trust my counsel,
Ful wel shal ich with þe do.	I will deal with you fairly.
For ich shal yeve þe to wive	For I will give you as a wife
2730 Þe fairest þing that is olive	The fairest thing that is alive,
Þat is Gunnild of Grimesby	Gunnild of Grimsby,
Grimes douther bi seint Davy	The daughter of Grim, by Saint David,[258]
Þat me forth broute and wel fedde	Who brought me up and kept me well,
And ut of Denmark with me fledde	And fled with me out of Denmark

256 *And that sholde ben born of wives*: i.e. everyone. The expression seems to have been common, for apparitions trick Macbeth by saying "none of woman born / shall harm Macbeth" (*Macbeth* IV.1.89-90), leading him into false confidence when Macduff turns out to be born by Caesarian. See also Stanzaic *Guy of Warwick*, 1288.

257 This seems to be the same Earl of Chester, Reyner, as the one who allies with Godrich earlier (2472), and apparently he has been rehabilitated. The reference might be meaningful, although there was no earl of Chester named Reyner, and Gunter is a generic name in the time period.

258 *Seint Davy*: Not King David of Israel, but David (c. 500-89) the patron saint of Wales. Associated with vegetarians and poets, he is probably here only to fit the rhyme. *Gunhildr* is Old Norse in etymology.

Me for to burwe fro mi ded.
Sikerlike þoru his red
Have ich lived in-to þis day.
Blissed worþe his soule ay!
I rede þat þu hire take
2740 And spuse and curteyse make
For she is fayr and she is fre
And al so hende so she may be.
Þertekene she is wel with me
Þat shal ich ful wel shewe þe
For ich give þe a give
Þat evere more hwil ich live
For hire shal-tu be with me dere.
Þat wile ich þat þis folc al here".
Þe erl ne wolde nouth ageyn
2750 Þe king be for knith ne sweyn
Ne of þe spusing seyen nay
But spusede þat ilke day.
Þat spusinge was god time maked
For it ne were nevere clad ne naked
In a þede samened two
Þat cam to-gidere livede so
So þey diden al here live.
He geten samen sones five
Þat were þe beste men at nede
2760 Þat mouthe riden on ani stede.
Hwan Gunnild was to Cestre brouth
Havelok þe gode ne for-gat nouth
Bertram þat was the erles kok.
Þat he ne dide callen ok
And seyde, "Frend so God me rede
Nu shaltu have riche mede
For wissing and þi gode dede
Þat tu me dides in ful gret nede.
For þanne y yede in mi cuwel
2770 And ich ne hauede bred ne sowel.
Ne y ne hauede no catel
Þou feddes and claddes me ful wel.
Have nu for-þi of Cornwayle
Þe erldom ildel with-uten fayle
And al þe lond þat Godrich held
Boþe in towne and ek in feld.
And þerto wile ich þat þu spuse
And fayre bring hire un-til huse
Grimes douther Leuiue þe hende
2780 For þider shal she with þe wende.

To rescue me from death.
Surely, through his good judgment
I have lived to this day.
May his soul be blessed forever!
I advise that you take her
And wed her, and do her courtesy,
For she is beautiful and she is noble,
And as gracious as she can be.
I will prove it to you in full that
I am well pleased with her by a token,
For I will give you a promise
That forevermore, while I live,
For her sake you shall be dear to me. This
I would like all these people to witness".
The earl did not refuse the king,
And neither knight nor attendant
Said anything against the match,
But they were wedded that same day. That
Marriage was made in a blessed moment,
For there were never in any land
Two who came together, clothed or naked,
Who lived in the way
That they did their whole lives.
They had five sons together,
Who were the best men in times of need
Who might ride on any steed.
When Gunnild was brought to Chester,
Havelok, the good man, did not forget
Bertram, who was the earl's cook.
He called him forward as well
And said, "Friend, so God help me,
You will have a rich reward
For your guidance and your kind deeds
That you did for me in my great need.
For then I walked in my cloak
And had neither bread nor sauce,
Nor did I have any possessions,
And you fed and clothed me well.
Take now the earldom of Cornwall,
Every acre, without a doubt,
And all the land that Godrich held,
Both in town and field as well.
And with that I give you to marry
Grim's daughter, Levi the gracious,
To bring her honorably to your house,
For she shall go with you there.

Hire semes curteys forto be	It is her very nature to be courteous,
For she is fayr so flour on tre.	For she is as fair as the flower on the tree.
Þe heu is swilk in hire ler	The color in her face
So þe rose in roser	Is like the rose in a rosebush
Hwan it is fayr sprad ut newe	When it has newly blossomed out
Ageyn þe sunne brith and lewe".	Toward the sun, bright and fresh".
And girde him sone with þe swerd	And he fit him with the sword
Of þe erldom bi-forn his ferd	Of the earldom, in front of his army,
And with his hond he made him knith	And with his hand he made him a knight
2790 And yaf him armes for þat was rith	And gave him arms, for that was proper,
And dide him þere sone wedde	And straightaway had him married
Hire þat was ful swete in bedde.	To Levi, who was so sweet in her bed.
After þat he spused wore	After they were married,
Wolde þe erl nouth dwelle þore	The earl did not wish to dwell there,
But sone nam until his lond	But soon made his way to his land
And seysed it al in his hond	And received it all into his hand,
And livede þer-inne he and his wif	And lived there, him and his wife,
An hundred winter in god lif.	For a hundred seasons in good health.
And gaten mani children samen	They had many children together,
2800 And liveden ay in blisse and gamen.	And lived forever in ease and pleasure.
Hwan þe maydens were spused boþe	When both of the maidens were married,
Havelok anon bigan ful rathe	Havelok at once began
His Denshe men to feste wel	To endow his Danish men well
Wit riche landes and catel	With rich lands and properties,
So þat he weren alle riche	So that they were all prosperous,
For he was large and nouth chinche.	For he was generous and never grudging.
Þer-after sone with his here	Soon after, he traveled with his army
For he to Lundone forto bere	To London to wear the crown,
Corune so þat it sawe	So that all would see,
2810 Henglishe ant Denshe heye and lowe	English and Danish, high and low,
Hwou he it bar with mikel pride	How he wore it with regal pride
For his barnage þat was unride.	Before his great baronage.
Þe feste of his coruning	The festival of his coronation
Lastede with gret joying	Lasted with great rejoicing
Fourti dawes and sumdel mo.	For forty days and somewhat more.
Þo bigunnen þe Denshe to go	Then the Danes began to go
Un-to þe king to aske leve.	To the king to ask permission to leave.
And he ne wolde hem nouth greve	He did not want to aggrieve them,
For he saw þat he woren yare	For he saw that they were anxious
2820 In-to Denmark for to fare	To journey home to Denmark,
But gaf hem leve sone anon	But gave them permission soon after
And bitauhte hem seint Johan	And entrusted them to Saint John,
And bad Ubbe his justise	And ordered Ubbe, his magistrate,
Þat he sholde on ilke wise	That he should govern and guard
Denemark yeme and gete so	Denmark in the same way,
Þat no pleynte come him to.	So that no complaint should come to him.

Hwan he wore parted alle samen	When they had all departed together,
Havelok bi-lefte wit joie and gamen	Havelok dwelled with joy and pleasure
In Engelond and was þer-inne	In England and was king there
2830 Sixti winter king with winne.	In peace for sixty years.
And Goldeboru quen þat I wene	And as for Queen Goldeboro, I know that
So mikel love was hem bitwene	So much love was between them
Þat al þe werd spak of hem two.	That all the world spoke of the two.
He lovede hire and she him so	He loved her and she loved him
Þat neyþer oþe mithe be	So that neither one could be separated
For oþer ne no joie se	From the other, nor have any happiness
But yf he were to-gidere boþe.	Unless they were together.
Nevere yete ne weren he wroþe	They were never angry with each other,
For here love was ay newe.	For their love was always new.
2840 Nevere yete wordes ne grewe	Harsh words never grew between them
Bitwene hem hwar-of ne lathe	That might lead to any hostility
Mithe rise ne no wrathe.	Or any wrath.
He geten children hem bi-twene	They had many children together,
Sones and douthres rith fivetene	Sons and daughters, fifteen in all,
Hwar-of þe sones were kinges alle	Of whom the sons were all kings
So wolde God it sholde bifalle	If God should have it happen,
And þe douhtres alle quenes.	And the daughters all queens.
Him stondes wel þat god child strenes.	'He stands well who has good children!'
Nu have ye herd þe gest al þoru	Now you have heard the story through
2850 Of Havelok and of Goldeborw	Of Havelok and Goldeboro,
Hw he weren born and hw fedde	How they were born and how they fared,
And hwou he woren with wronge ledde	And how they were treated wrongly
In here youþe with trecherie	In their youth with treachery,
With tresoun and with felounye	With treason, and with felony;
And hwou þe swikes haueden thit	And how the traitors intended
Reven hem þat was here rith	To rob them of what was their right,
And hwou he weren wreken wel.	And how they were well avenged.
Have ich sey you everildel.	I have told you every bit.
And forþi ich wolde biseken you	For that, I now beg of all of you
2860 Þat haven herd þe rim nu	Who have heard the tale now,
Þat ilke of you with gode wille	That each of you, in good faith,
Seye a pater-noster stille	Will say the Lord's Prayer quietly
For him þat haueth þe rym maked	For him who made these words
And þer-fore fele nihtes waked	And stayed awake many nights,
Þat Jhesu Crist his soule bringe	That Jesus Christ would bring his soul
Bi-forn His fader at his endinge.	Before His Father at his ending.
2867 Amen.	Amen.

King Horn

King Horn is perhaps the oldest surviving English romance, dating to about 1225-1285. While the stereotype of insular romances as inferior abridgments of French ones is unfair, it is unfortunately the case here. *Horn* is shorter and has a rougher cadence compared to the *Romance of Horn*, an earlier Anglo-Norman version of about 1170, which is considerably longer and more sophisticated. Nevertheless, the no-nonsense sparseness of the poem gives it a quick action, as Horn progresses from being exiled by invading heathens who have killed his royal father, to being raised in a southern court where he attains knighthood and the heart of the king's daughter, Rimenhild, to his adventures in pursuit of her along with his heritage.

Although the two romances are found in the same MS, unlike the detail of geography, politics, and stepfamily in *Havelok*, in *Horn* the focus is completely on the protagonist. Horn has the demeanor and gravitas of a king even as a boy, and the energy of the play lies in him forcing his external circumstances to match his regal inner self-actualization. In a regional and possibly later variant on the poem, *Horn Childe and Maiden Rimnild* (Auchinleck, NLS Adv. MS 19.2.1, c. 1330), the secondary characters and setting have more clarity and rationalization. Yet *Horn*'s strength is that its unstinting emphasis on the hero gives it a strong structural clarity and neat linear plot progress.

Victorian scholarship of *Horn* was chiefly interested in the manuscript stemma, as well as a still-unresolved mystery: where on earth are *Westernesse* and *Suddene*? Despite some ingenious solutions, their locations have never been compellingly found, and the map given here is only a surmisal based on possible name-links. Yet an interesting clue emerges: as Thomas Liszka details in a chapter in *The Texts and Contexts of Oxford, Bodleian Library, MS Laud Misc. 108*, while the dating remains contested it has generally crept later into the late 1200s, placing it in Edward I's reign. Edward,

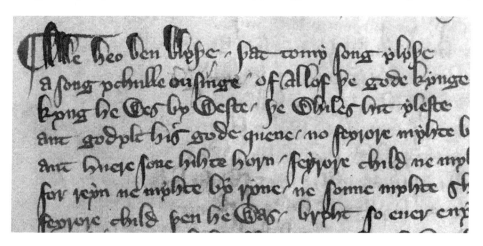

First lines of King Horn, from British Library MS Harley 2253, f.83r.

unlike his cartoonish depiction as an sour, cynical tactition in *Braveheart*, patronized music and arts with his wife Eleanor; his reign was also one of suppressing never-ending rebellions in Wales and Scotland. Might *Horn* be meant as a flattering portrait of a charismatic leader with a passionate, devoted queen, while tactfully fuzzying the northwestern geography which gave Edward so much trouble?

King Horn survives in three manuscripts: Bodleian MS Laud Misc. 108 (c. 1300), Cambridge University Library MS Gg.4.27.2 (c. 1300), and British Library MS Harley 2253 (c. 1325). I take as my text source George H. McKnight, *King Horn, Floriz and Blancheflur, The Assumption of Our Lady* (London: EETS, 1901 [1866]), comparing occasionally to other editions. Chief among these are Joseph Hall, *King Horn: A Middle English Romance*, 1901; Walter H. French & Charles B. Hale, eds., *Middle English Metrical Romances*, 1930; Rosamund Allen, *King Horn*, 1984; and Ronald B. Herzman, Graham Drake, and Eve Salisbury, eds., *King Horn. Four Romances of England*, 1999 (http://www.lib.rochester.edu/camelot/teams/hornfrm.htm).

C: Cambridge
L: Laud Misc. 108
H: Harley 2253

1C Alle beon he bliþe	May all be glad
Þat to my song lyþe!	Who listen to my tale!
A sang ich schal ȝou singe	I will sing you a song
Of Murry þe Kinge.	About Murray the King.
King he was biweste	He was a king in the far west
So longe so hit laste.	As long as his life lasted.
Godhild het his quen;	His queen was named Godhild;
Faire ne miȝte non ben.	No one could be more beautiful!
He hadde a sone þat het Horn;	He had a son called Horn.[259]
10 Fairer ne miȝte non beo born,	No one could be born more handsome,
Ne no rein upon birine,	No one who had rain fall on them
Ne sunne upon bischine.	Or the sun shine on them.
Fairer nis non þane he was:	There was no fairer child than he was.
He was briȝt so þe glas;	He was as bright as glass;
He was whit so þe flur;	He was as white as a flower;
Rose red was his colur.	His features were red like a rose.[260]
. . . .	. . . .
L He was fayr and eke bold,	He was fair and brave as well,[261]
And of fiftene winter hold.	And fifteen years old.
. . . .	. . . .
C In none kinge riche	In no other kingdom
20 Nas non his iliche.	Was there anyone like him.
Twelf feren he hadde	He had twelve companions
Þat alle wiþ him ladde,	Who always went with him,
Alle riche mannes sones,	All noble men's sons,
And alle hi were faire gomes,	And all of them were fine boys
Wiþ him for to pleie,	For him to enjoy time with.
And mest he luvede tweie;	And he loved two the most–
Þat on him het Haþulf child,	One of them was called Child Athulf,[262]
And þat oþer Fikenild.	And the other Fickenhild.
Aþulf was þe beste,	Athulf was the best,
30 And Fikenylde þe werste.	And Fickenhild the worst.
Hit was upon a someres day,	It was on a summer's day,
Also ich ȝou telle may,	As I can tell you as well,
Murri þe gode King	When Murray, the good king,
Rod on his pleing	Rode for leisure
Bi þe se side,	By the seaside,

---

259 Garbaty points out that, unlike many medieval romances, Murray, Godhild, Horn, and others in the text do not seem to refer to or represent any known historical figures. Thomas J. Garbaty, *King Horn, Medieval English Literature* (Long Grove, Il: Waveland, 1984), note to line 4.

260 The poet connects Horn's features to his mother's. Herzman et al. cite Hall, who comments that such language is usually reserved for women, and he has "not found anything quite like it used for a hero of romance". Joseph Hall, *King Horn: A Middle English Romance* (Oxford: Clarendon, 1901), 93.

261 In a few places here Cambridge has no gap but the line feels defective without additions from Laud.

262 *Hathulf child*: ME *child* as a post-positive adjective usually indicates not childhood but the role of apprentice knight, similar to the titles page and squire, though it can also be initial (Childe Roland). Normally boys began as pages very young and became squires around age fourteen.

Ase he was woned ride.	As he was accustomed to do.
. . . .	. . . .
L Wiþ him riden bote two -	There were only two riding with him;
Al to fewe ware þo!	They were all too few!
. . . .	. . . .
He fond bi þe stronde,	He noticed along the shore
40 Arived on his londe,	Fifteen ships
Schipes fiftene	That had arrived on his land
Wiþ Sarazins kene	With zealous Saracens.
He axede what hi soȝte	He asked what they were looking for
Oþer to londe broȝte.	Or what they brought to the land.
A payn hit of herde,	A pagan heard him
And hym wel sone answarede:	And answered him brusquely,
"Þy lond folk we schulle slon,	"We will kill the people of your land,
And alle þat Crist luveþ upon	And all who have love for Christ,
And þe selve riȝt anon.	And yourself right away.
50 Ne shaltu todai henne gon".	You will not leave here today".
Þe king aliȝte of his stede,	The king dismounted from his steed,
For þo he havede nede,	For he needed the help
And his gode kniȝtes two;	Of his two good knights.
Al to fewe he hadde þo.	He had all too few then!
Swerd hi gunne gripe	They began to grip swords
And togadere smite.	And strike against each other.
Hy smyten under schelde	They struck under shields
Þat sume hit yfelde.	So that some were brought down,
Þe king hadde al to fewe	But the king had all too few
60 Togenes so fele schrewe;	Against so many villains.
So wele miȝten yþe	They could too easily
Bringe hem þre to diþe.	Deliver the three to death.
Þe pains come to londe	The pagans came to the land
And neme hit in here honde	And took it into their hand.
Þat folc hi gunne quelle,	They began to kill the people
And churchen for to felle.	And to destroy churches.
Þer ne moste libbe	No one might live,
Þe fremde ne þe sibbe.	Whether friend or family,
Bute hi here laȝe asoke,	Unless they renounced their faith
70 And to here toke.	And took theirs.
Of alle wymmanne	Of all women,
Wurst was Godhild þanne.	The most miserable was Godhild.
For Murri heo weop sore	She wept bitterly for Murray
And for Horn ȝute more.	And for Horn even more.
He wente ut of halle	She fled out of the hall,
Fram hire maidenes alle	Away from all her maidens,
Under a roche of stone	Into a cave of stone
Þer heo livede alone.	Where she lived alone.
Þer heo servede Gode	There she served God

80	Aȝenes þe paynes forbode.	Against the pagans' injunction.
	Þer he servede Criste	There she served Christ,
	Þat no payn hit ne wiste.	So that no pagan knew of it.
	Evre heo bad for Horn child	She continually prayed for Child Horn,
	Þat Jesu Crist him beo myld.	That Jesus Christ might be kind to him.
	Horn was in paynes honde	Horn was in pagan hands
	Wiþ his feren of þe londe.	With his companions from the land.
	Muchel was his fairhede,	His noble grace stood out,
	For Jhesu Crist him makede.	For Jesus Christ had made him so.
	Payns him wolde slen,	The pagans would have killed him
90	Oþer al quic flen,	Or flayed him alive,
	Ȝef his fairnesse nere:	If not for his beauty;
	Þe children alle aslaȝe were.	The children would all be slain.
	Þanne spak on admirad -	Then one admiral spoke
	Of wordes he was bald, -	Who was bold in words:
	"Horn, þu art well kene,	"Horn, you are masterful,
	And þat is wel isene.	That is clear to see.
	Þu art gret and strong,	You are great and strong,
	Fair and evene long;	Handsome and tall.
	Þu schalt waxe more	You will grow bigger
100	Bi fulle seve ȝere.	Before seven years more.
	Yef þu mote to live go	If you were to leave alive,
	And þine feren also,	With your company as well,
	Ȝef hit so bi falle,	It might so happen that
	Ȝe scholde slen us alle:	You would slay us all.
	Þarvore þu most to stere,	Therefore you are headed for the sea,
	Þu and þine ifere;	You and your companions.
	To schupe schulle ȝe funde,	You will be set adrift on the ship,
	And sinke to þe grunde.	And sink to the bottom.
	Þe se ȝou schal adrenche,	The sea will drown you,
110	Ne schal hit us noȝt of þinche.	And we will have no regret for it.
	For if þu were alive,	For if you were alive,
	Wiþ swerd oþer wiþ knive,	We would all die,
	We scholden alle deie,	And you would avenge your father,
	And þi fader deþ abeie".	With sword or with knife".
	Þe children hi broȝte to stronde,	The boys were brought to the shore,
	Wringinde here honde,	Wringing their hands,
	Into schupes borde	And boarded the boat
	At þe furste worde.	At the first command.[263]
	Ofte hadde Horn beo wo,	Often Horn had been sorrowful,
120	Ac nevre wurs þan him was þo.	But never worse than he was then.
	Þe se bigan to flowe,	The sea began to rise,

---

263 The boys are set adrift and expected to drown. Tradition held that the sinful would die but the innocent would receive providential aid, as Bevis does (Herzman et al.). As with Godard and Havelok (519-36), the Saracens perhaps believe they will avoid sinning, as the *water* will be responsible for the boys' deaths. In the *Man of Law's Tale* Custance's heathen mothers-in-law set her adrift twice for similar reasons (*CT* II.439-41 and 799-802).

And Horn child to rowe;
Þe se þat schup so fasste drof
Þe children dradde þerof.
Hi wenden to wisse
Of here lif to misse,
Al þe day and al þe niȝt
Til hit sprang dailiȝt,
Til Horn saȝ on þe stronde
130 Men gon in þe londe.
"Feren", quaþ he, "ȝonge,
Ich telle ȝou tiþinge:
Ich here foȝeles singe
And þat gras him springe.
Bliþe beo we on lyve;
Ure schup is on ryve".
Of schup hi gunne funde,
And setten fout to grunde.
Bi þe se side
140 Hi leten þat schup ride.
Þanne spak him child Horn,
In Suddene he was iborn:
"Schup bi þe se flode,
Daies have þu gode.
Bi þe se brinke,
No water þe na drinke.
Ȝef þu cume to Suddene,
Gret þu wel of myne kenne,
Gret þu wel my moder,
150 Godhild, Quen þe gode,
And seie þe paene king,
Jesu Cristes wiþering,
Þat ich am hol and fer
On þis lond arived her;
And seie þat hei schal fonde
Þe dent of myne honde".
Þe children ȝede to tune,
Bi dales and bi dune.
Hy metten wiþ Almair King,
160 Crist ȝeven him His blessing

And Child Horn began to sail.[264]
The sea drove that ship so fast
That the children were terrified.
They expected for certain
To lose their lives,
Through all the day and all the night
Until daylight had sprung,
Until Horn saw on the shore
Men walking about the land.
"Fellows", he said, "lads,
I will tell you some good news!
I hear birds singing
And see the grass growing.
Let us be happy to be alive!
Our boat is on the shore".
They hurried off the boat
And set their feet on the ground
By the seaside,
Letting the boat drift.
Then Child Horn, born in
The Southlands, addressed it:[265]
"Boat on the ocean tide,
May you have good days
On the brink of the sea.
May you drink no water!
If you return to the Southlands,
Greet my family well.
Greet my mother well,
Godhild, the good queen,
And tell the heathen king,
Jesus Christ's enemy,
That I am safe and sound
And have arrived here on this land.
And say that they will feel
The strike of my hand!"
The children walked to the town,
Over hills and over valleys.
They met with King Almair.
May Christ give him His blessing!

---

264 Rowe: Herzman et al. render this as *rue*, i.e. Horn began to regret the sea waves, but several manuscripts have *rowen* and for Horn to take charge makes more sense within the poem's sentiments.

265 *Suddene*: Scholars do not agree where this is and have posited areas in southern England as well as Sweden and Suðdene, i.e. southern Denmark. Like the character names, the locations may be as fanciful as 'Riverdale' in an *Archie* comic. See also the notes to line 161 and 697.

King of Westernesse
Crist ʒive him muchel blisse!
He him spac to Horn child
Wordes þat were mild:
"Whannes beo ʒe, faire gumes,
Þat her to londe beoþ icume,
Alle þrottene,
Of bodie swiþe kene?
Bi God þat me makede,
170 A swich fair verade
Ne sauʒ ich in none stunde,
Bi westene londe:
Seie me wat ʒe seche".
Horn spak here speche,
He spak for hem alle,
Vor so hit moste bivalle:
He was þe faireste
And of wit þe beste.
"We beoþ of Suddenne,
180 Icome of gode kenne,
Of Cristene blode,
And kynges swþe gode.
Payns þer gunne arive
And duden hem of lyve.
Hi sloʒen and todroʒe
Cristene men inoʒe.
So Crist me mote rede,
Us he dude lede
Into a galeie,
190 Wiþ þe se to pleie,
Dai hit is igon and oþer,
Wiþute sail and roþer:
Ure schip bigan to swymme
To þis londes brymme.
Nu þu miʒt us slen and binde
Ore honde bihynde.
Bute ʒef hit beo þi wille,
Helpe þat we ne spille".
Þanne spak þe gode kyng
200 I wis he nas no niþing
"Seie me, child, what is þi name?
Ne schaltu have bute game".

He was king of the Westlands.[266]
May Christ give him great peace!
He spoke to Child Horn
With words that were kind:
"Where are you from, fair lads,
That you have come here,
All thirteen of you,
With such hardy bodies?
By God who made me,
I never saw such a noble group
In any time
In western lands.
Tell me what you are looking for".
Horn made a speech there.
He spoke for them all,
For it was most fitting,
As he was the fairest
And quickest of wits.
"We are from the Southlands.
I come from a good family,
Of Christian blood,
And a highly honored king.
Pagans have arrived there
And taken his life.
They have slain and torn apart
Christian men enough!
So help me Christ,
They had us led
Onto a galley
To take our chances on the sea.
One day passed, and another,
Without sail or rudder.
Our boat began to drift
Toward the shore of this land.
You might slay us now or bind
Our hands behind us.
But if it is your will,
Help us so that we do not die".
The good king spoke then.
I know he was no villain.
"Tell me, child, what is your name?
You will have nothing but leisure".

---

266 *Westernesse*: Like Suddene, this seems to ambiguously mean western England. Schofield suggests the Isle of Man based on the French manuscript where the queen flees to Ardenne, a Manx word and now The Ard (18-19). William H. Schofield, *The Story of Horn and Rimenhild* (Baltimore: Modern Language Association of America, 1903). But see the note to line 697 for different clues.

Þe child him answerde,	The boy answered him
Sone so he hit herde:	As soon as he heard the king:
"Horn ich am ihote,	"I am called Horn.
Icomen ut of þe bote,	I came out of the boat
Fram þe se side.	From the sea side.
Kyng, wel mote þe tide".	Sire, may you have good fortune".
Þanne hym spak þe gode king,	Then the good king spoke to him,
210 "Well bruc þu þin evening.	"May your name carry well![267]
Horn, þu go wel schulle	Horn, you will travel well
Bi dales and bi hulle;	By valley and by hill.
Horn, þu lude sune,	Horn, you will loudly sound
Bi dales and bi dune;	By plain and by dune.
So schal þi name springe	Your name will resound
Fram kynge to kynge,	From king to king,
And þi fairnesse	And your nobility will echo
Abute Westernesse,	Around the Westlands.
Þe strengþe of þine honde	The strength of your hand
220 Into evrech londe.	Will be known in every land.
Horn, þu art so swete,	Horn, you are so sweet,
Ne may ich þe forlete".	I cannot abandon you".
Hom rod Aylmar þe Kyng	Almair the king rode home with
And Horn mid him, his fundling,	Horn alongside him, his foundling,
And alle his ifere,	And all his companions
Þat were him so dere.	Who were so dear to him.
Þe kyng com into halle	The king came into the hall
Among his kniȝtes alle;	Among all of his knights.
Forþ he clupede Aþelbrus,	He called forth Athelbruce,
230 Þat was stiward of his hus.	Who was steward of his house.
"Stiward, tak nu here	"Steward, now take here
My fundlyng for to lere	My foundling, to teach him
Of þine mestere,	Your trade,
Of wude and of rivere,	Of hunting and hawking,
And tech him to harpe	And teach him to harp
Wiþ his nayles scharpe,	With his fingernails sharp;
Bivore me to kerve,	And to carve meat before me
And of þe cupe serve.	And to serve from the cup.[268]
Þu tech him of alle þe liste	Tutor him in all the skills
240 Þat þu evre of wiste,	That you ever learned,
And his feiren þou wise	And guide his companions
In to oþere servise.	Into other services.
Horn þu undervonge	Take charge of Horn
And tech him of harpe and songe".	And train him in harp and song".

---

267 *Well bruc thu þin evening*: Garbaty has *well bruc thu thi neuening*, "may you long enjoy your name". The king is making a series of puns on Horn's name, that his 'sound' or reputation will travel widely.

268 These are traditional duties of the squire, and Chaucer's squire similarly serves by cutting meat "biforn his fader at the table" (*CT* I.100).

Ailbrus gan lere	Athelbruce began to teach
Horn and his yfere.	Horn and his company.
Horn in herte laȝte	Horn took to heart
Al þat he him taȝte.	All that he taught him
In þe curt and ute,	In the court and outside it.
250 And elles al abute	And every man around
Luvede men Horn child,	Loved Child Horn,
And mest him luvede Rymenhild,	And Rimenhild loved him the most,
Þe kynges oȝene doghter.	The king's own daughter.
He was mest in þoȝte;	He was first in her thoughts.
Heo luvede so Horn child	She loved Child Horn so much
Þat neȝ heo gan wexe wild:	That she nearly grew mad.
For heo ne miȝte at borde	For she could not speak a word
Wiþ him speke no worde,	With him at the table
Ne noȝt in þe halle	Or in the hall
260 Among þe kniȝtes alle,	Among all the knights,
Ne nowhar in non oþere stede.	Or anywhere in another place.
Of folk heo hadde drede:	She was afraid of being seen.
Bi daie ne bi niȝte	By day and by night,
Wiþ him speke ne miȝte.	She could not speak with him.
Hire soreȝe ne hire pine	Neither her sorrow nor her pain
Ne miȝte nevre fine.	Might ever have an end.
In heorte heo hadde wo,	She had longing in her heart,
And þus hire biþoȝte þo:	And so she decided then
Heo sende hire sonde	She would send her word
270 Aþelbrus to honde,	To Althelbruce's hand,
Þat he come hire to,	That he should come to her,
And also scholde Horn do,	And Horn as well,
Al in to bure,	Together into her bedroom,
For heo gan to lure;	For she had begun to look pale.
And þe sonde seide	And the message said
Þat sik lai þat maide,	That the maiden lay sick,
And bad him come swiþe	And asked him to come quickly
For heo nas noþing bliþe.	For she had no happiness.
Þe stuard was in herte wo,	The steward was distressed at heart,
280 For he nuste what to do.	For he did not know what to do.
Wat Rymenhild hure þoȝte	What Rimenheld's intentions were
Gret wunder him þuȝte,	Seemed very mysterious to him,
Abute Horn þe ȝonge	To bring the young Horn
To bure for to bringe.	Into her chamber.
He þoȝte upon his mode	He turned it over in his mind
Hit nas for none gode:	But it was for no good.
He tok him anoþer,	He took someone else with him,
Aþulf, Hornes broþer.	Athulf, Horn's brother in arms.
"Aþulf", he sede, "riȝt anon	"Athulf", he said, "you will go
290 Þu schalt wiþ me to bure gon	With me right away to her room

To speke wiþ Rymenhild stille	To speak with Rimenhild privately
And witen hure wille.	And find out her will.
In Hornes ilike	In Horn's likeness
Þu schalt hure biswike:	You will fool her.
Sore ich me ofdrede	I am sorely afraid
Heo wolde Horn misrede".	She might lead Horn astray".
Aþelbrus gan Aþulf lede,	Athelbruce escorted Athulf
And into bure wiþ him ȝede:	And went with him into the bower.
Anon upon Aþulf child	Upon that, Rimenhild began
300 Rymenhild gan wexe wild:	To grow unrestrained with Athulf.
Heo wende þat Horn hit were	She thought it was Horn
Þat heo havede þere:	That she had there with her.
Heo sette him on bedde;	She set him on the bed
Wiþ Aþulf child he wedde;	And began to woo Athulf.
On hire armes tweie	She embraced him
Aþulf heo gan leie.	In her two arms.
"Horn", quaþ heo, "wel longe	"Horn", she said, "for the longest time
Ich habbe þe luved stronge.	I have loved you passionately.
Þu schalt þi trewþe pliȝte	You must swear your faithfulness
310 On myn hond her riȝte,	On my hand right here,
Me to spuse holde,	To hold me as your spouse,
And ich þe lord to wolde".	And for me to have you as lord".
Aþulf sede on hire ire	Athulf whispered in her ear,
So stille so hit were,	As gently as possible,
"Þi tale nu þu lynne,	"Stop your talking now,
For Horn nis noȝt her inne.	For Horn is not in here.
Ne beo we noȝt iliche:	We are not alike;
Horn is fairer and riche,	Horn is more handsome and strong,
Fairer bi one ribbe	Fairer by a rib
320 Þane eni man þat libbe:	Than any man that lives!
Þeȝ Horn were under molde	Even if Horn were under the earth
Oþer elles wher he wolde	Or wherever else he was,
Oþer henne a þusend mile,	Or a thousand miles from here,
Ich nolde him ne þe bigile".	I cannot deceive him or you!"
Rymenhild hire biwente,	Rimenhild changed her mood,
And Aþelbrus fule heo schente.	And cursed Athelbruce foully.
"Hennes þu go, þu fule þeof,	"Get out of here, you foul thief!
Ne wurstu me nevre more leof;	You will never again be dear to me.
Went ut of my bur,	Leave my room,
330 Wiþ muchel mesaventur.	With cursed luck!
Schame mote þu fonge	May shame undo you
And on hiȝe rode anhonge.	And hang you high on the gallows!
Ne spek ich noght wiþ Horn:	I have not spoken to Horn.
Nis he noȝt so unorn;	He is not so plain!
Horn is fairer þane beo he:	Horn is fairer than this man is.
Wiþ muchel schame mote þu deie".	May you die in great disgrace!"

Aþelbrus in a stunde
Fel anon to grunde.
"Lefdi min oȝe,
340 Liþe me a litel þroȝe!
Lust whi ich wonde
Bringe þe Horn to honde.
For Horn is fair and riche,
Nis no whar his iliche.
Aylmar, þe gode Kyng,
Dude him on mi lokyng.
Ȝef Horn were her abute,
Sore y me dute
Wiþ him ȝe wolden pleie
350 Bitwex ȝou selve tweie.
Þanne scholde wiþuten oþe
Þe kyng maken us wroþe.
Rymenhild, forȝef me þi tene,
Lefdi, my quene,
And Horn ich schal þe fecche,
Wham so hit recche".
Rymenhild, ȝef he cuþe,
Gan lynne wiþ hire muþe.
Heo makede hire wel bliþe;
360 Wel was hire þat siþe.
"Go nu", quaþ heo, "sone,
And send him after none,
On a squieres wise.
Whane þe kyng arise
To wude for to pleie,
Nis non þat him biwreie.
He schal wiþ me bileve
Til hit beo nir eve,
To haven of him mi wille;
370 After ne recche ich what me telle".
Aylbrus wende hire fro;
Horn in halle fond he þo
Bifore þe kyng on benche,
Wyn for to schenche.
"Horn", quaþ he, "so hende,
To bure nu þu wende,
After mete stille,

In an instant, Athelbruce
Fell to the ground.
"My dear lady,
Listen to me for a moment!
Hear why I hesitated
To bring Horn to your hand.
For Horn is fair and rich,
And there is no one his equal anywhere.
Almair, the good king,
Placed him in my care.
If Horn were around here,
I would be sorely worried
That you would go too far[269]
With the two of you alone.
Then, beyond question,
The king would make us sorry!
Rimenhild, forgive me your anger,
Lady, my queen,
And I will bring you Horn,
No matter who cares about it".
Rimenhild, as much as she could,
Kept her mouth quiet.
She made herself cheerful and
Things were well with her then.
"Go now", she said, "at once,
And send him after noon[270]
In a squire's disguise.
When the king rises
To hunt in the woods,
There is no one who will betray him.
He will stay with me
Until it is nearly night,
So that I have my will with him.
I don't care what is said about me after!"
Athelbruce departed from her.
He found Horn in the hall,
On a bench before the king
To pour him wine.
"Horn", he said, "so handsome,
Go to the chamber
After the meal, quietly,

---

269 *Ȝe wolden pleie*: *Play* in ME covers a variety of meanings, from innocent merriment to battle to sexual intercourse. Athelbruce is delicately suggesting that young passion would get the better of both of them. His concern is that the king would view the seduction of his daughter as treason, as also happens in *Amis and Amiloun*. But see line 365 below where *pleie* simply refers to the king hunting for fun.

270 *None*: The poet probably means the older medieval sense of *nona hora*, 3 PM. See the note to line 327 in *Athelston*.

	Wiþ Rymenhild to dwelle;	To stay with Rimenhild.
	Wordes swþe bolde,	If you have bold words,
380	In herte þu hem holde.	Hold them in your heart.
	Horn, beo me wel trewe;	Horn, be true to my counsel
	Ne schal hit þe nevre rewe".	And you will never regret it".[271]
	Horn in herte leide	Horn took to heart
	Al þat he him seide;	All that he said to him.
	He ȝeode in wel riȝte	He went right away
	To Rymenhild þe briȝte.	To Rimenhild the beautiful.
	On knes he him sette,	He set himself on his knees
	And sweteliche hure grette.	And greeted her elegantly.
	Of his feire siȝte	From his fair appearance
390	Al þe bur gan liȝte.	All the room began to glow.
	He spac faire speche -	He spoke a pleasing speech;
	Ne dorte him noman teche.	He needed no man to teach him!
	"Wel þu sitte and softe,	"How graciously and softly you sit,
	Rymenhild þe briȝte,	Shining Rimenhild,
	Wiþ þine maidenes sixe	With your six maidens
	Þat þe sitteþ nixte.	That you sit next to.
	Kinges stuard ure	Our king's steward
	Sende me in to bure;	Sent me to your room,
	Wiþ þe speke ihc scholde.	Saying I am to speak with you.
400	Seie me what þu woldest:	Tell me what you wish
	Seie, and ich schal here	To say, and I shall hear
	What þi wille were".	What your will is".
	Rymenhild up gan stonde	Rimenhild stood up
	And tok him bi þe honde:	And took him by the hand.
	Heo sette him on pelle	She set him on a fur spread
	Of wyn to drinke his fulle:	And gave him wine to drink his fill.
	Heo makede him faire chere	She showed him good cheer
	And tok him abute þe swere.	And took him about the neck.
	Ofte heo him custe,	She continually kissed him,
410	So wel so hire luste.	As much as she pleased.[272]
	. . . .	. . . .
H	"Welcome Horn", þus sayde	"Welcome, Horn!",
	Rymenild þat mayde.	Maid Rimenhild cooed.
	"An even ant a morewe,	"By day and by night,
	For þe ich habbe sorewe.	For you I am in sorrow.
	For þe y have no reste,	For you I can have no rest,
	Ne slepe me ne lyste".	Nor can I find a way to sleep".
	. . . .	. . . .
C	"Horn", heo sede, "wiþute strif,	"Horn", she said, "without refusing,
	Þu schalt have me to þi wif.	You must have me for your wife.
	Horn, have of me rewþe,	Horn, have pity on me,

---

271 MS Harleian 2253, *Shal þe nout arewe*, gives a better sense of Athelbruce's warning to Horn.
272 Rimenhild's wooing seems abrupt here, and Hall believes the copyist has missed some lines (note to 410, p. 118).

420 And plist me þi trewþe.	And pledge me your promise".
Horn þo him biþoȝte	Horn thought to himself
What he speke miȝte.	What he might say.
"Crist", quaþ he, "þe wisse,	"May Christ guide you", he said,
And ȝive þe hevene blisse	And give you Heaven's joy
Of þine husebonde,	In your husband,
Wher he beo in londe.	Wherever he is in the land!
Ich am ibore to lowe	I was born too low
Such wimman to knowe.	To have such a woman.
Ich am icome of þralle	I come from a peasant's home
430 And fundling bifalle.	And ended up an orphan.
Ne feolle hit þe of cunde	It would not be proper for you
To spuse beo me bunde.	To wed me as a spouse.
Hit nere no fair wedding	It would not be a fair wedding
Bitwexe a þral and a king".	Between a slave and a king".
Þo gan Rymenhild mislyke	Rimenhild was distaught then
And sore gan to sike:	And began to sigh bitterly.
Armes heo gan buȝe;	Her arms began to bow
Adun heo feol iswoȝe.	And she fell down in a swoon.
Horn in herte was ful wo	Horn was grieved in his heart
440 And tok hire on his armes two.	And took her in his two arms.
He gan hire for to kesse	He began to kiss her
Wel ofte mid ywisse.	Many times, with passion.
"Lemman", he sede, "dere,	"Darling", he said, "dear one,
Þin herte nu þu stere.	Take charge of your heart now.
Help me to kniȝte	Help me to become knighted,
Bi al þine miȝte,	With all your might,
To my lord þe king	By my lord the king
Þat he me ȝive dubbing:	So that he will give me dubbing.[273]
Þanne is mi þralhod	Then my serfdom
450 I went in to kniȝthod	Will be turned into knighthood
And I schal wexe more,	And I will grow to more, dear,
And do, lemman, þi lore".	And obey your bidding".
Rymenhild, þat swete þing,	Rimenhild, that sweet thing,
Wakede of hire swoȝning.	Woke from her swoon.
"Horn", quaþ heo, "wel sone	"Horn", she said, "very soon
Þat schal beon idone.	That will be done!
Þu schalt beo dubbed kniȝt	You will be dubbed a knight
Are come seve niȝt.	Before seven nights have passed.
Have her þis cuppe	Take this cup here,
460 And þis ryng þer uppe	And this ring with it,
To Aylbrus þe stuard,	To Athelbruce the steward,
And se he holde foreward.	And see that he keeps his word.

---

273 Hall points out that a commoner being knighted would have been acceptable under the laws of Ethelred but would have been rare by the thirteenth century (note to 439). Horn is of course already royal, though he possibly wishes to minimize the king's potential anger if he accedes to Rimenhild's desires.

Seie ich him biseche,	Say that I pleaded,
Wiþ loveliche speche,	With words of affection,[274]
Þat he adun falle	For him to fall down
Bifore þe king in halle,	Before the king in the hall
And bidde þe king ariȝte	And ask the king directly
Dubbe þe to kniȝte.	To dub you a knight at once.
Wiþ selver and wiþ golde	He will be well-rewarded
470 Hit wurþ him wel iȝolde.	With silver and with gold.
Crist him lene spede	May Christ grant him success
Þin erende to bede".	In pursuing your case".
Horn tok his leve,	Horn took his leave,
For hit was neȝ eve.	For it was nearly evening.
Aþelbrus he soȝte	He looked for Athelbruce
And ȝaf him þat he broȝte,	And gave him what he brought
And tolde him ful ȝare	And told him quickly
Hu he hadde ifare,	How he had fared,
And sede him his nede,	And told him his desires,
480 And bihet him his mede.	And promised him his reward.
Aþelbrus also swiþe	Athelbruce, just as quickly,
Wente to halle blive.	Went promptly to the hall.
"Kyng", he sede, "þu leste	"Sire", he said, "do listen
A tale mid þe beste.	To a word as good as the best.
Þu schalt bere crune	Tomorrow you will bear
Tomoreȝe in þis tune;	Your crown in this town;
Tomoreȝe is þi feste:	Tomorrow is your feast.
Þer bihoveþ geste.	It is fitting to enjoy yourself.
Hit nere noȝt for loren	It would not be a wasted effort
490 For to kniȝti child Horn,	To knight Child Horn
Þine armes for to welde:	To bear your arms.
God kniȝt he schal yelde".	He will make a good knight".
Þe king sede sone,	The king soon replied,
"Þat is wel idone.	"That is a good idea.
Horn me wel iquemeþ;	I am well pleased with Horn.
God kniȝt him bisemeþ.	It seems he will be a fine knight.
He schal have mi dubbing	He will have my dubbing
And afterward mi derling.	And will always be be my favorite.
And alle his feren twelf	And as for his twelve companions,
500 He schal kniȝten himself:	He will knight them himself.
Alle he schal hem kniȝte	He will dub them all
Bifore me þis niȝte".	Before me this next morning".[275]
Til þe liȝt of day sprang	Until the light of day sprang,

---

274 *With loveliche speche:* Who the 'loving words' are for is not clear, and ME has not yet worked out conventions of indirect speech. Rimenhild seemingly asks Horn to tell Athelbruce that she is asking him with fondness. Herzman et al. also suggest that the king is meant to understand that she is asking him with a daughter's affection.

275 *Þis niȝte:* A confusing line. After this speech the king knights them at sunrise (505). The meaning may be "within the next nightfall." ME often poetically uses nights to count days, as Rimenhild does in line 458.

Ailmar him þuȝte lang.
Þe day bigan to springe;
Horn com bivore þe kinge,
Mid his twelf yfere,
Sume hi were luþere.
Horn he dubbede to kniȝte
510 Wiþ swerd and spures briȝte.
He sette him on a stede whit:
Þer nas no kniȝt hym ilik.
He smot him a litel wiȝt
And bed him beon a god kniȝt.
Aþulf fel a knes þar
Bivore þe King Aylmar.
"King", he sede, "so kene
Grante me a bene:
Nu is kniȝt Sire Horn
520 Þat in Suddene was iboren;
Lord he is of londe
Over us þat bi him stonde;
Þin armes he haþ and scheld
To fiȝte wiþ upon þe feld:
Let him us alle kniȝte
For þat is ure riȝte".
Aylmar sede sone ywis,
"Do nu þat þi wille is".
Horn adun liȝte
530 And makede hem alle kniȝtes.
Murie was þe feste
Al of faire gestes:
Ac Rymenhild nas noȝt þer,
And þat hire þuȝte seve ȝer.
After Horn heo sente,
And he to bure wente.
Nolde he noȝt go one;
Aþulf was his mone.
Rymenhild on flore stod:
540 Hornes come hire þuȝte god:
And sede, "Welcome, Sire Horn,
And Aþulf kniȝt þe biforn.
Kniȝt, nu is þi time
For to sitte bi me.
Do nu þat þu er of spake:

Almair was deep in thought.
The day began to spring.
Horn came before the king
With his twelve companions,
Though some of them were wicked.
He dubbed Horn a knight
With a sword and shining spurs.
He set him on a white steed;
There was no knight like him.
He struck him a light blow[276]
And charged him to be a worthy knight.
Athulf fell on his knees there
Before King Almair.
"Sire, so valiant", he said,
"Grant me my plea.
Now Sir Horn is a knight,
Who was born in the Southlands.
He is lord of the land
Over all of us who stand near him.
He has your arms and shield
To fight with on the field.
Let him knight us all,
For that is our right".
Almair answered at once, in truth,
"Do now what your will is".
Horn knelt down
And made them all knights.
The feast was merry,
Filled with fine entertainments.
But Rimenhild was not there,
And it seemed like seven years to her.[277]
She sent for Horn,
And he went to her chamber.
But he would not go alone,
As Athulf was his companion.
Rimenhild stood on the floor;
She was pleased with Horn's coming,
And said, "Welcome, Sir Horn,
And Sir Athulf before you!
Knight, now is the time
For you to sit by me.
Do now what you spoke about before;

276 *He smot him a litel wight*: Dubbing by tapping a kneeling knight with a sword is a late medieval development. Dubbing originally involved a firm box on the ear, cheek, or neck (as is probably the case here) or an embrace around the neck. See also Hall's note (p. 126).

277 *Seve ȝer*: The poet is fond of sevens, and this may simply be an indefinite expression meaning "a very long time".

To þi wif þu me take.
Ef þu art trewe of dedes,
Do nu ase þu sedes.
Nu þu hast wille þine,
550　Unbind me of my pine".
"Rymenhild", quaþ he, "beo stille!
Ihc wulle don al þi wille,
Also hit mot bitide.
Mid spere I schal furst ride,
And mi kniȝthod prove,
Ar ihc þe ginne to woȝe.
We beþ kniȝtes yonge,
Of o dai al isprunge;
And of ure mestere
560　So is þe manere:
Wiþ sume oþere kniȝte
Wel for his lemman fiȝte
Or he eni wif take;
For þi me stondeþ þe more rape.
Today, so Crist me blesse,
Ihc wulle do pruesse,
For þi luve in þe felde
Mid spere and mid schelde.
If ihc come to lyve,
570　Ihc schal þe take to wyve".
"Kniȝt", quaþ heo, "trewe,
Ihc wene ihc mai þe leve:
Tak nu her þis gold ring:
God him is þe dubbing;
Þer is upon þe ringe
Igrave 'Rymenhild þe ȝonge':
Þer nis non betere anonder sunne
Þat eni man of telle cunne.
For my luve þu hit were
580　And on þi finger þu him bere.
Þe stones beoþ of suche grace
Þat þu ne schalt in none place
Of none duntes beon ofdrad,
Ne on bataille beon amad,
Ef þu loke þeran
And þenke upon þi lemman.
And Sire Aþulf, þi broþer,
He schal have anoþer.
Horn, ich þe biseche
590　Wiþ loveliche speche,
Crist ȝeve god erndinge

Take me to be your wife.
If you are true to your words,
Do now as you promised.
Now that you have your will,
Release me from my pining".
"Rimenhild", he said, "be still!
I will do all that you want
When the time is right.
I will first ride with a spear
And prove my knighthood
Before I begin to court you.
We are both young knights,
Sprung up in one day,
And this is the custom
Of our profession:
It is proper that one should fight
With some other knight
Before he takes a wife.
For you I go in greater haste.
Today, so may Christ bless me,
I will prove my valor,
For your love, in the field,
With spear and shield.
If I come back alive,
I will make you my wife".
"Knight so true", she answered,
"I know that I can trust you.
Take this gold ring here.
The detailing on it is fine;
On the ring is engraved
'Rimenhild the Young'.
There is none better under the sun
That any man can speak of.
Wear it for my love,
And bear it on your finger.
The stones are of such power
That you need not, in any place,
Be afraid of any blows,
Nor be maddened in battle,
If you look upon it
And think of your beloved.
And Sir Athulf, your brother,
He will have the other.
Horn, I plead for you,
With loving words,
That Christ give you a good finish

Middle English	Modern English
Þe aȝen to bringe". Þe kniȝt hire gan kesse, And heo him to blesse. Leve at hire he nam, And in to halle cam: Þe kniȝtes ȝeden to table, And Horne ȝede to stable: Þar he tok his gode fole, 600 Also blak so eny cole.	And bring you back again". The knight kissed her And she blessed him. He took his leave of her And came into the hall. The knights went to dinner, And Horn went to the stable. There he found his fine horse, As black as any coal.

. . . .

Middle English	Modern English
L In armes he him schredde And hys fole he fedde.	He clothed himself in armor, And fed his steed.

. . . .

Middle English	Modern English
C Þe fole schok þe brunie Þat al þe curt gan denie. Þe fole bigan to springe, And Horn murie to singe. Horn rod in a while More þan a myle. He fond o schup stonde 610 Wiþ heþene honde. He axede what hi soȝte Oþer to londe broȝte. An hund him gan bihelde Þat spac wordes belde: "Þis lond we wulleȝ winne And sle þat þer is inne". Horn gan his swerd gripe And on his arme wype. Þe Sarazins he smatte 620 Þat his blod hatte; At evreche dunte Þe heved of wente; Þo gunne þe hundes gone Abute Horn a lone: He lokede on þe ringe, And þoȝte on Rimenilde; He sloȝ þer on haste On hundred bi þe laste, Ne miȝte noman telle 630 Þat folc þat he gan quelle. Of alle þat were alive,	The foal shook its armor[278] So that it echoed through the court. The horse began to spring, And Horn began to sing merrily. In a while Horn had ridden More than a mile. He found an anchored ship, Filled with heathen hounds. He asked what they were looking for Or had brought to the land. One pagan dog beheld him, Who spoke belligerent words: "We will conquer this land And slay those who are in it". Horn gripped his sword And wiped it on his arm. He struck at the Saracens So that his blood grew hot. With every blow A head flew off. Then the hounds began To surround the lone Horn.[279] He looked on the ring And thought of Rimenhild. He slayed there in his fury At least a hundred! Nor might anyone count The men that he cut down. Of all who had arrived,[280]

---

278 *The fole schok the brunie*: Horses were commonly armored only after the late twelfth century (Hall, note to 591). Horn is
    knighted on a white steed (511) and so either this is a slip or he has several horses.

279 *A lone*: Or, *al one*, perhaps meaning the Saracens act as one in surrounding Horn.

280 *Alive*: Harleian 2253 MS has *aryve*.

Ne miȝte þer non þrive.   Not a one would succeed there.
Horn tok þe maisteres heved,   Horn took the leader's head,
Þat he hadde him bireved   Which he had lost because of him,
And sette hit on his swerde,   And set it on his sword,
Anoven at þan orde.   On top of the point.
He verde hom into halle,   He traveled home into the hall
Among þe kniȝtes alle.   Among all the knights.
"Kyng", he sede, "wel þu sitte,   "Sire", he announced, "you may sit easily
640 And alle þine knightes mitte.   With all your knights beside you!
Today, after mi dubbing,   Today, after my dubbing,
So I rod on my pleing   As I rode for pleasure,
I fond o schup rowe   I found a ship grounded
Þo hit gan to flowe,   Where the waters began,
Al wiþ Sarazines kyn,   Filled with Saracen kin
And none londisse men   And unknown foreign men,
To dai for to pine   Planning to harm and kill
Þe and alle þine.   You and all that is yours.
Hi gonne me assaille;   They tried to attack me,
650 Mi swerd me nolde faille.   But my sword would not fail me.
I smot hem alle to grunde,   I struck them all to the ground
Oþer ȝaf hem diþes wunde.   Or gave them deadly wounds.
Þat heved I þe bringe   I bring you the head
Of þe maister kinge.   Of the chief king.
Nu is þi wile iȝolde,   Now your effort is rewarded,
King, þat þu me knigȝi woldest".   Sire, for making me a knight".
A moreȝe þo þe day gan springe,   In the morning when day began to spring,
Þe king him rod an huntinge.   The king rode out to go hunting.
At hom lefte Fikenhild,   Fickenhild was left home,
660 Þat was þe wurste moder child.   Who was the worst mother's child.
Horn ferde into bure   Horn went into the bower
To sen aventure.   To pass some time.
He saȝ Rymenild sitte   He found Rimenhild pining
Also heo were of witte.   As if she were out of her wits.
Heo sat on þe sunne   She sat in the window sun
Wiþ tieres al birunne.   With tears running down.
Horn sede, "Lef, þin ore!   Horn said, "Dear, tell me your heart!
Wi wepestu so sore?"   Why are you crying so bitterly?"
Heo sede, "Noȝt I ne wepe,   She said, "I am not weeping for nothing.
670 Bute ase I lay aslepe   But as I lay asleep dreaming,
To þe se my net I caste,   I cast my net to the sea,
And hit nolde noȝt ilaste;   And it would not stay together.
A gret fiss at þe furste   At the first moment a great fish
Mi net he gan to berste.   Began to burst through my net.
Ihc wene þat ihc schal leose   I believe that I will lose
Þe fiss þat ihc wolde cheose".   The fish that I wish to choose".
"Crist", quaþ Horn, "and Seint Stevene   Horn replied, "May Christ and Saint

Turne þine swevene.	Stephen amend your dream!
Ne schal I þe biswike,	I will not deceive you,
680 Ne do þat þe mislike.	Nor do what displeases you.
I schal me make þin owe	I will make myself your own,
To holden and to knowe	To hold and to be known
For everech oþere wiȝte,	To every other person,
And þarto mi treuþe I þe pliȝte".	And to that I pledge my oath".
Muchel was þe ruþe	There was great dismay
Þat was at þare truþe,	In that betrothal,
For Rymenhild weop ille,	For Rimenhild wept sorely
And Horn let þe tires stille.	Until Horn stopped her tears.
"Lemman, quaþ he, "dere,	"Lover", he said, "dear heart,
690 Þu schalt more ihere.	There is more to hear.
Þi sweven schal wende	Your dream will show that
Oþer sum man schal us schende.	Some other man will harm us.
Þe fiss þat brak þe lyne,	The fish that broke the line,
Ywis he doþ us pine.	Truly, he will cause us pain.
Þat schal don us tene,	That result will bring us grief,
And wurþ wel sone isene".	And will soon be seen".
Aylmar rod bi Sture,	Almair rode by the Stour,[281]
And Horn lai in bure.	And Horn lay in the room.
Fykenhild hadde envye	Fickenhild was jealous
700 And sede þes folye:	And spoke these lies:
"Aylmar, ihc þe warne	"Almair, I must warn you:
Horn þe wule berne.	Horn will destroy you.
Ihc herde whar he sede,	I heard what he said,
And his swerd forþ leide,	And his sword is laid ready
To bringe þe of lyve,	To take your life
And take Rymenhild to wyve.	And to take Rimenhild as his wife.
He liþ in bure	He is lying in her chamber,
Under coverture	Under the bedcovers
By Rymenhild þi doȝter,	With your daughter Rimenhild,
710 And so he doþ wel ofte.	And he does this often.
And þider þu go al riȝt,	If you go there straightaway,
Þer þu him finde miȝt.	You will find him there.
Þu do him ut of londe,	Banish him out of the land
Oþer he doþ þe schonde!"	Before he brings you to ruin!"
Aylmar aȝen gan turne	Almair turned and went back
Wel modi and wel murne.	In great anger and distress.
He fond Horn in arme	He found Horn in her arms,
On Rymenhilde barme.	In Rimenhild's embrace.
"Awey ut", he sede, "fule þeof,	"Away, out", he said, "foul thief!

---

281 *Sture:* Herzman et al. and Garbaty claim this is the Mersey, but there is a River Stour running through Stourport-on-Severn and Kidderminster, near Worcester. If this is 'southern' to the poet, perhaps Westernesse is much further northwest, only limited by Ireland. *Suddene* might then refer to southern stretches of the Danelaw, but Worcester was part of Mercia and not occupied by the Danes. Laud only has *toure.*

720 Ne wurstu me nevremore leof!	You will never be dear to me again!
Wend ut of my bure	Get out of this room
Wiþ muchel messaventure.	With cursed fortune!
Wel sone bute þu flitte,	Unless you flee at once,
Wiþ swerde ich þee anhitte.	I will strike you with my sword![282]
Wend ut of my londe,	Get out of my land,
Oþer þu schalt have schonde".	Or you will have greater shame!"
. . . .	. . . .
L Horn cam in to stable,	Horn went into the stable,
Wel modi for þe fable.	Greatly saddened by the false report.
. . . .	. . . .
C Horn sadelede his stede	Horn saddled his steed
730 And his armes he gan sprede.	And laid out his arms.
His brunie he gan lace	He began to lace his chainmail,
So he scholde, in to place.	As is proper, into its place.
His swerd he gan fonge:	He seized his sword
Nabod he noʒt to longe.	And did not linger long;
He ʒede forþ blive	He went forth quickly
To Rymenhild his wyve.	To Rimenhild, his betrothed.
He sede, "Lemman derling,	He said, "Darling, dear one,
Nu havestu þi swevening.	Now you have your dream.
Þe fiss þat þi net rente,	The fish that tore your net
740 Fram þe he me sente.	Has now been sent away from you.
Rymenhild, have wel godne day:	Rimenhild, goodbye.
No leng abiden I ne may.	I cannot stay any longer,
In to uncuþe londe,	But will go to unknown lands
Wel more for to fonde;	To find a new life.
I schal wune þere	I will stay there
Fulle seve ʒere.	A full seven years.
At seve ʒeres ende,	At the end of seven years,
ʒef I ne come ne sende,	If I do not come or send word,
Tak þe husebonde;	Take some husband
750 For me þu ne wonde.	And do not wait for me.
In armes þu me fonge,	Take me in your arms
And kes me wel longe".	And kiss me for a while".
Heo custe him wel a stunde	She kissed him for a long time
And Rymenhild feol to grunde.	And Rimenhild swooned to the ground.
Horn tok his leve;	Horn took his leave;
Ne miʒte he no leng bileve.	He could not stay any longer.
He tok Aþulf, his fere,	He embraced his friend
Al abute þe swere,	Athulf about the neck
And sede, "Knight so trewe,	And said, "Knight so true,
760 Kep wel mi luve newe.	Keep my love as fresh as new.
Þu nevre me ne forsoke:	Do not ever forsake me!

---

282 This exposure scene is similar to the duke's discovery of Amis and Belisaunt, or even of the emir and Floris and Blancheflor. The king is relatively lenient here in not attempting to execute Horn by his own hand in a rage as the duke and emir do.

Rymenhild þu kep and loke.   Protect and look after Rimenhild".

His stede he gan bistride,   He mounted his steed

And forþ he gan ride.   And began to ride forth.

To þe havene he ferde,   He traveled to the harbor

And a god schup he hurede,   And hired a sturdy ship

Þat him scholde londe   That would take him

In westene londe.   To western lands.

Aþulf weop wiþ iȝe   Athulf wept from his eyes

770   And al þat him isiȝe.   In seeing all this.

. . . .

L   Þe whyȝt him gan stonde,   The sea breeze carried him

And drof til Hirelonde.   And drove him to Ireland.

. . . .

C   To londe he him sette   He set foot on land

And fot on stirop sette.   And put his feet in stirrups.

He fond bi þe weie   He found, on his way,

Kynges sones tweie;   The king's two sons.

Þat on him het Harild,   One called himself Harold

And þat oþer Berild.   And the other Berild.

Berild gan him preie   Berild asked of him

780   Þat he scholde him seie   That he would say

What his name were   What his name was,

And what he wolde þere.   And what he was doing there.

"Cutberd", he sede, "ich hote,   "Cutbeard is my name", he said.[283]

Icomen ut of þe bote,   "I come from out of a boat

Wel feor fram biweste   From far away on the western coast[284]

To seche mine beste".   To seek my fortune".

Berild gan him nier ride   Bereld rode nearer him

And tok him by þe bridel: And took him by the bridle.

"Wel beo þu, kniȝt, ifounde;   "You are welcome here, knight!

790   Wiþ me þu lef a stunde.   Stay with me a while.

Also mote I sterve,   As sure as I must die,

Þe king þu schalt serve.   You shall serve the king!

Ne saȝ I nevre my lyve   I never saw such a fair knight

So fair kniȝt aryve".   Arrive here in all my life".

Cutberd heo ladde in to halle,   They led Cutbeard into the hall

And hi a kne gan falle: And fell on their knees.

He sette him a knewelyng   They set themselves kneeling

And grette wel þe gode king.   And courteously greeted the good king.

Þanne sede Berild sone,   Then Bereld said at once,

---

283 *Cutberd*: The name may not have any significance, and Harleian MS 2253 has *Godmod*. Garbaty posits an influence from the legend of the Anglo-Saxon bishop Saint Cuthbert (c. 634-687), who was also set adrift and landed in Galloway, Scotland (his note to 773). For more on possible borrowings from saints' legends, see Irene P. McKeehan, "The Book of the Nativity of St. Cuthbert", *PMLA* 48 (1933): 981-99.

284 *Biweste*: 'by way of the west' or 'from the west' does not make sense from the perspective of Ireland. The poet perhaps means 'western England' or 'west Danelaw'.

800	"Sire King, of him þu hast to done;
	Bitak him þi lond to werie;
	Ne schal hit noman derie,
	For he is þe faireste man
	Þat evre ȝut on þi londe cam".
	Þanne sede þe king so dere,
	"Welcome beo þu here.
	Go nu, Berild, swiþe,
	And make him ful bliþe.
	And whan þu farst to woȝe,
810	Tak him þine glove:
	Iment þu havest to wyve,
	Awai he schal þe dryve;
	For Cutberdes fairhede
	Ne schal þee nevre wel spede".
	Hit was at Cristemasse,
	Neiþer more ne lasse;

. . . .

L	Þe King hym makede a feste,
	Wyt hyse knyctes beste,

. . . .

C	Þer cam in at none
820	A geaunt swþe sone,
	Iarmed fram paynyme
	And seide þes ryme:
	"Site stille, Sire Kyng,
	And herkne þis tyþyng:
	Her buþ paens arived;
	Wel mo þane five
	Her beoþ on þe sonde,
	King, upon þy londe;
	On of hem wile fiȝte
830	Aghen þre kniȝtes.
	Ȝef oþer þre slen ure,
	Al þis lond beo ȝoure;
	Ȝef ure on overcomeþ ȝour þreo,
	Al þis lond schal ure beo.
	Tomoreȝe be þe fiȝtinge,
	Whane þe light of daye springe".
	Þanne sede þe Kyng Þurston,
	"Cutberd schal beo þat on;
	Berild schal beo þat oþer,
840	Þe þridde Alrid his broþer;

"Sire King, you have work for him.
Entrust him to defend your land.
No man will harm him,
For he is the noblest man
That ever yet came to this land".
Then the dear king said,
"You are welcome here.
Go now, Berild, quickly,
And make him at ease.
And when you go courting,
Give him your glove to carry.[285]
If you intend to marry someone,
He will outshine you!
Because of Cutbeard's manliness
You would surely never succeed".
It was on Christmas Day,
Neither before or after,

. . . .

That the king held a feast
With his finest knights,

. . . .

When at midafternoon a giant
Abruptly came inside,
Armed from pagan lands,
Who said this challenge:
"Be still, Sire King,
And listen to what I say.
Pagan warriors have arrived,
Well more than five.
They are on the shore,
King, on your land.
Tomorrow one of them will fight
Against three of your knights.
If the three slay our one,
This land will remain yours.
If our one overcomes your three,
All this kingdom will be ours.
Tomorrow will be the battle,
When the light of day springs".
King Thurston said after,
"Cutbeard will be one,
And Berild will be the other,
And Alfred, his brother, the third.

---

285 *Tak him þine glove*: The meaning of the line is opaque. The king perhaps praises Horn's handsomeness and teases his son by saying that Berild should give Horn his glove when he is courting a woman to show that Horn is not a competitor, as otherwise Berild will be outclassed. See Herzman et al. and Hall, note to lines 793-7.

For hi beoþ þe strengeste
And of armes þe beste.
Bute what schal us to rede?
Ihc wene we beþ alle dede".
Cutberd sat at borde
And sede þes wordes:
"Sire King, hit nis no riȝte
On wiþ þre to fiȝte:
Aȝen one hunde,
850 Þre Cristen men to fonde.
Sire, I schal alone,
Wiþute more ymone,
Wiþ mi swerd wel eþe
Bringe hem þre to deþe".
Þe king aros amoreȝe,
Þat hadde muchel sorȝe;
And Cutberd ros of bedde,
Wiþ armes he him schredde:
Horn his brunie gan on caste,
860 And lacede hit wel faste,
And cam to þe kinge
At his up risinge.
"King", he sede, "cum to felde,
For to bihelde
Hu we fiȝte schulle,
And togare go wulle".
Riȝt at prime tide
Hi gunnen ut ride
And funden on a grene
870 A geaunt swþe kene,
His feren him biside
Hore deþ to abide.
Þe ilke bataille
Cutberd gan asaille:
He ȝaf dentes inoȝe;
Þe kniȝtes felle iswoȝe.
His dent he gan wiþdraȝe,
For hi were neȝ aslaȝe;
And sede, "Kniȝts, nu ȝe reste
880 One while ef ȝou leste".
Hi sede hi nevre nadde
Of kniȝte dentes so harde,
. . . .
L   Bute of þe King Mory,
Þat wes so swyþe stordy.
. . . .

For they are the strongest
And the finest in arms.
But what shall we do?
I expect we will all be dead!"
Cutbeard sat at the table
And said these words:
"Sire King, it is not right
For one to fight with three,
For three Christian men
To take on one heathen hound.
Sire, I will go alone,
Without any other companions.
With my sword I will easily
Bring the three of them to death".
In the morning, the king rose,
With great misgivings,
And Cutbeard got out of bed
And fitted himself with arms.
He cast on his chainmail coat
And laced it tightly,
And came to the king
When he had risen up.
"Sire", he said, "come to the field
To behold
How the fighting will go,
And we will go together".
Right at the first light,
They rode out
And met on the green.
The giant was very eager,
With his companions by him,
Waiting to bring on their deaths.
Cutbeard began to fight
The agreed battle.
He struck blows enough,
And the warriors became faint.
He began to ease off his strikes,
For they were nearly slain,
And said, "Sirs, you may rest now
For a while if you like".
They said they had never had
Such hard blows from a knight,
. . . .
Except from King Murray,
Who was also so hardy.
. . . .

C	He was of Hornes kunne,	He was from Horn's family,
	Iborn in Suddene.	Born in the Southlands.
	Horn him gan to agrise,	Horn began to shudder,
	And his blod arise.	And his blood rose.
	Bivo him saȝ he stonde	He saw standing before him the men
890	Þat driven him of lond	Who had driven him from his land
	And þat his fader sloȝ.	And killed his father.
	To him his swerd he droȝ.	He drew his sword to himself.
	He lokede on his rynge	He looked at his ring,
	And þoȝte on Rymenhilde.	And thought of Rimenhild.
	He smot him þureȝ þe herte,	He stabbed them through their chests,
	Þat sore him gan to smerte.	Which pained them harshly.
	Þe paens þat er were so sturne	The pagans, who were so fierce earlier,
	Hi gunne awei urne;	Began to run away.

. . . .

L	To schip he wolden ȝerne,	They wished to flee on their ships,
900	And Cubert hem gan werne,	And Horn moved to deny them,
	And seyde, "Kyng, so þou have reste,	And said, "Sire, to give you peace,
	Clep nou forþ ofi þi beste,	Call forth your best men,
	And sle we þyse hounden,	And we will slay these dogs
	Here we henne founden".	Who have come here!"

. . . .

C	Horn and his compaynye	Horn and his company
	Gunne after hem wel swiþe hiȝe	Took after them in great haste
	And sloȝen alle þe hundes	And slaughtered all the hounds
	Er hi here schipes funde.	Before they could reach their ships.
	To deþe he hem alle broȝte.	He brought them all to death;
910	His fader deþ wel dere hi boȝte.	They paid dearly for his father's murder.
	Of alle þe kynges kniȝtes	Of all the king's knights,
	Ne scaþede wer no wiȝte,	Not a person was hurt
	Bute his sones tweie	Except for his two sons,
	Bifore him he sagh deie.	Whom he saw die before him.
	Þe king bigan to grete	The king began to weep
	And teres for to lete.	And to let tears fall.
	Me leiden hem in bare	Men laid them on a funeral bier
	And burden hem ful ȝare.	And buried them right away.

. . . .

H	In a chirche of lym ant ston	In a chapel of lime and stone,
920	Me buriede hem wiþ ryche won.	Men interred them with rich goods.

. . . .

C	Þe king com into halle	The king came into the hall
	Among his kniȝtes alle.	Among all of his knights.
	"Horn", he sede, "I seie þe,	"Horn", he said, "I say to you,
	Do as I schal rede þe.	Do as I will advise you.
	Aslaȝen beþ mine heirs,	Both of my heirs are dead,
	And þu art kniȝt of muchel pris,	And you are a knight of great fame,

And of grete strengþe,	And of great strength,
And fair o bodie lengþe.	And fair, with a tall body.
Mi rengne þu schalt welde,	You will rule my kingdom
930 And to spuse helde	And will have for a wife
Reynild, mi doȝter,	Renild, my daughter,
Þat sitteþ on þe lofte".	Who waits upstairs".
"O Sire King, wiþ wronge	"Oh, Sire King, it would be wrong
Scholte ihc hit underfonge,	For me to accept
Þi doȝter, þat ȝe me bede,	Your daughter that you offer me,
Ower rengne for to lede.	Or to govern your realm.
Wel more ihc schal þe serve,	It is better that I serve you,
Sire Kyng, or þu sterve.	Sire, until you die.[286]
Þi sorwe schal wende	Your sorrows will be relieved
940 Or seve ȝeres ende.	Before seven years' end.
Whanne hit is wente,	When they have passed,
Sire King, ȝef me mi rente.	Sire, give me my reward.
Whanne I þi doȝter ȝerne,	If I ask for your daughter then,
Ne shaltu me hire werne".	You will not refuse me".
Cutberd wonede þere	Cutbeard lived there
Fulle seve ȝere	For a full seven years,
Þat to Rymenild he ne sente	And neither sent word to Rimenhild
Ne him self ne wente.	Nor did he journey himself.
Rymenild was in Westernesse	Rimenhild was in the Westlands
950 Wiþ wel muchel sorinesse.	In great sorrow.
A king þer gan arive	Another king arrived there
Þat wolde hire have to wyve;	Who wanted to have her as his wife.
Aton he was wiþ þe king	He was in accord with the king
Of þat ilke wedding.	On the matter of the wedding.
Þe daies were schorte,	The day was so close
Þat Rimenhild ne dorste	That Rimenhild did not dare
Leten in none wise.	To obstruct it in any way.
A writ he dude devise;	She dictated a letter,
Aþulf hit dude write,	And it was written by Athulf,
960 Þat Horn ne luvede noȝt lite.	Who did not love Horn lightly.
Heo sende hire sonde	She sent her messenger
To evereche londe	To every land
To seche Horn þe kniȝt,	To seek Horn the knight,
Þer me him finde miȝte.	Wherever he might find him.
Horn noȝt þerof ne herde	Horn heard nothing of it
Til o day þat he ferde	Until one day when he went
To wude for to schete.	Into the woods to hunt,
A knave he gan imete.	And he met a boy there.
Horn seden, "Leve fere,	Horn said, "Dear fellow,
970 What sechestu here?"	What are you looking for here?"

---

286 *Sterve*: in OE and ME *starve* has the more general meaning of 'die' (cf. German *sterben*). It only later gained the more specific meaning of dying of hunger.

"Kniȝt, if beo þi wille,	"Knight, if it is your will,
I mai þe sone telle.	I will soon tell you.
I seche fram biweste	I come from the English coast
Horn of Westernesse	Seeking Horn of the Westlands
For a maiden Rymenhild,	For a maiden, Rimenhild,
Þat for him gan wexe wild.	Who is growing mad for his sake.
A king hire wile wedde	A king will marry her
And bringe to his bedde,	And bring her to his bed,
King Modi of Reynes,	King Moody of Furness,[287]
980 On of Hornes enemis.	One of Horn's enemies.
Ihc habbe walke wide,	I have walked far
Bi þe se side;	Along the sea side.
Nis he nowar ifunde.	He is nowhere to be found.
Walawai þe stunde!	Alas the hour!
Wailaway þe while!	Alas the time!
Nu wurþ Rymenild bigiled".	Now Rimenhild has been deceived!"
Horn iherde wiþ his ires,	Horn heard with his own ears
And spak wiþ bidere tires:	And said through bitter tears,
"Knave, wel þe bitide!	"Lad, good fortune is with you!
990 Horn stondeþ þe biside.	Horn stands in front of you.
Aȝen to hure þu turne	Turn back to her again
And seie þat heo nu murne,	And tell her not to mourn,
For I schal beo þer bitime,	For I will be there in good time,
A Soneday by prime".	On Sunday by sunrise".
Þe knave was wel bliþe	The youth was very glad
And highede aȝen blive.	And hurried back quickly.
Þe se bigan to þroȝe	But the sea began to surge
Under hire woȝe.	Under Rimenhild's walls,
Þe knave þere gan adrinke	And the boy capsized there.
1000 Rymenhild hit miȝte of þinke	Rimenhild felt aware of this,
. . . .	. . . .
H Þe see him con ded þrowe	That the sea's rush had killed him
Under hire chambre wowe.	Under her chamber walls.
. . . .	. . . .
C Rymenhild undude þe durepin	She undid the door bolt
Of þe hus þer heo was in,	Of the house that she was in,
To loke wiþ hire iȝe	To look with her eyes
If heo oȝt of Horn isiȝe:	If she could see anything of Horn.
Þo fond heo þe knave adrent,	When she found the drowned boy
Þat heo hadde for Horn isent,	That she had sent for Horn,
And þat scholde Horn bringe.	Who was to bring him home,
1010 Hire fingres heo gan wringe.	She began to wring her hands.
Horn cam to Þurston þe King	Horn went to Thurston the king

287 *Reynes*: Perhaps Furness, Lancashire, in the Lake District. Schofield argues that the French MS has *Fenice* and that the English *Reynis* might be a corruption (15).

And tolde him þis tiþing.
Þo he was iknowe
Þat Rimenhild was his oȝe;
Of his gode kenne
Þe King of Suddenne,
And hu he sloȝ in felde
Þat his fader quelde,
And seide, "King þe wise,
1020 Ȝeld me mi servise.
Rymenhild help me winne,
Þat þu noȝt ne linne:
And I schal do to spuse
Þi doȝter wel to huse:
Heo schal to spuse have
Aþulf, mi gode felaȝe,
God kniȝt mid þe beste
And þe treweste".
Þe king sede so stille,
1030 "Horn, have nu þi wille".
He dude writes sende
Into Yrlonde
After kniȝtes liȝte,
Irisse men to fiȝte.
To Horn come inoȝe
Þat to schupe droȝe.
Horn dude him in þe weie
On a god galeie.
Þe wind him gan to blowe
1040 In a litel þroȝe.
Þe se bigan to posse
Riȝt in to Westernesse.
Hi strike seil and maste
And ankere gunne caste,
Or eny day was sprunge
Oþer belle irunge.
Þe word bigan to springe
Of Rymenhilde weddinge.
Horn was in þe watere,
1050 Ne miȝte he come no latere.
He let his schup stonde,
And ȝede to londe.
His folk he dude abide
Under wude side.
Horn him ȝede alone

And told him this news.
Then he was made aware
How Rimenhild was Horn's own,
About Horn's noble father,
The king of the Southlands,
And how he killed on the field
The men who murdered his father.
Horn said, "Wise king,
Reward me for my service.
Help me to win Rimenhild
And do not fail me,
And I will have your daughter
Married into a good family.
She will have for a husband
Athulf, my best friend,
A good knight among the best,
And the truest".
The king said gently,
"Horn, have your will now".
He had letters sent
Around Ireland
For able knights,
Fighting Irish men.
Enough came to Horn
And boarded the ship,
And Horn got underway
In a strong galley.
The wind began to blow
In a little while.
The sea began to drive them
Right into the Westlands.
They struck the sail and mast,
And cast off their anchor
Before another day had sprung
Or a bell was rung.
The word began to spread
Of Rimenhild's wedding.
Horn was on the sea
And could not come any later.
He let his ship stand anchored
And went ashore.
He had his company wait
Under cover of the woods;
Horn made his way alone,

Also he sprunge of stone.	As if he had sprung from the rocks.[288]
A palmere he þar mette	He met a pilgrim there
And faire hine grette:	And greeted him courteously:
"Palmere, þu schalt me telle	"Pilgrim, you must tell me
1060 Al of þine spelle".	All that is happening".
He sede upon his tale,	He said in his conversation,
"I come fram o brudale;	"I've come from a bridal feast.[289]
Ihc was at o wedding	I was at the wedding
Of a maide Rymenhild:	Of a maiden, Rimenhild.
. . . .	. . . .
L Fram honder chyrche wowe	Under the church walls nearby
Þe gan louerd owe	She wedded a husband.[290]
Ne miȝte hye hyt dreye	She could not dry the tears
Þat hye wep wyt eye.	That she wept from her eyes.
He seyde þat hye nolde	She said that she would not
1070 Be spoused myd golde.	Be married with a gold ring,
Hye hadde hosbonde	For she had a husband,
Þey be nere nawt in londe.	Even if he was in another land.
Mody myd strencþe hyre hadde	Moody married her by force
And in to toure ladde	And had her brought to the tower,
Into a strong halle,	Into a strong hall
Whit inne kastel walle.	Within the castle walls.
. . . .	. . . .
C Þer I was atte ȝate,	I was there at the gate,
Nolde hi me in late.	But they would not let me in.
Modi ihote hadde	Moody had ordered men
1080 To bure þat me hire ladde.	To take her to her bower.
Away I gan glide;	I slipped away,
Þat deol I nolde abide.	For I could not endure the sadness.
Þe bride wepeþ sore,	The bride cries bitterly,
And þat is muche deole".	And that is a great pity".
Quaþ Horn, "So Crist me rede,	Horn said, "So help me Christ,
We schulle chaungi wede.	We will exchange clothes!
Have her cloþes myne	Take my clothing here,
And tak me þi sclavyne,	And give me your cloak.
Today I schal þer drinke	Today I will drink there
1090 Þat some hit schulle ofþinke".	To something others will regret".
His sclavyn he dude dun legge,	The pilgrim laid down his cloak

---

288 *Also he sprunge of stone:* Garbaty mentions "an ancient belief that the first men originated from stones, singly, and hence were solitary" (note to line 1034). Hall gives as examples Teutonic legends and the *Odyssey*, xix.162-3, where Penelope tells the beggar, "You must have ancestors, for you did not spring from a tree or a rock".

289 Garbaty notes that pilgrims, who collected palm branches in the Holy Lands and were thus called palmers, were welcome guests at celebrations as they entertained everyone with their adventures. Refusing visitors during a wedding, as Moody does, was in very poor taste (his note to 1037, 1052).

290 The lines from Laud make the sequence clearer: the pilgrim observed the public church ceremony before being shooed away from the reception. They also emphasize that Riminhild is married unwillingly and thus the marriage is both invalid and unconsummated.

And tok hit on his rigge,
He tok Horn his cloþes;
Þat nere him noȝt loþe.
Horn tok burdon and scrippe
And wrong his lippe.
He makede him a ful chere,
And al bicolmede his swere.
He makede him unbicomelich
1100 Hes he nas nevremore ilich.
He com to þe gateward,
Þat him answerede hard:
Horn bad undo softe
Mani tyme and ofte;
Ne miȝte he awynne
Þat he come þerinne.
Horn gan to þe ȝate turne
And þat wiket unspurne.
Þe boye hit scholde abugge.
1110 Horn þrew him over þe brigge
Þat his ribbes him tobrake,
And swþe com in atte gate.
He sette him wel loȝe
In beggeres rowe;
He lokede him abute
Wiþ his colmie snute;
He seȝ Rymenhild sitte
Ase heo were of witte,
Sore wepinge and ȝerne;
1120 Ne miȝte hure no man wurne.
He lokede in eche halke;
Ne seȝ he nowhar walke
Aþulf his felawe,
Þat he cuþe knowe.
Aþulf was in þe ture,
Abute for to pure
After his comynge,
Ȝef schup him wolde bringe.
He seȝ þe se flowe
1130 And Horn nowar rowe.
He sede upon his songe:
"Horn, nu þu ert wel longe.

And took Horn's clothes,
And put them on his back.
They were not displeasing to him!
Horn took the staff and bag
And twisted his lip.
He gave himself a foul appearance
And dirtied up his neck.
He made himself unsightly
As he had never looked before.
He came to the gatekeeper,
Who answered him coldly.
Horn asked him kindly to open it,
Many times repeatedly.
He did not gain permission
So that he might come in.
Horn finally turned to the gate
And kicked out the wicket.
The oaf would pay for it!
Horn threw him over the bridge
So that his ribs cracked,
And swiftly came through the gate.[291]
He set himself down low,
Among a row of beggars.
He looked about him
With his dirty snout.[292]
He saw Rimenhild pining
As if she were out of her wits,
Weeping sadly and earnestly.
No man might console her.
He looked in each corner,
But he did not see his friend
Athulf walking anywhere,
As far as he could tell.
Athulf was in the tower,
Keeping a lookout
For his coming,
If a ship were to bring him.
He saw the ocean flow
And Horn nowhere on it.
He said in singing,
"Horn, you are slow to come.

---

291 Horn's violence seems extreme here, but maiming an ungracious or rude gatekeeper seems to be a common romance trope, and is also found in *Gamelyn* and *Bevis of Hampton*. In the latter the porter is killed.

292 *Colmie*: Rosamund Allen postulates that this refers to the sea-coal dust which would have been a part of trade in the capital, a lexical clue which might link the poem to the London court. Rosamund Allen, *King Horn* (New York: Garland, 1984), 113.

Rymenhild þu me toke	You entrusted Rimenhild to me,
Þat I scholde loke;	That I should look after her.
Ihc habbe kept hure evre;	I have always watched over her.
Com nu oþer nevre.	Come now or never!
I ne may no leng hure kepe.	I cannot protect her any longer,
For soreȝe nu I wepe".	And now I weep for sorrow".
Rymenhild ros of benche,	Rimenhild rose from the bench
1140 Wyn for to schenche,	To pour some wine
After mete in sale,	With the dinner in the hall,
Boþe wyn and ale.	Both wine and ale.[293]
On horn heo bar anhonde,	She carried a drinking horn in hand,
So laȝe was in londe.	As was the custom in the land.
Kniȝtes and squier	Knights and squires
Alle dronken of þe ber,	All drank the beer,
Bute Horn alone	All except for Horn alone,
Nadde þerof no mone.	Who had no share of it.
Horn sat upon þe grunde;	Horn sat on the ground
1150 Him þuȝte he was ibunde.	As though he were tied down to it.
He sede, "Quen so hende,	He said, "Gracious queen,
To meward þu wende;	Come toward me.
Þu ȝef us wiþ þe furste;	Give us some first.
Þe beggeres beoþ ofþurste".	The beggars are thirsty".
Hure horn heo leide adun,	She laid down her horn
And fulde him of a brun	And filled a bowl with a gallon
His bolle of a galun;	Of beer from a brown jug,
For heo wende he were a glotoun.	For she assumed he was a drunkard.
Heo seide, "Have þis cuppe,	She said, "Drink your cup,
1160 And þis þing þeruppe.	And this portion as well.
Ne saȝ ich nevre, so ich wene,	I never saw, so far as I know,
Beggere þat were so kene".	A beggar that was so bold".
Horn tok hit his ifere	Horn gave it to his companion
And sede, "Quen so dere,	And said, "Dear queen,
Wyn nelle ihc muche ne lite	I do not want much wine,
But of cuppe white.	Only a cupful of white.
Þu wenest I beo a beggere,	You believe I am a beggar,
And ihc am a fissere,	But I am a fisherman
Wel feor icome by este	Who has come far eastward
1170 For fissen at þi feste.	To fish at your feast.
Mi net liþ her bi honde,	My net lies nearby at hand
Bi a wel fair stronde.	Along a fair shore.
Hit haþ ileie þere	It has laid there
Fulle seve ȝere.	For a full seven years.
Ich am icome to loke	I have come to find out
Ef eni fiss hit toke.	If it has captured any fish,

---

293 Pouring alcohol for the king and his guests is not a servile task but Rimenhild's royal privilege. In *Beowulf*, Hrothgar's wife Wealhþeow ceremoniously fills the warriors' cups in the mead hall (622-4).

Ihc am icome to fisse;
Drink to me of disse.
Drink to Horn of horne.
1180 Feor ihc am jorne".
Rymenhild him gan bihelde;
Hire heorte bigan to chelde.
Ne knew heo noȝt his fissing,
Ne Horn hymselve noþing.
Ac wunder hire gan þinke
Whi he bad to Horn drinke.
Heo fulde hire horn wiþ wyn
And dronk to þe pilegrym.
Heo sede, "Drink þi fulle,
1190 And suþþe þu me telle
If þu evre isiȝe
Horn under wude liȝe".
Horn dronk of horn a stunde
And þreu þe ring to grunde.
. . . .

L   He seyde, "Quen, nou seche
Qwat is in þy drenche".
Rymild ȝede to boure
Wyt hyre maydenes foure.
. . . .

C   Þo fond heo what heo wolde,
1200 A ring igraven of golde
Þat Horn of hure hadde;
Sore hure dradde
Þat Horn isterve were,
For þe ring was þere.
Þo sente heo a damesele
After þe palmere;
"Palmere", quaþ heo, "trewe,
Þe ring þat þu þrewe,
Þu seie whar þu hit nome,
1210 And whi þu hider come".
He sede, "Bi Seint Gile,
Ihc habbe go mani mile,
Wel feor by ȝonde weste
To seche my beste.
I fond Horn child stonde
To schupeward in londe.
He sede he wolde agesse
To arive in Westernesse.
Þe schip nam to þe flode
1220 Wiþ me and Horn þe gode;

For I have come as a fisherman.
Drink to me from your dish!
Drink to Horn with your horn,
For I have journeyed far".
Rimenheld looked at him
And her heart began to quake.
She did not understand his fishing
Or recognize Horn himself,
But she thought it so mysterious
That she invited Horn to drink.
She filled her horn with wine,
And drank to the pilgrim.
She said, "Drink your fill,
And tell me the truth,
If you ever saw
Horn lying in the woods".
Horn drank from the horn a while
And dropped his ring to the bottom.
. . . .

He said, "Queen, look for
What is in your drink".
Rimenhild went to her chamber
With her four maidens.
. . . .

She found what she wished for,
The ring engraved of gold
That she had given Horn.
She sorely dreaded
That Horn was dead,
For the ring was there.
Then she sent a maiden
To bring her the pilgrim.
"Pilgrim", she said, "be truthful
About the ring that you dropped.
Say where you got it
And why you have come here".
He said, "By Saint Giles,
I have traveled many miles,
Far beyond the west
To seek my fortune.
I found Child Horn on land
Waiting to board a ship.
He said he was journeying
To return to the Westlands.
The ship took to the waters
With me and good Horn.

Horn was sik and deide,	Horn was sick and dying,
And faire he me preide:	And entreated me courteously,
'Go wiþ þe ringe	'Go take the ring
To Rymenhild þe ȝonge'.	To Rimenhild the Young'.
Ofte he hit custe,	He continually kissed it.
God ȝeve his saule reste!"	May God give his soul rest!"
Rymenhild sede at þe furste,	Rimenhild exclaimed at once,
"Herte, nu þu berste,	"Heart, now burst,
For Horn nastu namore,	For you no longer have Horn,
1230 Þat þe haþ pined so sore".	Who has hurt you so sorely".
Heo feol on hire bedde,	She fell on her bed,
Þer heo knif hudde,	Where she had hidden a knife
To sle wiþ king loþe	To slay the loathed king
And hureselve boþe	And herself as well
In þat ulke niȝte,	On that same night
If Horn come ne miȝte.	If Horn would not come.
To herte knif heo sette,	She set the knife to her heart
Ac Horn anon hire kepte.	But Horn quickly caught her.
He wipede þat blake of his swere,	He wiped the soot off his neck
1240 And sede, "Quen, so swete and dere,	And said, "Queen, so sweet and dear,
Ihc am Horn þin oȝe.	I am your own Horn!
Ne canstu me noȝt knowe?	Don't you recognize me?
Ihc am Horn of Westernesse;	I am Horn of the Westlands.
In armes þu me cusse".	Kiss me in your arms!"
Hi custe hem mid ywisse	They kissed each other, certainly,
And makeden muche blisse.	And had great joy.
"Rymenhild", he sede, "y wende	"Rimenhild", he said, "I must go
Adun to þe wudes ende:	Down to the woods' end.
Þer beþ myne kniȝtes	My knights are there,
1250 Redi to fiȝte;	Ready to fight,
Iarmed under cloþe,	Armed under their clothes.
Hi schulle make wroþe	They will make the king
Þe king and his geste	And his guests who have
Þat come to þe feste.	Come to the feast displeased!
Today I schal hem teche	Today I will teach them
And sore hem areche".	And correct them harshly".
Horn sprong ut of halle	Horn sprang out of the hall
And let his sclavin falle.	And let his cloak fall.
Þe quen ȝede to bure	The queen ran to the chamber
1260 And fond Aþulf in ture.	And found Athulf in the tower.
"Aþulf", heo sede, "be bliþe	"Athulf", she said, "be glad,
And to Horn þu go wel swiþe.	And go to Horn quickly!
He is under wude boȝe	He is under the forest boughs
And wiþ him kniȝtes inoȝe".	With knights enough with him".
Aþulf bigan to springe	Athulf began to hurry
For þe tiþinge.	Because of the news,

After Horn he arnde anon,
Also þat hors miȝte gon.
He him overtok ywis;
1270 Hi makede swiþe muchel blis.
Horn tok his preie
And dude him in þe weie.
He com in wel sone:
Þe ȝates were undone.
Iarmed ful þikke
Fram fote to þe nekke,
Alle þat were þerin
Biþute his twelf ferin
And þe King Aylmare,
1280 He dude hem alle to kare,
Þat at þe feste were;
Here lif hi lete þere.
Horn ne dude no wunder
Of Fikenhildes false tunge.
Hi sworen oþes holde,
Þat nevre ne scholde
Horn nevre bitraie,
Þegh he at diþe laie.
Hi runge þe belle
1290 Þe wedlak for to felle;
Horn him ȝede wiþ his
To þe kinges palais,
Þer was bridale swete,
For riche men þer ete.
Telle ne miȝte tunge
Þat gle þat þer was sunge.
Horn sat on chaere,
And bad hem alle ihere.
"King", he sede, "þu luste
1300 A tale mid þe beste.
I ne seie hit for no blame:
Horn is mi name.
Þu me to kniȝt hove,
And knigȝthod have proved.
To þe, king, men seide
Þat I þe bitraide;
Þu makedest me fleme,
And þi lond to reme;
Þu wendest þat I wroȝte
1310 Þat I nevre ne þoȝte,
Bi Rymenhild for to ligge,
And þat I wiþsegge.

And ran after Horn as quickly
As a horse might gallop.
In fact, he overtook him.
They made great rejoicing.
Horn called his band
And set them on their way.
Very soon he came in;
The gates were undone.
Armed heavily
From head to foot,
He made sorry
Everyone who was inside
At the celebration,
Except for his twelve companions
And King Almair.
They forfeited their lives there!
Yet Horn took no vengeance
On Fickenhild's false tongue.
He swore oaths of loyalty,
That he would
Never betray Horn,
Even if death threatened.
They rang the bell
To celebrate the wedding.
Horn went with his men
To the king's palace.
There was a sweet wedding feast
For the fine men who ate there.
No tongue might tell
Of the joys that were sung there.
Horn sat on the throne,
And asked them all to listen.
"Sire King", he said, "listen to
A word among the best.
I do not speak to blame you.
Horn is my name.
You raised me to be a knight,
And I have proven my knighthood.
Men said to you, king,
That I betrayed you.
You made me flee
And to leave your land.
You believed that I had done
What I would never think of,
To lay with Rimenhild,
And that I deny!

Ne schal ich hit biginne,	Nor will I think to do so
Til I Suddene winne.	Until I win the Southlands.
Þu kep hure a stunde,	Keep her for a time,
Þe while þat I funde	While I attempt
In to min heritage,	To recover my heritage
And to mi baronage.	And my own baronage.
Þat lond I schal ofreche	I will take that land
1320 And do mi fader wreche.	And wreak vengeance for my father.
I schal beo king of tune,	I will be lord of that town,
And bere kinges crune;	And bear a king's crown.
Þanne schal Rymenhilde	Then Rimenhild will
Ligge bi þe kinge".	Lie with a king!"
Horn gan to schupe draȝe	Horn took to the ship
Wiþ his Irisse felaȝes,	With his Irish fellows,
Aþulf wiþ him, his broþer:	With his brother Athulf by him.
Nolde he non oþer.	He did not want any others.
Þat schup bigan to crude;	The ship began to move
1330 Þe wind him bleu lude;	And the wind blew loudly.
Biþinne daies five	Within five days
Þat schup gan arive	The ship arrived
Abute middelniȝte.	Around midnight.
Horn him ȝede wel riȝte;	Horn set forth right away.
He tok Aþulf bi honde	He took Athulf by the hand
And up he ȝede to londe.	And went up onto the shore.
Hi founde under schelde	Under a shield they found a knight
A kniȝt hende in felde.	Who was valiant on the battlefield.

. . . .

L Op þe schelde was drawe	On the shield was drawn
1340 A crowch of Jhesu Cristes lawe.	A cross of the faith of Jesus Christ.[294]

. . . .

C Þe kniȝt him aslepe lay	The knight lay asleep
Al biside þe way.	Along the pathway.
Horn him gan to take	Horn took hold of him
And sede, "Kniȝt, awake!	And said, "Knight, wake up!
Seie what þu kepest?	What you are guarding,
And whi þu her slepest?	And why you are sleeping there?
Me þinkþ bi þine crois liȝte,	I assume by your shining cross
Þat þu longest to ure Driȝte.	That you belong to our Lord.
Bute þu wule me schewe,	But unless you tell me,
1350 I schal þe tohewe".	I will hack you to pieces".
Þe gode kniȝt up aros;	The good knight rose up;
Of þe wordes him gros.	He was terrified by the words.
He sede, "Ihc serve aghenes my wille	He pleaded, "Against my will,[295]

---

294 Lines from Laud emphasize that the knight retains his Christian faith in spite of the Saracens. For some reason the Cambridge manuscript omits numerous religious references from the narrative.

295 *Serve*: McKnight has *have*, which makes no sense.

Payns ful ylle.
Ihc was Cristene a while:
Þo icom to þis ille
Sarazins blake,
Þat dude me forsake.
On Crist ihc wolde bileve.
1360 On him hi makede me reve
To kepe þis passage
Fram Horn þat is of age,
Þat wunieþ biweste,
Kniȝt wiþ þe beste;
Hi sloȝe wiþ here honde
Þe king of þis londe,
And wiþ him fele hundred,
And þerof is wunder
Þat he ne comeþ to fiȝte.
1370 God sende him þe riȝte,
And wind him hider drive
To bringe hem of live.
He sloȝen Kyng Murry,
Hornes fader, king hendy.
Horn hi ut of londe sente;
Twelf felaȝes wiþ him wente,
Among hem Aþulf þe gode,
Min oȝene child, my leve fode.
Ef Horn child is hol and sund,
1380 And Aþulf biþute wund,
He luveþ him so dere,
And is him so stere.
Miȝte I seon hem tweie,
For joie I scholde deie".
"Kniȝt, beo þanne bliþe
Mest of alle siþe;
Horn and Aþulf his fere
Boþe hi ben here".
To Horn he gan gon
1390 And grette him anon.
Muche joie hi makede þere
Þe while hi togadere were.

I serve evil pagans!
I was once a Christian.
Then black Saracens[296]
Came to this island,[297]
Who made me abandon my faith.
Otherwise I would follow Christ.
They made me a guard
To protect this passage
From Horn, who is of age
And lives in the Westlands,
A knight among the best.
By their hands they killed
The king of this land,
And with him many hundreds.
It is a mystery that he
Has not returned to fight!
May God send him the right,
And the wind to drive him here,
To take away their lives!
They slaughtered King Murray,
Horn's father, a gracious king.
They exiled Horn out of the land;
Twelve fellows went with him,
Among them Athulf the good,
My own child, my dear son.
If Child Horn is whole and sound,
And Athulf is without harm–
He loved my son so dearly that
He was like a guiding star to him!–
If I could see the two of them,
I would die for joy".
"Then rejoice, knight,
More than ever before!
Horn and Athulf his friend
Are both standing here".
He rushed to Horn
And embraced him at once.
They made great joy there
While they were together.

---

296 *Þis ille*: The 'isle' has been read as a locational clue meaning the Isle of Man, although England itself is often poetically referred to as such: "this sceptered isle".

297 *Sarazins blake*: Who are the poem's Saracens? Diane Speed (580) notes that 'black' did not have the denotation of 'wicked' at this time, which suggests that the Saracens are Africans or Arabs. In *Horn et Rimenhild* the invaders explicitly are Muslims from Persia, but no such peoples ever reached England. Some claim the poet means Vikings, as *Horn* is the first known ME text to use the word *Saracen* (Speed, 566), but the Norsemen had no interest in suppressing Christianity. Like the geographical references, the poem may be intentionally vague in giving Horn a generic and bestial antagonist. Diane Speed, "The Saracens of *King Horn*", *Speculum* 65:3 (1990): 564-66.

"Childre", he sede, "hu habbe ye fare?"
"Þat ich you seȝ, hit is ful ȝare.
Wulle ȝe þis lond winne
And sle þat þer is inne?"
He sede, "Leve Horn child,
Ȝitt lyveþ þi moder Godhild:
Of joie heo miste
1400 If heo þee alive wiste".
Horn sede on his rime,
"Iblessed beo þe time
I com to Suddene
Wiþ mine Irisse menne:
We schulle þe hundes teche
To speken ure speche.
Alle we hem schulle sle,
And al quic hem fle".
Horn gan his horn to blowe;
1410 His folk hit gan iknowe;
Hi comen ut of stere,
Fram Hornes banere;
Hi sloghen and fuȝten,
Þe niȝt and þe uȝten.
Þe Sarazins cunde
Ne lefde þer non in þende.
Horn let wurche
Chapeles and chirche;
He let belles ringe
1420 And masses let singe.
He com to his moder halle
In a roche walle.
Corn he let serie,
And makede feste merie;
Murye lif he wroghte.
Rymenhild hit dere boghte.
Fikenhild was prut on herte,
And þat him dude smerte.
Ȝonge he ȝaf and elde
1430 Mid him for to helde.
Ston he dude lede,
Þer he hopede spede,
Strong castel he let sette,
Mid see him biflette;

"My boys", he said, "how have you fared?
It is a long time since I saw you!
Will you win back this land
And slay those who rule it?"
He continued, "Dear Child Horn,
Your mother Godhild still lives.
She would have great joy
If she knew you were alive".
Horn said in his speech,
"Blessed be the time
When I came to the Southlands
With my Irish men!
We will teach the hounds
To speak as we want![298]
We will slaughter them all
And flay them alive".
Horn began to sound his horn
And his men heard it.
They came out of the stern,
From under Horn's banner.
They killed and fought
From night until morning.
Of the Saracens' kind,
None were left in the end.[299]
Horn ordered that chapels
And churches be built;
He had bells rung,
And masses sung.
He came to his mother's hall
In the rock cliffside,
Where he had food readied
And held a merry feast.
He made their lives glad,
But Rimenhild paid dearly for it.
For Fickenhild was proud at heart
And it would bring them trouble.
He gave money to young and old
To build alliances with him.
He had stone brought in,
Hoping for success there
By having a strong castle built,
Filled around with sea water.

---

298 *To speken ure speche*: Hall interprets this as a euphemism for "we will teach them a humiliating lesson" (note to 1366, his lineation), whereas Garbaty is more prosaic: "they will meet our spoken terms" (his note to 1380).

299 Herzman et al. make 1415-16 a simple sentence, so that the Saracens leave nothing in the end for the locals, but it does not seem to fit contextually here.

Þer ne miȝte liȝte	No one might land there,
Bute foȝel wiþ fliȝte.	Except for birds in flight,
Bute whanne þe se wiþdroȝe,	But when the sea drew back,
Miȝte come men ynoȝe.	Men enough might come.
Fikenhild gan wende	Fickenhild turned his attention
1440 Rymenhild to schende.	To shaming Rimenhild.
To woȝe he gan hure ȝerne;	He began to court her intensely;
Þe kyng ne dorste him werne.	The king did not dare prevent him.
Rymenhild was ful of mode;	Rimenhild was sick at heart,
He wep teres of blode.	And she wept tears of blood.
Þat niȝt Horn gan swete	That night Horn become feverish
And hevie for tomete	And began to have nightmares
Of Rymenhild, his make,	About Rimenhild, his mate.
Into schupe was itake.	She was taken onto a ship;
Þe schup bigan to blenche:	The boat began to capsize,
1450 His lemman scholde adrenche.	And his lover was about to drown.
Rymenhild wiþ hire honde	Rimenhild wished to swim back
Wolde up to londe;	To land with her arms,
Fikenhild aȝen hire pelte	But Fickenhild threw her back
Wiþ his swerdes hilte.	With his sword's hilt.
Horn him wok of slape	Horn woke from his sleep
So a man þat hadde rape.	Like a man in urgent haste.
"Aþulf", he sede, "felaȝe,	"Athulf", he said, "my brother,
To schupe we mote draȝe.	We must get on board the ship!
Fikenhild me haþ idon under	Fickenhild has deceived me
1460 And Rymenhild to do wunder.	And has put Rimenhild in danger.
Crist, for his wundes five,	May Christ, for his five wounds,
Toniȝt me þuder drive".	Drive us toward there tonight!"
Horn gan to schupe ride,	Horn set off on his ship
His feren him biside.	With his companions beside him.
Fikenhild, or þe dai gan springe,	Fickenhild, before the day sprang,
Al riȝt he ferde to þe kinge,	Went straightaway to the king
After Rymenhild þe briȝte,	To ask for shining Rimenhild,
To wedden hire bi niȝte.	To marry her by night.
He ladde hure bi þe derke	He sent her in the darkness
1470 Into his nywe werke.	Into his new fortress.
Þe feste hi bigunne,	The wedding feast began
Er þat ros þe sunne.	Before the sun had even risen.[300]
Er þane Horn hit wiste,	And before Horn knew of it,
Tofore þe sunne upriste,	Before the sun was up,
His schup stod under ture	His ship stood under the tower
At Rymenhilde bure.	Near Rimenhild's chamber.
Rymenhild litel weneþ heo	Rimenhild little suspected

---

300 Again, Rimenhild's forced marriage is not consummated, as Fickenhild is apparently more interested in the feasting than in his new bride, which gives Horn enough time to sail back to Suddene.

Þat Horn þanne alive beo.	That Horn was alive.
Þe castel þei ne knewe,	They did not know the castle,
1480 For he was so nywe.	For it was so new.
Horn fond sittinde Arnoldin,	Then Horn found Arnold,
Þat was Aþulfes cosin,	Who was Athulf's cousin,
Þat þer was in þat tide,	Who was at that moment
Horn for tabide.	Sitting and waiting for Horn.
"Horn kniȝt", he sede, "kinges sone,	"Sir Horn", he said, "royal son,[301]
Wel beo þu to londe icome.	Welcome to this land!
Today haþ ywedde Fikenhild	This morning Fickenhild has married
Þi swete lemman Rymenhild.	Your sweet lover Rimenhild.
Ne schal I þe lie:	I will not lie to you;
1490 He haþ giled þe twie.	He has deceived you twice.
Þis tur he let make	He had this tower made,
Al for þine sake.	All for your sake.
Ne mai þer come inne	No man may get inside
Noman wiþ none ginne.	By any contriving.
Horn, nu Crist þe wisse,	Horn, may Christ guide you now
Of Rymenhild þat þu ne misse".	So that you do not lose Rimenhild".
Horn cuþe al þe liste	Horn knew all the tricks
Þat eni man of wiste.	That any man might know of.
Harpe he gan schewe,	He brought out a harp,
1500 And tok felaȝes fewe,	And took a few fellows,
Of kniȝtes swiþe snelle	Very keen knights, who disguised
Þat schrudde hem at wille.	Themselves as they wished.
Hi ȝeden bi þe gravel	They went along the sand
Toward þe castel.	Toward the castle.
Hi gunne murie singe	They began to sing merrily
And makede here gleowinge.	And made harping music.
Rymenhild hit gan ihere	Rimenhild heard it
And axede what hi were.	And asked who they were.
Hi sede hi weren harpurs	They replied that they were harpists
1510 And sume were gigours.	And some were fiddlers.
He dude Horn in late	They let Horn in
Riȝt at halle gate.	Right through the hall gate.
He sette him on þe benche,	He set himself on the bench
His harpe for to clenche.	And grasped his harp.
He makede Rymenhilde lay,	He played Rimenhild a lay,
And heo makede walaway.	And made her a lament.
Rymenhild feol yswoȝe	Rimenhild fell in a swoon then;
Ne was þer non þat louȝe.	There was no one there who laughed!
Hit smot to Hornes herte	It pierced to Horn's heart
1520 So bitere þat hit smerte.	So bitterly that it pained him.
He lokede on þe ringe	He looked on the ring

301 *Kinges sone*: The phrase fits the rhyme, but neither *Horn* nor *Havelok* ever uses Anglo-Norman 'prince', and the MED has no uses recorded for it until after 1300.

And þoʒte on Rymenhilde:
He ʒede up to borde
Wiþ gode swerdes orde:
Fikenhildes crune
Þer he fulde adune,
And al his men a rowe,
Hi dude adun þrowe.
Whanne hi weren aslaʒe
1530 Fikenhild hi dude todraʒe.
Horn makede Arnoldin þare
King after King Aylmare
Of al Westernesse
For his meoknesse.
Þe king and his homage
ʒeven Arnoldin trewage.
Horn tok Rymenhild bi þe honde
And ladde hure to þe stronde,
And ladde wiþ him Aþelbrus,
1540 Þe gode stuard of his hus.
Þe se bigan to flowe,
And Horn gan to rowe.
Hi gunne for to arive
Þer King Modi was sire.
Aþelbrus he makede þer king
For his gode teching:
He ʒaf alle þe kniʒtes ore
For Horn kniʒtes lore.
Horn gan for to ride;
1550 Þe wind him blew wel wide.
He arivede in Yrlonde,
Þer he wo fonde,
Ther he dude Athulf child
Wedden maide Reynild.
Horn com to Suddenne
Among al his kenne;
Rymenhild he makede his quene;
So hit miʒte wel beon.
Al folk hem miʒte rewe
1560 That loveden hem so trewe:
Nu ben hi boþe dede -

And thought of Rimenhild.
He went up to the table
With a good sword edge.
He made Fickenhild's head
Fall to the ground there,
And struck down
All his men in a row;
And when they were dead,
He cut apart Fickenhild.
There Horn made Arnold king
To follow King Almair,
Of all the Westlands,
For his gentleness.
The king and his vassals
Gave Arnold tribute.[302]
Horn took Rimenhild by the hand
And led her to the shore,
And took along Athelbruce,
The good steward of the house.
The sea began to flow,
And Horn began to sail.
They arrived where
King Moody had been lord.
He made Athelbruce their king,
For his good teaching;
He gave all the knights clemency
Because of Sir Horn's counsel.
Horn sailed away again,
And the wind blew him far away.
He arrived in Ireland, where he
Had found bittersweet fortune.[303]
There he had young Athulf
Wed maid Reynild.
Then Horn came home to the Southlands,
Among all of his kin.
He made Rimenhild his queen
So that all might be well.
All the people who loved them truly
Might grieve for them now,
For now they are both dead.

---

302 In Cambridge the sense is that the aged Almair will be succeeded by Arnold as king and that the knights pay respect to him. Hall suggests a possible darker reading of Laud Misc. 108, where 1536 is *utrage* instead of *truage*. If so, Almair is deposed and the narrative would read more like "Horn made Arnold king there, after King Almair, the knights, and the baronage did him all kinds of outrage". Yet Harleian 2253 agrees more with Cambridge in that Horn has earlier reconciled with Almair (1299-1324).

303 Garbaty explains this confusing line: *fonde* does not refer to Horn's last arrival in Ireland but his first, where he finds refuge but also woe because of the deaths of Harild and Berild (note to 1526).

Crist to hevene hem lede!
Her endeth the tale of Horn
That fair was and noȝt unorn.
Make we us glade evre among,
For thus him endeth Hornes song.
Jesus, þat is of hevene king,
Ȝeve us alle His swete blessing.

1569 Amen.

May Christ lead them to Heaven!
Here ends the tale of Horn,
Who was noble and never cowardly.
Let us now together be glad,
For thus ends Horn's song.
May Jesus, who is Heaven's king,
Give us all His sweet blessing.

Amen.

Sir Degare

Clerical opinions of medieval romance seemingly range from bemused indulgence to active moral condemnation over its secular and exotic themes. Yet modern claims that medieval romances were salacious and transgressive often betray the agendas of critics more than the texts. English insular romances seldom conform to the prescriptive definition of courtly love as adulterous, and sex usually reflects traditional morality in its (non) depiction. A wide stylistic divide separates most medieval romances from the filthy *Dame Sirith* or other fabliaux, or the suggestive riddles of the Exeter book.

Yet *Sir Degare* has perhaps more carnality than most English romances; even the maiden Degare courts emphasizes that he can have her 'bodi' at will if he defeats a violent suitor. Worse, there are the queasy subthemes of rape and incest. In *Havelok*, under Athelwold anyone "wo so dide maydne shame" (83) has his limbs cut off. The Wife of Bath's "lusty bacheler" violates a maiden and initially faces a death sentence, a penalty going far beyond contemporary punishments which would have seen sexual assault as more a property crime necessitating fines. But the knight in *Degare* seems a strangely well-mannered rapist who speaks kindly and reassuringly to the princess, announcing "damaisele, welcome mote thou be!" (102) before taking her virginity by violent force.

Nevertheless, the fictive frame of the poem seems to cheerily excuse the knight's sexual assault as the enchanted action of a fairy knight. Degare even apologizes to his father for mistakenly fighting him, and the king has no objections to the princess later marrying the man who has given him a bastard grandson. Influenced by its possible origins as a Breton lay, magic infuses the poem in protective swords, dwarves, and monstrous giant-knights. All this co-exists with both the regular romance trappings of dragons and jousts as well as Degare's upbringing in a hermitage with the monks who father him. While the princess does accidentally marry her own son, the mistake

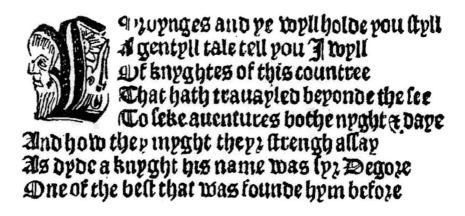

From black-letter edition by Wynkyn de Worde

is recognized before anything happens and the marriage is annuled, and so what seems well on the way to an Oedipan tragedy ends with the formal romance accoutrements of marriage and lands.

Sir Degare is well-preserved in six manuscripts, though unfortunately all incomplete: Auchinleck, Adv. MS 19.2.1 (c. 1330), British Library MS Egerton 2862 (c. 1400), Cambridge University Library MS Ff. 2.38 (c. 1450), Bodleian Library MS Rawlinson Poetry 34 (c. 1450), Bodleian Library MS Douce 261 (dated 1561), and British Library Add. MS 27879 (dated 1650). There are also several sixteenth-century print editions. I take as my text source David Laing, ed., *Sire Degarre, a Metrical Romance of the End of the Thirteenth Century* (Edinburgh: Abbotsford Club, 1849), comparing it to the Auchinleck images. The last missing lines are supplied by a black-letter edition by Wynkyn de Worde, Oxford, Bodleian Library; New York, Pierpont Morgan Library (c. 1512). A few lines are also added from Cambridge and Egerton.

A: Auchinleck
W: Wynkyn de Worde
E: Egerton 2862
C: Cambridge Ff. 2.38

1 C	Lystenyþ lordyngys gente and fre	Listen, lordings, noble and generous,
	Y will yow telle of Syr Degarre.	And I will tell you about Sir Degare.
	Knyȝtys þat were some tyme in lande	There were once in this land knights,
A	Ferli fele wolde fonde	A wondrous number, who would
	And sechen aventoures bi niȝt and dai	By day and night seek out adventures
	Hou ȝhe miȝte here strengthe asai.	To see how they might test their valor.
	So dede a knyȝt Sire Degarree.	So did one knight, Sir Degare.
	Ich wille ȝou telle wat man was he.	I will tell you what kind of man he was.
	In Litel Bretaygne was a kyng	In Brittany there was a king[304]
10	Of gret poer in alle þing	With great might in all things,
	Stif in armes under scheld	Firm in arms wielded under his shield,
	And mochel idouted in þe feld.	And greatly feared on the field.
	Þer nas no man verraiment	There was no man, truly,
	Þat miȝte in werre ne in tornament	Who faced him in war or tournament
	Ne in justes for no þing	Or in jousts who might by any means
	Him out of his sadel bring	Force him out of his saddle
	Ne out of his stirop bringe his fot	Or bring his feet out of his stirrups,
	So strong he was of bon and blod.	So strong was he in body and blood.
	Þis kyng ne hadde non oþer hair	This king had no heir,
20	But a maidenchild fre and fair.	Other than a young maiden, noble and fair.
	Here gentiresse and here beaute	Her gentility and her beauty
	Was moche renound in ich countre.	Were renowned in every land.
	Þis maiden he loved als his lif.	He loved this maiden as much as his life.
	Of hire was ded þe quene his wif	The queen, his wife, had died having her,
	In travailing here lif ȝhe les.	For she had lost her life in childbirth.
	And þo þe maiden of age wes	And when the maiden was of age,
	Kynges sones to him speke	The sons of kings asked him,
	Emperours and dukes eke	Emperors and dukes as well,
	To haven his doughter in mariage	To have his daughter in marriage,
30	For love of here heritage.	For the love of their heritage.
	Ac þe kyng answered ever	But the king always answered
	Þat no man schal here halden ever	That no man should ever have her
	But ȝif he mai in turneying	Unless he could throw him
	Him out of his sadel bring	Out of his saddle in tourneying,
	And maken him lesen hise stiropes bayne.	And make him lose both his stirrups.
	. . . .	. . . .
C	Mani assayed and myȝte not gayne.	Many tried and could not succeed.
	That ryche kynge every ȝere wolde	Every year that noble king would
	A solempne feste make and holde	Proclaim and hold a magnificent feast
	On his wyvys mynnyng day	On the memorial day of his wife,[305]

---

304 *Litel Bretaygne*: This may either refer to 'Little Britain'– Brittany, or more specifically the northwest tip between Brest and Quimper. The poet may simply be giving the lay a suitably mythical Celtic setting, as there are few other placename clues and some versions set the poem in England.

305 *Mynnyng day*: A 'minding day' was a day "set apart for prayers and penances for the soul of a dead person" (French & Hale 289). As in many of these romances, building a religious house for prayers for the dead was common among the nobility. Walter H. French and Charles B. Hale, ed., *The Middle English Metrical Romances* (New York: Russell & Russell, 1964 [1930]).

40	Þat was beryed in an abbay	Who was buried in an abbey
	In a foreste there besyde.	In a forest nearby.
	With grete meyne he wolde ryde	With a great company he would ride
	To do dyryges and masses boþe	And perform a dirge and mass as well,
	Pore to fede and naked to cloþe	Feed the poor and clothe the naked,
	And offeryng brynge grete plente.	Bring offerings, in great plenty,
	And fede þe covent wyth every deynte.	And support the convent with every need.
	So on a day the kyng yede to that abbey	So one day the king went to the abbey
	And many ȝede wyth hym that day.	And many traveled there with him.

. . . .

A	Toward þe abbai als he com ride	As he came riding toward the abbey,
50	And mani knyȝtes bi his side	With many knights by his side,
	His doughter also bi him rod.	His daughter also rode with him.
	Amidde þe forest hii abod	As they journeyed in the forest,
	Here chaumberleyn ȝhe clepede hire to	She called her chamberlain to her,
	And oþer dammaiseles two	And two other maidens,
	And seide þat hii moste aliȝte	And said that they needed to dismount to
	To don here nedes and hire riȝte.	Relieve themselves, as their natural right.[306]
	Þai aliȝt adoune alle þre	All three of them dismounted,
	Tweie damaiseles and sche	The two damsels and her,
	And longe while þer abiden	And paused there a long while
60	Til al þe folk was forht iriden.	Until all the company had ridden past.
	Þai wolden up and after wolde	They wanted to mount and ride after them,
	And couþen nowt here way holde.	But could not find their way.
	Þe wode was rough and þikke iwis	The woods were rough and thick, I know,
	And þai token þe wai amys.	And they took the wrong way.
	Þai moste souht and riden west	They should have gone south but rode west,
	Into þe þikke of þe forest.	Into the thick of the forest.
	Into a launde hii ben icome	They came into a land
	And habbeȝ wel undernome	And saw clearly
	Þat þai were amis igon.	That they had gone astray.
70	Þai liȝt adoune everichon	Each of them dismounted
	And cleped and criede al ifere	And called and shouted together,
	Ac no man miȝt hem ihere.	But no man heard them well enough.
	Þai nist what hem was best to don.	They did not know what was best to do.
	Þe weder was hot bifor þe non.	The weather was hot before noon.
	Hii leien hem doun upon a grene	They laid themselves down on a green,
	Under a chastein-tre ich wene	Under a chestnut tree, as I know,[307]
	And fillen aslepe everichone	And everyone fell asleep
	Bote þe damaisele alone.	Except for the princess alone.

---

306 *To don here nedes and hire righte*: the poet considers answering nature's call "a natural right". *Sir Degaré*, ed. Anne Laskaya and Eve Salisbury, *The Middle English Breton Lays* (Kalamazoo, MI: Medieval Institute Publications, 1995), http://www.lib. rochester.edu/camelot/teams/degarfrm.htm.

307 *Chastein tre*: Laskaya and Salisbury point out that chestnut trees not only represent Christian chastity but serve as a medial point between reality and fairy otherworlds. Like Queen Herodis in *Sir Orfeo*, the maidens fall asleep, but here the princess does not.

	3he wente aboute and gaderede floures	She walked about and gathered flowers
80	And herknede song of wilde foules.	And listened to the songs of wild birds.
	So fer in þe launde 3he goht iwis	She strayed so far in the land, indeed,
	Þat 3he ne wot nevere whare 3e is.	That she did not know where she was.
	To hire maidenes 3he wolde anon	She wanted to go back at once to her ladies,
	Ac hi ne wiste never wat wei to gon.	But she did not know which way to walk.
	Whenne hi wende best to hem terne	Wherever she thought it best to turn,
	Aweiward þan hi go3 wel 3erne.	In her hurrying she ended up further away.

. . . .

C	And callyd and cryed evyr more	She called out and continually shouted,
	And wepyd and wrynged hur handys sore	And wept and wrung her hands sorely.

. . . .

A	"Allas", hi seide, "þat I was boren!	"Alas", she said, "that I was ever born!
90	Nou ich wot ich am forloren!	Now I know that I am lost!
	Wilde bestes me wille3 togrinde	Wild beasts will chew me up
	Or ani man me schulle finde!"	Before any man will find me!"[308]
	Þan segh hi swich a si3t!	Then she saw such a sight!
	Toward hire comen a kni3t	Toward her came a knight,
	Gentil 3ong and jolif man	A graceful, young, and handsome man,
	A robe of scarlet he hadde upon.	With a robe of scarlet upon him.
	His visage was feir his bodi ech weies	His face and body were fair in every way,
	Of countenaunce ri3t curteis	And his appearance was perfectly noble,
	Wel farende legges fot and honde.	With well-shaped legs, feet, and hands.
100	Þer nas non in al þe kynges londe	There was no one in all the king's land
	More apert man þan was he.	Who was more elegant than he was.
	"Damaisele welcome mote þou be!	"My lady, may you be welcome!
	Be þou afered of none wih3te.	Do not be afraid of anyone here.
	Iich am comen here a fairi-kny3te.	I have come here as a fairy knight.
	Mi kynde is armes for to were	Our nature is to bear arms,
	On horse to ride wi3 scheld and spere	And to ride on horse with shield and spear,
	Forþi afered be þou nowt!	And so do not be worried!
	I ne have nowt but mi swerd ibrout.	I have brought nothing but my sword.
	Iich have iloved þe mani a yer	I have loved you for many a year,
110	And now we be3 us selve her.	And now we are here by ourselves.
	Þou best mi lemman ar þou go	You will be my lover before you go,
	Weþer þe like3 wel or wo".	Whether you like it or not".
	Þo no þing ne coude do 3he	There was nothing she could do
	But wep and criede and wolde fle.	But cry and shout and try to flee,
	And he anon gan hire atholde	But he seized her at once
	And dide his wille what he wolde.	And did his will as he desired.[309]

---

308   In medieval thought forests did not suggest restful places of communion with nature but danger and foreboding. Medieval devils were accordingly green and not red. An audience would likely sympathize with the princess' fears at being lost.

309   In *Sir Orfeo* the queen is abducted by the fairy king, but here the princess is raped. Laskaya and Salisbury note that actual sexual assault is rare in medieval romance, and notes the connection to the Wife of Bath's Tale. Loomis states that no other analogue of the Loathly Lady story has a rape incident and posits that Chaucer might have been reminded of Degare. Laura Hibbard Loomis, "Chaucer and the Breton Lays of the Auchinleck", *Studies in Philology* 38:1 (1941): 30-1.

He binam hire here maidenhod
And seththen up toforen hire stod.
"Lemman", he seide, "gent and fre,
120 Mid schilde I wot þat þou schalt be.
Siker ich wot hit worht a knave.
Forþi mi swerd þou sschalt have.
And whenne þat he is of elde
Þat he mai him self biwelde
Tak him þe swerd and bidde him fonde
To sechen his fader in eche londe.
Þe swerd his god and auenaunt.
Lo as I faught wiȝ a geaunt
I brak þe point in his hed
130 And siththen when þat he was ded,
I tok hit out and have hit her,
Redi in min aumener.
Ȝit peraventure time biȝ
Þat mi sone mete me wiȝ
Be mi swerd I mai him kenne.
Have god dai! I mot gon henne".
Þe kniȝt passede as he cam.
Al wepende þe swerd ȝhe nam
And com hom sore sikend
140 And fond here maidenes al slepend.
Þe swerd ȝhe hidde als ȝhe miȝte
And awaked hem in hiȝte
And doht hem to horse anon
And gonne to ride everichon.
Þanne seghen hi ate last
Tweie squiers come prikend fast.
Fram þe kyng þai weren isent
To white whider his doughter went.
Þai browt hire into þe riȝte wai
150 And comen faire to þe abbay.
And doȝ þe servise in alle þingges
Mani masse and riche offringes.
And whanne þe servise was al idone
And ipassed over þe none
Þe kyng to his castel gan ride
His doughter rod bi his side
And ȝemeȝ his kyngdom overal
Stoutliche as a god king schall.
Ac whan ech man was glad and blithe
160 His doughter siked an sorewed swithe.
Here wombe greted more and more.
Þer while ȝhe miȝte ȝe hidde here sore.

He took away her maidenhead,
And afterward he stood over her.
"Lover", he said, "noble and free,
I know that you will be with child,
And I know for sure it will be a boy.
For this you shall take my sword.
And when he is of age,
So that he may protect himself,
Give him the sword, and tell him to try
To seek his father in every land.
The sword is firm and powerful.
Listen, for as I fought with a giant,
I broke the point in his head.
And later, when he was dead,
I took it out and have it here,
Ready in my pouch.
If by chance the time comes
That my son meets with me,
I will know him by my sword.
Good day to you! I must go on".
The knight disappeared, just as he came.
All in tears, she took the sword,
And came back sighing bitterly
And found her maidens all asleep.
She hid the sword as best she could,
And awakened them in haste,
And ordered them to their horses at once
And for everyone to ride.
Then at last she saw
Two squires coming, galloping swiftly.
They were sent from the king
To find out where his daughter went.
They showed her the right way
And they came properly to the abbey.
They did every part of the service,
With many masses and rich offerings.
And when the ceremony was all done,
And the afternoon was past,
The king rode back to the castle,
And his daughter rode by his side,
And he ruled over all his kingdom,
Proudly, as a good king does.
But when each man was glad and at ease,
His daughter sighed and grieved sorely.
Her womb grew greater and greater.
While she could, she hid herself miserably.

On a dai as hi wepende set	One day as she sat weeping,
On of hire maidenes hit underȝet.	One of her maidens noticed it.
"Ma dame", ȝhe seide, "par charite	"Madam", she said, "for charity's sake,
Whi wepe ye now telleȝ hit me".	Why are you crying, now tell me".
"A gentil maiden kinde icoren	"Oh, gentle maiden, chosen of the best,
Help me oþer ich am forloren.	Help me, for otherwise I am lost.
Ich have ever ȝete ben meke and milde.	I have always been obedient and mild.
170 Lo now ich am wiȝ quike schilde!	But listen, now I am with a living child!
Ȝif ani man hit underȝete	If anyone knew about it,
Men wolde sai bi sti and strete	People would say my father the king
Þat mi fader þe king hit wan	Had me near some pigsty or back alley,[310]
And I ne was nevere aqueint wiȝ man!	For I was never intimate with any man!
And ȝif he hit him selve wite	And if he himself learns of it,
Swich sorewe schal to him smite	It will strike his heart with such sorrow
Þat never bliȝe schal he be	That he will never be happy again,
For al his joie is in me".	For all his joy is in me".
And tolde here altogeder þer	And she told her there in full
180 Hou hit was biȝete and wher.	How and where the child was fathered.
"Madame", quad þe maide, "ne care þou nowt.	"Madam", said the maid, "don't be anxious.
Stille awai hit schal be browt.	It will be quietly taken away.[311]
No man schal wite in Godes riche	No man in God's realm will know
Whar hit bicomeȝ but þou and iche".	Where it went but you and I".
Her time come ȝhe was unbounde	Her time came and she was unburdened
And delivred al mid sounde.	And delivered, all in sound health.
A knave schild þer was ibore	A baby boy was born there;
Glad was þe moder þarfore.	The mother was glad for it.
Þe maiden servede here at wille	The maid served her in her needs,
190 Wond þat child in cloþes stille	Silently wrapped the child in clothes,
And laid hit in a cradel anon	And laid it at once in a cradle,
And was al prest þarwiȝ to gon.	And was all ready to leave.
Ȝhit his moder was him hold.	Yet his mother was faithful to him.
Four pound ȝhe tok of gold	She took four pounds of gold,
And ten of selver also	And ten of silver as well,
Under his fote ȝhe laid hit þo	And she laid it under his feet
For swich þinges hit mihove.	For such things as it might help with.
And seththen ȝe tok a paire glove	And then she took a pair of gloves
Þat here lemman here sente of fairi-londe	That her lover had sent her from fairyland,
200 Þat nolde on no manne honde	Which would not fit any man's hand,
Ne on child ne on womman ȝhe nolde	Nor on any child or a woman,

---

310 *Bi sti and strete*: MED defines *sti* as a pigsty but also as a place of degradation. But compare MS Digby No. 86 "Love is sofft, love is swet, love is goed": "Love hath his stiwart by sti and by strete". The poet may intend some irony in that Degare later does marry his mother, though without knowledge or consummation.

311 John Boswell, in *The Kindness of Strangers: The Abandonment of Children in Western Europe from Late Antiquity to the Renaissance* (Chicago: University of Chicago Press, 1998), states that child abandonment for economic or social reasons was endemic in the ancient and medieval world and may have been as high as 20-40% of all live births in some periods. Babies were abandoned to religious houses and often took church positions or became servants to nobility, although many landed in brothels. The maid seems suspiciously knowledgeable about how to discreetly deal with just such a situation.

But on hire selve wel ʒhe wolde.	Except on herself, as she knew well.
Þe gloven ʒe put under his hade	She put the gloves under his head,
And siththen a letter ʒhe wrot and made	And then she wrote out a letter,
And knit hit wiʒ a selkene þred	And tied it with a silk thread
Aboute his nekke wel God sped	About his neck for God's blessing
Þat who hit founde sscholde iwite	That whoever found it would see
Þan was in þe lettre þous iwrite:	What was thus written in the letter:
'Par charite ʒif ani god man	'For charity's sake, if any good man
210	Þis helples child finde can	Can save this helpless child,
Lat Cristen hit wiʒ prestes honde	Let him be christened by a priest's hand,
And bringgen hit to live in londe	And raise him to live in the land,
For hit is comen of gentil blod.	For he has come from noble blood.
Helpeʒ hit wiʒ his owen god	Help him using his own goods,
Wiʒ tresor þat under his fet lis.	With the treasure that lies under his feet.
And ten ʒer eld whan þat he his	And when he is ten years old,
Takeʒ him þis ilke gloven two	Give him these two gloves here
And biddeʒ him wharevere he go	And instruct him, wherever he goes,
Þat he ne lovie no womman in londe	Not to love any woman in the land
220	But þis gloves willen on hire honde.	Until these gloves go on her hands.
For siker on honde nelle þai nere	For certain, they will never fit any hand
But on his moder þat him bere'.	Except his mother who bore him'.
Þe maiden tok þe child here mide	The maid took the child with her
Stille awai in aventide.	And stole away in the evening.
· ·	· ·
C	Sche passyd ovyr a wylde hethe	She passed over wild meadows,
Thorow felde and wode for the sche goyth	And went through fields and woods,
· ·	· ·
A	Alle þe winteres longe niʒt.	All the long winter's night. The
Þe weder was cler þe mone liʒt.	Weather was clear, the moon was bright.
Þan warhiʒ ʒe war anon	After a while she was aware
230	Of an hermitage in a ston	Of a hermitage in a cliffside
An holi man had þer his woniyng.	Where a holy man had his dwelling.
Þider ʒhe wente on heying	She went there in haste
An sette þe cradel at his dore	And set the cradle at his door,
And durste abide no lengore	Not daring to wait any longer,
And passede forʒ anonriʒt.	And passed on right away.
Hom ʒhe com in þat oþer niʒt	She came home the next day
And fond þe leuedi al drupni	And found the lady all despondent,
Sore wepinde and was sori.	Weeping bitterly and full of sorrow.
And tolde hire altogeder þer	She told her in full there
240	Hou ʒhe had iben and wher.	How she had fared and where she had been.
Þe hermite aros erliche þo	The hermit rose early,
And his knave was uppe also	And his servant was up as well,
And seide ifere here matines	And they said their matins together
And servede God and Hise seins.	And worshipped God and His saints.
Þe litel child þai herde crie	They heard the little child crying

	And clepede after help on hie.	And called for help in haste.[312]
	Þe holi man his dore undede	The holy man unfastened his door
	And fond þe cradel in þe stede.	And found the cradle on the step.
	He tok up þe cloþes anon	He lifted up the cloths at once
250	And biheld þe litel grom.	And saw the little boy.
	He tok þe letter and radde wel sone	He took and quickly read the letter
	Þat tolde him þat he scholde done.	Which told him what he should do.
	Þe heremite held up boþe his honde	The hermit held up both his hands
	And þonked God of al His sonde	And thanked God for all His blessings,
	And bar þat child into his chapel	And carried the baby into his chapel,
	And for joie he rong his bel.	And rang his bell for joy.
	He dede up þe gloven and þe tresour	He put away the gloves and the treasure
	And Cristned þe child wiȝ gret honour	And baptized the child with great honor
	In þe name of þe Trinite.	In the name of the Trinity.
260	He hit nemnede Degarre.	He named him Degare.
	Degarre nowt elles ne is	Degare meant nothing else
	But þing þat not never whar it is	But something that is unknown,
	Or þe þing þat is neȝ forlorn also.	A thing that was almost lost.[313]
	Forþi þe schild he nemnede þous þo.	For this the child was named so.
	Þe heremite þat was holi of lif	The hermit, who led a holy life,
	Hadde a soster þat was a wif.	Had a sister who was a wife.
	A riche marchaunt of þat countre	A rich merchant of that land
	Hadde hire ispoused into þat cite.	Had taken her into the city.
	To hire þat schild he sente þo	He sent the child to her,
270	Bi his knave and þe silver also	And the silver as well, by his servant,
	And bad here take gode hede	And asked her to take good care
	Hit to forster and to fede	To foster and raise him,
	And ȝif God Almiȝti wolde	And if God Almighty would
	Ten ȝer his lif holde	Give him ten years of life,
	Aȝen to him hi scholde hit wise	She should arrange for him to return,
	He hit wolde teche of clergise.	And he would teach him the clergy.
	Þe litel child Degarre	The little child Degare
	Was ibrout into þat cite.	Was brought into the city.
	Þe wif and hire louerd ifere	The wife and her husband together
280	Kept hit ase hit here owen were.	Kept him as if he were their own.
	Bi þat hit was ten ȝer old	By the time he was ten years old,
	Hit was a fair child and a bold	He was a fair and spirited child,
	Wel inorissched god and hende.	Well-raised, kind, and courteous.
	Was non betere in al þat ende.	There was no one better in all the land.
	He wende wel þat þe gode man	He fully thought that the good man
	Had ben his fader þat him wan	Was his father who had begotten him,
	And þe wif his moder also	And the woman his mother also,
	And þe hermite his unkel bo.	And the hermit his uncle as well.

---

312 *On hie*: Or, possibly "They called for help from on high". C has *in hye*. See also line 232.

313 French *égaré* has the meaning of *misplaced* or *strayed*, and Laskaya and Salisbury give the meaning of Degarre as "almost lost".

And whan þe ten ȝer was ispent	And when the tenth year had passed,
290 To þe hermitage he was sent.	He was sent to the hermitage.
And he was glad him to se	The hermit was glad to see him,
He was so feir and so fre.	For he was so fair and so noble.
He tauȝte him of clerkes lore	He taught him the lore of clerics[314]
Oþer ten wynter oþer more.	For another ten years or more.
And he was of twenti yer	And when he was in his twentieth year,
Staleworth he was of swich pouer	He was sturdy and of such might
Þat þer ne was man in þat lond	That there was no man in the land
Þat o breid him miȝt astond.	Who could stand one blow from him.
Þo þe hermite seȝ wiȝouten les	Then the hermit said, without a lie,
300 Man for him self þat he wes	That he was ready to be his own man,
Staleworht to don ech werk	To do all things with steadfastness,
And of his elde so god a clerk.	And was for his age so fine a clerk.
He tok him his florines and his gloves	He gave him his gold coins and gloves[315]
Þat he had kept to hise bihoves	That he had kept to fulfill his needs,
Ac þe ten pound of starlings	Except for the ten pounds of silver,
Were ispended in his fostrings.	Which were spent in raising him.
He tok him þe letter to rede	He gave him the letter to read,
And biheld al þe dede.	And watched all that happened.
"O leve hem par charite	"Oh, dear uncle, for charity's sake,
310 Was þis letter mad for me?"	Was this letter written for me?"
"Ȝe bi oure Lord us helpe schal	"Yes, by our Lord who helps us,
Þus hit was", and told him al.	So it was", and he told him everything.
He knelede adoun also swiȝe	The youth knelt down as quickly
And þonked þe ermite of his live	And thanked the hermit for his life,
And swor he nolde stinte no stounde	And swore he would not lose a moment
Til he his kinrede hadde ifounde.	Until he had found his kin.
For in þe lettre was þous iwrite	For in the letter it was so written
Þat bi þe gloven he sscholde iwite	That by the gloves he would know
Wich were his moder and who	Who his mother was,
320 Ȝhif þat sche livede þo	If she were still alive,
For on hire honden hii wolde	For they would fit on her hands
And on non oþer hii nolde.	And would go on no other's.
Half þe florines he ȝaf þe hermite	He gave the hermit half the gold
And halvendel he tok him mide	And took the other half with him,
And nam his leve and wolde go.	And made his goodbye and readied to go.
"Nai", seide þe hermite, "schaltu no.	"No", said the hermit, "you must not.
To seche þi ken miȝtou nowt dure	Your search for your kin will not last
Wiȝouten hors and god armure".	Without a horse and strong armor".
"Nai", quod he, "bi Hevene-kyng	"No", he replied, "by Heaven's king,
330 Ich wil have first anoþer þing".	I will have other help first".

---

314 *Clerkes lore:* Degare is receiving a Latin education. He is evidently not being groomed for priestly vows but for a lay position.

315 *Florines:* Florins were gold coins first minted in Florence in 1252, and issued in England only once by Edward III in 1344. Several European countries had their own florins but not France.

He hew adoun boþe grete and grim
To beren in his hond wiȝ him
A god sapling of an ok.
Whan he þarwiȝ ȝaf a strok
Ac wer he never so strong a man
Ne so gode armes hadde upon
Þat he ne scholde falle to grounde.
Swich a bourdon to him he founde.
Þo þenne God he him bitawt

340 And aiþer fram oþer wepyng rawt.
Child Degarre wente his wai
Þourgh þe forest al þat dai.
No man he ne herd ne non he seȝ
Til hit was non ipassed heȝ.
Þanne he herde a noise kete
In o valai an dintes grete.
Blive þider he gan to te
What hit ware he wolde ise.
An herl of þe countre stout and fers

350 Wiȝ a kniȝt and four squiers
Hadde ihonted a der oþer two
And al here houndes weren ago.
Þan was þar a dragon grim
Ful of filth and of venim
Wiȝ wide þrote and teȝ grete
And wynges bitere wiȝ to bete.
As a lyoun he hadde fet
And his tail was long and gret.
. . . .

360E Bytwyx the taile and his hed
Were twoo and fourty longe fete!
His body was also a wyn tonne
When that bryȝt shyneþ the sonne.
He was as bryȝt as eny glas
And harder than stele ywys he was.
. . . .

A Þe smoke com of his nose awai
Ase fer out of a chimenai.
Þe knyȝt and squiers he had torent
Man and hors to deþe chent.

370 Þe dragon þe erl assaile gan
And defended him as a man
And stoutliche leid on wiȝ his swerd

He chopped down a stout oak trunk,
Both huge and forbidding,[316]
To carry in his hand with him.
When he gave a blow with it
There would never be a strong man
Wearing fine arms upon himself
Who would not fall to the ground.
He made for himself such a weapon.
Then he commended the hermit to God
And each left the other, weeping.
Child Degare made his way
Through the forest all that day.
He heard no man, nor did he see anyone
Until it was well into the afternoon.
Then he heard a loud noise
In a valley and a great clashing.
He hurried that way excitedly,
Wanting to see what it was.
An earl of the countryside, hardy and fierce,
With a knight and four squires,
Had hunted a deer or two,
And all their hounds were gone.
A fearsome dragon had appeared,
Full of filth and venom,
With a wide throat and huge teeth,
And wings to beat cruelly with.
He had feet like a lion,
And his tail was long and massive.

Between his tail and his head
It was forty-two long feet!
His body was like a wine barrel
When it shines brightly in the sun.
He was as bright as any diamond
And harder than any steel, I know.

The smoke came from his nose
Like a fire out of a chimney.
He had torn apart the knight and squires
And sent man and horse to their deaths.
The earl had begun to attack the dragon,
And he defended himself as a man,
And laid on stoutly with his sword,

---

316 Degare declines a knight's gear in favor of an oak club as a sign of humility, as does Havelok, who fights with a door bar.
Oaks had significance both as objects of worship in the pagan Celtic world and as Christian symbols of faith and virtue.
See George Ferguson, *Signs & Symbols in Christian Art* (London: Zwemmer, 1955). See also the note to line 384.

And stronge strokes on him gerd.
Ac alle his dentes ne greved him nowt.
His hide was hard so iren wrout.
Þerl flei fram tre to tre
Fein he wolde fram him be
And þe dragon him gan asail.
Þe doughti erl in þat batail
380 Ofsegh þis child Degarre
"Ha help!" he seide, "par charite!"
Þe dragoun seʒ þe child com.
He laft þe erl and to him nom
Blowinde and ʒeniend also
Als he him wolde swolewe þo.
Ac Degarre was ful strong.
He tok his bat gret and long
And in þe forehefd he him batereʒ
Þat al þe forehefd he tospatereʒ.
390 He fil adoun anonriʒt
And frapte his tail wiʒ gret miʒt
Upon Degarres side
Þat up so doun he gan to glide.
Ac he stert up ase a man
And wiʒ his bat leide upan
And al tofrusst him ech a bon
Þat he lai ded stille as a ston.
Þ'erl knelede adoun bilive
And ʒonked þe child of his live
400 And maked him wiʒ him gon
To his castel riʒt anon
And wel at hese he him made.
And proferd him al þat he hade
Rentes tresor an eke lond
For to holden in his hond.
Þanne answerede Degarre
"Lat come ferst bifor me
Þi leuedi and oþer wimmen bold
Maidenes and widues ʒonge and olde
410 And oþer damoiseles swete.
ʒif mine gloven beʒ to hem mete
For to done upon here honde
Þanne ich wil take þi londe.
And ʒif þai ben nowt so
Iich wille take mi leve and go".

And struck him with harsh blows.
But all his strokes gave him no harm.
His hide was as tough as wrought iron.
The earl fled from tree to tree,
Wanting only to escape from him,
But the dragon began to attack him.
In that battle the hardy earl
Saw Child Degare, and shouted,
"Hey! Help! For charity's sake!"
The dragon saw Degare coming.
He left the earl and turned to him,
Blowing and gaping as well,[317]
Wanting to swallow him there.
But Degare was very strong.
He took his club, great and long,
And battered him on the forehead
So that he shattered his skull.
The dragon at once fell down
And slapped his tail with great force
Against Degare's sides,
So that he was thrown upside down.
But Degare leaped up like a man
And laid on with his club,
And crushed each bone of his
So that he lay dead, as still as a stone.
The earl knelt down humbly
And thanked the youth for his life,
And had him go with him
To his castle straightaway,
And made him well at ease.
He offered him all that he had,
Income, treasure, and lands as well,
To hold in his hand.
Degare answered then,
"First let your lady come before me,
With other noble women,
Maidens and widows, young and old,
And other sweet damsels.
If my glove is suitable
To fit on their hands,
Then I will accept your lands.
And if it is not so,
I will take my leave and go".

---

317 *ʒeniend*: Yawning, not in boredom but in stretching his mouth to swallow Degare. French and Hale state that "monsters usually could not be injured with manmade weapons; they had to be fought with their own (see also the sword in *Beowulf*) or with primitive things like the club here, or even with bare hands" (299). Degare's choice of an oak is providential.

	Alle wimman were forht ibrowt	All the women were brought forth,
	Wide cuntreis and forht isowt.	Sought from lands far and wide.
	Ech þe gloven assaie bigan	Each attempted to try on the gloves,
	Ac non ne miȝte don hem on.	But none could put them on.
420	He tok his gloven and up hem dede	He took his gloves and put them away
	And nam his leve in þat stede.	And made his goodbye in that hall.
	Þe erl was gentil man of blod	The earl was a refined man of courtesy,
	And ȝaf him a stede ful god	And gave him a very sturdy steed
	And noble armure riche and fin	And noble armor, rich and strong,
	When he wolde armen him þerin.	For when he wished to arm himself,
	And a palefrai to riden an	And a palfrey to ride on,
	And a knave to ben his man.	And a servant to be his man.
	And ȝaf him a swerd briȝt	He gave him a shining sword,
	And dubbed him þer to knyȝt	And dubbed him a knight there,
430	And swor bi God Almiȝti	And swore by God Almighty
	Þat he was better worthi	That he was far more worthy
	To usen hors and armes also	To have a horse and arms as well
	Þan wiȝ his bat aboute to go.	Than to walk about with his club.[318]
	Sire Degarre was wel blithe	Sir Degare was well pleased,
	And þanked þe erl mani a siþe.	And thanked the earl many times.
	And lep upon palefrai hiis	He leaped upon his palfrey
	And doht him forȝ in his wai.	And went forth on his way.
	Upon his stede riȝte his man	His squire rode upon his steed,
	And ledde his armes als he wel can.	And carried his arms as he knew well to.
440	Mani a jorne þai ride and sette.	They rode and set upon many a journey.
	So on a dai gret folk þei mette	And so one day they met a great crowd,
	Erles and barouns of renoun	With earls and barons of renown,
	Þat come fram a cite-toun.	Who came from a fortress city.
	He asked a seriaunt what tiding	He asked an officer for news, where
	And whennes hii come and what is þis þing.	They came from and what this was about.
	"Sire", he seide, "verraiment	"Sir", he said, "in truth,
	We come framward a parlement.	We've come from an assembly.
	Þe king a gret counseil þer made	The king called a great council
	For nedes þat he to don hade.	For needs he had to fulfill.
450	Whan þe parlement was plener	When the meeting was in full session,
	He lette crie fer and ner	He had it proclaimed, near and far,
	Ȝif ani man were of armes so bold	That if any man were so bold in arms
	Þat wiȝ þe kinge justi wold	That he would joust with the king,
	. . . .	. . . .
C	And he myȝt for any thynge	And that he might by any cause
	Hym owte of hys sadull brynge,	Throw him out of his saddle,
	. . . .	. . . .
A	He scholde have in mariage	He would have his daughter

---

318 *Go*: *go* in romance often has the modern nuance of general action, but here the regular ME meaning of *walk* is likely intended. Compare Chaucer's plea "go, litel bok, go" (*Troilus* V.1786). For general *go* OE also had *wendan*, indirectly leading to PDE past simple *went*.

His dowter and his heritage
Þat is a kingdom god and fair.
For he ne had non oþer hair.
460 Ac no man ne dar graunte þerto.
For mani hit assaieȝ and mai nowt do
Mani erl and mani baroun
Kniȝtes and squiers of renoun.
Ac ech man þat him justeȝ wiȝ tit
Haþ of him a foul despit.
Some he brekeȝ þe nekke anon
And of some þe rig-bon.
Some þourgh þe bodi he girt.
Ech is maimed oþer ihirt.
470 Ac noman mai don him no þing
Swich wonder chaunce haþ þe king".
Sire Degarre þous þenche gan
"Ich am a staleworht man

. . . .

C   And am now in my ȝonge blode
And have armour wondur gode,

. . . .

A   And of min owen ich have a stede
Swerd and spere and riche wede.
And ȝif ich felle þe kyng adoun
Evere ich have wonnen renoun.
480 And þei þat he me herte sore
No man wot wer ich was bore.
Wheþer deȝ oþer lif me bitide
Aȝen þe king ich wille ride!"
In þe cite his in he takeȝ
And resteȝ him and meri makeȝ.
On a dai wiȝ þe king he mette
And knelede adoun and him grette.
"Sire king", he saide, "of muchel miȝt
Mi louerd me sende hider nou riȝt
490 For to warne you þat he
Bi þi leve wolde juste wiȝ þe
And winne þi dowter ȝif he mai
As þe cri was þis enderdai.
Justes he had to þe inome".
"De par deus", quaþ þe king, "he is welcome!
Be he baroun be he erl
Be he burgeis be he cherl
No man wil I forsake.

In marriage along with his heritage,
For he has no other heir.
That's a kingdom, good and fair!
But no man dared accept the challenge,
For many have tried and could not do it,
Many earls and many barons,
And knights and squires of renown.
But each man who jousted with him
Has promptly earned disgrace from him.
With some he broke their neck at once,
And some their back-bone.
Some he thrusts through their body.
Each is maimed or hurt.
But the king has such amazing fortune
That no man can do him any harm".
Sir Degare began to think to himself,
"I am a sturdy man,

. . . .

And am in the prime of my youth
And have wonderfully fine armor,

. . . .

And I have a steed of my own,
Sword and spear, and rich clothes.
And if I take down the king,
I will have won fame for ever.
And if he hurts me badly,
No man knows where I was born.
Whether life or death awaits me,
I will ride against the king!"
He took a room in the city
And rested and amused himself.
One day he met with the king,
And knelt down and greeted him.
"Sire king, of great might", he said,
My lord has sent me here directly[319]
To inform you that, with your approval,
He wishes to joust with you,
And win your daughter, if he may,
In answer to the call the other day.
He will prepare to joust with you".
"By God, he's welcome!" cried the king.
Whether he's a baron or earl,
Or townsman or peasant,
I will overlook no man!

---

319 Why Degare needs to pose as a messenger for his lord is not clear, and presumably is etiquette. All MSS have this impersonation but in C the king replies "thou art welcome", seemingly addressing Degare himself.

He þat winneʒ al sschal take!"
500 Amorewe þe justes was iset.
Þe king him purveid wel þe bet
And Degarre ne knew no man.
Ac al his trust is God upon.
Erliche to churche þan wente he
Þe masse he herde of þe Trinite.
To þe Fader he offreʒ hon florine
And to þe Sone an oþer also fine
And to þe Holi Gost þe þridde.
Þe prest for him ful ʒerne gan bidde.
510 And to þe servise was idon
To his in he wente wel son
And let him armi wel afin
In god armes to justi in.
His gode stede he gan bistride
His squier bar his sschaft biside.
In þe feld þe king he abide gan
As he com ridend wiʒ mani a man
Stoutliche out of þe cite-toun
Wiʒ mani a lord of gret renoun.
520 Ac al þat in þe felde beʒ
Þat þe justes iseʒ
Seide þat hi never ʒit iseʒe
So pert a man wiʒ here egʒe
As was þis gentil Degarre.
Ac no man wiste whennes was he.
Boþe þai gonne to justi þan
Ac Degarre can nowt þeron.
Þe king haþ þe gretter schaft
And kan inowgh of þe craft
530 To breke his nekke he had iment.
In þe helm he set his dent
Þat þe schaft al tosprong.
Ac Degarre was so strong
Þat in þe sadel stille he set
And in þe stiropes held his fet.
For soþe I seie wiʒoute lesing
He ne couþe nammore of justing!
"Allas!" quaþ þe king, "Allas!
Me ne fil nevere swich a cas
540 Þat man þat ich miʒte hitte
After mi stroke miʒte sitte!"
He takeʒ a wel gretter tre
And swor so he moste iþe.
"ʒif his nekke nel nowt atwo

He that wins shall take all!"
The joust was set for the morning. The
King outfitted himself in the best manner,
While Degare had no man's support.
But all his trust was in God.
He went early to church
And heard the mass of the Trinity.
To the Father he offered one gold coin,
And to the Son another just as fine,
And to the Holy Ghost the third.
The priest prayed for him fervently.
And when the service was done,
He went at once to his inn
And had himself well-armed
With good armor to joust in.
He mounted his fine steed,
And his squire carried his lance alongside.
On the field he waited for the king,
Who came riding stoutly,
Out of the city walls with many men,
With many a lord of great fame.
But everyone who was on the field
Who saw the joust
Said that they had never before seen
With their eyes so distinguished a man
As this noble Degare was.
But no man knew where he came from.
Both of them began to battle then,
Though Degare did not know how to joust.
The king had the larger lance
And knew the craft in full;
He intended to break Degare's neck.
He landed his blow in the helmet
So that the shaft splintered apart.
But Degare was so strong
That he sat still in the saddle
And held his feet in the stirrups.
I tell the truth, without a lie,
He know no more about jousting than that!
"Alas!" cried the king, "alas!
Such a thing has never happened to me,
That any man I might hit
Would sit there after my charge!"
He seized a much larger lance
And swore that he would succeed.
"If his neck isn't broken,

His rigg schal ar ich hennes go!"
He rod eft wiȝ gret raundoun
And þought to beren him adoun
And girt Degarre anon
Riȝt aȝein þe brest-bon.
550 Þe schaft was stef and wonder god
And Degarre stede astod
And al biforen he ros on heghȝ.
And þo was he ifallen neghȝ
But as God Almiȝti wold
Þe schaft brak and miȝt nowt hold.
And Degarre his cours outritte
And was agramed out of his witte.
"Allas", quaþ he, "for vilaynie!
Þe king me haþ ismiten þrie
560 And I ne touchede him nowt ȝete.
Nou I schal avise me bette!"
He turned his stede wiȝ herte grim
And rod to þe king and he to him
And togider þai gert ful riȝt
And in þe scheldes here strokes piȝt
Þat þe speres al toriueȝ
And upriȝt to here honde sliveȝ.
Þat alle þe lordings þat þer ben
Þat þe justing miȝte sen
570 Seiden hi ne seȝe never wiȝ egȝe
Man þat mighte so longe dreghȝe
In wraþþe for no þing
Sitten a strok of here king.
"Ac he his doughti for þe nones
A strong man of bodi and bones!"
Þe king wiȝ egre mod gan speke
"Do bring me a schaft þat wil nowt breke!
A be mi trewþe he schal adoun
Þai he be strengere þan Sampson
580 And þei he be þe bare qued
He schal adoune maugre his heued!"
He tok a schaft was gret and long
Þe schild anoþer also strong
And to þe king wel evene he rit.
Þe king faileȝ and he him smit.
His schaft was strong and god wiȝal
And wel scharped þe coronal.

His backbone will be before I leave here!"
He rode again with wild abandon
And thought to throw him down,
And struck Degare at once,
Right against the breast-bone.
The shaft was firm and wondrously strong,
But Degare held his ground,
And as before he reared up high.
And although Degare was nearly fallen,
As God Almighty wished,
The shaft broke and would not hold.
Degare changed his course
And was angered out of his wits.
"Alas", he said, "for the crime of it!
The king has struck me twice,
And I have not touched him at all yet.
Now I will make a better plan!"
He turned his steed with a fierce heart
And rode to the king, and he did to him,
And they crashed straight on together,
And blows were struck on shields
So that the spears were broken apart
And split right up to their hands.
All the lords who were there
And could see the jousting
Said they never saw with their eyes
A man who could endure so long,
Who could in combat, for anything,
Withstand a blow from their king.
"But he shows courage for the occasion,
A strong man in flesh and bones!"
The king was in a furious rage and said,
"Go, bring me a shaft that will not break!
Now, by my word, he will go down
Even if he is stronger than Sampson,
Or he is the naked devil himself,[320]
He will fall, in spite of his might!"
He took a shaft that was huge and long,
And Degare took another just as strong,
And he met the king in mid-course.
The king wavered and Degare struck him.
His shaft was strong and firm throughout,
And the spear head was well-sharpened.

---

320 *The bare qued*: 'Naked evil'. Laskaya and Salisbury explain that this is a euphemism for the devil, who cannot be named for
fear of attracting him, just as the denizens of Hogwarts are reluctant to name Voldemort. The *Havelok* poet does not seem
to share these qualms and compares both Godrich and Godard to *Sathanas* (1141, 2357). C & W also have *devyll*.

He smot þe kyng in þe lainer
He miȝt flit noþer fer ne ner.
590 Þe king was strong and harde sat.
Þe stede ros up biforn wiȝ þat
And sire Degarre so þriste him þan
Þat maugre whoso grochche bigan
Out of þe sadel he him cast
Tail over top riȝt ate last.
Þan was þer long houting and cri
Þe king was sor asschamed forþi.
Þe lordinges comen wiȝ miȝt and mein
And broughte þe king on horse aȝein
600 An seide wiȝ o criing iwis
"Child Degarre haþ wonne þe pris!"
Þan was þe damaisele sori
For hi wiste wel forwhi
Þat hi scholde ispoused ben
To a kniȝt þat sche never had sen
And lede here lif wiȝ swich a man
Þat sche ne wot who him wan
No in what londe he was ibore.
Carful was Þe leuedi þerfore.
610 Þan seide þe king to Degarre
"Min hende sone com hider to me.
And þou were also gentil a man
As þou semest wiȝ siȝt upan
And ase wel couþest wisdomes do
As þou art staleworht man þerto
Me þouwte mi kingdom is wel biset.
Ac be þou werse be þou bet
Covenaunt ich wille þe holde.
Lo her biforn mi barons bolde
620 Mi douwter I take þe bi þe hond
And seise þe her in al mi lond.
King þou schalt ben after me.
God graunte þe godman forto be!"
Þan was þe child glad and bliȝe
And þonked þe kyng mani a sithe.
Gret purveaunce þan was þer iwrout.
To churche þai were togidere ibrout
And spoused þat leuedi verraiment

He stabbed the king in the armor straps;
He could not flee, neither near or far.
Yet the king was strong and sat firmly.
With that his steed reared before him,
And Sir Degare thrust at him,
So that despite whoever began the grudge,
He threw the king out of the saddle,
And finally, head over feet.
There was a long shouting and crying then,
And the king was sorely ashamed for it.
The lords came in force with their company
And brought the king to his horse again,
And said with one shout, in truth,
"Child Degare has won the prize!"[321]
Then the princess was saddened,
For she knew well what had happened,
That she had been promised
To a knight that she had never seen,
To lead her life with such a man that
She did not know who had fathered him,
Nor in what land he had been born.
And so the lady was miserable.
Then the king said to Degare,
"My noble son, come here to me.[322]
If you are as decent a man
As you seem to my sight,
And as skilful in wise deeds
As you are rugged and manly,
I think my kingdom will be well served.
But whether you are better or worse,
I will hold my agreement with you.
See, here before my brave barons,
I give you my daughter's hand,
And award her to you with all my land.
You will be king after me.
God grant that you be a good man!"
Then Degare was glad and joyful,
And thanked the king many times.
Great preparations were made.
They were brought together to church,
And he married that lady, truly,

---

321 *Child Degarre*: Though Degare has already been knighted (429), for him to be called *child* (knight-in-training) even as a young adult is commonplace and not an insult. The lords may also see Degare's youth and do not know his full rank.

322 *Min hende sone*: The king means 'young man', perhaps with some affection, and the audience might sense or later realize the irony that Degare is the king's grandson.

Under holi sacrament.

630   Lo what chaunse and wonder strong
      Bitideʒ mani a man wiʒ wrong
      Þat comeʒ into an uncouþe þede
      And spouseʒ wif for ani mede
      And knowes no þing of hire kin
      Ne sche of his neiþer more ne min
      And beʒ iwedded togider to libbe
      Par aventure and beʒ neghʒ sibbe!
      So dede Sire Degarre þe bold
      Spoused þere his moder
640   And þat hende leuedi also
      Here owene sone was spoused to
      Þat sche upon here bodi bar.
      Lo what aventure fil hem þar!
      But God þat alle þingge mai stere
      Wolde nowt þat þai sinned ifere.
      To chirche þai wente wiʒ barouns bolde
      A riche feste þai gonne to holde.
      And wan was wel ipassed non
      And þe dai was al idon
650   To bedde þai scholde wende þat fre
      Þe dammaisele and sire Degarre.
      He stod stille and biþouwte him þan
      Hou þe hermite þe holi man
      Bad he scholde no womman take
      For faired ne for riches sake
      But ʒhe miʒte þis gloves two
      Liʒtliche on hire hondes do.
      "Allas allas!" þan saide he
      "What meschaunce is comen to me?
660   A wai! Witles wrechche ich am!
      Iich hadde levere þan þis kingdam
      Þat is iseised into min hond
      Þat ich ware faire out of þis lond!"
      He wrang his hondes and was sori
      Ac no man wiste þer forewi.
      Þe king parceyved and saide þo
      "Sire Degarre wi farest þou so?
      Is þer ani þing don ille
      Spoken or seid aʒen þi wille?"
670   "ʒa sire", he saide, "bi Hevene-king!
      Ichal never for no spousing

Under the holy sacrament.
See what fate and great wonder it is,
That fortune should befall a man
Who comes into an unknown land,
And takes a wife for whatever reward,
Knowing nothing of her family,
Nor she of his, neither more nor less,
And to be wedded to live together,
And by chance to be close kin!
Thus did Sir Degare the bold
Wed his own mother there,
And that gracious lady as well
Was married to her own son,
Whom she bore from her own body.
See what chance brought them there!
But God, who may guide all matters,
Would not have them sin together.
They went to church with noble barons,
And a rich feast was held for them.
And when the afternoon had long passed
And the day was all done,
They had to go to bed, that noble pair,
The princess and Sir Degare.
But he stood still and thought to himself
How the hermit, the holy man,
Ordered that he should take no woman,
For beauty or for riches,
Until she might put the two gloves
Easily on her hands.
"Alas, alas!" he said then,
"What misfortune has come to me?
Oh, woe! I am a witless wretch!
I would rather be gone from this land,
Than have this kingdom
That was given into my hand!"
He wrung his hands and was miserable,
But no one knew why.
The king noticed him and said then,
"Sir Degare, why do you behave so?
Has anything wrong been done or spoken,
Or said against your will?"
"No, Sire", he said, "by Heaven's king![323]
But while I live I can never consort

---

323 *ʒa sire*: What Degare is grammatically assenting to here seems confusing. W has "nay, Lord". See also *Floris*, 574.

	Þerwhiles I live wiȝ wimman dele	With a woman in marriage,[324]
	Widue ne wif ne dammeisele	Not a widow or wife or maiden,
	But ȝhe þis gloves mai take and fonde	Unless she takes and tries these gloves
	And liȝtlich drawen upon hire honde".	And draws them lightly on her hands".
	His ȝonge bride þat gan here	His young bride overheard that,
	And al for þout chaunged hire chere	And in realization her expression changed,
	And ate laste gan to turne here mod.	And at last her mood turned.
	Here visage wex ase red ase blod.	Her face blushed as red as blood.
680	Ȝhe knew þo gloves þat wer hire.	She knew those gloves were hers.
	"Schewe hem hider leve sire".	"Show them here, dear sir".
	Sche tok þe gloves in þat stede	She took the gloves in that moment
	And liȝtliche on hire hondes dede	And put them easily on her hands,
	And fil adoun wiȝ reuli cri	And fell down in a doleful cry,
	And seide, "God mercy merci!	And said, "God, have mercy, mercy!
	Þou art mi sone hast spoused me her	You are my boy who has married me here,
	And ich am sone þi moder der!	And son, I am your dear mother!
	Ich hadde þe loren ich have þe founde.	I had lost you, and I have found you.
	Blessed be Jhesu Crist þat stounde!"	Jesus Christ be blessed that moment!"
690	Sire Degarre tok his moder þo	Then Sir Degare took his mother
	And helde here in his armes two	And held her in his two arms,
	Keste and clepte here mani a siþe.	Kissing and embracing her many times.
	Þat hit was sche he was ful bliþe.	He was joyful, for it was her.
	Þe kyng gret wonder hadde	The king had great puzzlement then
	What þat noise was þat þai made	Over the fuss that they made,
	And mervailed of hire crying	And wondered about her crying
	And seide, "Doughter what is þis þing?'	And said, "Daughter, what is going on?"
	"Fader", ȝhe seide, "þou schalt ihere.	"Father", she said, "you will hear it all.
	Þou wenest þat ich a maiden were	You thought that I was a maiden,
700	Ac certes nay sire ich am non.	But for sure, Sire, I am not.
	Twenti winter nou hit is gon	Twenty years have passed now
	Þat mi maidenhed I les	Since I lost my virginity
	In a forest as I wes.	When I was in the forest.
	And þis is mi sone God hit wot.	And this is my son, God knows.
	Bi þis gloves wel ich wot".	By these gloves I know it well".
	Ȝhe told him al þat soþe þer	She told him all the truth there,
	Hou þe child was geten and wher	How the child was fathered, and where,
	And hou þat he was boren also	And how he was born as well,
	To þe hermitage ȝhe sente him þo	How she sent him to the hermitage,
710	And seþthen herd of him no þing.	And after then heard nothing of him.
	"But þanked be Jhesu Hevene-king	"But Jesus be thanked, Heaven's king,
	Iich have ifounde him olive!	I have found him alive!

---

324 *With wimman dele*: The MED states that *dele* with can mean sexual intercourse. While it fits the situation, Degare is probably not saying this to the king about his daughter.

Ich am his moder and ek his wive!"	I am his mother and also his wife!"[325]
"Leve moder", seide Sire Degarre,	"My dear mother", said Sir Degare,
"Telle me þe sothe par charite	"Tell me the truth, for charity's sake.
Into what londe I mai terne	What land I may turn to,
To seke mi fader swithe and ȝerne".	Quickly and eagerly, to find my father?"
"Sone", ȝhe saide, "bi Hevene-kyng	"Son", she said, "by Heaven's king,
I can þe of him telle no þing	I can tell you nothing of him,
720 But þo þat he fram me rauȝt	Except that when he departed from me,
His owen swerd he me bitauȝt	He entrusted me with his own sword,
And bad ich scholde take hit þe forþan	And ordered that I should give it to you
Ȝif þou livedest and were a man".	If you lived to become a man".
Þe swerd sche fet forht anonriȝt	She fetched the sword right away,
And Degarre hit outpliȝt.	And Degare pulled it out.
Brod and long and heui hit wes.	It was broad and long and heavy.
In þat kyngdom no swich nes.	There was nothing like it in that kingdom.
Þan seide Degarre forþan	With that, Degare said,
"Whoso hit auȝt he was a man!	"Whoever owned it, he was a man!
730 Nou ich have þat I kepe	Now that I have it in my possession,
Niȝt ne dai nel ich slepe	I will not rest day or night
Til þat I mi fader see	Until I see my father,
Ȝif God wile þat hit so be".	If God wills that it be so".
. . . .	. . . .
W Then sayd the kynge, "My next kinne,	Then the king said, "My heir, I will
I wyl gyve the knyghtes with the to wynne".	Send knights with you for your success".
"Syr", he sayd, "gramercye than;	"Sire", he answered, "my great thanks.
With me shall go no other man".	But no other man shall go with me".
. . . .	. . . .
A In þe cite he reste al niȝt.	He slept all night in the city.
Amorewe whan hit was dailiȝt	In the morning when it was daylight,
740 He aros and herde his masse	He rose and heard mass
He diȝte him and forȝ gan passe.	And he readied himself and went forth.
Of al þat cite þan moste non	In all the city there was no one
Neiþer wiȝ him riden ne gon	Who might ride or go with him,
But his knave to take hede	Except his attendant, to take care
To his armour and his stede.	Of his armor and his steed.
Forȝ he rod in his wai	He rode forth on his way through
Mani a pas and mani jurnai.	Many a pass and many a journey.
So longe he passede into west	He traveled west for a long time,
Þat he com into þeld forest	Until he came into the ancient forest
750 Þer he was biȝeten som while.	Where he had been conceived before.
Þerinne he rideȝ mani a mile	He rode in it many a mile,

---

325 *Ich am his moder and ek his wive*: Again, while this line seems *ewwy* to the point of risible for a modern reader, the important point for a medieval audience is that the accidental marriage is recognized as a mistake and not consummated. This permits the quick annulment at the end (1136-7). Laskaya and Salisbury point out that *The Legend of Pope Gregory*, an Auchinleck text and a possible influence on *Degare*, also features a hero set adrift at birth who returns home to unwittingly marry his mother. Both stories suggest the Oedipal myth, but neither are tragedies.

Mani a dai he ride gan	And went on for many a day,
No quik best he fond of man.	Meeting no living beast that was tame.
Ac mani wilde bestes he seghʒ	But he saw many wild animals,
And foules singen on heghʒ.	And birds singing from on high.
So longe he drouwʒ to þe niʒt	It continued until the fall of night,
Þe sonne was adoune riʒt.	When the sun had gone down.
Toward toun he wolde ride	He wanted to ride toward town,
But he nist never bi wiche side.	But he did not know which way to go.
760 Þenne he seʒ a water cler	Then he saw clear waters,
And amidde a river	And alongside the river,
A fair castel of lim and ston.	A stately castle of lime and mortar.
Oþer wonyng was þer non.	There was no other dwelling.
To his knave he seide, "Tide wat tide	He said to his man, "Come what comes,
O fote forþer nel I ride	I will not ride one foot farther,
Ac here abide wille we	But we will stay here
And aske herberewe par charite	And ask for shelter for charity's sake,
ʒif ani quik man be here on live".	If there is anyone alive staying here".
To þe water þai come als swiþe.	They came to the water as quickly.
770 Þe bregge was adoune þo	The bridge was down,
And þe gate open also	And the gate was open as well,
And into þe castel he gan spede.	And they sped into the castle.
First he stabled up his stede	First he stabled his horse
He taiede up his palefrai.	And tied up his palfrey.
Inouʒ he fond of hote and hai.	They found plenty of oats and hay.
He bad his grom on heying	He ordered his groom in haste
Kepen wel al here þing.	To keep all their things well.
He passed up into þe halle	He went up into the hall,
Biheld aboute and gan to calle	Looked around, and began to call out,
780 Ac neiþer on lond ne on heʒ	But he saw no living person,
No quik man he ne seʒ.	Either on the ground floor or higher.
Amidde þe halle flore	In the middle of the hall floor
A fir was bet stark an store.	A fire had been lit, strong and blazing.
"Par fai", he saide, "ich am al sure	"By my faith", he said, "I am sure
He þat bette þat fure	That whoever made that fire
Wil comen hom ʒit to niʒt.	Will come home tonight yet.
Abiden ich wille a litel wiʒt".	I will wait a little while".
He sat adoun upon þe dais	He sat down on the platform,
And he warmed him wel eche wais.	And warmed himself well all over.
790 And he biheld and undernam	Then he noticed and saw,
Hou in at þe dore cam	Coming in through the door,
Four dammaiseles gent and fre.	Four ladies, noble and elegant.
Ech was itakked to þe kne.	Each was bare-legged from the knee down.
Þe two bowen and arewen bere	Two carried bows and arrows,
Þe oþer two icharged were	And the others were laden
Wiʒ venesoun riche and god.	With venison, rich and fine.
And Degarre up stod	Sir Degare stood up

	And gret hem wel fair apliȝt.	And greeted them very courteously,
	Ac þai answerede no wiȝt.	But they did not answer at all.
800	But yede into chaumbre anon	They only advanced into their rooms
	And barred þe dore after son.	And barred the door right after.
	Sone þerafter wiȝalle	Following that, soon after
	Þer com a dwerw into þe halle	A dwarf came into the hall,
	Four fet of lengthe was in him.	With no more than four feet in him.
	His visage was stout and grim	His appearance was firm and severe;
	Boþe his berd and his fax	Both his beard and his hair
	Was crisp and ȝhalew as wax.	Were crisp and yellow like wax.
	Grete sscholdres and quarre	With large, square shoulders,
	Riȝt stoutliche loked he.	He looked very stout.
810	Mochele were hise fet and honde	His feet and hands were as huge
	Ase þe meste man of þe londe.	As the biggest man in the land.
	He was iclothed wel ariȝt	He was clothed very finely,
	His schon icouped as a kniȝt.	With his shoes scored like a knight's.[326]
	He hadde on a sorcot overt	He had on an open overcoat,
	Iforred wiȝ blaunchener apert.	Trimmed elegantly with white fur.
	Sire Degarre him biheld and lowgȝ	Sir Degare saw him and laughed,
	And gret him fair inowgȝ	And greeted him politely enough,
	Ac he ne answerede nevere a word.	But he did not answer a word.
	But sette trestles and laid þe bord.	He only set supports and laid the table,
820	And torches in þe halle he liȝte	And lit torches in the hall,
	And redi to þe soper diȝte.	And prepared to make supper.
	Þan þer com out of þe bour	Then there came out of the rooms
	A dammeisele of gret honour.	A young lady of great honor.
	In þe lond non fairer nas.	There was no one fairer in the land.
	In a diapre cloþed ȝhe was	She was dressed in patterned clothes,
	Wiȝ hire come maidenes tene	And ten maidens came with her,
	Some in scarlet some in grene	Some in scarlet, some in green,[327]
	Gent of bodi of semblaunt swete.	Delicate in body, and sweet in appearance,
	And Degarre hem gan grete.	And Degare went to greet them.
830	Ac hi ne answerede no wiȝt	But they answered no one
	But ȝede to þe soper anonriȝt.	And only went right to their supper.
	"Certes", quaþ sire Degarre	"For certain", said Sir Degare,
	"Ich have hem gret and hi nowt me.	"I greeted them, and they did not answer.
	But þai be dombe bi and bi	Unless they are mute, by and by,
	Þai schul speke first ar I!"	They shall speak first before I do!"
	Þe leuedi þat was of rode so briȝt	The lady, who had so bright a face,

---

326 *His sschon icouped as a knight*: Laskaya and Salisbury cite both French and Hall, who state that this was a fashion where the upper part of shoes were scored to show the bright colors of the stockings underneath (p. 311), and Laing, who notes that early editors dated the poem to the early thirteenth century from this style. David Laing, ed., *Sire Degarre, a Metrical Romance of the End of the Thirteenth Century* (Edinburgh: Abbotsford Club, 1849). Romance dwarves are typically brusque.

327 *Some in scarlet, some in grene*: Scarlet could refer either to a type of woolen cloth or to the hue, though both had connotations of luxury or authority, being the color of cardinals' robes. Green was again an ominous color suggesting wild nature. Medieval clothing, even for peasants, was not as drab as the modern stereotype suggests, but there is a special air of mystique to the attire here.

Amidde ʒhe sat anonriʒt	Sat right down in the middle,
And on aiþer half maidenes five.	With five maidens on either side.
Þe dwerw hem servede also blive	The dwarf served them swiftly
840 Wiʒ riche metes and wel idiʒt.	With rich foods, sumptuously prepared.
Þe coppe he filleʒ wiʒ alle his miʒt.	He filled the cups with all his energy.
Sire Degarre couþe of curteisie.	Sir Degare knew court manners.
He set a chaier bifore þe leuedie	He set a chair before the lady
And þerin him selve set	And sat himself there,
And tok a knif and carf his met.	And took a knife and carved his meat.
At þe soper litel at he	He ate lightly of the supper,
But biheld þe leuedi fre	Only beholding the gracious lady,
And seʒ ase feir a wimman	Seeing as beautiful a woman
Als he hevere loked an	As he had ever looked upon,
850 Þat al his herte and his þout	So that all his heart and his mind
Hire to love was ibrowt.	Were moved to love for her.
And þo þai hadde souped anowʒ	And when they had eaten enough,
Þe dwerw com and þe cloʒ he drouʒ.	The dwarf came and drew the tablecloth.
Þe leuedis wessche everichon	Each one of the ladies washed
And ʒede to chaumbre quik anon.	And went right away to her chamber.
. . . .	. . . .
W "Trewly", quod Degore, "and after I wyl	"Truly", mused Degare, "I'll follow after
To loke on that lady all my fyll;	To gaze at that lady as much as I desire.
Who that me warneth, he shall a-by	Whoever prevents me will pay for it,
Or to do him make a sory crye".	Or I will make him cry out in regret!"
. . . .	. . . .
860 A Up at þe gres his wai he nom	Degare made his way up the stairs
Into þe chaumbre he com ful sone.	And quickly followed into the room.
Þe leuedi on here bed set	The lady sat on her bed
And a maide at here fet	With a maid at her feet, who played
And harpede notes gode and fine.	Music on a harp, sweet and fine.
Anoþer brouʒte spices and wine.	Another brought spices and wine.
Upon þe bedde he set adoun	He sat down upon the bed
To here of þe harpe soun.	To listen to the harp's sound.
For murthe of þe notes so sschille	From enjoyment of the beautiful notes,
He fel adoun on slepe stille	He fell down into a sound sleep,
870 So he slep al þat niʒt.	And so he slept all that night.
Þe leuedi wreiʒ him warm apliʒt	The lady tucked him in warmly, I know,
And a pilewer under his heued dede	And placed a pillow under his head,
And ʒede to bedde in þat stede.	And went to bed in that place.
Amorewe whan hit was dai-liʒt	In the morning, when it was daylight,
Sche was uppe and redi diʒt.	She was up and already dressed.
Faire sche awaked him þo.	Then she woke him up gently.
"Aris", sche seide, "graiʒ þe and go".	"Get up", she said, "dress yourself and go".
And saide þus in here game	And she added playfully,
"Þou art worþ to suffri schame	"You deserve to suffer shame,
880 Þat al niʒt as a best sleptest	For sleeping like a beast all night and not

And non of mine maidenes ne keptest".
"O gentil leuedi", seide Degarre
"For Godes love for3if hit me!
Certes þe murie harpe hit made.
Elles misdo nowt I ne hade.
Ac tel me leuedi so hende
Ar ich out of þi chaumber wende
Who is louerd of þis lond
And who þis castel haþ in hond?
890 Wether þou be widue or wif
Or maiden 3it of clene lif?
And whi her be so fele wimman
Allone wi3outen ani man?"
Þe dameisele sore si3te
And bigan to wepen anonri3te.
"Sire wel fain ich telle þe wolde
3if evere þe better be me sscholde.
Mi fader was a riche baroun
And hadde mani a tour and toun.
900 He ne hadde no child but me.
Ich was his hair of þis cuntre.
In mene ich hadde mani a kni3t
And squiers þat were gode and li3t
And staleworht men of mester
To serve in court fer and ner.
Ac þanne is þar herebiside
A sterne kni3t iknawe ful wide.
Ich wene in Bretaine þer be non
So strong a man so he is on.
910 He had ilove me ful 3ore
Ac in herte nevere more
Ne mi3te ich lovie him a3ein.
But whenne he segh3e þer was no gein
He was aboute wi3 maistri
For to ravisse me awai.
Mine kni3tes wolde defende me
And ofte fow3ten hi and he.
Þe best he slowgh þe firste dai
And seþen an oþer par ma fai
920 And seþen þe þridde and þe ferþe
Þe beste þat mi3te gon on erthe!
Mine squiers þat weren so stoute
Bi foure bi fiue þai riden oute

Taking care of any of my maidens".[328]
"Oh, gentle lady", said Degare,
"For the love of God, forgive me!
For sure, the beautiful harping caused it.
Otherwise I would not have behaved so.
But tell me, noble lady,
Before I go out of this room,
Who is lord of this land,
And who has this castle in hand?
Are you a widow or a wife,
Or still a maiden, pure in body?
And why are there so many women here,
Alone, without any man?"
The damsel sighed sorely,
And immediately began to cry.
"Sir, I would gladly tell you
If it might ever do me any good.
My father was a rich baron
And had many a tower and town.
He had no children but me.
I was the heir of his country.
In my company I had many knights,
And squires who were good and able,
And sturdy men of skill,
To serve the court near and far.
But then there came around here
A cruel knight who is widely known.
I believe there is no one in Brittany
So strong a man as he is.
He had loved me for a long time,
But I could never in my heart
Love him in return.
But when he saw there was no use,
He was ready to ravish
Me away with force.
My knights attempted to defend me,
And they continually fought with him.
He slaughtered the best the first day,
And then a second, by my faith,
And then the third and fourth,
The best that might walk on earth!
My squires who were so strong,
Rode out, by four, by five,

---

328 Derek Brewer feels that the lady is gently mocking Degare's virility for having "paid no attention to the ladies" (253). Derek Brewer, "Medieval Literature, Folk Tale, and Traditional Literature", *Dutch Quarterly Review of Anglo-American Letters* 11:4 (1981): 243-56.

On hors armed wel anow3.
His houen bodi he hem slough.
Mine men of mester he slough alle
And oþer pages of mine halle.
Þerfore ich am sore agast
Lest he wynne me ate last".

930 Wi3 þis word sche fil to grounde
And lai aswone a wel gret stounde.
Hire maidenes to hire come
And in hire armes up hire nome.
He beheld þe leuedi wi3 gret pite.
"Loveli madame", quaþ he
"On of þine ich am here.
Ich wille þe help be mi powere".
"3he sire", 3he saide, "þan al mi lond
Ich wil þe 3ive into þin hond

940 And at þi wille bodi mine
3if þou mi3t wreke me of hine".
Þo was he glad al for to fi3te
Ac wel gladere þat he mi3te
Have þe leuedi so bri3t
3if he slough þat oþer kni3t.
And als þai stod and spak ifere
A maiden cried wi3 reuful chere
"Her come3 oure enemi faste us ate!
Drauwe þe bregge and sschet þe 3ate

950 Or he wil slen ous everichone!"
Sire Degarre stirt up anon
And at a window him se3
Wel i-armed on hors high.
A fairer bodi þan he was on
In armes ne segh he never non.
Sire Degarre armed him blive
And on a stede gan out drive.
Wi3 a spere gret of gayn
To þe kni3t he rit a3ein.

960 Þe kni3te spere al tosprong
Ac Degarre was so strong
And so harde to him þrast
But þe kni3t sat so fast
Þat þe stede rigge tobrek
And fel to grounde and he ek.
But anon stirt up þe kni3t
And drou3 out his swerd bri3t.
"Ali3t!" he saide, "adoun anon!
To fi3t þou sschalt afote gon.

On horses, armed well enough.
He destroyed them by his own hand.
He killed all of my masterful men
And other pages in my hall.
For this I am sorely afraid
That he might finally overcome me".
With these words she fell to the ground
And lay in a faint for a good while.
Her maidens came to her
And took her up in their arms.
He looked at the lady with great pity.
"My lovely lady", he said,
"I am here as one of your own.
I will help you by my own power".
"Sir, yes", she said, "then I will give you
All of my land into your hand,
As well as my body, at your will,
If you can avenge me of him".
Then he was glad to be able to fight,
And even gladder that he might
Have the lady so bright
If he could slay that other knight.
And as they stood and spoke together,
A maiden cried, with a doleful voice,
"Here comes our enemy toward us fast!
Raise the bridge and shut the gate,
Or he will slay every one of us!"
Sir Degare started up at once
And saw him through a window,
Well armed and high on his horse.
He never saw a mightier body
In arms than he was.
Sir Degare armed himself swiftly
And drove out on his steed.
With a spear of great force
He rode toward the knight.
The knight broke the spear into pieces;
But Degare was so strong
And thrust on him so hard,
That because the knight sat so firmly,
The horse's backbone was broken
And it fell to the ground with him.
But the knight jumped up at once
And drew out his bright sword.
"Get down!" he shouted, "dismount now!
To fight me you must go on foot.

970 For þou hast slawe mi stede	Because you have slain my steed,
Deȝ-dint schal be þi mede!	A death blow will be your reward!
Ac þine stede sle I nille	I don't want to slay your horse;
Ac on fote fiȝte ich wille!"	I want to fight you on foot!"
Þan on fote þai toke þe fiȝt	Then they took the fight to the ground,
And hewe togidere wiȝ brondes briȝt.	And clashed together with shining blades.
Þe kniȝt ȝaf Sire Degarre	The knight gave Sir Degare
Sterne strokes gret plente	Harsh blows in great plenty,
And he him aȝen also	And he struck him in return as well,
Þat helm and scheld cleve atwo.	So that helmet and shield were cut in two.
980 Þe kniȝt was agreued sore	The knight was sorely angered
Þat his armour toburste þore.	That his armor was broken there.
A strok he ȝaf Sire Degarre	He gave Sir Degare a stroke
Þat to grounde fallen is he.	That brought him to the ground.
But he stirt up anonriȝt	But he jumped up right away
And swich a strok he ȝaf þe kniȝt	And gave the knight such a blow,
Upon his heued so harde iset	So powerfully set upon his head,
Þat helm and heued and bacinet	Through helmet and steel and head,
Þat ate brest stod þe dent.	That the stroke only stopped at the breast.
Ded he fil doun verraiment.	He fell down dead, in truth.
990 Þe leuedi lai in o kernel	The lady stayed in the barricade
And biheld þe batail everi del.	And saw every moment of the battle.
Ȝhe ne was never er so bliþe	She was never before so happy
Sche þankede God fele sithe.	And thanked God many times.
Sire Degarre com into castel	Sir Degare came into the castle
Aȝein him com þe dammaisel	And the damsel came to him
And þonked him swiþe of þat dede.	And thanked him swiftly for his deeds.
Into chaumber sche gan him lede	She led him into her chamber
And unarmed him anon	And unarmed him at once,
And set him hire bed upon.	And set him upon her bed.
. . . .	. . . .
1000W She toke hym in her arms two	She took him in her two arms
And kyssed hym a hundred tymes and mo	And kissed him a hundred times and more
. . . .	. . . .
A And saide, "Sire par charite	And said, "Sir, for charity's sake,
I þe prai dwel wiȝ me	I beg you to stay with me,
And al mi lond ich wil þe ȝive	And I will give you all my land,
And mi selve whil þat I live".	And myself, while I live".
"Grant merci dame", saide Degarre	"Many thanks, my lady", said Degare,
"Of þe gode þou bedest me.	"For all the good that you offer me.
Wende ich wille into oþer londe	But I will travel to other lands,
More of haventours for to fonde.	To find more adventures.
1010 And be þis twelve moneþ be go	And after twelve months have passed,
Aȝein ich wil come þe to".	I will come back again to you".
Þe leuedi made moche mourning	The lady made great mourning
For þe kniȝtes departing	Over the knight's departing,

And ȝaf him a stede god and sur
Gold and silver and god armur
And bitauȝt him Jhesu Hevene-king.
And sore þai wepen at here parting.
Forht wente Sire Degarre
Þurh mani a divers cuntre.
1020 Evermor he rod west.
So in a dale of o forest
He mette wiȝ a douȝti kniȝt
Upon a stede god and liȝt
In armes þat were riche and sur
Wiȝ þe sscheld of asur
And þre bor-heuedes þerin
Wel ipainted wiȝ gold fin.
Sire Degarre anonriȝt
Hendeliche grette þe kniȝt
1030 And saide, "Sire God wiȝ þe be".
And þous aȝein answerede he
"Velaun, wat dost þou here
In mi forest to chase mi dere?"
Degarre answerede wiȝ wordes meke
"Sire þine der nought I ne seke.
Iich am an aunterous kniȝt
For to seche werre and fiȝt".
Þe kniȝt saide, "Wiȝouten fail
Ȝif þou comest to seke batail
1040 Here þou hast þi per ifounde!
Arme þe swiþe in þis stounde!"
Sire Degarre and his squier
Armed him in riche atir
Wiȝ an helm riche for þe nones.
Was ful of precious stones
Þat þe maide him ȝaf saun fail
For whom he did raþer batail.
A scheld he kest aboute his swere
Þat was of armes riche and dere
1050 Wiȝ þre maidenes heuedes of silver briȝt
Wiȝ crounes of gold precious of siȝt.
A schaft he tok þat was nowt smal
Wiȝ a kene coronal.
His squier tok anoþer spere

And gave him a steed, fine and sure,
Gold and silver, and strong armor,
And entrusted him to Jesus, Heaven's king.
They wept bitterly at their parting.
Sir Degare went forth
Through many a different land,
Always riding west.
And so one day in a forest valley
He met with a sturdy knight
On a steed, strong and lively,
In arms that were rich and firm,
With a shield of azure
With three boars' heads on them,[329]
Finely painted with costly gold.
At once Sir Degare
Politely greeted the knight
And said, "God be with you, sir".
But he answered in return,
"Villain, what are you doing here[330]
In my forest, hunting my deer?"
Degare replied with mild words,
"Sir, I do not want any of your deer.
I am a faithful knight,
Out to seek adventure and combat".
The knight said, "Without a doubt,
If you've come to seek battle,
You've found your match here!
Arm yourself fast in this place!"
Sir Degare, with his squire,
Armed himself in rich clothing,
With a fine helmet for the occasion.
It was full of precious stones
That the maiden gave him, without doubt,
For the foe he battled earlier.
He put a shield about his neck
Which had rich and precious ornaments,
With three maidens' heads of bright silver,
And with costly-looking crowns of gold.
He took a shaft which was not small,
With a keen point.
His squire grasped another spear

---

329 *Thre bor-hevedes*: Having boars' heads on a crest was common in Celtic heraldry and in many other nations, perhaps
suggesting either the fierceness of the boar or a hunter who had defeated them.

330 *Velaun*: Deer poaching was a serious crime in private forests. The knight may mean *villain* as 'bad guy', or its original
meaning of a rural peasant, making the infraction even more grave. See Roger B. Manning, "Unlawful Hunting in England,
1500-1640", *Forest & Conservation History* 38:1 (1994): 16-23.

Bi his louerd he gan hit bere.
Lo swich aventure he gan betide!
Þe sone aȝein þe fader gan ride
And noiþer ne knew oþer no wiȝt!
Nou beginneȝ þe firste fiȝt.
1060 Sire Degarre tok his cours þare
Aȝen his fader a schaft he bare.
To bere him doun he hadde imint
Riȝt in þe sscheld he set his dint.
Þe schaft brak to peces al
And in þe sscheld sat þe coronal.
Anoþer cours þai gonne take.
Þe fader tok for þe sones sake
A schaft þat was gret and long
And he anoþer also strong.
1070 Togider þai riden wiȝ gret raundoun
And aiþer bar oþer adoun.
Wiȝ dintes þat þai smiten þere
Here stede-rigges toborsten were.
Afote þai gonne fiȝt ifere
And laiden on wiȝ swerdes clere.
Þe fader amerveiled wes
Whi his swerd was pointles
And seide to his sone apliȝt
"Herkne to me a litel wiȝt!
1080 Wher were þou boren, in what lond?"
"In Litel Bretaigne ich understond.
Kingges doughter sone witouten les
Ac I not wo mi fader wes".
"What is þi name?" þan saide he.
"Certes men clepeȝ me Degarre".
"O Degarre sone mine!
Certes ich am fader þine!
And bi þi swerd I knowe hit here.
Þe point is in min aumenere".
1090 He tok þe point and set þerto.
Degarre fel iswone þo
And his fader sikerli
Also he gan swony.
And whanne of swone arisen were
Þe sone cride merci þere
His owen fader of his misdede
And he him to his castel gan lede
And bad him dwelle wiȝ him ai.
"Certes sire", he saide, "nai".
1100 Ac ȝif hit ȝoure wille were

And carried it alongside his lord.
See what fortune awaited them!
The son began to ride against the father,
And neither knew who the other was!
Now the first charge began.
Sir Degare took his course there,
Bearing a lance against his father.
He intended to bear him down
And set his aim right on the shield.
The shaft broke into pieces,
And left the point in the shield.
They began to take another charge.
To attack the son, the father seized
A lance which was great and long,
And Degare took another just as strong.
They rode together with great spirit,
But neither bore the other down.
With the blows that they struck there,
Their horses' backs were broken.
They started to battle on foot,
And laid on with shining swords.
The father was puzzled
As to why Degare's sword was pointless,
And said to his son, fittingly,
"Listen to me for a moment!
Where were you born, in what land?"
"In Brittany, as I understand.
I am a king's daughter's son, without a lie,
But I do not know who my father was".
"What is your name?" he then asked.
"For certain, men call me Degare".
"Oh, Degare, my son!
For certain, I am your father!
And I know it by your sword here.
The point is in my pouch".
He took the point and set it on.
Degare was overcome then,
And his father, certainly,
Also began to faint.
And when they rose from their shock,
The son asked for forgiveness there
For his offence against his father,
And he invited Degare to his castle
And asked him to stay with him forever.
"For certain, sir, no", Degare said.
"But, if it is your will,

To mi moder we wende ifere
For ʒhe is in gret mourning".
"Bleþelich", quaþ he, "bi Hevene-kyng!"
. . . .

W   So longe the have spoke togither
     Both the sonne and the father,
     That they be ryght well at one,
     The father and the sonne alone.
     Syr Degore and his father dere
     Into Englande they rode in fere.
1110 They were both armed and wel dighte
     As it behoveth everye knyght.
     They rode forth on theyr journey
     Many a myle of that contrey
     And on theyr way they rode full fast
     Into England they came at the laste.
     When they might England se
     They drewe thyther as they wold be.
     When they were to the palayes come
     They were welcome all and seme
1120 And they behelde over all.
     The ladye them spyed over a wall.
     And when the ladye saw that syght
     She went to them with all her myght
     And ryght well sche them knewe
     And then sche chaunged all her hewe
     And sayd, "My dere sonne Degore
     Thou hast thy father brought with thee!"
     "Trewly madame", then sayd he
     "Full well I wote it is he".
1130 "Nowe thanked be God then!" sayd the kynge.
     "For nowe I knowe without leasynge
     Who is Degores father in dede".
     The lady sowned in that stede.
     And soone after sykerlye
     The knyght wedded that lady.
     She and her sonne was departed atwin
     For he and sche were to nye kynne.
     Forthe then went Syr Degore
     With the kynge and his menye
1140 His father and his mother dere.
     Unto the castell they went in fere
     Where as dwelled that lady bright
     That he had wonne in right

We will go together to my mother,
For she is in great distress".
"Gladly", he said, "by Heaven's king!"
. . . .

They spoke together for so long,
Both the son and the father,
Until they were fully reconciled,
The father and the son alone.
Sir Degare and his dear father
Rode together into Brittany.[331]
They were both armed and finely dressed,
As is proper for every knight.
They rode forth on their journey,
Many a mile of that country.
And along their way they rode quickly
Until at last they came to Brittany.
When they had sight of Brittany,
They set forth as they had intended.
When they had come to the palace,
They were welcomed by one and all
And they beheld everything.
The lady had espied them over a wall,
And when the lady saw that sight
She hurried to them with all her might.
She knew them very well,
And at once her color changed entirely
And she said, "My dear son, Degare,
You have brought your father with you!"
"Truly, madam", he said then,
"I know very well that it is him".
"Now may God be thanked!", said the king.
"For now I know, without a lie,
Who Sir Degare's father is indeed".
The lady fell faint at that moment.
And soon after, to be sure,
The knight wedded that lady.
She and her son's marriage was annulled,
For he and she were too close of kin.
Then Sir Degare went forth
With the king and his retinue,
And his father and dear mother.
They went together into the castle
Where that shining lady lived
That he had won rightfully,

---

331 At line 1103 Auchinleck stops, as a final page is missing, and no period MSS preserve the ending. The later black letter
    version transfers the setting to England, but *Brittany* is maintained here for consistency.

And wedded her with great solempnite
Before all the lordes of that countre.
Thus came the knyght out of his care.
God geve us grace wel to fare
And that we upon Domes day
Come to the blysse that lasteth aye.

1150 Amen.

And he married her with great ceremony
In front of all the lords in that country.
Thus the knight came out of his troubles.
May God give us grace to fare as well,
So that we, upon Judgment Day,
Will come to the bliss that lasts eternally.

Amen.

Works Cited

"Currency Converter". *UK National Archives*. http://www.nationalarchives.gov.uk/currency/

Allen, Rosamund. *King Horn*. New York: Garland, 1984.

Ascham, Roger. *Toxophilus*. In *English Works,* edited by W.A. Wright. Cambridge, 1904.

Bakhtin, Mikhail M. "Epic and Novel". *The Dialogic Imagination*. Ed. and trans. Michael Holquist and Caryl Emerson. Austin: University of Texas Press, 1981.

Barbour, Harriot B. *Old English Tales Retold*. New York: MacMillan, 1924.

Battaglia, Denise, and Esther Kaufmann, et al. "You Can Say You to Me: English Politeness from the Middle Ages up to Now". Conference paper. *eHistLing* 1 (2004).

Battles, Dominique. *Cultural Difference and Material Culture in Middle English Romance: Normans and Saxons*. New York: Routledge, 2013.

Baugh, Albert C. "Improvisation in the Middle English Romance". *Proceedings of the American Philosophical Society* 103:3 (1959): 418-454.

--. "The Middle English Romance: Some Questions of Creation, Presentation, and Preservation". *Speculum* 42:1 (1967): 1-31.

Bellamy, J. *The Law of Treason in England in the Later Middle Ages*. Cambridge: University Press, 1970.

Benson, Larry D., and John Leyerle, ed. *Chivalric Literature*. Kalamazoo: The Board of the Medieval Institute, 1980.

Benson, Larry D., ed. *The Riverside Chaucer*. 3rd ed. Boston: Houghton Mifflin, 1987.

Beowulf, trans. Howell D. Chickering, Jr. Toronto: Anchor Books, 1977.

Boswell, John. *The Kindness of Strangers: The Abandonment of Children in Western Europe from Late Antiquity to the Renaissance*. Chicago: University of Chicago Press, 1998.

Bowers, John M. *The Politics of Pearl: Court Poetry in the Age of Richard II*. Cambridge: D.S. Brewer, 2001.

Bradbury, Nancy M. "Chaucerian Minstrelsy: *Sir Thopas, Troilus and Criseyde* and English Metrical Romance". In *Tradition and Transformation in Medieval Romance*, edited by Rosalind Field, 115-24. Cambridge: D.S. Brewer, 1999.

Brewer, Derek. "Medieval Literature, Folk Tale, and Traditional Literature". *Dutch Quarterly Review of Anglo-American Letters* 11.4 (1981): 243-56.

Burnley, David, and Alison Wiggins, eds. *Auchinleck Manuscript*. National Library of Scotland. http://digital.nls.uk/auchinleck

Burrow, John A. "'Alterity' and Middle English Literature". *Review of English Studies* 50:200 (1999): 483-492.

Childress, Diana T. "Between Romance and Legend: 'Secular Hagiography' in Middle English Literature". *Philological Quarterly* 57 (1978): 311-22.

Connors, Robert J. "The Rhetoric of Citation Systems, Part I: The Development of Annotation Structures from the Renaissance to 1900". *Rhetoric Review* 17:1 (1998): 35.

Couch, Julie N. "The Vulnerable Hero: *Havelok* and the Revision of Romance". *Chaucer Review* 42:3 (2008): 330-52.

Crane, Ronald S. "The Vogue of *Guy of Warwick* from the Close of the Middle Ages to the Romantic Revival". *PMLA* 30:2 (1915): 125-194.

Crane, Susan. *Gender and Romance in Chaucer's Canterbury Tales*. Princeton: University Press, 1994.

--. *Insular Romance: Politics, Faith, and Culture in Anglo-Norman and Middle English Literature*. Berkeley: University of California Press, 1986.

Curry, Walter C. *The Middle English Ideal of Personal Beauty*. Baltimore: J.H. Furst, 1916.

Dabhoiwala, Faramerz. *The Origins of Sex: A History of the First Sexual Revolution*. New York: Oxford University Press, 2012.

Darton, F.J.H. *A Wonder Book of Old Romances*. London: Wells Gardner Darton, 1907.

Delaney, Sheila. "A, A, and B: Coding Same-Sex Union in *Amis and Amiloun*". In *Pulp Fictions of Medieval England*, 63-81.

--. *Medieval Literary Politics*. Manchester: University Press, 1990.

Dickerson, A. Inskip. "The Subplot of the Messenger in *Athelston*". *Papers on Language & Literature* 12 (1976): 115-24.

Du Méril, Édélestand, ed. *Floire et Blanceflor, Poèmes du 13è Siècle*. Paris: 1856. *Internet Archive*. http://www.archive.org/details/floireetblancefl00floiuoft

Eckert, Kenneth D. "*Amis and Amiloun*: A Spiritual Journey and the Failure of Treuþe". *Literature & Theology* 27:3 (2013), 285-96.

--. "Growing Up in the Middle English *Floris and Blancheflor*". *The Explicator* 70:4 (2012), 243-247.

--. "Numerological and Structural Symbolism in the Auchinleck Stanzaic *Guy of Warwick*". *English Studies* 95:8 (2014), 849-859.

--. "Three Types of 'Messengers' in the Middle English *Athelston*". *ANQ* 26:4 (2013), 219-225.

Ellis, George. *Specimens of Early English Metrical Romances*. 3 vols. London: 1811 (1805).

Ferguson, George. *Signs & Symbols in Christian Art*. London: Zwemmer, 1955.

Field, Rosalind, ed. *Tradition and Transformation in Medieval Romance*. Cambridge: D.S. Brewer, 1999.

Finlayson, John. "Definitions of Middle English Romance, Part I". *Chaucer Review* 15:1 (1980): 44-62.

-- "The Marvellous in Middle English Romance, Part II". *Chaucer Review* 33:4 (1999): 168-81.

Florio, John, trans. *The Essayes of Michael Lord of Montaigne*. 2 vols. London, 1603.

Ford, John C. "A New Conception of Poetic Formulae Based on Prototype Theory and the Mental Template". *Neuphilologishche Mitteilungen* 103 (2002): 218–24.

Foster, Edward E., ed. *Amis and Amiloun, Robert of Cisyle, and Sir Amadace*. Kalamazoo, MI: Medieval Institute Publications, 1997. http://www.lib.rochester. edu/camelot/teams/amisfr.htm

French, Walter H., and Charles B. Hale, eds. *Middle English Metrical Romances*. New York: Russell & Russell, 1964 (1930).

Frye, Northrop. *Anatomy of Criticism: Four Essays*. Princeton: University Press, 1957.

Garbaty, Thomas J. *Medieval English Literature*. Long Grove, Il: Waveland, 1984.

Gibbon, Edward. *History of the Decline and Fall of the Roman Empire*. London, 1782.

Glosecki, Stephen O. "Beowulf and the Wills: Traces of Totemism?" *Philological Quarterly* 78:1/2 (1999): 15-47.

Graden, Pamela. "The Romance Mode". In *Form and Style in Early English Literature*. London: Methuen, 1971. 212-272.

Green, R.F. *A Crisis of Truth: Literature and Law in Ricardian England*. Philadelphia: University of Pennsylvania Press, 1999.

Grieve, Patricia E. *Floire and Blancheflor and the European Romance*. Cambridge: University Press, 1997.

Hall, Joseph. *King Horn: A Middle English Romance*. Oxford: University Press, 1901.

Hanna, Ralph. *London Literature, 1300-1380*. Cambridge: University Press, 2005.

Herzman, Ronald B., Graham Drake, and Eve Salisbury, eds. *Athelston*. In *Four Romances of England*. Kalamazoo, MI: Medieval Institute Publications, 1999. http://www.lib.rochester.edu/camelot/teams/athelfrm.htm

--. *Bevis of Hampton*. In *Four Romances of England*. http://www.lib.rochester.edu/ camelot/teams/bevisfrm.htm

--. *Havelok the Dane*. In *Four Romances of England*. http://www.lib.rochester.edu/ camelot/teams/danefrm.htm

--. *King Horn*. In *Four Romances of England*. http://www.lib.rochester.edu/camelot/ teams/hornfrm.htm

Hodges, Kenneth. "Medieval Sourcebook: Medieval Prices". *Fordham University Center for Medieval Studies*. Mirrored at http://faculty.goucher.edu/eng240/ medieval_prices.html

Holford, Matthew L. "History and Politics in *Horn Child and Maiden Rimnild*". *Review of English Studies* 57:229 (2006): 149-168.

Hudson, Harriet E. "Construction of Class, Family, and Gender in Some Middle English Popular Romances". In *Class and Gender in Early English Literature*, edited by Britton J. Harwood and Gillian R. Overing, 76-94. Indianapolis: Indiana University Press, 1994.

Jameson, Fredric. *The Political Unconscious: Narrative as a Socially Symbolic Act*. New York: Cornell University Press, 1981.

Jebson, Tony, ed. *Anglo-Saxon Chronicle, Manuscript E: Bodleian MS Laud 636*. Accessed at http://asc.jebbo.co.uk/e/e-L.html

Jordan, Robert M. "Chaucerian Romance?" *Yale French Studies* 51 (1974): 223-34.

Ker, W.P. *Epic and Romance* (1908). New York: Dover Publications, 1957.

Knight, Stephen, and Thomas H. Ohlgren, eds. *The Tale of Gamelyn*. In *Robin Hood and Other Outlaw Tales*. Kalamazoo, MI: Medieval Institute Publications, 1997. http://www.lib.rochester.edu/camelot/teams/gamelyn.htm

Kölbing, Eugen, ed. *Amis and Amiloun, Altenglische Biblioteck 2*. Heilbronn: Henninger, 1884.

Kooper, Erik, ed. *Floris and Blancheflour*. In *Sentimental and Humorous Romances*. Kalamazoo, MI: Medieval Institute Publications, 2006. http://www.lib.rochester.edu/camelot/teams/ekfbfrm.htm

Kratins, Ojars. "The Middle English *Amis and Amiloun*: Chivalric Romance or Secular Hagiography?" *PMLA* 81 (1966): 347-54.

Laing, David. *A Penni Worth of Witte: Florice and Blaunchflour: And Other Pieces of Ancient English Poetry*. Edinburgh: Abbotsford Club, 1857.

--. *Sire Degarre, a Metrical Romance of the End of the Thirteenth Century*. Edinburgh: Abbotsford Club, 1849.

Lang, Andrew, ed. *The Red Romance Book*. New York: Longmans and Green, 1921.

Laskaya, Anne, and Eve Salisbury, ed. *Sir Degaré*. In *The Middle English Breton Lays*. Kalamazoo, MI: Medieval Institute Publications, 1995. http://www.lib.rochester.edu/camelot/teams/degarfrm.htm

--. *Sir Orfeo*. In *The Middle English Breton Lays*. Kalamazoo, MI: Medieval Institute Publications, 1995. http://www.lib.rochester.edu/camelot/teams/orfeofrm.htm

Leeson, Peter T. "Ordeals". George Mason University. http://www.peterleeson.com/Ordeals.pdf

Levine, Robert. "Who Composed *Havelok* For Whom?" *Yearbook of English Studies* 22 (1992): 95-104.

Liszka, Thomas R. "Talk in the Camps: On the Dating Of the *South English Legendary, Havelok the Dane*, and *King Horn* in Oxford, Bodleian Library, MS Laud Misc. 108". In *The Texts and Contexts of Oxford, Bodleian Library, MS Laud Misc. 108*, edited by Kimberly Bell and Julie N. Couch, 31-50. Leiden: Brill, 2011.

Liuzza, Roy Michael. "Representation and Readership in the ME *Havelok*", *Journal of English and Germanic Philology* 93 (1994): 504-519.

Loomis, Laura A. Hibbard. "*Athelston*, a Westminster Legend". *PMLA* 36:2 (1921): 223-244.

--. "Chaucer and the Breton Lays of the Auchinleck MS". *Studies in Philology* 38:1 (1941): 14-33.

--. "The Auchinleck Manuscript and a Possible London Bookshop of 1330-1340". *PMLA* 57:3 (1942): 595-627.

Los, Bettelou. "The Loss of the Indefinite Pronoun Man: Syntactic Change and Information Structure". In *English Historical Syntax and Morphology*, edited by Teresa Fanego, María J. López-Couso, and Javier Pérez-Guerra, 181-202. Amsterdam: John Benjamins, 2002.

MacEdward, Leach, ed. *Amis and Amiloun*. Early English Text Society OS 20. London: Oxford University Press, 1937.

McDonald, Nicola, ed. *Pulp Fictions of Medieval England.* Manchester: University Press, 2004.

McKeehan, Irene P. "The Book of the Nativity of St. Cuthbert". *PMLA* 48 (1933): 981-99.

McKnight, George H. *King Horn, Floriz and Blancheflur, The Assumption of Our Lady* (1866). London: EETS, 1901.

Manning, Roger B. "Unlawful Hunting in England, 1500-1640". *Forest & Conservation History* 38:1 (1994): 16-23.

Meech, Sanford B. "A Collection of Proverbs in Rawlinson MS D 328". *Modern Philology* 38:2 (1940): 113-132.

Mehl, Dieter. *The Middle English Romances of the Thirteenth and Fourteenth Centuries.* London: Routledge and Kegan Paul, 1967.

Meres, Francis. *Palladis Tamia, Wits Treasury* (1598). In *Elizabethan Critical Essays*, edited by Gregory Smith. Oxford: Clarendon, 1904.

Meyer, Paul, and Gaston Paris. *Romania: Recueil Trimestriel.* Paris: Mario Roques, 1921.

Michel, Francisque X., ed. *Horn et Rimenhild*. Paris: Bannatyne Club Par Maulde Et Renou, 1845.

Michel, M. Francisque, ed. *Lai D'Havelok Le Danois.* Paris: Silvestre, 1834.

Mills, Maldwyn. "*Havelok* and the Brutal Fisherman". *Medium Aevum* 36 (1967): 219-30.

Millward, Celia M. *A Biography of the English Language.* Orlando, FL: Harcourt Brace Jovanovich, 1988.

Milton, John. Introduction ("The Verse") to *Paradise Lost* (1674). In *The Norton Anthology of English Literature, The Sixteenth Century and Early Seventeenth Century Vol. B,* eighth ed., edited by Stephen Greenblatt. New York: W.W. Norton, 2006.

Nashe, Thomas. *The Anatomy of Absurdity* (1589). In *The Works of Thomas Nashe,* vol. III, edited by Ronald B. McKerrow. London, 1905.

Osborn, Marijane. *Nine Medieval Romances of Magic: Re-Rhymed in Modern English*. Peterborough, Ont.: Broadview, 2010.

Owst, G.R. *Literature and Pulpit in Medieval England*. Cambridge: University Press, 1933.

Pearsall, Derek. *The Life of Geoffrey Chaucer*. Cambridge: Basil Blackwell, 1992.

--. "The Pleasure of Popular Romance: A Prefatory Essay". In *Medieval Romance, Medieval Contexts*, edited by Rhiannon Purdie and Michael Cichon, 9-18. Cambridge: D.S. Brewer, 2011.

--. "Understanding Middle English Romance". *Review* 2 (1980): 105-25.

Peck, Russell A. "Number as Cosmic Language". In *Essays in the Numerical Criticism of Medieval Literature*, edited by Carolyn D. Eckhardt, 15-64. Lewisburg, PA: Bucknell University Press, 1980.

Prestwich, Michael. *Plantagenet England 1225-1360*. New York: Oford University Press, 2005.

Putter, Ad, and Jane Gilbert Jane, ed. *The Spirit of Medieval English Popular Romance*. Harlow: Longman, 2000.

Reiss, Edmund. "Symbolic Detail in Medieval Narrative: *Floris & Blancheflour*". *Papers on Language & Literature* 7 (1971): 339-50.

Rowe, Elizabeth A. "The Female Body Politic and the Miscarriage of Justice in *Athelston*". *Studies in the Age of Chaucer* 17 (1995): 79-98.

Said, Edward W. *Orientalism: Western Conceptions of the Orient*. London: Routledge & Kegan Paul, 1978.

Schofield, William H. *The Story of Horn and Rimenhild*. Baltimore: Modern Language Association of America, 1903.

Seaman, Myra. "Engendering Genre in Middle English Romance: Performing the Feminine in *Sir Beves of Hamtoun*". *Studies in Philology* 98:1 (2001): 49-75.

Shannon, Edgar F., Jr. "Mediaeval Law in the *Tale of Gamelyn*". *Speculum* 26:3 (1951): 458-64.

Shippey, T.A. "The *Tale of Gamelyn*: Class Warfare and the Embarrassments of Genre". In *The Spirit of Medieval English Popular Romance*, 78-96.

Skeat, Walter W., ed. *The Lay of Havelok the Dane*. London: EETS, 1868.

Smithers, G.V., ed. *Havelok*. Oxford: Clarendon, 1987.

Speed, Diane. "The Saracens of *King Horn*". *Speculum* 65:3 (1990): 564-66.

Strohm, Paul. *Social Chaucer*. Cambridge, MA: Harvard, 1989.

Swanton, Michael J. *English Literature Before Chaucer*. New York: Longman Group, 1987.

Tait, James. *The Medieval English Borough*. Manchester: University Press, 1968 (1936).

Tatlock, J.S.P. "Epic Formulas, Especially in Layamon". *PMLA* 38:3 (1923): 494-529.

--. "The *Canterbury Tales* in 1400". *PMLA* 50:1 (1935): 100-139.

Taylor, A.B. *Floris and Blancheflor: A Middle English Romance*. Oxford: Clarendon, 1927.

Treharne, Elaine M. "Romanticizing the Past in the Middle English *Athelston*". *Review of English Studies* 50:197 (1999): 1-21.

Trounce, A. Mcintyre, ed. *Athelston: A Middle English Romance*. EETS O.S. 224. London: Oxford University Press, 1951.

Tucker, Susie I. "Sixty as an Indefinite Number in Middle English". *Review of English Studies* 25:98 (1949): 152-153.

Whistler, Charles W. Preface to *Havelok the Dane: A Legend of Old Grimsby and Lincoln*. T. Nelson and Sons, 1899.

Wiggins, Alison, ed. *Stanzaic Guy of Warwick*. Kalamazoo, MI: Medieval Institute Publications, 2004. http://www.lib.rochester.edu/camelot/teams/guywfrm.htm

Wilcox, Rebecca. "Romancing the East: Greeks and Saracens in *Guy of Warwick*". In *Pulp Fictions of Medieval England*, 217-40.

Woolgar, C.M. *The Great Household in Late Medieval England*. New Haven, CT: Yale University Press, 1999.

Wright, Thomas, and James O. Halliwell. *Reliquiae Antiquae*. Vol. 2. London: John Russell Smith, 1845.

Zupitza, Julius. "Die Romanze von *Athelston*". *Englische Studien* 13 (1883): 331-414.

Index